# PATENT LAW IN GREATER CHINA

## ELGAR INTELLECTUAL PROPERTY LAW AND PRACTICE

**Series Editors:** Trevor Cook, *Partner, Bird & Bird* and Johanna Gibson, *Herchel Smith Professor of Intellectual Property Law, Queen Mary University of London*

The *Elgar Intellectual Property Law and Practice* series is a library of works by leading practitioners and scholars covering discrete areas of law in the field of intellectual property. Each title will describe the law in detail, but will also be deeply analytical, highlighting and unpicking the legal issues that are most critical and relevant to practice. Designed to be detailed, focused reference works, the books in this series aim to offer an authoritative statement on the law and practice in key topics within the field, from *Trade Marks* to *Pharmaceuticals*, from *Patent Standards* to *Trade Secrecy* and from *IP Licensing* to *IP Valuation.*

Titles in this series include:

The Law and Regulation of Franchising in the EU
*Mark Abell*

The Protection of Geographical Indications
*Michael Blakeney*

Patent Law in Greater China
*Edited by Stefan Luginbuehl and Peter Ganea*

# PATENT LAW IN GREATER CHINA

Edited by

STEFAN LUGINBUEHL

*PhD, Attorney at Law, Lawyer, European Patent Office, Germany*

PETER GANEA

*PhD, Lecturer and Researcher, Interdisciplinary Centre for East Asian Studies (IZO), Goethe University Frankfurt, Germany*

ELGAR INTELLECTUAL PROPERTY LAW AND PRACTICE

**Edward Elgar**
Cheltenham, UK • Northampton, MA, USA

Illustration on page vi:

满月 'Full Moon'

王伯鹿 by Wang Bo-Lu

Published by
Edward Elgar Publishing Limited
The Lypiatts
15 Lansdown Road
Cheltenham
Glos GL50 2JA
UK

Edward Elgar Publishing, Inc.
William Pratt House
9 Dewey Court
Northampton
Massachusetts 01060
USA

A catalogue record for this book
is available from the British Library

Library of Congress Control Number: 2014932520

This book is available electronically in the ElgarOnline.com Law Subject Collection,
E-ISBN 978 1 78195 484 3

MIX
Paper from responsible sources
FSC® C013056
FSC www.fsc.org

ISBN 978 1 78195 483 6

Typeset by Columns Design XML Ltd, Reading
Printed and bound in Great Britain by T.J. International Ltd, Padstow

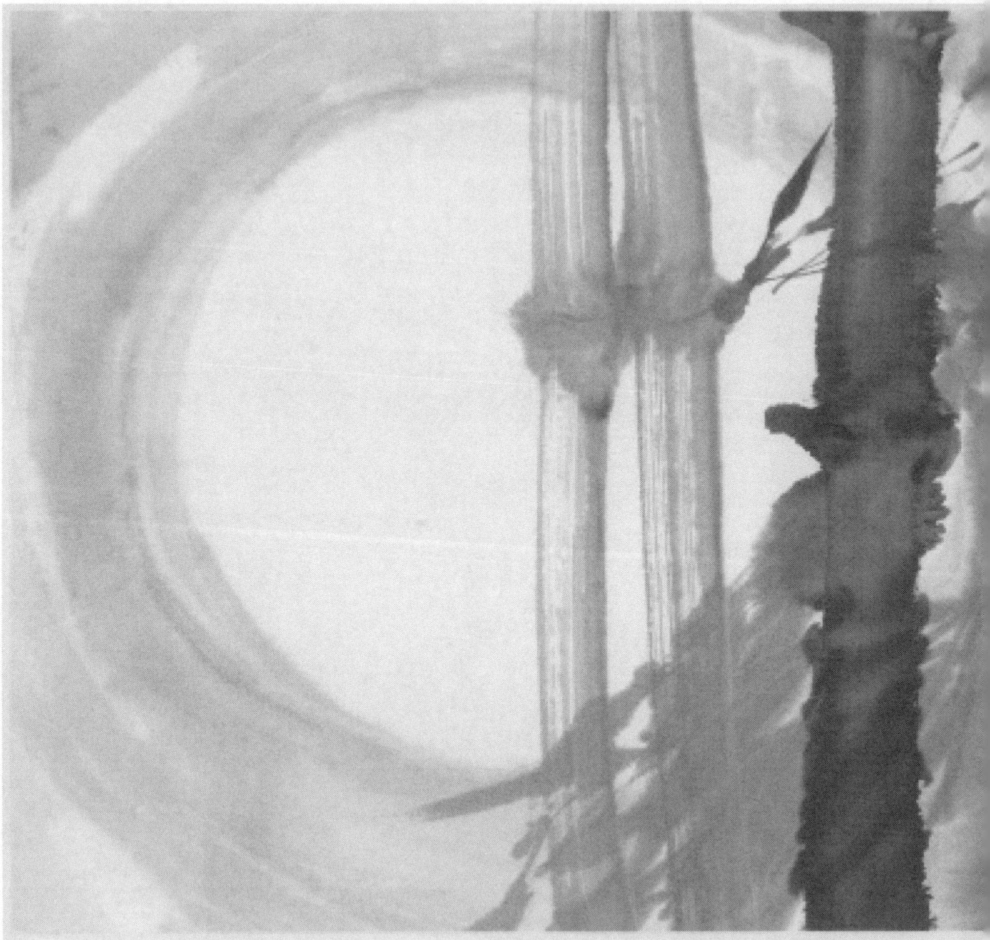

# CONTENTS

# EXTENDED TABLE OF CONTENTS

## PART B SUBSTANTIVE PATENT LAW

## PART H PATENT PROTECTION IN HONG KONG SAR



## PART I PATENT PROTECTION IN MACAU SAR

# CONTRIBUTORS

**Christopher Bailey**, LL.M. (Edinburgh), Partner at Rouse, China.

**Bu Yuanshi,** PhD, LL.M. (Harvard), Chair of International Economic Law with special focus on East Asia, University of Freiburg, Germany.

**Cao Jingjing**, PhD, LL.M. (Munich), Senior Associate at Taylor Wessing, China.

**Chen Wenping**, Patent Attorney at King & Wood Mallesons, China.

**Douglas Clark**, Barrister, Hong Kong.

**Cui Guobin**, PhD, B.Sc., LLM, J.S.D. (Peking University), LL.M. (Yale University), full-time associate professor at Tsinghua University School of Law, China.

**Christian Czychowski**, PhD, Professor, Attorney at Law, Partner at Boehmert & Boehmert, Germany.

**Deng Ming**, PhD, Patent Attorney, Director of China Patent Agent (H.K.) Ltd., Munich Office, Germany.

**Peter Ganea**, PhD, programme coordinator and lecturer at Goethe University Frankfurt, Germany.

**Heinz Goddar**, PhD, Professor, Patent Attorney, Partner at Boehmert & Boehmert, Germany.

**Nils Heide**, PhD, Attorney at Law, Specialized Lawyer for Intellectual Property Law, Partner at Gleiss & Große, lecturer at Esslingen University of Applied Sciences, Germany.

**Lee Su-Hua**, PhD, Associate Professor, College of Law, National Taipei University, Taiwan.

**Li Jian**, PhD, Presiding Judge, Supreme People's Court of the People's Republic of China.

**Li Yonghong**, Vice President of the Patent Re-examination Board of State Intellectual Property Organization (SIPO), China.

**Liu Kung-Chung**, PhD, Professor, Institutum Iurisprudentia, Academia Sinica, Institute of Law for Science and Technology, National Tsing Hua University, Taiwan.

**Stefan Luginbuehl**, PhD, Attorney at Law, Lawyer at the European Patent Office, Germany.

**Ma Qian**, PhD, LL.M. (Saarland University), LL.B. (Jilin University P.R.China), Foreign Lawyer at Clifford Chance, Germany.

**Toby Mak**, PhD, Patent Attorney at Tee & Howe IP Attorneys, China.

**Jan Bernd Nordemann**, PhD, LL.M. (Cantab.), Professor, Attorney at Law, Partner at Boehmert & Boehmert, Germany.

**Thomas Pattloch**, PhD, LL.M. Eur., Lawyer, Partner at Taylor Wessing, Germany.

**Oliver Pfaffenzeller**, PhD, Patent Attorney, Principal IP Counsel at Siemens, Germany.

**Berrit Roth**, MA (Chinese Studies), Junior Barrister ('Referendarin'), PhD candidate at University of Freiburg, Germany, former research assistant at Clifford Chance, Germany, current recipient of a PhD scholarship of the Konrad-Adenauer-Stiftung, a renowned political foundation in Germany.

**Carlos D. Simões**, Partner, DSL Lawyers, Macau.

**Lucy Wang**, B.Sc., LL.M (Peking University), LL.M. (China University of Political Science and Law P.R.China), LL.M (John Marshall Law School, USA), Patent Attorney, Head of China Patent Group at Rouse, China.

**Beat Weibel**, M.Sc., LL.M., Patent Attorney, Chief IP Counsel and Group Senior Vice President at Siemens, Germany.

# PREFACE

Within only 30 years, the People's Republic of China has developed a full-fledged and functioning patent system which fulfills international standards and the policy needs of China: In the course of its emergence, the Chinese legislature and judiciary had constantly been under the challenge to align foreign demands to adhere to international standards with the domestic interest. The present patent system forms such a compromise which makes utmost use of the remaining flexibilities under the international treaty system, so as to accommodate concerns related to national technological development.

The present book aims to provide the reader with a comprehensive overview of Chinese patent law and practice, and the challenges posed by the Chinese patent system. The distinctive feature of the book is that it provides an introduction to the political and legal background of important patent-related issues and combines comprehensiveness and in-depth reasoning on current challenges faced by practitioners in their daily work. That is, the general structure of the book follows the structure of traditional treaties on patent law, but in its subchapters our authors concentrate on certain aspects which have turned out to be of high practical relevance or which are currently debated.

We, the editors, are proud to have gathered together a group of highly renowned specialists in their fields, predominantly practitioners who are active in China but also a number of academics and judges. All of them have displayed not only their China-related experience but also their capability of reflecting their observations on legal and practical issues in China against the situation in Europe and other important jurisdictions.

The contributions bring to light increasing levels of legal certainty in various areas of the patent examination process and the enforcement of patent rights in China. Be it the communication between examiners and applicants in the course of patent examination or the mode of claim interpretation in the course of patent litigation, it becomes obvious that in many areas, administrators and judges base their judgments on established practices or guidelines, for example, the Supreme People's Court's interpretations on certain aspects of patent litigation, which enshrine such practices. Even though not all of these established practices are in the very interest of users, one should not underestimate the positive effects of such enhanced transparency and predictability of administrative and judicial decision making on both Chinese and foreign parties.

Finally, it should be noted that whereas the focus of our observations is on the People's Republic of China, we have also striven for comprehensiveness in regional respects. Therefore, the book includes overviews of patent legislation and practice in the Special Administrative Regions of Hong Kong and Macau, and on the challenges posed by the recent reforms to the patent system of Chinese Taipei (Taiwan). Furthermore, the book provides an introduction to the utility model and design protection systems of China which complement the patent system.

The editors express their own views and would like to stress that any opinions expressed in this book are those of the respective authors and do not necessarily reflect the views of the editors or their employers.

Finally, the editors would like to thank the staff and management of Edward Elgar for investing all their editorial expertise to polish this book into publishable shape.

The Editors
Peter Ganea and Stefan Luginbuehl

*Note: Chinese names are written in traditional form throughout, that is, family name placed first, followed by the given name. However, names of Chinese authors of publications in Western languages are quoted as they appear in connection with the respective publication.*

# ABBREVIATIONS AND ACRONYMS

| | |
|---|---|
| ADR | Alternative Dispute Resolution |
| AMEAs | Anti-Monopoly Law Enforcement Authorities |
| AML | Anti-Monopoly Law |
| ANSI | American National Standards Institute |
| ArbEG | Gesetz über Arbeitnehmererfindungen (Employee's Inventions Act, Germany) |
| Art./Arts. | Article/Articles |
| AVS | Audio Video Standard |
| CH | Country code for: Switzerland (Confoederatio Helvetica) |
| CIELA | China IP Litigation Analysis, <http://www.ciela.cn/> |
| CIPA | The Chartered Institute of Patent Attorneys |
| CJEU | Court of Justice of the EU |
| CN | Country code for: China |
| DE | Country code for: Germany (Deutschland) |
| DSE | Macau SAR Department of Economic Services |
| EPC | Convention on the grant of European patents (European Patent Convention) of 5.10.1973, last revised on 29.11.2000 |
| EPO | European Patent Office |
| et al. | et alii: and others |
| et seq. | et sequens: and following |
| ETSI | European Telecommunications Standards Institute |
| EU | European Union |
| EUCCC | The European Union Chamber of Commerce in China |
| EWCA civ | England and Wales Court of Appeal (Civil Division) |
| Fed. Cir. | US Court of Appeals for the Federal Circuit |
| FR | Country code for: France |

| | |
|---|---|
| FRAND | Fair, reasonable, and non-discriminatory terms |
| HCA | High Court Action |
| HK SAR | Code for: Hong Kong Special Administrative Region |
| ibid. | ibidem: in the same book or in the same decision |
| id. | idem: the same author |
| IEEE | Institute of Electrical and Electronics Engineers |
| IGRS | Intelligent Grouping and Resource Sharing working group |
| IPO | Macau SAR Intellectual Property Office |
| IP5 Offices | The world's five largest Intellectual Property Offices – The European Patent Office (EPO), the Japan Patent Office (JPO), the Korean Intellectual Property Office (KIPO), the State Intellectual Property Office of the PRC (SIPO) and the United States Patent and Trademark Office (USPTO) |
| It. | Item |
| ITU | International Telecommunication Union |
| JPO | The Japan Patent Office |
| KIPO | Korean Intellectual Property Office |
| LLC | Limited liability company |
| LLP | Limited liability partnership |
| MMLC | Managing Markets and Legal Consulting Group |
| MOFCOM | Ministry of Commerce of the PRC |
| MOP$ | Macau Pataca (currency of Macau SAR) |
| NDRC | National Development and Reform Commission |
| No./no. | Number |
| Paris Convention | Paris Convention for the Protection of Industrial Property of 20.3.1883 |
| PCT | Patent Cooperation Treaty of 19.6.1970, amended on 28.9.1979, modified on 3.2.1984, and on 3.10.2001 |
| PPH | Patent Prosecution Highway |
| PRB | Patent Re-examination Board of SIPO |
| PRC | People's Republic of China |
| R. | Rule |
| RAND | reasonable and non-discriminatory terms |
| Rep. | Reports |

| | |
|---|---|
| RMB | Renminbi; Chinese Yuan (currency of PRC) |
| SAIC | State Administration for Industry and Commerce of the PRC |
| SAR | Special Administrative Region |
| Sec./s. | Section |
| SEP | Standard-essential patent |
| Ser. | Series |
| SFDA | China State Drug and Food Administration |
| SIPO | State Intellectual Property Office of the People's Republic of China |
| SME | Small- and medium-sized enterprise |
| SPC | Supreme People's Court of the PRC |
| SSO | Standard setting organisation |
| T ../.. | Decision of an EPO Technical Board of Appeal |
| TFEU | Treaty on the Functioning of the EU |
| TFTA | The Taiwan Fair Trade Act of 4.2.1991 |
| TFTC | Taiwanese Fair Trade Commission |
| TIPO | Taiwan Intellectual Property Office |
| TRIPS/TRIPs Agreement | Agreement on Trade-Related Aspects of Intellectual Property Rights, including Trade in Counterfeit Goods of 5.4.1994 |
| UK | Country code for: United Kingdom |
| UKHL | UK House of Lords |
| US | Country code for: United States of America |
| USA | United States of America |
| USPTO | US Patent and Trademark Office |
| *v/vs* | versus |
| vol. | Volume |
| VPP | Vereinigung von Fachleuten auf dem Gebiet des gewerblichen Rechtsschutzes (Association of Intellectual Property Experts, Germany) |
| WTO | World Trade Organisation |

## ABBREVIATIONS AND ACRONYMS OF BLOGS, BOOKS, DOCUMENTS AND PERIODICALS

| | |
|---|---|
| All ER | All England Law Reports (UK) |
| *Antitrust L.J.* | Antitrust Law Journal (USA) |
| *Chi.-Kent J. Intell. Prop* | Chicago-Kent Journal of Intellectual Property (USA) |
| *CLP* | China Law & Practice (CN) |
| *CPA newsletter* | China Patent Agent Newsletter (CN) |
| *CPI Antitrust Chronicle* | Competition Policy International Antitrust Chronicle (USA) |
| *Duke J. Comp. & Int'I L.* | Duke Journal of Comparative and International Law (USA) |
| *Electronic IP* | Electronic Intellectual Property (CN) |
| *EIPR* | European Intellectual Property Review (UK) |
| *Fed. Circuit B. J.* | Federal Circuit Bar Journal (USA) |
| *F.Supp.* | Federal Reporter, Supplement (USA) |
| F.3d | Federal Reporter; 3rd ser. (USA) |
| *Fordham Int'l L.J.* | Fordham International Law Journal (USA) |
| FSR | Fleet Street Reports (UK) |
| *Ga. J. Int'l & Comp. l.* | Georgia Journal of International and Comparative Law (USA) |
| *GRUR* | Gewerblicher Rechtsschutz und Urheberrecht (DE) |
| *GRUR Int.* | Gewerblicher Rechtsschutz und Urheberrecht Internationaler Teil (DE) |
| *GRUR-RR* | Gewerblicher Rechtsschutz und Urheberrecht-Rechtsprechungsreport (DE) |
| *Harv.B.R.* | Harvard Business Review (USA) |
| HKC | Hong Kong Cases (HK SAR) |
| HKLR | Hong Kong Law Reports (HK SAR) |
| HKLRD | Hong Kong Law Reports and Digest (HK SAR) |
| *iam blog* | Intellectual Asset Management, <http://www.iam-magazine.com/blog/> |

| | |
|---|---|
| *IIC* | International Review of Industrial Property and Copyright Law (DE) |
| *Ind.J. Global Legal Stud.* | Indiana Journal of Global Legal Studies (USA) |
| *IP* | Intellectual Property (CN) |
| IPKat | IPKat blogger, <http://ipkitten.blogspot.de/> |
| *IPQ* | Intellectual Property Quarterly (UK) |
| *IStR-LB* | Internationales Steuerrecht und deren Länderbericht (DE) |
| *J. Marshall Rev. Intell. Prop. L.* | The John Marshall Review of Intellectual Property Law (USA) |
| *JIPLP* | Journal of Intellectual Property Law & Practice (UK) |
| *JPTOS* | Journal of the Patent and Trademark Office Society (USA) |
| *JWIP* | The Journal of World Intellectual Property (CH/UK) |
| *Mitt.* | Mitteilungen der deutschen Patentanwälte (DE) |
| *Nw. J. Tech & Intell. Prop.* | Northwestern Journal of Technology and Property (USA) |
| *NZA* | Neue Zeitschrift für Arbeitsrecht (DE) |
| *OJ EPO* | Official Journal of the European Patent Office (EPO) |
| *OJ EU* | Official Journal of the EU (EU) |
| *pi* | Propriétés intellectuelles (FR) |
| *RIW* | Recht der Internationalen Wirtschaft (DE) |
| RPC | Reports on Patent, Design and Trademark cases (UK) |
| *sic!* | Zeitschrift für Immaterialgüter-, Informations- und Wettbewerbsrecht (CH) |
| U.S. | List of United States Supreme Court cases |
| *VPP-Rdbr* | Rundbrief der Vereinigung von Fachleuten auf dem Gebiet des gewerblichen Rechtsschutzes (DE) |
| WIPR | World Intellectual Property Report (USA/UK) |
| WLR | Weekly Law Reports (UK) |
| WRP | Wettbewerb in Recht und Praxis (DE) |

# TABLE OF CASES

**Key**:

| | |
|---|---|
| CFI | Court of First Instance (EU) |
| Ch | Div Chancery Division (UK) |
| CJEU | Court of Justice of the European Union, named as ECJ – European Court of Justice before 1 December 2009 |
| HL | House of Lords (UK) |
| PRB | Patent Re-examination Board (China) |
| HKCA | Hong Kong Court of Appeal |
| TFTC | Taiwanese Fair Trade Commission |

## CHINA, PEOPLE'S REPUBLIC OF

### People's Court decisions

## Ministry of Commerce merger control decisions



## Patent Reexamination Board



# CHINESE TAIPEI (TAIWAN)



# EUROPEAN COURT OF JUSTICE

## EUROPEAN PATENT OFFICE, BOARDS OF APPEAL



## FRANCE



## GERMANY

## HONG KONG SAR



## JAPAN



## THE NETHERLANDS

## UNITED KINGDOM



## UNITED STATES OF AMERICA

# TABLE OF LEGISLATION

**Key**:

| | |
|---|---|
| PRC | People's Republic of China |
| SAIC | State Administration for Industry and Commerce of the PRC |
| SAR | Special Administrative Region |
| TFEU | Treaty on the Functioning of the European Union |
| TFTC | Taiwanese Fair Trade Commission |

## CHINA, PEOPLE'S REPUBLIC OF

### Primary legislation

## Secondary legislation

## CHINESE TAIPEI (TAIWAN)

### Primary legislation

## Secondary legislation



## GERMANY

## HONG KONG SAR

### Primary legislation



### Secondary legislation



## INTERNATIONAL (INCL. EUROPEAN UNION)

### Conventions and Treaties

## Secondary legislation

## MACAU SAR



## UNITED KINGDOM

### Primary legislation



## UNITED STATES OF AMERICA

# Part A

# PATENT PROTECTION IN THE PEOPLE'S REPUBLIC OF CHINA

# 1

# CHINA'S PATENT POLICY[1]


## Stefan Luginbuehl[2]




## A. INTRODUCTION

1.01 Since the 1970s, when Deng Xiao Ping opened up the country to foreign investment and limited private competition, and introduced the 'socialist market reform', China has – with an official annual GDP growth rate of nigh on 10 per cent – become the fastest-growing economy in human history. With its attractive labour conditions, including the low wages associated with its huge population, and more open policies for foreign direct investment,[3] China has developed at a rapid rate into the country for labour-intensive low-technology manufacturing.[4] At the beginning of the new millennium it was difficult to find a product which was not made in the People's Republic of China. However, as the century progressed, the Chinese government came to recognise that sustainable growth could only continue at this pace – and China become a global

1 See also Stefan Luginbuehl and Thomas Pattloch, 'China's New Patent Policy', [2011] **33** *EIPR 274*; Stefan Luginbuehl and Thomas Pattloch, 'The Awakening of the Chinese Patent Dragon – The Revised Chinese Patent Act 2009', [2011] **42** *IIC* 130.

2 Any views expressed in this article are those of the author and do not necessarily reflect the views of the European Patent Office. The author would like to thank Christine Kämmer and Stephan Worack for their great support concerning the establishment of the graphs in this article.

3 Cf. Chunlai Chen, *Foreign Direct Investment in China*, Cheltenham, UK and Northampton, MA, USA: Edward Elgar 2011, 5.

4 Cf. John L. Orcutt and Hong Shen, *Shaping China's Innovation Future*, Cheltenham, UK and Northampton, MA, USA: Edward Elgar 2010, p. vii.

player and the world's biggest economy[5] – if the country was transformed from a manufacturing economy to a manufacturing and knowledge-based economy.[6] The establishment of a strong intellectual property system creating wealth for China and encouraging investment in research and development (R&D) was deemed to be an important part of this transformation.

**1.02** To this end, it was important to strengthen the independent innovation capacity of Chinese companies, to enable them to create and protect their own IP rights and free themselves from what was often considered the dominance[7] of IP rights owned by foreign companies, who could set the conditions for the manufacture of their protected products and request licensing fees which left Chinese producers with little profit.[8]

**1.03** At the same time, in order to become a knowledge- and service-based economy, China needs access to technological information from developed economies and consequently has to establish an environment which will attract companies from such economies to invest and produce in China. Studies have revealed that foreign direct investment (FDI) to China from developed countries possessing advanced technology and production techniques was and is still limited.[9] In order to improve this situation and to become more innovative, the Chinese government introduced a mandatory work plan in 2008 to bring the country to the level of its European, US and Asian competitors by 2020. This plan is known as the National Intellectual Property Strategy (NIPS).

## B. THE NATIONAL INTELLECTUAL PROPERTY STRATEGY (NIPS)

**1.04** The adoption of the NIPS was the first time in China that intellectual property had been the subject of an approved policy strategy at the highest political level, and was an indication of the importance that China had begun to attach to this

5 China passed Japan as the second largest economy in 2010. The OECD expects that China will be the world's largest economy as early as 2016, see OECD, 'Looking to 2060: Long-term growth prospects for the world', 2012, available at <www.oecd.org>.

6 See Wen Jiabao, opening speech at the world economic forum in Tianjin on 13 September 2010 who stated that China should develop from a big production country to a strong production and innovation country.

7 Peter Ganea, 'China's Amended Legal Regime on Patents for Inventions and Utility Models', [2010] **5** *JIPLP* 650, 651.

8 Cf. for example as regards DVD player manufacturing: Ying Zhan and Xuezhong Zhu, 'Intellectual Property Right Abuses in the Patent Licensing of Technology Standards from Developed Countries to Developing Countries: A Study of Some Typical Cases from China', [2007] **10** *JWIP* 187, 192; 'China unveils home-grown DVD standard', *Managing IP, Weekly News* – 13 September 2007.

9 Cf. Chunlai Chen, above note 3, 170 et seq., 279 et seq.

subject. Before the NIPS[10] was approved by the State Council, in-depth research and consultation was carried out, particularly with various branches of government and government ministries.

The NIPS includes details of the guiding principles, strategic goals, strategic focuses and specific tasks involved, with timelines for achieving them.

As a strategic goal it was made clear that: **1.05**

> By 2020, China will become a country with a comparatively high level in terms of the creation, utilization, protection and administration of IPRs. The legal environment for IPRs is much better, market entities are much better at the creation, utilization, protection and administration of IPRs, the public awareness of intellectual property is increased greatly, the quality and quantity of the self-relied intellectual property are able to effectively support the effort to make China an innovative country, the role of the intellectual property system in promoting economic development, the culture prosperity and social progress in China become very apparent.

There is no doubt about the patent policy's fundamental role in all this, a role **1.06** which was confirmed in November 2010 when the Chinese State Intellectual Property Office (SIPO) published the National Patent Development Strategy 2011–2020 (NPDS).[11]

The NPDS includes detailed measures aimed at enabling China to develop into a powerful country in patent terms.

The following sections deal only with the major patent policy measures which are determined in the NIPS and the NPDS:

- revise the patent law and constantly improve it,
- increase the capacity to create domestic innovation ('indigenous innovation'), and
- improve the general enforcement of patent rights.

10 For an outline of the NIPS published in English, see http://www.chinaipr.gov.cn/policyarticle/policy/documents/200806/241260_1.html.

11 'China sets 10-year plan to boost patent industry', *China Daily*, 11 November 2010; 'China announces plans to own key patents in newly emerging and traditional industries', *iam blog*, November 2010, www.iam-magazine.com.

## 1. The revision of the patent law and its constant improvement

**1.07** The third revision of the Chinese Patent Act[12] was the first important measure of the patent policy triggered by the NIPS which was implemented. The revision was concluded on 1 February 2010 with the entry into force of the Implementing Regulations and the amended Patent Examination Guidelines. The 'Interpretation of the Supreme People's Court on Several Issues concerning the Application of Law in the Trial of Patent Infringement Dispute Cases (applicable for all lower courts)'[13] contains important information on interpreting substantive law for lower-level courts.

**1.08** The two previous revisions of the Patent Act[14] – in 1992[15] and 2000 – were designed to construct a legal framework to attract foreign investors[16] and prepare the ground for joining, first, the Patent Cooperation Treaty (PCT)[17] and then the WTO, which meant that the law had to be compliant with the TRIPs Agreement.[18]

**1.09** By contrast, the third revision followed China's own economic, technological and cultural interests.[19] The revision was aimed at meeting a number of general objectives derived from the goals of the NIPS:

- to improve patent quality,
- to safeguard national security and other 'substantial interests',
- to improve the balance between patent protection and the public interest, and

12 For this history see EU-CHINA IPR 2, *Third revision of China's Patent Law, Legal texts and documents on the drafting process 2006–2008*, 31.

13 Fashi (2009) No. 21 of the Supreme People's Court. The Judicial Interpretation came into force on 1 January 2010.

14 For a historical overview see Zhang Ping, 'Review and perspective of the Chinese patent system', in Ryo Shimanami (ed.), *The Future of the Patent System*, Cheltenham, UK and Northampton, MA, USA: Edward Elgar 2012, 308, 309 et seq.

15 Cf. Ping-Hsun (Quincy) Chen, 'China as a Technology Exporter: A Question Mark after the Third Amendment of the China Patent Law in 2009', [2012] **34** *EIPR* 853, 855.

16 Cf. Andrea Wechsler, Volksrepublik China – Verabschiedung der dritten chinesischen Patentrechtsreform durch den Nationalen Volkskongress', **2009** *GRUR Int* 275.

17 Guo Shoukang and Zuo Xiadong, 'Are Chinese intellectual property laws consistent with the TRIPs Agreement?', in Paul Torremans, Hailing Shan and Johan Erauw (eds.), *Intellectual Property and TRIPS Compliance in China*, Cheltenham, UK and Northampton, MA, USA: Edward Elgar 2007, 11 and 12; Qian Ma and Ge Jiang, 'Die dritte Revision des Patentgesetzes der Volksrepublik China', **2010** *RIW* 446; Yuanshi Bu, *Patentrecht und Technologietransfer in China,* München et al.: Verlag C.H. Beck/Helbing Lichtenhahn Verlag, 2010, N 10.

18 Chiang Ling Li, 'Recent Chinese Patent Reform', [2001] **4** *JWIP* 919; Peter Ganea, 'Die Neuregelung des chinesischen Patentrechts', **2002** *GRUR Int* 686, 687; Wang Yanhong, 'Enhance Patent Protection, Promote Scientific and Technological Innovation – The Introduction to the Second Revision of the Chinese Patent Act', AIPPI Journal, Extra Issue 2001, 29; Gordon Gao, Dixon Zhang and Fang Qi, *Intellectual Property Rights in China*, Hong Kong: Sweet & Maxwell, 2011, 3 et seq.

19 See also Zhang Ping, above note 14, 308, 316 and Yuanshi Bu, above note 17, N 10.

- to put in place measures to improve patent enforcement and prevent the unlawful use of rights.[20]

### (a) Changes in the Patent Act aimed at improving patent quality

Patent quality has been a problem for many years. The revised Act contains numerous changes intended to rectify this. 1.10

First, it introduced the absolute novelty standard.[21] Under the old law, novelty was only destroyed if the technology had been used or was known in China (domestic use or knowledge of the invention), or had already been published, either inside or outside China.[22] This new standard allows SIPO to reject patent applications and revoke patents (or utility models) which were no more than a copy of prior art used abroad.[23] However, in practice this would appear not to be that easy (see the issue of utility models under 2 below.).

The revised law also makes it clear that the subject-matter determined in a patent application is novelty-destroying vis-à-vis a subsequently filed application by the same applicant including the same subject-matter if the first application was published after the subsequent application ('conflicting applications').[24] Under the old law, the subject-matter of the earlier filed application was not novelty-destroying in such a situation (see also *Bu*, Chapter 3). 1.11

Furthermore, in order to avoid inventions being protected for more than 20 years, under the revised Patent Act an application for a utility model and a patent for the same invention can only be filed on the same day, and the applicant must abandon the previously obtained utility model right in order to have the patent granted.[25] 1.12

---

20 See also Explanatory notes from SIPO, (I) Legislative objective of the patent law, in EU-CHINA IPR 2, *Third revision of China's Patent Law, Legal texts and documents on the drafting process 2006–2008*, 50, and Explanatory notes from LAO, *ibid.*, 150 f.

21 Art. 22(5) Chinese Patent Act.

22 See Benjamin Bai, Anthony Chen, Chiang Ling Li, Mark Cohen and Ann W. Chen, 'The radical third amendment', *Managing IP*, China IP Focus 2009, 21; Weishi Li, 'All change for China', Patent World Issue # 213, June 2009, 18; Yali Shao, 'Latest patent changes analysed', *Managing IP*, Asia-Pacific IP Focus 2007, 25; Jay Sha, 'Third time lucky', *Managing IP*, China IP Focus 2007, 29, 30.

23 Cf. also Peter Ganea, above note 7, 650, 652.

24 See Art. 22(2) Chinese Patent Act. See also Luo Li, 'Reflection on the Principle of Prohibition of Double Patenting', in Christian Harmsen, Oliver Jan Jüngst and Felix Rödiger (eds.), *Festschrift für Wolfgang von Meibom zum 65. Geburtstag*, Carl Heymanns Verlag 2010, 285 et seq.

25 Art. 9(1) Chinese Patent Act and R. 41(2) Implementing Regulations to the Chinese Patent Act. See also Luo Li, above note 24, 291.

### (b) Improved protection of national and public interests

**1.13** The most important amendment in terms of improved protection of national interests is the introduction of the confidentiality examination. This examination gives SIPO an overview of the technical areas in which research is being carried out in China and the core technical areas involved.[26] According to Article 20(1) Chinese Patent Act, any entity or individual intending to file a patent application abroad for an invention completed in China first has to apply to SIPO for a prior confidentiality examination. The applicant is only allowed to file abroad once SIPO gives its approval (for more information, see *Luginbuehl*, Chapter 11).

**1.14** The revised Patent Act also introduced a mandatory declaration of the source of genetic resources in patent applications for inventions based on such resources. This addition was designed to provide greater protection for the considerable genetic diversity in China.[27] Article 26(5) Chinese Patent Act stipulates that an applicant who files a patent application for an invention completed on the basis of genetic resources must indicate the direct and original source of those resources (see also in this regard *Bu*, Chapter 3 and *Chen*, Chapter 4). Usually, the genetic material will be from a gene bank, which would be given as the direct source and which should also be able to provide details of the original source of the genetic material. If the applicant is unable to indicate the source he must provide an explanation. Under Article 5 Chinese Patent Act, non-compliance with the rules on the acquisition and use of genetic resources will result in refusal of the application, or revocation of any patent granted.

**1.15** In addition, the Chinese Patent Act now includes the so-called 'Bolar exemption',[28] under which generic products can be launched more quickly after expiry of the patent protecting the generic drug or medical apparatus than would normally be the case, as the company producing the drug or apparatus can perform the necessary studies and tests for administrative approval during the patent's term without infringing it.

**1.16** The strengthening of compulsory licensing[29] is another of the stated aims of the NIPS, so, under the revised Patent Act, the grounds for compulsory licensing have been extended. On the one hand, it is now possible to obtain a compulsory licence to exploit the patent if the patent holder has not exploited or has not

26 See also the critical remarks by Ping-Hsun (Quincy) Chen, 'China as a Technology Exporter: A Question Mark after the Third Amendment of the China Patent Law in 2009', [2012] **34** *EIPR* 853, 862 et seq.

27 See also Hu Kaizhong, 'An Analysis of Determination of Level of Intellectual Property in China', [2008] **30** *EIPR* 515, 519 f.

28 Art. 69(5) Chinese Patent Act.

29 See No. 20 NIPS.

sufficiently exploited the patent without justifiable reason within three years from the date of grant or four years from the filing date.[30] Exploitation of the patent is deemed to be insufficient if the patent holder or his licensee exploits the patent in a manner or on a scale that fails to meet the domestic demands for the patented product or process.[31] On the other hand, where the exercise of patent rights is considered to be a monopolistic act under the anti-monopoly law, a compulsory licence may be granted to reduce or eliminate the adverse consequences of this act for competition.[32] Furthermore, the Doha Declaration on the TRIPs Agreement and Public Health[33] has also been implemented in the Chinese Patent Act. It is now possible to obtain a compulsory licence to manufacture a patented drug and export it to a state which is eligible to import the drug under the Doha Declaration. So far, no such licence has been issued.

Finally, it is also worth mentioning that the revision introduced the international exhaustion of patent rights.[34] In other words, importing patented goods does not constitute infringement if the goods have been put on the market anywhere in the world with the consent of the patent holder. The principle of international exhaustion should be removed from the law once the price for Chinese patent products in China is higher than in other countries.[35] **1.17**

### *(c) Measures to improve the enforcement of patent rights*

The revised Patent Act stipulates how damages can be claimed in civil proceedings and defines a mandatory hierarchy of computational methods.[36] The first level on which compensation is determined is on the basis of the patent holder's actual losses. If these are difficult to ascertain, the next calculation is based on the infringer's profits. Then comes an appropriate multiple licence fee and, finally, statutory damages, which have been doubled from their previous maximum to RMB 1 million (approx. €120,000). It is in fact standard practice in many regions to claim statutory damages in patent infringement cases, mainly because of the strict evidential requirements in Chinese courts. It is now **1.18**

30 Art. 48(1) Chinese Patent Act, see also Art. 5A(4) Paris Convention.

31 R. 73(1) Implementing Regulations to the Chinese Patent Act.

32 Art 48(2) Chinese Patent Act.

33 See further information at www.wto.org/english/tratop_e/dda_e/dohaexplained_e.htm. See also Jenny Wakely, 'Compulsory Licensing under TRIPS: An Effective Tool to Increase Access to Medicines in Developing and Least Developed Countries?', [2011] **33** *EIPR* 299; Duncan Matthews, 'From the August 30, 2003 WTO Decision to the December 6, 2005 Agreement on an Amendment to TRIPS: Improving Access to Medicines in Developing Countries?', [2006] **2** *IPQ* 91; Alfredo Barona, 'TRIPS and Access of Developing Countries to Essential Medicines – Hands Tied?', **2006** *Mitt.* 402.

34 Art. 69(1) Chinese Patent Act.

35 More about the exhaustion of patent rights in China, see *Ganea*, Chapter 16.

36 Art. 65 Chinese Patent Act.

also possible under the revised law to request interim injunctions and measures to preserve evidence.[37]

### *(d) Fourth revision of the Patent Act*

**1.19** In August 2012 SIPO tabled a proposal for new revision of the Patent Act. The proposed changes aim at the further improvement of the enforcement of patent rights. For this purpose it is, inter alia, suggested that the administrative enforcement of patent rights should again be strengthened. In particular damages and compensation could be awarded in administrative proceedings. Furthermore, the introduction of punitive damages which would be three times the costs the patent infringer would have had to pay if he had entered into a licensing agreement and to give immediate effect to decisions of the Patent Re-examination Board in relation to patent validity decisions is suggested. The proposals were criticised by high-level Chinese experts. Mainly the proposal to strengthen the administrative proceedings vis-à-vis the court litigation was identified as problematic. It is thus questionable whether these proposals will become law.

## 2. The indigenous innovation (*zizhu chuangxin*) policy and the problem of utility models

**1.20** The NIPS provides that by 2013:

> China will rank among the advanced countries of the world in terms of the patents for inventions granted to domestic applicants while the number of overseas patent applications by Chinese applicants should greatly increase.

The NPDS also states that, by 2015:

> the annual quantity of applying for patents, utility models and designs will reach 2 million. China will rank among the top two in the world in terms of annual number of patents for inventions granted to the domestic applicants, and the quality of patents filed will further improve … [38]

This policy of self-developed and self-owned technology is usually referred to as 'indigenous innovation'.[39]

---

37 See Arts. 66 and 67 Chinese Patent Act.

38 See III. Strategic Goals, National Patent Development Strategy (2011–2020).

39 See in this regard also Zhang Ping, above note 14, 308, 343 ff and Fashi (2011) No. 18 of the Supreme People's Court.

Now, five years after the adoption of the NIPS and its implementation at central and local level, the strategy is bearing fruit, and it looks as if this crucial goal of the Chinese patent policy can be reached. The number of applications for invention patents (in China the term 'patent' includes patents, utility models and designs) filed with SIPO rose in 2012 to an impressive 652,777. Of these, 535,313 were filed by Chinese applicants (see Figure 1.1). This is an increase of more than 250 per cent since 2008, and almost 600 per cent since 2005. **1.21**

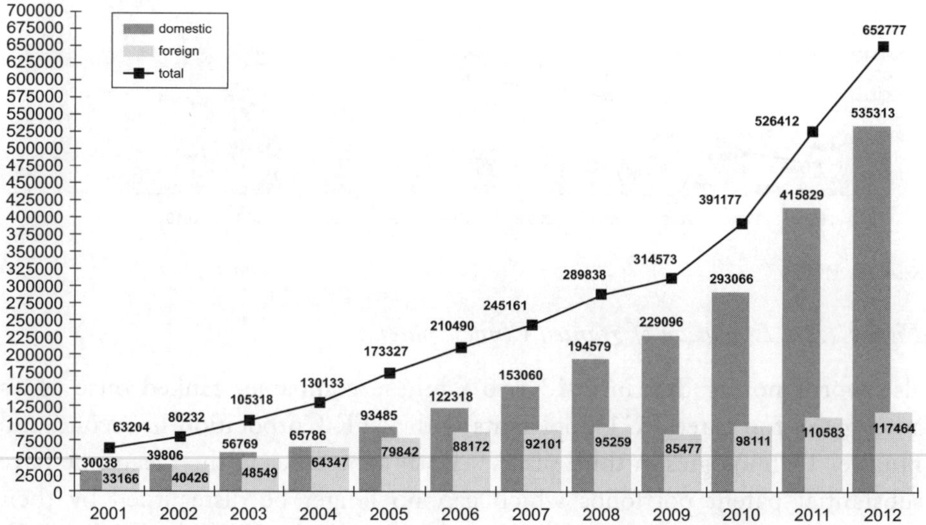


*Source:* EPO

*Figure 1.1 Evolution of Chinese patent applications*

Furthermore, the grant rate of SIPO, which is in fact more important than the number of applications, has also risen significantly in the past few years. In 2008, SIPO still granted slightly more patents to foreign applicants (47,116) than to domestic applicants (46,590). In 2012 it granted 143,847 patents to Chinese applicants, almost double that of its foreign competitors and an increase of more than 300 per cent vis-à-vis 2008 (see Figure 1.2). **1.22**

As far as patent applications filed abroad are concerned, in 2013 China became the third largest user of the PCT system passing Germany, with 21,516 filings.[40] This represents a 15.5 per cent growth vis-à-vis 2012[41] and an increase of 86 per cent vis-à-vis 2005,[42] when 2,499 filings were of Chinese origin. It is **1.23**

40 WIPO, Who filed the most PCT patent applications in 2013?, available at www.wipo.org.

41 WIPO, 2013 PCT Yearly Review, 27, available at http://www.wipo.int.

42 WIPO, The International Patent System in 2006, PCT Yearly Review, available at http://www.wipo.int.

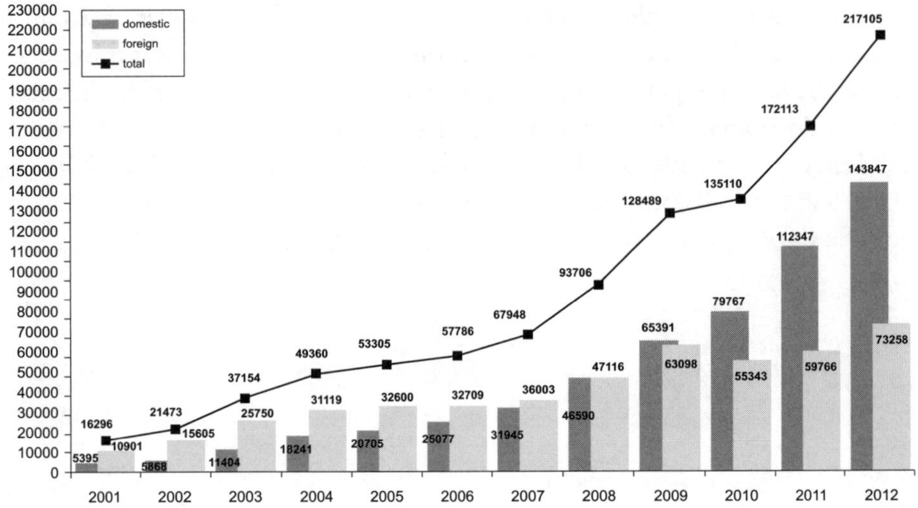


*Source:* EPO

*Figure 1.2 Evolution of granted Chinese patents*

also worth noting that in 2013 two Chinese companies ranked once again among the top three PCT applicants with ZTE Corporation in second and Huawei Technologies in third place.[43] Both companies in the meantime have substantial patent portfolios which can no longer be disregarded by their competitors. They have high-level in-house expertise and highly developed IP (in particular patents), which is professionally managed, commercialised and used as strategic value,[44] even against each other.[45] This is no coincidence. Both companies are active in key technology sectors defined by the state and both get support from the Chinese government. The preferential treatment of chosen enterprises[46] in particular, and Chinese companies in general, by the Chinese

43 WIPO, Who filed the most PCT patent applications in 2013?, available at www.wipo.org.

44 Cf. 'Huawei: From the PLA [People's Liberation Army] to global telecoms', *Managing Intellectual Property*, 25 March 2013; Peter Leung, 'ZTE and IBM discuss their international patent strategies', *Managing Patents*, 21 June 2012.

45 In a decision rendered by the Paris District Court on 28 March 2013, Huawei was ordered to pay €100,000 in damages to ZTE after dismissing the company's infringement claim on grounds of lack of novelty over a data card patent, see Emma Barraclough, 'Paris Court Rules in Chinese Patent Row', *Managing Intellectual Property*, 2 April 2013. The court followed similar rulings by the German Federal Patent Court where the patent was revoked. Huawei sued ZTE for infringement of its patents before many European courts. The Düsseldorf district court stayed one case at the end of March 2013 and referred questions to the Court of Justice of the EU concerning the interpretation of EU competition law, in particular on whether the approach taken by Germany on FRAND licensing is in line with EU competition law (case C-170/13).

46 Dan Prud'homme, 'Dulling the Cutting-Edge: How Patent-Related Policies and Practices Hamper Innovation in China', August 2012, 13, available at www.europeanchamber.com.cn

government has provoked criticism,[47] with the result that the government had to withdraw its plans to support and enhance domestic companies by reserving preferential treatment in government procurement procedures for indigenously innovated products.[48]

Support for Chinese companies in obtaining patents in core areas of technology with the aim of facilitating the development of China's new and high-tech industries in key sectors is one of the tasks laid down in the NIPS.[49] With a view to making a stronger push for more patents in these technical areas, on 1 August 2012 SIPO introduced administrative measures aimed at prioritising the examination of patent applications, inter alia, relating to innovations in these areas.[50] If a request for prioritised examination is granted, SIPO will issue the first office action within 30 working days from the date of acceptance of the request[51], aiming at completing the examination procedure within one year.[52]

What is more, SIPO takes part in a number of Patent Prosecution Highway (PPH) bilateral programmes with other patent offices, such as the German Patent and Trade Mark Office, the JPO, KIPO and the USPTO.[53] Furthermore, SIPO participates in a PPH pilot programme within the IP5 Offices and within a global framework, and in a PPH pilot programme with eased requirements. Under the PPH[54] an application whose claims have been determined to be patentable in the office of first filing is eligible – at the applicant's request – for accelerated examination in the office of second filing using a simple procedure. Chinese applicants thus have access to accelerated examination before the PPH partner offices if they first file an application with SIPO and SIPO holds at least one claim to be patentable. 1.24

47 As regards subsidies for Huawei on electric vehicles see for example: http://greenworldinvestor.com/2010/08/04/china-to-create-green-vehicle-national-champions-with-a-100-billion-yuan-subsidy/.

48 See Stefan Luginbuehl and Thomas Pattloch, 'China's New Patent Policy', above note 1, 274.

49 See National Patent Development Strategy (2011–2020) No. 16, which qualifies biology, medicine, information, new materials, advanced manufacturing, new energy, oceanography, resources, environmental protection, modern agriculture, modern transportation, aeronautics and astronautics as key sectors.

50 Administrative Measures on Prioritized Examination of Invention Patent Applications, Order No. 65 of SIPO, promulgated on 19 June 2012 and implemented on 1 August 2012.

51 R. 10, Administrative Measures on Prioritized Examination of Invention Patent Applications, Order No. 65 of SIPO, promulgated on 19 June 2012 and implemented on 1 August 2012.

52 Patent Protection and Enforcement in the PRC, 28 January 2014, Bird & Bird, A report commissioned by Huawei Technologies, 11.

53 See also Toby Mak, 'Patent Prosecution Highway in China', **2013** *CIPA Journal* 388.

54 For more information see http://www.jpo.go.jp/ppph-portal/index.htm.

**1.25** Although there is still a high concentration of patent filings from just a few Chinese firms,[55] the figures indicate that Chinese companies, universities and research institutions[56] are becoming increasingly aware of the commercial potential of creating innovation. This is the result not only of far-reaching awareness campaigns run by the government, but also of the attractive incentives afforded to Chinese applicants. Apart from tax reductions (15 per cent[57] instead of 25 per cent corporate income tax) for new and high-technology enterprises which have demonstrated that they are in the possession of IP protected core technology, many fees are reimbursable for Chinese companies and Chinese companies with foreign partners. An innovative government-financed patent pledge and loan system[58] and other subsidies,[59] as well as financial assistance for SMEs applying for patents outside of China,[60] bonuses or promotions for employees who apply for patents,[61] and career incentives at universities,[62] are also provided, as mandated by China's patent policy.[63]

**1.26** However, there are several factors which would suggest that the innovative capability of Chinese companies has remained limited up to date. On the one hand, it is not rarely stated by patent professionals that many patent applications filed by Chinese in China are still of low quality.[64]

On the other hand, the number of international applications by Chinese companies is only 4 per cent of the number of domestic applications. This indicates that only a very limited selection of applications are also filed outside

---

55 Cf. Dan Prud'homme, above note 46; Virna Chung and Justin Kung in a study identified just 33 Chinese companies with what they qualified as having a world-class approach to IP, see Virna Chung and Justin Kung, 'Meet the China IP Champions', *Intellectual Asset Management*, January/February 2013, www.iam-magazine.com, 49, 51.

56 Six of the top ten patent applicants in China are academic institutions, cf. Tom Duke, 'The domestic context to Chinese overseas patent applications', **2013** *CIPA Journal* 450, 453.

57 Thomas T. Moga, 'China's Utility Model Patent System: Innovation Driver or Deterrent', Asia, U.S. Chamber of Commerce, November 2012, 17.

58 Zuo Yuru, Dianzi Zhishi Chanquan, 10 November 2010, 48 et seq.

59 Thomas T. Moga, above note 57, 17 f; Tom Duke, above note 56, 453.

60 In Wuhan, for example SMEs receive €2,500 for the deposit of a Chinese patent application and €12,500 for the deposit of an international application if they qualify as an 'innovative company', cf. http://breese.blogs.com/pi/2013/11/chine.html; cf. also Michael Standard, 'China Sets New Financial Incentives to Encourage Patent Application Abroad', 07/2012, *WIPR* 8.

61 Patent Protection and Enforcement in the PRC, above note 52, 26.

62 See Annsley Merelle Ward, 'Why do Chinese academics file so many patents?', IPKat, 1 February 2011, http://ipkitten.blogspot.com/2011/02/why-do-chinese-academics-file-so-many.html.

63 Cf. NPDS No. 4; R 100 Implementing Regulations to the Chinese Patent Act, *Measures of Reduction of Expenses for patent,* promulgated by SIPO on 12 October 2006.

64 Cf. Toby Mak, 'Recent moves to enhance the quality of patents in China', **2014** *CIPA Journal* 99; see also Dan Prud'homme, above note 46, 49, suggests that 67% of patent applications are ultimately not granted.

of China (although the number of filings is steadily increasing).[65] This is also underlined by the relatively low number of patent grants to Chinese abroad. In 2013, the EPO, for example, granted 941 patents to Chinese applicants. By contrast it granted 14,880 patents to US, 13,425 to German and 12,135 to Japanese applicants. In the US too the number of patents granted to Chinese applicants is limited compared to the number of grants to applicants from other countries.[66]

Furthermore, in China most patents awarded to Chinese only have an average life-span of five years, that is, they are dropped earlier than patents owned by non-Chinese, which are, on average, in force for nine years.[67] This seems to indicate that patent protected Chinese-owned inventions are less valuable. Additionally, studies have revealed that Chinese patents are rarely cited in patent application literature and non-patent literature, which would suggest that their importance with regard to the state of the art is limited.[68] What is more, the utility model figures indicate that the pre-determined patent application targets which have to be reached by Chinese companies in the race for innovation lead to a situation where quantity takes precedence over quality.[69] In other words, the innovation capability of Chinese enterprises and universities has not evolved as fast as the Chinese government envisaged, or at least not at the pace of the benchmarked application figures. **1.27**

The number of applications and grants for utility models has literally exploded in the past few years. However, due to the fact that utility models are not examined substantively they are often simply copies of existing state of the art, or they involve only slight modifications to protected innovations which do not fulfil the requirements of inventive step, which is already at a lower level compared to patents (see *Bu*, Chapter 3). In 2012, SIPO registered 566,750 utility models to Chinese applicants. In just four years, there was an increase of more than 250 per cent although the number of 203,802 registered utility models in 2009 was already relatively high for utility models (see Figure 1.3).[70] **1.28**

65 In 2013, the EPO received 4,056 applications from China: 871 Euro-direct and 3,185 PCT applications entering the regional phase. This is an increase of 8,4% vis-à-vis 2012 and an increase of 97,7% vis-à-vis 2010. The growth in patent applications from China is consequently slowing down.

66 In 2013, 5,030 US patents were granted to applicants from China, more than half of them going to just ten companies, see 'Why aren't Chinese companies Filing in the US?', 30 January 2014, <www.managingip.com>.

67 Cf. Dan Prud'homme, above note 46, 51, referring to L. Gao, M.Li and Y.Cheng, et al. (2011, September), *Report on the Quality for Invention in China*, Beijing Intellectual Property Rights Institute and Tom Duke, above note 56, 453.

68 Cf. Dan Prud'homme, above note 46, 53.

69 Cf. Song Shenxia and Liu Linlin, 'Inventors needed', *Global Times*, 17 March 2013; John L. Orcutt and Hong Shen, above note 4, 65; Toby Mak, above note 64, 100.

70 In Germany for example there were 15,491 applications for utility models in 2012 which is a decrease of almost 4% vis-à-vis 2011, see annual report of the German Patent and Trade Mark Office 2012, 19. In contrast, in 2012

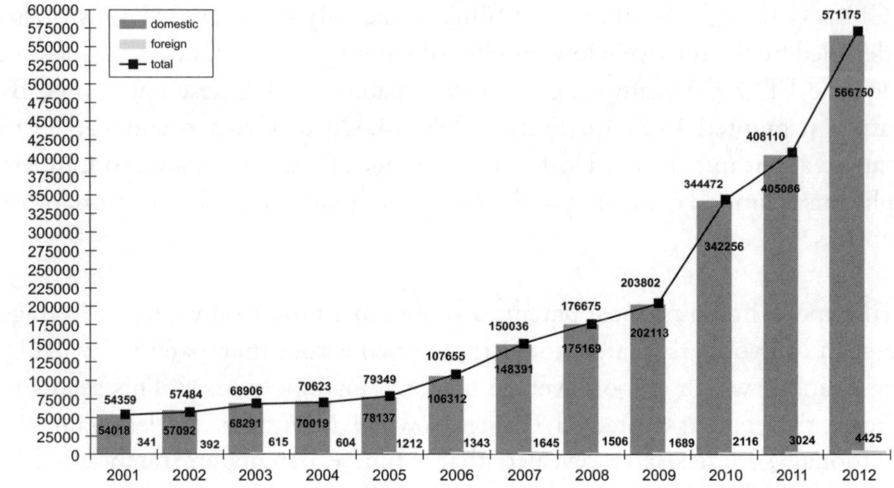


*Source:* EPO

*Figure 1.3 Evolution of Chinese utility model registrations*

**1.29** This trend looks like continuing: in 2012, Chinese applicants filed 734,437 requests for the registration of utility models, which is an increase of more than 230 per cent over 2009. In contrast, in 2012 applicants from outside of China only filed 5,853 applications for utility models (see Figure 1.4).

**1.30** Although more and more non-Chinese applicants are applying for utility models, the statistics show that the huge increase in the number of utility models accounts predominantly for Chinese applicants. This suggests that the Chinese government's incentives, quotas and awards are geared towards increasing the number of utility model filings instead of invention patent applications. Utility models are thus also used as a catalyst to enable government-set targets to be reached. As long as a utility model does not have to meet any requirements as to quality to entitle its holder to subsidies or tax breaks the number of utility model applications will further increase. However, the many low-quality utility models[71] ('junk patents')[72] flooding the market – even under the absolute novelty scheme introduced in the revised patent law – seem more suited to hampering or even paralysing innovation rather than

---

the German Patent and Trademark Office received 61,311 patent applications which was an increase of almost 3% vis-à-vis 2011, see annual report of the German Patent and Trade Mark Office 2012, 5, available at www.dpma.de/english/service/publications/index.html.

71 See also Peter Leung, 'China's utility model growing pains', *Managing IP*, 10 June 2013.

72 See inter alia Jörg-Michael Scheil, 'Die strategische Bedeutung von Patentnichtigkeitsanträgen in China', **2013** *Mitt.* 263, 268.

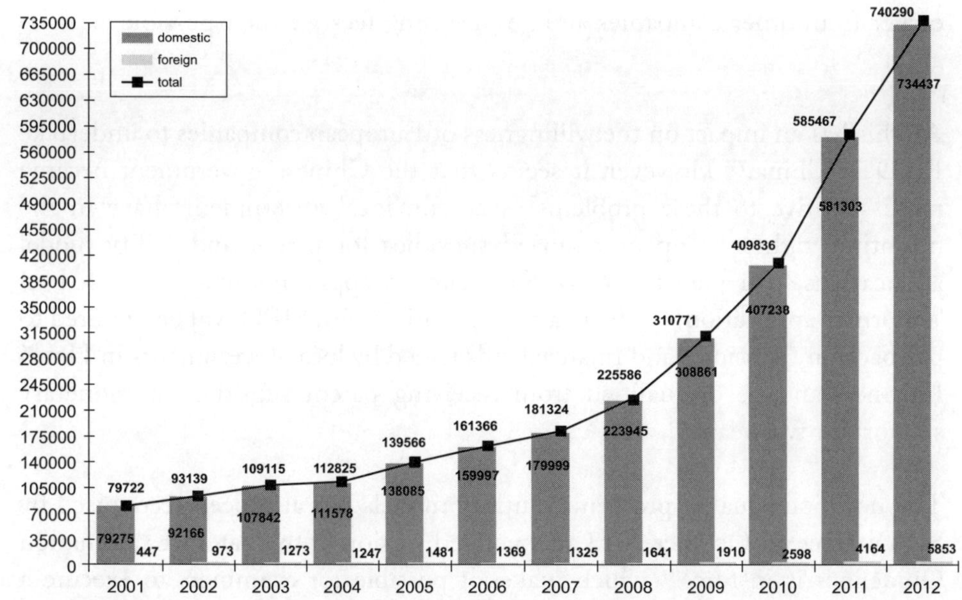


*Source:* EPO

*Figure 1.4 Evolution of Chinese utility model applications*

fostering it. Such 'utility model thickets' are not only problematic for Chinese companies that would like to be innovative, but also for foreign investors, who are increasingly confronted with high costs:

- for monitoring and evaluating the utility models[73] that could be a potential danger for the exploitation of a company's own patent rights, as well as
- for possible negotiations and settlements with the owners of the utility models,[74] and/or
- for possible litigation, in order to invalidate the utility models.[75]

This seems also fertile ground for a possible development of so-called 'patent trolls', that is, of 'patent assertion entities' which are not active in the technological area at stake and which have only the intention to 'extort' their often weak patent and utility model rights which they have acquired **1.31**

73 It is not rare that companies active in certain technical areas are faced with 800 new utility models per month in the same technical field.

74 Often utility models are simply bought in order to avoid litigation.

75 Thomas T. Moga, above note 57, 20 f.

earlier from other companies and get licensing fees for their possible exploitation.[76]

**1.32** All this has an impact on the willingness of European companies to undertake R&D in China.[77] However, it seems that the Chinese government became more sensitive to these problems as certain local governments have in the meantime tightened up or removed subsidies for patent and utility model applications,[78] or plan to do so. For example, applicants who have filed an 'abnormal' application[79] or bad-faith application with SIPO will be required to pay back any subsidies and financial aids issued by local governments in Hebei Province, and be disqualified from receiving patent subsidies or monetary support for two years.[80]

The notorious quality problem of utility models has also been recognised by SIPO: Since 15 October 2013 an amended version of the Patent Examination Guidelines is in force[81] which makes it possible for examiners to execute a preliminary examination and reject utility model applications if they obviously lacked novelty, that is, if they obviously contain copied prior art, or if they were a repeat submission of a patent application with substantially identical content.[82] To this end, the examiner is able to conduct a search or otherwise gather documents to determine whether the application lacked novelty. Furthermore, one of the objectives set out by SIPO in its promotion plan for the implementation of the NIPS in 2013[83] is to encourage inventors to transfer their focus from quantity to quality. Measures include implementing a revised evaluation system for the State Technological Award and guiding evaluation experts towards a more quality-based approach.[84] These and other steps to improve the patent quality in China were endorsed by a SIPO opinion on patent quality issued on 25 December 2013. They include taking account of the number of patents (not utility models) and the grant rate in order to determine whether the patent

76 Cf. for example Sujitha Subramanian, 'Patent Trolls in Thickets: Who is Fishing Under the Bridge?' [2008] **30** *EIPR* 182; Christian Osterrieth, 'Patent-Trolls in Europa – braucht das Patentrecht neue Grenzen?' **2009** *GRUR* 540.

77 Cf. in 2010 EU enterprises invested only 2% of their foreign R&D investment in China, Dan Prud'homme, above note 46, 57 f.

78 'China's crucial struggle to raise patent quality', *iam blog*, 23 April 2013, www.iam-magazine.com.

79 There is no official definition of what an 'abnormal' application means. However, this should include simple copies of published patent applications, patents and utility models.

80 [2013] **7** *China IP newsletter* of the British embassy to China, available at https://www.gov.uk/government/publications/china-ip-newsletter.

81 See <http://www.sipo.gov.cn/zwgg/jl/201311/t20131106_876947.html>.

82 See Part I, Chapter 2, Section 11 and 13 Patent Examination Guidelines.

83 Promotion plan for the Implementation of the National Intellectual Property Strategy in 2013, 21 March 2013, available at http://english.sipo.gov.cn/.

84 Ibid.

application targets set were reached, limiting subsidies to granted patents and taking measures against illegal patent attorney work and low-price competition in this area.[85] Time will tell whether these measures will be sufficient to stop the run on utility models[86] and to steer Chinese applicants towards a more sophisticated protection of their inventions.[87]

### 3. Improvement of patent rights enforcement in general

The accession of China to the WTO strengthened the role of the judiciary in patent litigation.[88] However, even after the Patent Law reform of 2000, the system of dual enforcement was retained. In other words, patent rights holders involved in patent infringement cases can choose between civil and administrative enforcement, the main difference being that damages, as well as provisional and protective measures, can only be requested from the courts. From 2001 to 2007, Chinese courts dealt with more than 17,700 patent cases,[89] gaining valuable experience in IPR enforcement. Nevertheless, the NIPS includes the further improvement of IP law enforcement as one of its goals.[90] **1.33**

From 2008 to 2010, that is, in three years, it seems that the number of patent cases has reached almost the same figure as in the previous eight years[91] and the speed and quality of the proceedings[92] and judgments have improved. In a 2012 survey of British businesses active in China, 61 per cent of those questioned felt that IP protection against infringement was 'effective' or 'very effective'.[93] Most European companies and lawyers active in China share the view that litigation and customs enforcement have significantly improved in recent years.[94] CIELA,[95] an IP litigation platform which provides a database of more than **1.34**

85 See http://www.sipo.gov.cn/yw/2013/201312/t20131225_891833.html. Cf. also Toby Mak, above note 64.

86 See Martin Meng and Howard Hao, 'Application and protection of Chinese utility model patents', in *China: Managing the IP Lifecycle 2013*, 22, iam and World Trademark Review, who expect that the amendments of the examination guidelines will have no substantial impact in the utility model practice because prior art searches are not required by examiners.

87 See also the recommendations for an improved utility models system by Thomas T. Moga, above note 57, 30 ff and Dan Prud'homme, above note 46, 116 ff, available at www.europeanchamber.com.cn.

88 Cf. Thomas Pattloch, 'The enforcement of patent rights in China' in Christopher Heath and Laurence Petit (eds), *Patent Enforcement Worldwide*, Oxford: Hart Publishing 2005, 285.

89 Cf. Gordon Gao, Dixon Zhang and Fang Qi, above note 18, 4.

90 National Patent Development Strategy (2011–2020) No. 45 et seq.

91 Cf. Peter Ollier, 'China's IP Litigation Rises 40%', *Managing IP*, 28 April 2011. However, also see Patent Protection and Enforcement in the PRC, above note 52, 37, where it is indicated that the number of patent court cases has decreased over the past years.

92 Cf. Éric Sergheraert, Valérie Schwalek and Jining Shi, 'Étude statistique sur les actions en contrefaçon de brevet en Chine: des confirmations mais surtout des surprises!', [2013] **48** *p.i.* 271.

93 British Chamber of Commerce in China and China-Britain Business Council, British Business in China – 2012 Business climate survey, 23, available at www.cbbc.org.

94 See also Luke Minford and Aggie Liu, 'Follow the Leader', *Intellectual Property Magazine*, February 2013, 61.

95 www.ciela.cn.

23,000 IP cases (see also *Bailey and Wang*, Chapter 8), including 6,000 patent cases, reveals that first-instance proceedings before the top ten courts in China are usually concluded within between six and 14 months. Due to good *forum shopping*[96] opportunities plaintiffs can often choose the court which they feel will provide them with the best chance of success.[97] This is very important as there is still no fully independent judicial system in place in China. It is not unknown for local companies to be favoured over foreign companies, in particular in cases involving strategic or state-owned enterprises,[98] or where local companies hold a strong position at the seat of the court. Furthermore, the low damages awarded by the courts remain a problem for foreign companies litigating their patents in China.[99] Nevertheless, litigators state that foreign parties in big and important centres, such as Beijing, Guangzhou, Nanjing or Shanghai can expect dedicated judges, reasonable quality of decisions, swift proceedings, absence of obvious bias, protectionism or political interference, transparency[100] and reasonable costs.[101] Furthermore, statistics reveal that the success rate for foreign companies in patent cases before the first-instance courts is close to 80 per cent.[102] The problems thus seem to lie mainly at provincial level, where there is still a lack of legal certainty and experience, in particular in patent litigation involving more complex types of technology.[103]

However, it should be noted that in the past few years the administrative route has regained popularity as a means of enforcing patents. The main reasons seem to be that litigating patents before civil courts is getting more and more expensive, while administrative proceedings have become more structured and accessible. Furthermore, SIPO – which, together with the local patent administration authorities, is competent to handle administrative proceedings (see *Cao*, Chapter 12) – seems to have frequent success in bringing parties to mediation.[104] Depending on the case at issue, administrative proceedings may thus be a good alternative for enforcing patent rights in China.

---

96 As regards forum shopping related to patent litigation in general see Stefan Luginbuehl, *European Patent Law, Towards A Uniform Interpretation*, Cheltenham, UK and Northampton, MA, USA: Edward Elgar 2011, 42 et seq.

97 See also Beda Bischof and Hussein Noureddine, 'Chinesisches Haftpflichtrecht bei Immaterialgüterrechtsverletzungen', **2012** *sic!* 515, 525 f.

98 European Commission Staff working document, 'Report on the protection and enforcement of intellectual property rights in third countries', SWD(2013) 30 final, 8.

99 Patent Protection and Enforcement in the PRC, above note 52, 40 f.

100 See Luke Minford and Aggie Liu, above note 94, 61.

101 See Tim Smith, 'Patent Litigation: Forum Shopping Tactics in China', *China Patent Forum*, 31 May 2012, London.

102 See Tim Smith, above note 101; Patent Protection and Enforcement in the PRC, above note 52, 39.

103 See Patent Protection and Enforcement in the PRC, above note 52, 37 et seq.

104 See Patent Protection and Enforcement in the PRC, above note 52, 35. As regards mediation for patent disputes in general cf. Stefan Luginbuehl, *Uniform interpretation of European patent law with a special view on*

## C. SUMMARY AND CONCLUSION

1.35 China's IP policy is an important part of the country's overall economic policy for more growth and less dependence on foreign technology. The NIPS has set clear goals aimed at making China a highly competitive state with a strong knowledge-based economy by 2020. There is no doubt that China, with its many tens of thousands of scientists and engineers educated by top Chinese and Western universities every year, has great innovation potential. This is not least underscored by the many Chinese inventors currently active abroad, doing work for foreign corporations and institutions.[105]

1.36 However, it is clear that more time is needed before China can reach the innovation levels of its Western and Asian competitors in all the core technologies defined by the Chinese government. There is no doubt that the Middle Kingdom is on the right path to becoming the worldwide market leader in certain technological fields,[106] such as graphene.[107] A great deal of effort has also been put into the development of environmentally friendly technologies, an area where Chinese companies play an important role on the global market. However, in many core technologies there are already many patented innovations, often owned by international companies. Chinese firms thus need to develop inventions in 'peripheral' technologies and often get patents for so-called 'incremental' innovations (inventions for small innovation). Furthermore, they have to draft patent applications that do not infringe existing patents and, in particular, utility models.[108] This of course impacts on the speed of the move towards sustainable and commercial innovation.

Experts believe that the technology transfer rate, that is, the frequency with which inventions born of academic research reach the commercial market, is still too low in China and must be improved.[109] What is more, there is still

---

*the creation of a common patent court*, 185 et seq., available at http://igitur-archive.library.uu.nl/dissertations/2009-0901-200115/luginbuehl.pdf

105 'New guidelines shed light on approach to inventor remuneration in China', *iam blog*, July 2013, www.iam-magazine.com.

106 See Thomsen Reuters, 'Chinese Patenting, report on the current state of innovation in China', 2011.

107 [2013] **1** *China IP newsletter* of the British embassy to China, available at https://www.gov.uk/government/publications/china-ip-newsletter.

108 See Catherine Zheng in Peter Leung, 'China moves to curtail low-quality patents', *Managing Intellectual Property*, 28 February 2013, www.managingip.com.

109 'National lacks innovation despite patents, experts say', *China Daily*, 21 February 2014. As a consequence, the Beijing Municipal Government issued a 'Temporary Opinion on Promotion of Transformation of University Science & Technology Achievements' which aims at giving greater flexibility to universities and research institutions to commercialise technologies by relieving restrictions on transfer and licensing, see [2014] **2** *China IP newsletter* of the British embassy to China, available at https://www.gov.uk/government/publications/china-ip-newsletter.

limited innovation by Chinese companies in technical sectors that require big and long-term financial investments, such as the pharma sector. It is thus interesting to note that SIPO was criticised for protecting local pharmaceutical companies by making it more difficult for foreign applicants in this sector to get their patents granted.[110]

Nevertheless, the number of patent applications filed abroad is steadily increasing, as is the number of patents granted to Chinese applicants. Recent surveys have revealed that Chinese companies intend to file more patent applications abroad, where Europe seems to be the most popular target region.[111] This is a clear sign that China is on its way to becoming an increasingly innovative country with companies also active outside the domestic market.

**1.37** The current lack of innovation capacity and long-term patent strategies together with the mainly financial incentives to file for patents have resulted in a large number of utility model applications and registered utility models. This has led to a situation where truly innovative companies are increasingly being forced to spend large amounts of money on evaluating the different utility models in their technical area so as to avoid being drawn into litigation. But it also forces them to conclude amicable agreements with the owners of the utility models simply because it would be too much trouble to initiate litigation with regard to all of the utility models surrounding a technical area. This is endorsed by the fact that utility models have a lower standard as regards inventive step and are consequently more difficult to invalidate than patents.[112] It seems thus crucial that the level of inventive step for utility models is raised in China.[113]

The fact that more and more utility models are in force could also jeopardize competition and innovation which in turn might endanger China's drive to foster indigenous innovation. However, it is in many economies precisely SMEs and start-ups which need support and an appropriate environment to become and stay innovative. The same should be the case in China so as to enable China's ambitious innovation policy to reach through to the entire enterprise landscape, not only a few big players.[114]

---

110 Patent Protection and Enforcement in the PRC, above note 52, 28.

111 Cf. Peter Leung, 'The China In-House Survey: More Filings, Particularly in EU', *Managing Intellectual Property*, 23 October 2013, www.managingip.com.

112 See Meng Pu, 'A Comparative Study of Stability of Invention Patent and Utility Model Patent', [2014] **1** *China Patents & Trademarks* 38, 44.

113 See also Oliver Pfaffenzeller, Ming Deng and Xia Pfaffenzeller, 'Die Herausforderungen durch chinesische Gebrauchsmuster', **2014** *Mitt.* 101, 105.

114 See also in this regard, Emma Barraclough, 'Chinese IP Owners are not Always What You Expect', *Managing Intellectual Property*, 17 June 2013.

Additionally, the 'utility model thickets' and the possible development of 'trolls' might also provoke negative incentives on foreign companies who would like to exploit their inventions in China and as a consequence might be reluctant to invest in R&D in China. Consequently, it might be more difficult for China to have access to foreign technology which is crucial for the technological development of the Middle Kingdom. **1.38**

Another and possibly easier approach to securing foreign know-how and technology is to buy it. The NIPS clearly holds that Chinese entities should be encouraged to obtain intellectual property overseas.[115] **1.39**

In 2012, Chinese investors poured a total of $168 billion in FDI overseas, representing a nine times fold in only one decade,[116] gaining instant access to the technology of foreign enterprises. This trend is to impact especially on Europe, where Chinese companies can and are going to take advantage of the continuing economic crisis.

The following graph illustrates this sharp increase of Chinese direct investments in the EU during recent years. In 2012, the Chinese FDI stock in the EU amounted to around €77 billion, five times the amount that had been invested in the EU in 2004.

115 See No. 40 NIPS.

116 Data for Chinese (China and Hong Kong) Outbound Direct Investment 2012 and 2002 taken from the United Nations Conference on Trade and Development (UNCTAD) Statistics, available at: http://unctad.org/en/Pages/Statistics.aspx.

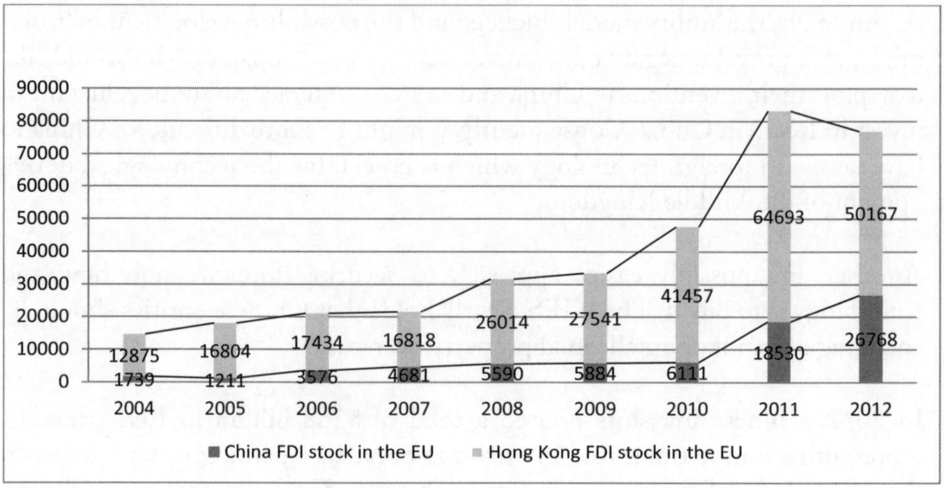


*Note:* Figures in million Euro

*Source:* Eurostat

*Figure 1.5 Chinese FDI stocks in the EU*

# 2

# TECHNOLOGY TRANSFER IN CHINA

**Beat Weibel**



## A. DEFINITION

There is no legal definition of 'technology transfer' in Chinese law, nor is there one specific law governing technology transfer. Rather, the term is used differently in different contexts and the relevant rules have to be looked up in a variety of laws and regulations.[1] **2.01**

As a general concept, technology transfer covers any act involving the transfer of – or investment into – technology, intellectual property (IP) rights, know-how, and so on from abroad into China ('import of technology'), or from China to abroad ('export of technology'). Of course it is also possible that technology is transferred within China from one company to another. This type of technology transfer is, however, not the subject of this chapter. **2.02**

The term 'technology transfer' can thus refer to the simple act of transferring a Chinese patent application from a Chinese company or inventor to a company **2.03**

1 Yuanshi Bu, *Patentrecht und Technologietransfer in China,* München et al.: Verlag C.H. Beck/Helbing Lichtenhahn Verlag, 2010, 181.

outside China, or it can cover a complicated creation of a joint venture (JV) in China between a foreign company and a local partner with the aim of starting developing technology for local market needs. Both are legally and practically treated as technology transfer and therefore have to be in line with the pertinent regulations.

**2.04** Technology transfer in general is not easy to grasp. Together with the dissemination of the relevant regulations concerning technology transfer and its general broad interpretation in China, it becomes even more important to define clearly what technology transfer is all about.

**2.05** Basically, there are two main issues that need to be defined in order to characterise technology transfer: scope and transfer.[2] 'Scope' means that the technology at stake needs to be defined very carefully. This covers not only the products and know-how, but also the IP rights related to the technology. Furthermore, it must be crystal clear what 'transfer' refers to: Is it the transfer of ownership of an IP right or just the right to exploit the technology and IP right (usually called a 'licence')? How long and for which purpose may the technology be exploited, and how is non-registered know-how transferred to the receiver (exchange of documents, training, qualified persons having the required know-how, and so on)?

**2.06** In order to conclude a simple patent licence agreement or transfer agreement it is required that these points are clearly determined. These points become even more important if one is dealing with the establishment of a complex JV where technology is used as an investment. The better the scope and means of the transfer are defined, the fewer misunderstandings there will be if the agreement needs to be interpreted.

**2.07** For some time, Chinese technology transfer regulations have been subject to complaints from the international business community because it is felt that the government unilaterally favours domestic companies. Accordingly, there are a number of studies dealing with the risks and potential concerns in terms of WTO compliance.[3] Keeping in mind that it is China's explicit goal to change

---

2 Dr. Arthur Wolff, *Besonderheiten und typische Probleme bei der Verhandlung von Technologietransfer/ Lizenzverträgen in China*, Wien: Rechtsanwälte Baier Böhm, 2010, 25.

3 Inter alia: *China's Laws, Regulations and Practices in the Areas of Technology Transfer, Trade-related Investment Measures, Subsidies and Intellectual Property Protection which Raise WTO Compliance Concerns*, Trade Lawyers Advisory Group, 2007; Bureau of Industry and Security U.S. Department of Commerce, *Technology Transfer to China*; Margot Schüler, *Technologietransfer nach China – ein unkalkulierbares Risiko für die Länder der Triade Europa, USA und Japan?*, Friedrich Ebert Stiftung, 2008.

from a manufacturing country to a strong innovative nation,[4] it becomes immediately clear that political aspects and objectives need to be taken into account when discussing technology transfer in China.

## B. LEGAL SOURCES

The main legal sources for technology transfer are: **2.08**

- Foreign Trade Act
- Regulations on Technology Import and Export Administration
- Measures for the Administration of Prohibited and Restricted Import of Technologies
- Measures for the Administration of Prohibited and Restricted Export of Technologies
- Catalogue of Technologies Prohibited and Restricted from Import
- Catalogue of Technologies Prohibited and Restricted from Export
- Patent Act and Regulation
- Foreign Investment Catalogue.

First of all, Chinese laws distinguish between technologies that are: **2.09**

- prohibited from import and export;
- restricted for import and export; and
- free to import and export (see Chapter 3 Foreign Trade Act).

Consequently, the first step for every technology transfer project is to determine **2.10** into which category the technology falls. Unfortunately, the catalogues which make it possible to determine whether the import or export of the technology at stake is restricted or prohibited are not officially available in an English translation. Therefore, it is recommended to seek the advice of local consultants. Furthermore, technology import and export are not treated exactly equally. Both restricted and free technologies have to undergo a registration and approval process.

It is interesting to note that the transfer of design patents does not need to be **2.11** approved or registered.[5] Therefore, it may be concluded that design patents – although also governed by the Chinese Patent Act – are not regarded as technology rights.

4 Ting Zhang, *Technology Transfer and IP Licensing in China*, China Business Solutions Ltd, 2008.

5 Yuanshi Bu, above note 1, 187.

**2.12** The Ministry of Commerce (MOFCOM) is the responsible authority for the registration and approval of technology import and export contracts. For patent transfers, the assignment has to be registered with the State Intellectual Property Office (SIPO).[6]

**2.13** Technology can also be brought into China via a foreign direct investment, either into a JV or a wholly foreign-owned enterprise (WFOE). Since there are restrictions for the establishment of a Chinese entity, the Foreign Investment Catalogue also needs to be consulted in such cases.[7]

## C. IMPORT AND EXPORT OF TECHNOLOGY

**2.14** For technology imports and exports in China, first of all it has to be determined whether the technology can be freely imported or whether it is restricted or prohibited. To this end, the corresponding catalogue has to be consulted. If a technology is not listed in the catalogue it may be imported without restrictions. If the technology is to be exported at a later stage, the export catalogue also needs to be consulted in order to prevent any problems later. The scope of the import and export catalogues, as well as the procedure for the different restricted technologies may vary. As a rule of thumb it can be said that the technology export regulations are stricter than the import regulations even though the current number of technologies that is prohibited from being imported (39 technology items) is larger than the figure for exports (33 technology items).[8]

**2.15** Rule 7 Regulation on Technology Import and Export Administration reads: 'The State encourages import of advanced and appropriate technology'. According to Yuanshi Bu's German translation, it should read 'applicable' technology rather than 'appropriate' technology.[9] The corresponding definition for exporting reads: 'the State encourages exporting well-developed industrialized technology'. The stricter definition for technology import is in line with the principles given in the import catalogue. It becomes clear that the import restrictions are directed at protecting domestic production and preventing negative impacts on national security and social public interest. The export restrictions are mainly directed at protecting national security interests, rural production and cultural heritage.

6 Art. 10 Chinese Patent Act and R. 14 Implementing Regulations to the Chinese Patent Act.

7 China IPR SME Helpdesk, *Technology Transfer to China, Guidance for Businesses*, available at www.china-iprhelpdesk.eu.

8 Catalogue of Technologies Prohibited or Restricted from Import/Export in China.

9 Yuanshi Bu, above note 1, 302.

As far as the proceedings are concerned, there is one important difference between technology import and export: Whereas negotiations for import of restricted technologies may already be carried out before or during the approval and registration process,[10] this is not allowed for technology export.[11] 2.16

All these differences make it clear that technology import is still favoured over technology export. The reason for this is that China wants to develop from a manufacturing to an innovation-based economy. Therefore, technology import is supported in the same way as domestic innovation. 2.17

## 1. Procedure for technology import

It goes without saying that prohibited technology may not be imported.[12] For restricted technologies, an application for technology import accompanied with the relevant documents (in particular, a description of the technology and project documentation, as well as possibly a draft contract) has to be submitted to MOFCOM. Within 30 days, MOFCOM will render a decision on preliminary approval and issue a so-called 'letter of intent'. The applicant may sign a contract for technology import with his/her foreign counterpart if he is in possession of such a letter of intent. The contract also has to be submitted to MOFCOM, where its authenticity is checked within 10 days. Although the wording of Rule 13 Regulations on Technology Import and Export Administration is not crystal clear, it suggests that it is only the Chinese party that may apply for the letter of intent and submit the contract. 2.18

If the parties have already concluded a contract covering a technology import, it may be submitted with the application. In this case, the deadline for approval by MOFCOM is 40 days. When the import of a restricted technology is approved, MOFCOM issues a technology import licence. The contract for the technology import takes effect on the date of the issuance of the technology import licence.[13] 2.19

If patents are transferred from a foreign patent owner to a Chinese patent owner, such assignments do not necessarily have to be registered at the SIPO as well. It is advisable, however, to register the change of ownership even though in China there is apparently no direct link between the registered owner and the 2.20

10 Rules 13, 14, 15 Regulations on Technology Import and Export Administration.

11 R. 31 Regulations on Technology Import and Export Administration: '[..] after obtaining the letter of intent […], the applicant may begin substantive negotiation, and conclude a contract for the technology export'.

12 R. 9 Regulations on Technology Import and Export Administration.

13 R. 16 Regulations on Technology Import and Export Administration.

right to sue. If patents are just licensed, the licence contract is the contract to be submitted to MOFCOM according to the procedure described above.

**2.21** For technology that can be imported freely, a registration of the underlying technology licence contract is not necessary to ensure that the contract takes effect. However, it is necessary to be able to make payments abroad.[14] Banks and custom authorities request the certificate of registration before they make or allow any payments. For the registration of the licence contract of technology free to import, MOFCOM requests an application, a copy of the agreement and documents certifying the legal status of the contract parties.

### 2. Procedure for technology export

**2.22** The procedure for the export of restricted technology is similar to that for technology import, with the exception that contract negotiations may only be started with the issuance of the preliminary approval (letter of intent). The deadlines to be respected by MOFCOM are 30 days for checking the technology and 10 days for checking a contract, respectively. However, if patents are transferred from a Chinese patent owner to a foreign patent owner, such assignments have to be registered at the SIPO as well.[15]

**2.23** The proceedings for technology free to export are similar to those for free import. Changes to the contract and its termination have to be reported to MOFCOM.

## D. CONTRACTUAL RESTRICTIONS

**2.24** In addition to the registration and approval process for technology import and export outlined above, there are a few contractual restrictions that a non-Chinese party considering undertaking technology transfer in China has to be aware of. After China's accession to the WTO on 11 December 2001, the situation improved substantially. However, in older contracts there may still be some clauses that are based on old mandatory regulations. For example, the term of a contract used to be restricted to ten years and the Chinese licensee was free to use the licensed technology after expiry of the agreement.[16] The latter restriction together with a restriction to extend confidentiality over the termination of an agreement are the main reasons why foreign parties complained that

14 R. 20 Regulations on Technology Import and Export Administration.

15 Art. 10 Chinese Patent Act.

16 Yuanshi Bu, above note 1, 186.

technology that was once licensed in China stayed there forever. Fortunately, these restrictions are no longer in force.

However, there are still a few restrictions with which foreign parties are usually not very familiar. In terms of clauses restricting competition, the situation is in the meantime similar to that in Western countries. The biggest deviations relate to the ownership of IP rights, improvements and confidentiality. All of these restrictions, if not properly dealt with in the contract, can severely weaken the position of the licensor. Accordingly, a technology transfer or licence contract with a Chinese partner has to be drafted very carefully. The licensor must always think of the worst case scenario, that is, what happens if the contract is breached or terminated and what options are available to protect the licensor's IP rights in such cases. Only the most important contractual restrictions for technology transfer contracts are explained below. **2.25**

As mentioned above, the main difficulty in drafting technology transfer contracts is to define the scope of the technology involved and of the transfer or right to use. As a general rule, the freedom of contract is quite advanced and in many cases contractual regulations may precede legal regulations (for example, for inventor remuneration). The number of mandatory legal requirements has decreased since the laws on technology transfer were adapted to WTO standards. **2.26**

### 1. Improvements

The licensor is not allowed to prohibit the licensee from making improvements, and the licensor may not request improvements made by the licensee to be assigned to the licensor.[17] The licensor may just request the licensee to grant a licence back on improvements. If an improvement clause in a licence contract violates this restriction, the clause becomes invalid and the licensee becomes free to develop improvements to the licensed technology without a licence back to the licensor. Additionally, Rule 27 Regulations on Technology Import and Export Administration clarifies that any improvement belongs to the party that made it. **2.27**

For licence agreements between two Chinese parties, the ownership of improvement can be freely agreed upon.[18] **2.28**

17 R. 29(3) Regulations on Technology Import and Export Administration.

18 Art. 354 Contract Act. Yuanshi Bu, above note 1, 204.

### 2. Confidentiality

**2.29** Confidentiality obligations have to be concluded specifically in each case. In general there is no secondary obligation to keep information confidential if this has not been specifically agreed upon.[19] Furthermore, confidentiality obligations expire with the termination of the contract or if the information is disclosed. Therefore, it is important to make sure in the contract that confidentiality obligations survive the agreement and the project that the technology transfer is intended for. However, with regard to the pre-stage of the contract, that is, contract negotiations, Article 43 of the Contract Act provides that business secrets acquired in the course of the establishment of a contract shall not be revealed or otherwise utilised in an unfair manner, and that a party which has breached such legal obligation shall be held liable for damages.

### 3. Reverse engineering

**2.30** Reverse engineering is generally allowed in China. Therefore, a good licence agreement should also include clauses about restricting reverse engineering, because otherwise the receiving party is free to gather information that the licensor does not want to disclose by reverse engineering.[20]

### 4. Non-challenge obligations and non-compete obligations

**2.31** Obligations restricting the licensee to challenge the validity of licensed IP rights are prohibited[21] in the same way as non-compete obligations which restrict the licensee's freedom to obtain comparable or competing technology from other sources.[22]

### 5. Contract manufacturing or development and commissioned IP

**2.32** Commissioned IP based on contract manufacturing or contract development belongs to the party that made it unless the contract states otherwise. Accordingly, ownership in commissioned IP must be clearly set out. Not only what is to be developed needs to be defined carefully, but also who will own it.[23] Contracts

19 R. 26 Regulations on Technology Import and Export Administration.

20 China IPR SME Helpdesk, *Technology Transfer to China, Guidance for Businesses* (above note 7).

21 Yuanshi Bu, above note 1, 205.

22 R. 29(4) Regulations on Technology Import and Export Administration.

23 Mia Qu, China Bulletin by King and Wood, *Intellectual Property Issues of Biomedical Outsourcing in the PRC*, August 2012.

assigning the right to file a patent application to a foreign party must be registered at SIPO.[24]

### 6. Other 'undue' restrictions

Further restrictions which can be prohibited if exercised in an undue manner are: 2.33

- obliging the licensee to purchase raw materials, parts and components, products or equipment from a specific source;
- restricting the quantity, variety or sales prices of the products manufactured by the licensee;
- restricting the licensee from utilising export and sales channels.[25]

These restrictions have to be taken seriously because it is unclear what 'if exercised in an undue manner' means. The wording leaves considerable room for interpretation by the authorities. Often, international companies agree to transfer technology to China but contractually restrict the Chinese partner from exporting the products which incorporate such technology to other markets. In view of the rationale to 'encourage technology export',[26] a broad interpretation of what is 'undue manner' cannot be excluded. This could lead to a factual ban of export restrictions. 2.34

Finally, obligations restricting the licensee from obtaining similar technology as supplied from other parties are not allowed.[27] 2.35

## E. POLITICAL ASPECTS

In the US, the opinion prevails that the Chinese regulations on technology transfer aim at enforcing access to proprietary technology 'from US companies engaged in normal business practices and joint ventures in China in exchange for access to China's market'.[28] In particular, China's accession to the WTO was accompanied by complaints that the Chinese technology and investment policy forced foreign parties to transfer their technology to China in exchange for the 2.36

24 Art. 10 Chinese Patent Act.
25 R. 29(5) to (7) Regulations on Technology Import and Export Administration.
26 R. 30 Regulations on Technology Import and Export Administration.
27 R. 29(4) Regulations on Technology Import and Export Administration.
28 Bureau of Industry and Security U.S. Department of Commerce, *Technology Transfer to China*, 1.

permission to invest in China.[29, 30] Meanwhile, however, there is a general consensus that the Chinese laws are no longer substantially inconsistent with the WTO obligations, in particular the TRIPS obligations.[31]

It is not the objective of this chapter to further analyse these allegations and concerns. Rather, a broader context will be provided, allowing a party involved in a technology transfer deal to better understand why there are still certain constraints in the Chinese legal system for technology transfer and how to take them into consideration.

**2.37** China's industrial policy shows a number of parallel developments with Japan and South Korea.[32] In order to compensate for deficits in R&D and technology development, in the 1990s the Chinese government implemented a policy which guided and encouraged foreign investment and technology transfer to China. During this phase, for example in the electronics industry, foreign partners were only permitted to actively participate in the Chinese market as minority partners in JV, and they were forced to transfer their technology to such JV.[33]

**2.38** In order to prevent the technology from flowing back, Chinese JV partners but also licensees in general were entitled to continued use of the licensed technology after termination of the licence contract. Foreign bidders in public procurement, for example, in the electric power production sector, were also required to submit detailed technical drawings to so-called 'test and certification institutes' and to intensively train the local people. Both measures aimed at transferring technology to Chinese companies and to ascertain that the state-owned JV partners, for example those which participated in the construction of the famous Three Gorges Dam, acquired the knowledge necessary to produce the same technology. A foreign technology licensor's first order was therefore very often its very last one, unless it managed to keep some core parts under its control or maintain a technological or qualitative advantage that forced the licensee to repeatedly seek a licence for the latest technology or to source certain critical parts from the technology owner.

---

29 Yuanshi Bu, above note 1, 188, 'forced technology transfer?'.

30 *China's Laws, Regulations and Practices in the Areas of Technology Transfer, Trade-related Investment Measures, Subsidies and Intellectual Property Protection which Raise WTO Compliance Concerns*, Trade Lawyers Advisory Group, 2007, 17.

31 *China's Laws, Regulations and Practices in the Areas of Technology Transfer, Trade-related Investment Measures, Subsidies and Intellectual Property Protection which Raise WTO Compliance Concerns*, above note 30, 2.

32 Margot Schüler, above note 3, 47.

33 Margot Schüler, above note 3, 71.

After the accession to the WTO, China started to focus more on quality investment and gave priority to advanced technologies.[34] Such policy is expressly laid out in the 11th five-year plan with regard to the utilisation of foreign investment. At the same time, China began to build and strengthen national champions with the capability to position themselves domestically, as well as on the international market.[35] Examples of such companies are Huawei or ZTE, which are presently among the leading PCT applicants[36] and are already serious players on the European market. 2.39

Simultaneously, the Chinese government boosted the number of domestic and foreign patent filings by providing subsidies to the applicants.[37, 38] These measures resulted in a tremendous increase in patent, utility model and design filings, in particular in China. A large proportion of these applications (1.2 million filings in 2010, 1.6 million in 2011 and over 2 million in 2012)[39] are unexamined utility model applications (see also *Luginbuehl*, Chapter 1). 2.40

The strategic aim of this policy is to incentivise local development and to create a kind of patent shield – often called the 'Great Wall of Patents' – for Chinese companies, as well as to provide them with a bargaining chip in international business negotiations or IP disputes. Invalidating such large numbers of unexamined utility models would entail a tremendous burden on foreign right holders, so this patent shield can be effectively used to neutralize patent infringement attacks from multi-national companies. The building-up of such piles of utility model patents is not only facilitated by subsidies from the Chinese government but also by the fact that the inventive step threshold is lower for utility model patent applications than for invention patent applications (see *Bu*, Chapter 3). 2.41

In order to further promote domestic R&D and the development of Intellectual Property, the High and New Technology Enterprises (HNTE) programme was established. This programme basically grants domestic enterprises a 10 per cent income tax advantage if they engage in R&D, own IP rights, have a high 2.42

34 *China's Laws, Regulations and Practices in the Areas of Technology Transfer, Trade-related Investment Measures, Subsidies and Intellectual Property Protection which Raise WTO Compliance Concerns,* above note 30, 21, 22.

35 Margot Schüler, above note 3, 49.

36 WIPO Statistics 2011.

37 David J. Kappos, Under Secretary of Commerce for IP and Director of the USPTO, 'A Public Discussion on Strategies for Engaging China', April 11, 2011, Fordham IP Law Institute – China, http://www.uspto.gov/news/speeches/2012/kappos_fordham.jsp.

38 Frederico Munari/Liang Xu, 'Are Patent Subsidies for SMEs Effective?', 6th Annual Conference of EPIP Association, Brussels, 8–9 September 2011.

39 Source: SIPO.

number of employees and a high number of scientists. Furthermore, another programme originally aimed at favouring companies which have their own intellectual property in public procurement by granting them a price advantage ('Indigenous Innovation Programme'). This programme, however, had to be abolished due to international complaints.

**2.43** In 2012, the Chinese government published a draft for a fourth amendment of the Chinese Patent Act for a public consultation. The aim of the amendment is to further strengthen patent enforcement. This is a clear signal that the IP system in China has, after its establishment in 1985, now reached a new phase. The first step required an IP system to be established, whereas the second phase focused on a better protection of patent rights. The third phase now concentrates on enforcement.

**2.44** Looking at this very short and rough overview of Chinese industry and technology policy since the 1990s, three main phases become obvious:[40]

*Table 2.1 Chinese industry and technology policy since the 1990s*

| 1990–2000 | 2001–2010 | 2011 onwards |
|---|---|---|
| Catching-up and building the ground for domestic R&D | Establishing and localising R&D; preparing ground for expansion into international markets | Expanding local R&D and exporting internationally |
| • Encouraged foreign direct investments<br>• Forced technology transfer, for example for public procurement projects and joint ventures<br>• Strengthened patent law in terms of protection | • Stimulating local R&D<br>• Promotion of high-tech industries<br>• First Chinese investments abroad<br>• Becoming independent from foreign direct investment and technology transfer<br>• Adapting patent law to WTO standards | • Expanding domestic R&D capacities<br>• Setting-up global market presence<br>• Broadening investments abroad<br>• Strengthening patent law in terms of enforcement |

**2.45** Technology transfer regulations in China therefore play a major political role and have greatly supported China's endeavours to catch-up with Western development and to increase productivity. In spite of the abolition of the

40 In more detail: Margot Schüler, above note 3, 50.

majority of rules and practices which put foreign right holders at a disadvantage, a certain favouring of local technology owners and R&D still has to be considered when negotiating technology transfer deals.

Together with the tremendous increase in patent filings by Chinese companies in China and abroad, it becomes clear that the Chinese IP system will be further strengthened in the future. Whereas the first steps were directed at supporting technological catch-up and stimulating technology development, future developments will aim at protecting the domestic IP against misappropriation by others and at supporting the export of technology by Chinese companies. 2.46

## F. BEST PRACTICES

### 1. Know the system

First of all, the system and its rules have to be understood. If a company is aware of the fact that it will be expected to support China's technological development in return for the opportunity to invest and participate in the huge Chinese market, it will find it easier to deliberately decide whether the risks connected with a market presence in China are worth taking. It has to be appreciated that the explicit purpose of the Chinese Regulation on Technology Import and Export Administration is to 'enhance national economic growth and social development'.[41] That is, the political motives behind the Regulation are not concealed and should therefore come as no surprise to foreign companies. 2.47

### 2. Decide which technology should be licensed

Knowing the rules as outlined above should facilitate the decision as to whether a technology should be transferred or not. In particular, it may not always be wise to transfer a core technology which resulted from substantial investment and which can be easily reproduced. 2.48

An alternative would be to create a wholly foreign-owned enterprise in China that manufactures critical components or takes care of the final assembly. This would allow the technology owner to keep control over the manufacturing and assembly process of critical elements protected by trade secrets. 2.49

41 R. 1 Regulation on Technology Import and Export Administration.

### 3. Select the right partner

**2.50** The selection of the right partner for a project which involves technology transfer is, of course, crucial as well. Although the situation has improved, some companies still complain about measures that inhibit market access by requiring the use of Chinese core technologies, or even require IP to be licensed to the Chinese partner.[42] In a deal with a state-owned partner there is usually not much of a choice. However, if the partner is privately owned, it may be beneficial if the partner is an established company that already has some experience in dealing with technology and that has no immediate incentive to compete with the technology provider. Furthermore, the partner should allow the technology provider to monitor production and to impose confidentiality restrictions on employees.

**2.51** Sometimes it is advisable to split up the technology at issue and to license it to different licensees with the final assembly being carried out under the control of the non-Chinese licensor and technology owner.

**2.52** In any case, the most preferable licensee is a JV, the majority of which is owned by the licensor, as such an ownership scheme enables the licensor to control the use of the technology and to play a dominant role in case of a dispute.

### 4. Patent protection

**2.53** Although the possibility of enforcing patents in China is still questioned by some commentators, patent protection is the key to legal protection of technology. In China, it should be kept in mind that the Patent Law does not only cover invention patents but also utility model and design protection. Design patents protect the outer appearance of a product. Therefore, design patents are the best choice for protection of products that are bound to be copied. Furthermore, design patents are not treated as an element of technology transfer, so the contractual freedom is larger. Utility models are not examined as to substance. Therefore, they should be used to protect simpler innovations which do not deserve full invention patent protection.

**2.54** It cannot be stressed enough that in order to have any chance at all of enforcing and protecting one's IP rights in China, a diversified patent protection covering invention patents, utility models and design patent is even more necessary than in other countries. This is because Chinese companies have in the meantime detected patent protection as a powerful business tool and are filing more patent

42 David J. Kappos, above note 37.

applications than domestic companies in any other nation in the world. Therefore, it is necessary to file invention, utility model or design patent applications even if one would not consider doing so in one's home country.

### 5. Know-how protection and confidentiality

2.55 Non-Disclosure Agreements (NDAs) are in the meantime widely used in China and also accepted by the courts.[43] To protect confidential know-how, NDAs are absolutely necessary. An NDA can be made even more restrictive by including a clause prohibiting the use of the transmitted information for other purposes than as granted by the licensor. A non-circumvention provision will provide additional security. Such clauses, however, would have to be balanced with the above-mentioned prohibited restrictions on improvements.

2.56 In order to avoid unwanted loopholes, confidentiality needs to be extended to employees of the partner, as well as to suppliers.

2.57 The big advantage of know-how and trade secret protection is that trade secrets are protected in most countries (by Article 39 TRIPS) without any procedural formalities. If a technology transfer contract therefore covers both patent rights and trade secrets, the infringement of the latter could be enforced outside China and even in countries where the technology is not patent protected at all. It is a typical situation that a licensor of technology seeks patent protection in Western countries and in China, whereas he does not envisage patent protection in other emerging countries.

2.58 Enforcement of trade secrets could therefore be a way to overcome the applicability of the restrictions mentioned at para. 2.33. This could, in particular, be a way of overcoming the interdiction to unduly restrict the transferred technology from exporting by preventing the licensee from exporting technology based on trade secret protection in the country the technology is exported to.

### 6. Contract

2.59 Secondary obligations are harder to enforce in China than in Western countries and there is not yet a long history of established case law. Therefore, contracts should be very clear with regard to mutual obligations, IP ownership, the scope and term of a licence and technology transfer, as well as confidentiality.

---

43 China IPR SME Helpdesk, *Guide to Using Contracts to Protect Your Intellectual Property Rights in China*, 4, available at www.china-iprhelpdesk.eu.

**2.60** As the structure of the Chinese language is different from the structures of Western, Indo-European languages,[44] the language used in the agreement is crucial. For instance, it does not make sense to draft overly long and complicated US-style agreements: Chinese readers are not used to complicated sentence structure, nor are they familiar with the common law principles behind it. Clear, straightforward, concise and complete language should be preferred.

**2.61** Choice of law and court are also very important. As Chinese courts tend to regard the law of the country where the licensee is located as applicable and therefore in most cases Chinese law,[45] it is advisable to agree upon an appropriate arbitration clause.

## G. OUTLOOK

**2.62** Whereas in the past, technology transfer in China was mainly understood as technology transfer *to* China, the future will see more and more technology transfer *from* China. In certain technical fields, Chinese companies are already worldwide competitive leaders and have understood that intellectual property rights are a powerful tool to protect their business against competition. Therefore, in future we will not only see an increasing number of Chinese companies ranking first in international patent filings, but this development will proceed hand in hand with a larger presence of Chinese companies in international markets. It is clear that the Chinese government will support this development. Therefore, it may well be that future articles about China and technology transfer will increasingly be about technology transfer from China and its implications for European and other Western businesses.[46]

44 For example, the placement of the object is very flexible, location comes before verb, prepositional phrases are placed before the verb, no use of tenses and conjugation, rather contextual time modifiers, no use of definite and indefinite articles, no plural forms for nouns.

45 *Das IPR des Geistigen Eigentums in der VR China*, Tübingen: Mohr Siebeck 2003, 158.

46 As Prime Minister Wen Jiabao had already said in 2004: 'Competition in the future is IP competition.'

# Part B

# SUBSTANTIVE PATENT LAW

# 3

# PREREQUISITES FOR PROTECTION

**Bu Yuanshi**



## A. PATENTABILITY

### 1. Definition of invention patents and utility models

According to Article 2(2), (3) Chinese Patent Act, an invention patent right refers to a new technical solution, developed for a product, process or the improvement thereof. Utility model rights are provided for new technical solutions proposed for the shape and structure of a product, or the combination thereof, which are fit for industrial applicability. **3.01**

### 2. Exclusion of patentability

Under certain circumstances or with respect to certain subject matter the patentability for invention patents and utility models is excluded by statute. The relevant provisions are Articles 5, 20(4) and 25 Chinese Patent Act. The **3.02** patentability is excluded regardless of the fact of whether the technical solution as provided for in the application filed with SIPO would otherwise meet the prerequisites for the grant of patent rights.

### *(a) Violation of law, contrary to social morality or detrimental to public interest*

**3.03** According to Article 5 Chinese Patent Act, the grant of patent rights is excluded if it would constitute a violation of law, be contrary to social morality or detrimental to public interest. Laws in the sense of Article 5 Chinese Patent Act include only statutes enacted by the National People's Congress (NPC) (laws in the narrow sense). Examples under Article 5 Chinese Patent Act are tools for gambling or for forging bank notes, invoices, identification cards, and seals. If only the exploitation of the technical solution, such as manufacturing, sale or utilisation of a product is legally restricted, this will not affect the patentability of the product or its manufacturing process, as is the case with weapons, for example.[1]

**3.04** The Patent Examination Guidelines contain detailed explanations regarding the two legal terms 'social morality' and 'public interest' and enumerate several examples. For instance, an artificial sexual organ or its substitute not designed for medical use, a process for modifying the genetic identity of the human being's germline or use of human embryos for industrial and commercial purposes, a process for cloning human beings, a process for modifying the genetic identity of animals which is apt to cause suffering to the animals, as long as it has no substantial value for the treatment of human beings or animals, can all be considered as contrary to social morality.[2] Examples of inventions detrimental to the public interest are inventions which cause significant environmental pollution or which are not able to use energy efficiently.[3]

### *(b) Inventions based on genetic resources*

**3.05** A patent would not be granted according to Article 5(2) Chinese Patent Act for a gene-related invention if the invention is based on genetic resources which were obtained or used illegally. The legality of the acquisition and use is judged in accordance with the relevant administrative provisions, namely the Animal Husbandry Law,[4] the Measures for the Examination and Approval of Entry and Exit and the Foreign Cooperative Research on the Application of Genetic

---

1 R. 10 Implementing Regulations to the Chinese Patent Act; origin in Art. 4quater Paris Convention.

2 Second Part, First Chapter, Section 3.1.2 Patent Examination Guidelines.

3 Second Part, First Chapter, Section 3.1.3 Patent Examination Guidelines.

4 畜牧法, promulgated by the Standing Committee of the National People's Congress on 29 May 2005, effective on 1 July 2006.

Resources of Livestock and Poultry[5] and the Interim Measures for the Administration of Human Genetic Resources.[6]

*(c) Non-patentable inventions*

3.06 According to Article 25 Chinese Patent Act, scientific discoveries, rules and measures for mental activities, methods for the diagnosis or treatment of diseases, animal and plant varieties, as well as substances obtained by means of nuclear transformation, are not patentable.

*(i) Scientific discoveries*

3.07 The revelations of substances, phenomena and transformation processes that exist in nature and that of their features, as well as laws of nature are called scientific discoveries. They are not patentable because no technical solution to solve a technical problem is embodied. If it is discovered that a pre-existing chemical material may be used for a certain purpose, for example for the treatment of a disease, this 'discovery' can, however, be protected as a use patent.

*(ii) Rules and methods for mental activities*

3.08 Rules and measures for mental activities are excluded from patent protection due to the absence of technical relevance. This includes technical means used, laws of applied nature, or if neither a technical problem is solved or a technical effect created. For this reason, computer programs and business methods are usually not patentable.[7]

*(iii) Methods for diagnosis or for therapeutic treatment of diseases*

3.09 Methods for diagnosis or for therapeutic treatment of diseases are excluded from patentability by the argument that physicians should be able to choose freely among the existing therapeutic methods for the treatment of patients from a humanistic point of view; in addition such inventions often lack industrial applicability.[8] However, equipment, devices, and products that are used to implement the methods for a diagnosis and treatment are patentable.

3.10 A method for diagnosis according to the Patent Examination Guidelines is a process of identifying, determining or eliminating the cause or the focus of the

5 畜禽遗传资源进出境和对外合作研究利用审批办法, promulgated by the State Council on 28 August 2008, effective 1 October 2008.

6 人类遗传资源管理暂行办法, promulgated by the General Office of the State Council upon the approval of the State Council on 10 June 1998, effective on 10 June 1998.

7 For details, see Second Part, Ninth Chapter Patent Examination Guidelines; for further reading, see Peter Ganea, 'The New Regulation of the Chinese Patent Act', **2002** *GRUR Int.* 686, 688 et seq.; Yu Xiang and Liu Shan, 'The New Developments in Patent Protection for Inventions Involving Computer Programs in China – A Study Based on the Newly Amended Chinese Patent Examination Guidelines', [2007] **38** *IIC* 659.

8 Second Part, First Chapter, Section 4.3 Patent Examination Guidelines.

disease which is practised directly on living human beings or animals. As far as the method is performed on the body of a living human being or animal or directly aims at obtaining diagnostic findings or determining the physical condition, it is excluded from patent protection, and thus offers no incentive for inventions in this area; this is being criticised by commentators.[9]

**3.11** Inventions that are not regarded as non-patentable diagnostic methods cover three sets of facts:[10]

(1) the object of a method of pathological anatomy is a dead human body or animal;
(2) the method does not directly aim at obtaining a diagnostic result or determining the physical condition but is instead used to obtain information as an intermediate result of the living human or animal body or to process such information;
(3) the method does not directly aim at obtaining a diagnostic result or determining the physical condition but is used for treating or testing issues, body fluids or excrements after they have been removed from the human body or animal and the information obtained is used as an intermediate result or the method is used for processing such information.

**3.12** According to the Patent Examination Guidelines the term 'treatment method' refers to a process of intercepting, relieving or eliminating the cause or focus of diseases so that the living human or animal body may recover or gain health or be relieved from pain.[11] The Patent Examination Guidelines offer an incomplete list of non-patentable therapeutic methods, such as:

(1) methods of surgical treatment, methods of treatment with medications or psychotherapeutics, or
(2) acupuncture, anesthesia, massage, Qi Gong, hypnosis, medicated bath, air bath, sun bath for the purpose of treatment.[12]

Methods that simply serve cosmetic purposes or facilitate improved well-being for human beings or animals that are not ill do not constitute treatment methods in the sense of Article 25 Chinese Patent Act.

9 Yongkang Yang, 'Comparison Among the Patent Laws of China, the United States, and the European Patent Convention Regarding Methods for the Diagnosis of Diseases', [2007] **89** *JPTOS* 887, 897, with proposals for improvement.
10 Second Part, First Chapter, Section 4.3.1.2 Patent Examination Guidelines.
11 Second Part, First Chapter, Section 4.3.2 Patent Examination Guidelines.
12 Second Part, First Chapter, Section 4.3.2.1 Patent Examination Guidelines.

Methods to manufacture prostheses or artificial limbs as well as methods of measurement in making prostheses or artificial limbs are patentable.[13] Also patentable are methods that facilitate the growth of animals, that is, those that improve the quality of meat or amount of wool of a sheep, methods to slaughter animals or methods to treat dead animal or human bodies. **3.13**

Methods for surgical treatment are not explicitly mentioned in the Patent Law but are patentable according to the Patent Examination Guidelines if either their object is not a living human being or animal or they do not serve therapeutic purposes. **3.14**

### *(iv) Animal species and plant varieties*

For all non-patentable animal species and plant varieties the term 'animals' refers to all living beings that do not synthesize (合成) themselves but are dependent on carbohydrates and proteins from nature to maintain their lives. The term 'plants' refers to all living beings that synthesise carbohydrates and proteins with the help of photosynthesis of water, $CO_2$ and mineral salt. Animals and plants thus maintain their own lives and are usually immovable. Microbiological substances therefore do not meet this exclusion criterion. However, animal species and plant varieties are not defined in the patent law. **3.15**

New plant varieties can be protected by the Regulation on the Protection of New Plant Varieties, whereas for new animal species there is no special protection. However, all new non-biological methods to cultivate animal species and plant varieties are patentable according to Article 25(2) Chinese Patent Act. Non-biological in this context means that not nature but technical usage is an essential factor for achieving the designated aim or effect, such as for example a method to increase milk production through radiotherapy. **3.16**

### *(v) Substances obtained by nuclear transmission*

The exclusion of patentability for substances obtained by nuclear transmission is based on the idea that otherwise essential national interests would be affected in the areas of economy, national defense, research, and public life. Allowing private persons or non-governmental actors to obtain patents in these fields would mean a private monopoly and would thus run contrary to this consideration.[14] However, devices and equipment to conduct nuclear transmission and their building components are patentable. **3.17**

13 Second Part, First Chapter, Section 4.3.2.2 Patent Examination Guidelines.

14 Second Part, First Chapter, Section 4.5 Patent Examination Guidelines.

### (d) Chinese inventions illegally filed for patents abroad

**3.18** Article 20(1) Chinese Patent Act provides that applications for patent inventions or utility models created in China shall be filed with SIPO for confidentiality examination before a patent application for the same invention is allowed to be filed outside China. In case of a violation of this requirement no Chinese patent will be granted for the invention[15] and the applicant will be exposed to disciplinary measures or criminal charges if state-secrets are disclosed thereby.[16] Whether an invention is deemed as created in China depends on whether the inventive step has been accomplished in China.[17]

**3.19** The confidentiality examination can be initiated as follows:

(1) If the applicant waives an application in China, he has to file an application for confidentiality examination and describe the technical solution in detail.
(2) In the case of filing a priority application in China, the application for the confidentiality examination is to be filed prior to the filing of patent applications outside China. Should the applicant not wish to disclose his application in China, he may withdraw the application within one year.[18]
(3) If the later application is a PCT-application, the requirements in the sense of Article 20(1) Chinese Patent Act are deemed as met with the filing of the PCT-application in China.[19]

**3.20** According to Article 4 Chinese Patent Act, a confidentiality examination has to be undertaken if the application affects national security or other significant national interests. The relationship between this confidentiality examination and that based on Article 20(1) Chinese Patent Act has been challenged by commentators[20] (for more details also see *Luginbuehl*, Chapter 11).

---

15 Art. 20(4) Chinese Patent Act.

16 Art. 71 Chinese Patent Act.

17 Department of SIPO for Regulations and Laws (ed.), *Introductory Remarks on the Third Revision of the Patent Act* (2009), 48; R. 8(1) Implementing Regulations to the Chinese Patent Act.

18 Wang Huimin and Song Yanqin, 'Short Discussion of the Provisions on the Assignment and Administration of Rights on Invention-Creations Produced in China after the Third Revision of the Patent Act', [2009] **7** *IP* 15, 21.

19 R. 8(3) Implementing Regulations to the Chinese Patent Act; for advantages and disadvantages, see Wang Huimin and Song Yanqin, above note 18.

20 Wang Huimin and Song Yanqin, above note 18, 20 et seq.

## B. PREREQUISITES FOR THE GRANT OF PATENT RIGHTS

A patent is granted if the statutory requirements of novelty, inventiveness and industrial applicability are fulfilled in accordance with Article 22 Chinese Patent Act. **3.21**

### 1. Novelty

An invention or utility model is deemed novel, if: **3.22**

(1) it does not belong to prior art; and
(2) there is no interference with another senior patent application.

This makes clear that conflicting patent applications do not constitute prior art under the Chinese Patent Act.

#### *(a) Prior art*

Prior art includes everything known to the public prior to the application date[21] (if priority is claimed, then the priority date).[22] Technical solutions that were published or publicly used in China and outside of China prior to the application date or were made available to the public by other means such as oral notice, belong to prior art. If an invention has only been made available to a certain circle of people (特定人) that is bound by explicit or implicit confidentiality governance, it is to be assumed that the invention is not yet publicly known. **3.23**

It was the patent law revision in 2009 that introduced the absolute novelty standard. Before that revision, a public use outside of China was incapable of destroying novelty. **3.24**

While the introduction of the concept of prior art constitutes a pure legislative-technical amendment, the adoption of the absolute novelty concept was very controversial. The necessity for the absolute novelty was justified by the legislator with the argument that the distinction between a disclosure by publication and a disclosure by means other than publication is in flux due to the proliferation of the internet.[23] In addition, it was argued that not only would public interest be contravened, but also the creation of invention would not be **3.25**

21 According to Art. 28 Chinese Patent Act, the filing date is either the day upon which the filing arrives at SIPO or the day of mailing in the case when the documents were sent by post to SIPO.

22 Art. 22(5) Chinese Patent Act.

23 Department of SIPO for Regulations and Laws, *Introductory Remarks on the Third Revision of the Patent Act* (2009), 50.

promoted if one technology that has already been publicly used outside of China were allowed to be patented in China.[24] This way, foreign enterprises would be no longer allowed to acquire patents on devices that have already entered into the public domain and reap unjustified gains. In addition, it would be possible to improve the quality of Chinese patents with the introduction of the absolute novelty concept.[25]

**3.26** On the other hand, it was argued that this change would only benefit foreign enterprises. Assuming that the incentive to obtain patent protection for a technology that has been publicly used abroad but has not yet been published is the same, foreign enterprises would be in a better position to do this due to their advanced knowledge than domestic enterprises. Should a Chinese enterprise manage to pre-empt foreign enterprises, its foreign competitors could much more easily collect counter evidence for a revocation of the patent.[26] The situation would be even worse if a Chinese enterprise invested in the development of certain technology and was then exposed to challenges from foreign competitors alleging that this technology has already been used publicly, albeit in a small circle outside of China.[27] It should be considered that SIPO is not in a position to examine oral disclosures or disclosures made by public use in the examination proceeding.

**3.27** A striking point in this discussion is that it is not based on thorough studies but rather on speculation, hypotheses and references to foreign experience. The precise impact of introducing the concept of absolute novelty remains to be seen. It is in any event remarkable that the absolute novelty concept is applicable both to invention patents and utility models and even exceeds the German requirement on utility models with respect to its strictness.

**3.28** The term 'disclosure by publication' is to be construed broadly. Not only scientific journals, textbooks, conference reports or newspaper articles, but also product catalogues, advertising flyers or the internet will be considered as publication media.[28] The only exclusion is confidential prints that are designated for internal circulation and are marked accordingly and whose readers are bound by confidentiality governance. With respect to non-official publication

24 Department of SIPO for Regulations and Laws, *Introductory Remarks on the Third Revision of the Patent Act* (2009), 51.

25 Tian Lipu, 'The Introduction of the Absolute Novelty Standard is Necessary for Patent Application' (专利申请加入绝对新颖性标准是必要的) (16 April 2009).

26 Guo Xiaoming, Shen Jianfeng and Wang Haibo, 'The Implications of the Third Revision of the Patent Act on the Telecommunication Industry', [2009] **5** *Electronic IP* 2009 28, 30.

27 Hu Zuohao et al., '"The life of the law has not been logic, it has been experience" – About the Compatibility of the Absolute Novelty Standard in China', [2009] **5** *Electronic IP* 20, 23.

28 Second Part, Third Chapter, Section 2.1.2.1 Patent Examination Guidelines.

mediums, however, there exists a practical difficulty in proving the date of publication.

A disclosure by use in the form of manufacturing, sale, importation and performance is prejudicial as to novelty if the content of the invention has been brought to the attention of the public. If the public is unable to take notice of the invention because the structure, effect or the material is not explained in terms of an average person skilled in the relevant technical field during the public performance, public use is denied. For this reason it should be assumed that there is a public use prejudicial as to novelty if an average professional of the relevant technical field is able to investigate the structure or the effect by disassembling a legally obtained product or device.[29] **3.29**

### (b) *Conflicting patent applications*

A conflicting patent application refers to the case in which an identical technical solution had already been filed with SIPO for invention patent or utility model patent prior to the application date and the content of the solution is made publicly available after the application date.[30] Conflicting patent applications include those cases in which a part of the technical solution was disclosed, and also a PCT-application that has already entered into the national phase in China and was filed before the application date and published on or after the publication date in Chinese. **3.30**

Conflicting patent applications are always senior applications filed by the same applicant or a third party. A conflicting patent application (抵触申请) does not belong to prior art because its content remains unknown to the public prior to the publication date, but is still prejudicial as to the novelty. The rule aims to avoid a situation where several identical patents for the same invention are granted to the same person or a third party. **3.31**

### (c) *Grace period*

Publications or a public use do not adversely affect novelty in accordance with Article 24 Chinese Patent Act if the invention was, within six months prior to the application date (if priority is claimed, then the priority date): **3.32**

(1) disclosed at an international exhibition sponsored or recognized by the Chinese government for the first time; or
(2) disclosed at a specified academic or technological conference for the first time; or

---

29 Second Part, Third Chapter, Section 2.1.2.2 Patent Examination Guidelines.
30 Art. 22(2) Chinese Patent Act.

(3) divulged by a third party without the consent of the applicant.

Article 24 Chinese Patent Act is applicable both to invention patent applications and utility model applications. The grace period is used extremely rarely and made up only 0.039 per cent of all applications from 1985–2006.[31]

**3.33** As a general rule, it should be noted that if a disclosure is made during the grace period stipulated in Article 24 Chinese Patent Act, the invention has already become prior art. The statutory assumption that these disclosures do not affect novelty benefits only the inventor. That means that if a third party, who accomplishes the same invention independently and files it within a grace period for patent before the first inventor has done this, then that third party is excluded from acquiring the patent, because it is illegitimate for such a third party to claim the benefit of the grace period. However, the third party may use his application to prevent the first inventor from acquiring the patent based on the first-to-file principle, according to which the patent will be granted to the first applicant. Applicants filing too late have to leave empty-handed. Therefore, in this situation, nobody may acquire the patent.

**3.34** Should the same invention be disclosed again during the grace period and there is no circumstance in the sense of Article 24 Chinese Patent Act, this disclosure is prejudicial as to novelty.[32] This is the case if a third party, who learned about the invention by legal means, discloses it during the grace period. Because no clear answer can be derived from Article 24 Chinese Patent Act, the scholarly opinion rejects the prejudicial effect of such disclosure in order to avoid an erosion of the purpose of the grace period.[33]

## 2. Inventiveness

### *(a) Definition*

**3.35** Inventiveness, also called 'inventive step' and 'non-obviousness', is stipulated as another requirement for patentability, so that the patent register will not be occupied by inferior inventions with minor improvements compared to prior art – the so-called 'junk patents'.

---

31 Wan Xiaoli, 'The Patent Novelty Grace Period in China in Comparative Perspective', [2009] **40** *IIC* 182, 183.

32 Second Part, Third Chapter, Section 5 Patent Examination Guidelines.

33 Yin Xintian, *Protection of the Patent Right* (2nd edn.), Intellectual Property Publishing House 2005, 38.

3.36 The inventiveness requires that, compared with the existing technologies, the invention has prominent substantive features (突出的实质性特点) and represents a notable progress (显著性的进步).[34] This phrase follows the model of the former Soviet Union and obviously differs from the American and European counterparts. However, the notion of prominent substantive features calls for nothing other than non-obviousness of the invention for a person of ordinary skills in the relevant technical domain (所属技术领域的技术人员).[35] With respect to utility models, the criteria for the inventiveness are set lower (see different opinion of *Mak*, Chapter 19). Merely substantive features (实质性特点) and progress (进步) are required. However, the gap between utility models and invention patents with regard to inventiveness is hard to quantify (see below).

3.37 For the determination of the inventiveness, the notion of a person skilled in the art is crucial. According to the Patent Examination Guidelines, this refers to a hypothetical person who possesses ordinary knowledge in the relevant technical domain existing prior to the application date, has access to the entire prior art, is in a position to conduct routine experiments and is not inventive himself.[36] It should be noted that this standard applies both to an invention and a utility model application.

*(b) Three-steps approach*

3.38 To assess inventiveness, the Patent Examination Guidelines stipulate the following three-steps approach: The first is to determine the closest prior art; the second is to determine the distinguishing features of the invention and the technical problem actually solved by the invention; and the third is to determine whether or not the claimed invention is obvious to a person skilled in the art.[37] While determining the closest prior art, the examiner is bound to first consider the identical or comparable technical field of the invention.[38] An invention is deemed obvious where there is a technical indication in the prior art to apply a technical means that is either identical to or bears no material difference to the technical means adopted by the invention, to solve the technical problem that is supposed to be solved by the invention, and may achieve identical or basically identical technical effect; in addition, the search for such a technical means does not require inventive efforts.[39] According to a ruling of the Supreme People's

34 Art. 22(3) Chinese Patent Act.
35 Second Part, Fourth Chapter, Section 2.2 of the Patent Examination Guidelines.
36 Second Part, Fourth Chapter, Section 2.4 of the Patent Examination Guidelines.
37 Second Part, Fourth Chapter, Section 3.2.2.1 of the Patent Examination Guidelines.
38 Liu Xiaojun, 'Technical Teaching in the Assessment of Inventiveness of Patents', [2012] **5** *IP* 45.
39 Liu Xiaojun, above note 38, 47.

Court in *Zhao et al. v Patent Reexamination and Adjudication Board*,[40] in determining inventiveness of an application for a utility model the examiner is usually bound to consider only the technical field indicated by the applicant and is allowed to take neighbouring technical fields into account only when the prior art provides an unambiguous technical indication (in the form of clear documentation) to adopt the distinguishing feature of the application with respect to the closest prior art.[41]

**3.39** If the distinguishing feature of an invention is common knowledge in the art, then the inventiveness is denied.[42] The scope of common knowledge in the art is still subject to controversy.[43] The narrowest approach, adopted by the Patent Examination Guidelines[44] and followed by the courts,[45] construes common knowledge as covering only general knowledge that is documented in textbooks, technical dictionaries or technical manuals. By contrast, the broadest construction extends the scope of common knowledge also to contents disclosed by patent documentation, technical journals and academic theses.[46]

### *(c) Notable progress*

**3.40** The requirement of notable progress appears to be confusing. At first glance, this concept appears to be alien to the European Patent Convention. This requirement refers to the positive technical effect that an invention may create. The requirement has almost no practical significance,[47] because it is met as soon as:

(1) an invention's accomplishments compared to the prior art are technically superior; or
(2) its solution is new and it is able to accomplish the same effect as a comparable technique of prior art; or

40 Case discussion by Qin Yuanming, [2012] **12** *People's Justice* 5.
41 Fang Ting et al., 'Difference between the Standard for Inventiveness with Respect to Utility Models and Invention Patents', [2012] **1** *China Invention & Patent* 100; Qin Yuanming, above note 40.
42 Second Part, Fourth Chapter, Section 3.2.1.1 Patent Examination Guidelines.
43 Jiao Yan, 'Scrutiny of "General Knowledge Known to the Public" in the Sense of the Patent Law', [2013] **1** *China Patents & Trademarks* 19.
44 Second Part, Eighth Chapter, Section 4.3.3 Patent Examination Guidelines.
45 Zhang Dongmei, 'The Evidence on Common Knowledge in Cases of Determining the Grant of Patents', [2012] **10** *IP* 32; Mao Jin and Liu Xinlei, 'Determination of Relevant Evidence in the Assessment of Inventiveness', [2012] **8** *China Invention & Patent*, 89.
46 Tong Shu, 'Determination of Common Knowledge Evidence in Administrative Patent Proceedings', [2011] **3** *China Patents & Trademarks* 40; criticized by Jiao Yan, above note 43, 21.
47 Xiaojun Liu, above note 38, 43.

(3) the invention has negative effect but is still able to accomplish an obviously positive effect.[48]

#### *(d) Indications for inventiveness*

According to the Patent Examination Guidelines, the following circumstances constitute indications for inventiveness: **3.41**

(1) the invention solves a known difficult problem, the solution to which has been sought without success for a long time;
(2) the invention overcomes a technical prejudice;
(3) the invention has surprising elements;
(4) the invention has achieved great economic success and the success is attributed to the technical features of the invention.[49]

### 3. Industrial applicability

Industrial applicability means that the object of an invention or a utility model may be manufactured or exploited in an industrial manner in the field of industry, agriculture, forest industry, fishery, culture, pharmaceutics, sports and transportation, and is able to create a positive (economic or technical) impact.[50] An invention does not comply with this requirement if it cannot be reproduced or contradicts the law of nature (for example a *Perpetuum Mobile*). Methods for surgery treatment for non-therapeutical purposes (because otherwise the invention would not be patentable at all) are deemed as not industrially applicable, because the objects of these inventions are living human beings or animals. The same is true with respect to methods for diagnosis that measure biological data on bodies of human beings or animals under extreme external conditions, such as coldness or low oxygen supply.[51] **3.42**

### 4. Prohibition on double-patenting

The prohibition on double-patenting (禁止重复授权) constitutes another important principle of patent law and is applicable to utility models as well.[52] This principle is aimed at avoiding a situation where two patents are awarded to the same invention. The first-to-file principle (先申请原则) and the conflicting patent applications principle also serve the same purpose, albeit from **3.43**

48 Second Part, Fourth Chapter, Section 3.2.2 Patent Examination Guidelines; Tang Zongshun, *A Course in Patent Law* (3rd edn.), Law Press, 2003, 94.

49 Second Part, Fourth Chapter, Section 5 Patent Examination Guidelines.

50 Art. 22(4) Chinese Patent Act; this corresponds with Art. 57 EPC, Art. 1(3) Paris Convention.

51 Second Part, Fifth Chapter, Section 3.2.5 Patent Examination Guidelines.

52 Art. 9(1), sentence 1 Chinese Patent Act.

different perspectives. With the prohibition of double-patenting, the extension of the duration of protection will be avoided,[53] which may otherwise occur if the same applicant files the same invention twice for patent and the patents are granted at different times.

### (a) Prohibition on double-patenting – first-to-file principle

**3.44** The first-to-file principle requires that a patent is awarded to the first applicant if two or more than two persons filed a patent for the same invention.[54] If two identical inventions or utility models were filed by two different applicants on the same application date (if priority is claimed, then the priority date), both applicants may try to solve the conflict through consultation. If the consultation is unsuccessful and the applicants fail to turn the applications into two different ones either by statements or amendments, then both applications are rejected.[55] A situation in which the earlier and the later application are filed by the same applicant constitutes a double-patenting, but cannot be barred by the first-to-file principle. To this end, the prohibition on double-patenting is necessary.

### (b) Prohibition on double-patenting – conflicting patent applications

**3.45** The prohibition on double-patenting differs from conflicting patent applications in that the later application will not lead to the award of a patent even if the conflicting application is abandoned by the applicant. In other words, the fate of the conflicting application is no longer relevant for the prevention of a later application, because the novelty requirement is not fulfilled with respect to the later application in case of a conflicting patent application.

**3.46** In addition, for the determination of conflicting patent applications, the patent claims as well as the specifications and the drawings will be considered; whereas with respect to the prohibition of double-patenting, only the patent claims are relevant.[56] Consequently, the award of a patent may not be prevented based on the prohibition on double-patenting if in the patent claims of the senior application, protection is claimed for a product and in the patent claims of the later application, protection is claimed for manufacturing methods, although in

53 Wei Zheng, 'Application of the Double Patenting Prohibition Doctrine from the Perspective of Shu Xuezhang Case', [2009] **1** *China Patent and Trademarks* 49.

54 Art. 9(2) Chinese Patent Act.

55 R. 41(1) Implementing Regulations to the Chinese Patent Act.

56 Second Part, Third Chapter 2.2 Patent Examination Guidelines; *Shu Xuezhang and Patent Reexamination and Adjudication Board v Jining Factory of Pressureless Boilers* (舒学章、国家知识产权局专利复审委员会与济宁无压锅炉厂发明专利权无效纠纷提审案), decision of the SPC dated of 14 July 2008, available at http://www.chinacourt.org/public/detail.php?id=330945.

the specifications of both applications, both the product and the manufacturing method have been disclosed.[57]

### (c) *Exception to the prohibition on double-patenting*

Prior to the introduction of the prohibition on double-patenting through the third revision of the patent law (Article 9(1) Chinese Patent Act), there was a long-lasting controversy concerning its significance and application.[58] According to one opinion, the prohibition on double-patenting precludes merely the existence of two valid patents for the same invention at the same time,[59] while the other opinion bars the award of a second patent for the same invention regardless of whether a patent granted at an earlier time has meanwhile expired.[60] It is now clarified with the third revision of the patent law that the case where the applicant applies simultaneously for utility model and patent on the same invention and SIPO awards first a utility model and then an invention patent under the condition that the applicant revokes the utility model constitutes a double-patenting. Such double-patenting is, however, permissible due to the exception stipulated in Article 9(1) sentence 2 Chinese Patent Act. **3.47**

This double-patenting is to be attributed to the administrative practice of SIPO since 1990. At that time SIPO was confronted with the difficulty of coping with the strongly increasing number of applications with limited personal resources. One consequence was that the average duration of examination reached six to seven years for the grant of invention patents. In order to reduce the backlog of pending applications, SIPO admitted the practice of staggered applications for invention patents and utility models on the same invention since 1995 in the Patent Examination Guidelines. Although the prohibition on double-patenting was not incorporated into the patent law, it had already been stipulated in the Patent Implementation Rules of 1992 and 2001. This is why the above-described practice was challenged for being incompatible with the prohibition on double-patenting.[61] The examination procedure has been expedited with the recruitment of additional examiners at the beginning of the 21st **3.48**

---

57 Department of SIPO for Regulations and Laws (ed.), *Introductory Remarks on the Third Revision of the Patent Act* (2009), 52.

58 According to Zhou Yunchuan, 'Judicial Praxis in Respect of Double Patenting', [2009] **1** *China Patents & Trademarks* 35; double-patenting cases were 6% of all patent invalidity cases tried at the first Intermediate Court Beijing between 2001 and 2007; for the legal situation prior to the third revision of the Patent Law, cf. Zhang Rongyan, 'On "Repatenting": Reflections on a Judicial Judgement', [2003] **4** *China Patents & Trademarks* 54.

59 The first Intermediate Court Beijing and the Supreme People's Court in the case of *Shu Xuezhang and Patent Reexamination and Adjudication Board v Jining Factory of Pressureless Boilers*.

60 The High Court Beijing in the case of *Shu Xuezhang and Patent Reexamination and Adjudication Board v Jining Factory of Pressureless Boilers*.

61 Department of SIPO for Regulations and Laws (ed.), *Introductory Remarks on the Third Revision of the Patent Act* (2009), 35 et seq.

century. Nevertheless, the maintenance of this practice was held necessary,[62] so that the exemption was nailed down statutorily in Article 9(1) sentence 2 Chinese Patent Act. In order to benefit from this exception, the following three preconditions are to be fulfilled:

**3.49** First, the applicant has to file an application for invention patent and utility model patent on the same day. The applicant is required to disclose the circumstance of double-patenting when filing the applications; without such an explicit declaration the application of Article 9(1) sentence 2 Chinese Patent Act is precluded.[63] The requirement of double application on the same day aims to prevent the extension of the patent term of over 20 years in total from the application date.[64] In literature it has been pointed out that an excess of the 20-year term is in any case impossible under the current patent law regime in the case of staggered patent filings. The senior application would hinder the later application as a conflicting application and thus, the requirement of simultaneous filings is therefore unnecessary.[65] The requirement must have probably been kept in the statute by mistake.[66] This notion is accurate to the extent that the internal priority may not be combined with the exemption of the prohibition on double-patenting.[67] On the same day means that the actual application dates must be identical.

**3.50** Second, the utility model patent may neither have expired nor been abandoned. In this way the public shall be able to rely on the fact that an already expired or abandoned utility model patent may not be revived through a new patent award.[68] For the same reason, the announcement of the grant of the utility model patent will be accompanied with the public notice that another identical patent application has been filed on the same date.[69] Should the utility model patent already have expired, then the application of Article 9(1) sentence 2 Chinese Patent Act is precluded. Indeed, this requirement appears unreasonable, as pointed out by commentators,[70] since it could be a coincidence or

---

62 Department of SIPO for Regulations and Laws (ed.), *Introductory Remarks on the Third Revision of the Patent Act* (2009), 36; Li Shunde, 'Comments on the Change of the Relevant Provisions on the Prohibition of Double-Patenting', [2009] **3** *Electronic IP* 20, 22.

63 R. 41 (2), half sentence 2 Implementing Regulations to the Chinese Patent Act.

64 Department of SIPO for Regulations and Laws (ed.), *Introductory Remarks on the Third Revision of the Patent Act (2009)*, 37.

65 Li Shunde , above note 62, 22.

66 Li Shunde, above note 62, 23.

67 R. 41(2) half sentence 1 Implementing Regulations of the Patent Law.

68 Department of SIPO for Regulations and Laws, above note 64, 36 et seq.

69 R. 41(3) Implementing Regulations to the Chinese Patent Act.

70 Li Chunhui, 'New Thoughts on the Question of Double-Patenting – Remarks on the Judgment of the Administrative Law Tribunal of the Supreme Court (2007) Xing Ti Zi No. 4 and Arts, 9, 22, 23 Patent Act', [2009] **5** *Electronic IP* 73, 77; Li Shunde, above note 62, 24.

SIPO's fault if the patent examination procedure is delayed excessively. The opposite approach – abandonment of the invention patent and maintenance of the utility model patent – is not covered by Article 9(1) sentence 2 Chinese Patent Act, because the legislature assumed that no reasonable patentee would abandon an invention patent with a longer protection term simply in order to maintain the corresponding utility model patent.[71]

Third, the applicant has to abandon the not expired utility model patent. In case no abandonment is declared or not timely declared, the invention patent application is deemed withdrawn. The utility model patent extinguishes on the day of the public announcement of the grant of the invention patent.[72] 3.51

### *(d) Consequences of double-patenting*

In case the prerequisites of Article 9(1) sentence 2 Chinese Patent Act are not met, the patentee has to abandon one patent in the invalidation proceeding, if both applications were awarded patents. Otherwise, the patent affected by the invalidation proceeding will be invalidated.[73] If two identical patents with an identical application date were awarded to two different patent proprietors, both proprietors may maintain one patent by abandonment of the other patent in the invalidation proceeding initiated by a third party.[74] If no one is willing to abandon his patent, then both patents will be invalidated. The situation, in which two applications of the same categories (invention patents, utility model patents or design patents) for the same invention were filed on the same day and one has been awarded and the other has not yet been awarded, is unclear. At this point, it is unclear whether Article 9(1) sentence 2 Chinese Patent Act is applicable accordingly.[75] 3.52

71 Department of SIPO for Regulations and Laws, above note 64, 37.
72 R. 41(5) Implementing Regulations to the Chinese Patent Act.
73 Fourth Part, Seventh Chapter, Section 2.2 Patent Examination Guidelines.
74 Fourth Part, Seventh Chapter, Section 3 Patent Examination Guidelines.
75 Li Chunhui, above note 70, 76 et seq.

# 4

# BIOTECHNOLOGICAL, CHEMICAL AND PHARMACEUTICAL INVENTIONS I: GENERAL

**Chen Wenping**



## A. INTRODUCTION

**4.01** Patent protection of chemical, pharmaceutical and biotechnological inventions in China differs quite significantly from the majority of Western jurisdictions, as compared to other technical fields. This is especially true with regard to two aspects. One is the scope of subject matter that is eligible for patent protection. The other is how broad a claim can be to be in line with law and practice, and how the description must be formulated to support an allowable claim.

**4.02** The first version of the Chinese Patent Act of 1984 did not provide patent protection for chemical, pharmaceutical or biological substances. Patent protection for these subject matters became available only after the first amendment to the Chinese Patent Act in 1993. From 1993 to 2006, the examination practice of the Chinese Patent Office (now SIPO) in relation to applications for such inventions was generally in line with the practice of other major patent jurisdictions. However, in 2006, stricter Guidelines for Patent Examination (hereinafter 'Guidelines') became applicable.

The 2006 version of the Guidelines, as well as its subsequent versions, emphasized that the predictability of an invention in the chemical field (including pharmaceutical and biotechnology) is generally low and that most of the technical effects have to be verified by experimental data. Based on this understanding, the examination practice of SIPO has become increasingly strict over the years. Meanwhile, the allowable scope of protection has become so limited in some cases that it has become virtually meaningless to seek protection for the invention at issue. Nevertheless, there is still some room for negotiations with the examiners concerning eligibility and reasonable scope of protection. It is clear, however, that it has become more challenging for patent practitioners to get the inventions of their clients protected in this area. **4.03**

Against this background, this chapter focuses on the eligible subject matter and the issue of enablement/support-from-description of the claims at stake. Additionally, the chapter will provide a brief overview of particular issues relating to pharmaceutical or biological inventions, such as executing clinical tests without infringing patent rights, data exclusivity, marketing exclusivity and patent linkage. **4.04**

## B. PATENTABLE SUBJECT MATTER

An invention has to consist of subject matter that is patentable in order to be eligible for patent protection. Article 2 Chinese Patent Act defines an invention as a new technical solution relating to a product, a process or improvement thereof. Therefore, the requirement that the invention has to be of a 'technical' nature is the most important prerequisite for patentability. Based on this principle and other legal, cultural, political and social considerations, there are important exceptions to patentability, which are set forth in the Chinese Patent Act, the Implementing Regulations and the Guidelines for Patent Examination. **4.05**

The subject matter which is eligible for patent protection is restricted in three ways. An invention is *prima facie* patentable if it does not fall within one of these three exclusions. **4.06**

### 1. Industrial applicability

**4.07** According to Article 22(4) Chinese Patent Act, a patentable invention must be capable of industrial application. An invention is capable of industrial application if it can be made or used in industry and can produce effective results. According to the Guidelines, such industry includes, for example, agriculture, forestry, fishery, or animal husbandry.

**4.08** An invention that can be made or used in industry is any exploitable technical solution that conforms to the laws of nature and possesses technical features.

**4.09** With regard to the requirement that the invention must produce effective results, it is only required that any economic, technical or social result can be expected by a person skilled in the art at the date of filing of the patent application. This latter requirement means that an invention has to exhibit a credible useful purpose.

**4.10** The Guidelines expressly deny the industrial applicability of inventions that:

- are not reproducible,
- are contrary to the laws of nature,
- relate to products produced under unique natural conditions,
- relate to surgical operations on human or animal bodies, and
- relate to methods of measuring physical parameters of human beings under extreme conditions.

**4.11** Although many new gene structures have been identified due to the rapid development of sequencing techniques, the functions of many of these genes remain unknown. Such genes or structures of genes are not patentable for lack of industrial applicability unless a useful purpose can be provided.

**4.12** The requirement of industrial applicability might be met even if the use of the gene is speculative. However, according to the Guidelines, where the establishment of the proposed technical solution depends on experimental verification, the suggested use for a biochemical material such as a DNA fragment, a gene, a peptide or a protein is only established if experimental evidence is provided.

**4.13** If the technical solution has a diagnostic or therapeutic purpose, sufficient qualitative or quantitative data raised by way of laboratory experiments, animal experiments or clinical experiments have to be submitted to prove that the proposed technical solution can achieve the desired purpose or effect.

Generally, a process for screening a specific microorganism from nature is qualified as not reproducible and therefore lacks industrial applicability. This qualification comes from uncertainty concerning the geographical location where the screening sample is taken, environmental change in the location, and the haphazard nature of the presence of the specific microorganism in the sample. However, if the applicant has sufficient evidence proving the reproducibility of the process, such process may be patentable. Similarly, since processes of artificial mutagenesis are usually based on random mutations of microorganisms under some physical or chemical conditions, such processes are normally deemed not to be industrially applicable, for lack of reproducibility. However, a process based on a site-directed mutagenesis or any other process resulting with certainty in the desired microorganism under specific conditions may be industrially applicable. **4.14**

Although processes for screening microorganisms from nature or for random mutagenesis are usually not patentable, new microorganisms screened from nature or obtained by random mutagenesis may be patentable if samples of such microorganisms are deposited according to the Chinese Patent Act. **4.15**

### 2. Violation of law, contrary to social morality or detrimental to public interest

According to Article 5 Chinese Patent Act, a patentable invention shall not be contrary to the laws of the State or social morality[1] or be detrimental to the public interest. This exclusion is limited to inventions that have purposes which are contrary to law or social morality or are detrimental to the public interest. Inventions that have useful effects cannot be deemed to fall into this exclusion if their misuse or abuse results in a situation in which the invention turns out to be contrary to law or detrimental to the public interest. Moreover, inventions shall not be considered as contrary to law simply because their exploitation is prohibited by law. **4.16**

#### *(a) Inventions contrary to the law*

Inventions relying on illegally obtained genetic resources are excluded for patentability under Article 5 Chinese Patent Act. As non-exclusive examples, the Guidelines mention two laws that set forth regulations for acquiring, handling and importing and exporting genetic resources. They are the Chinese Animal Husbandry Act and the Measures for Examination and Approval in Respect of the Entry and Exit of Genetic Resources of Livestock and Poultry **4.17**

1 Social morality is the moral standards generally accepted by the public. See Guidelines, Part II, Chapter 1, Section 3.2.1.

and in Respect of Research in Their Utilization in Cooperation with Foreign Entities. These laws require approval for exporting certain genetic resources. Patent applications concerning inventions based on genetic resources obtained in violation of the laws have to be rejected. If a patent for such an invention is granted, it can be revoked.

**4.18** In order to enforce this provision, the Chinese Patent Act generally requires under Article 26(5) that an applicant who files a patent application for an invention completed on the basis of genetic resources must indicate the direct and original source of the genetic resources in the patent application. The practical implementation of this provision caused much concern to applicants in the biotechnology field when it was introduced into the law during the third revision of the Chinese Patent Act. Fortunately, the Guidelines clarify that the applicant should disclose the source of the biological materials upon request of the examiner during the examination of the application. In practice, it is very rare for the examiners to issue such requests. The application can be rejected if the application fails to disclose the source of the relevant biological material. However, the lack of disclosure of the source of the genetic resource is not a ground for revocation.

*(b) Immoral inventions*

**4.19** The Guidelines clarify that the following inventions are not patentable under Article 5 Chinese Patent Act for being immoral:

(1) processes for cloning human beings and human beings cloned by such processes;
(2) processes for modifying the germline genetic identity of human beings;
(3) human bodies at various stages of their formation including germ cells oosperms, embryos;
(4) use of human embryos for industrial or commercial purposes;
(5) human embryonic stem cells and methods for producing the same;
(6) processes for modifying the genetic identity of animals which are likely to cause them suffering without any substantial medical benefits to man or animal.

### 3. Non-patentable inventions

**4.20** Article 25 Chinese Patent Act explicitly excludes the following among others from the scope of patentable subject matter: scientific discovery, methods for treatment or diagnosis of diseases, plant or animal varieties.

### (a) Scientific discoveries

A scientific discovery itself is not patentable. However, a technical solution based on the scientific discovery may be patentable. For example, the discovery that silver halide is sensitive to light is not patentable, whereas photosensitive film conceived based on this discovery and the process for making the same are patentable. **4.21**

A discovery of a previously unknown substance in its naturally occurring status is not patentable. However, products and processes resulting from the human effort in isolating or extracting the substance from its natural surroundings are *prima facie* patentable. For example, isolated or substantially purified antibiotics, proteins, genes or microorganisms are eligible for patent protection. One might therefore wonder whether genes are patentable. Under Chinese law, genes isolated or extracted from the natural environment including human genes and their fragments are patentable. **4.22**

### (b) Medical treatment and diagnostic methods

Methods for treatment and diagnosis of diseases in general are excluded from being patentable subject matter. **4.23**

#### (i) Methods for diagnosis

Before 2006, an in vitro method to diagnose diseases was patentable and many patents on this subject matter had been granted. However, the 2006 version of the Guidelines brought a change and declared that this method of diagnosis was not patentable as a category. The Guidelines set forth the criteria for determining whether a method qualifies as a diagnostic method: a diagnostic method (1) is practiced on the human or animal body; and (2) has the immediate purpose of obtaining diagnostic results. **4.24**

It is always difficult to argue that a method based on either of these criteria does not have a diagnostic purpose.

For the requirement of practicing on the human or animal body, the Guidelines further expand the scope by providing that a method practiced on in vitro samples such as tissue, body liquids or excretion separated from the human or animal body will also be deemed to be a diagnostic method if the direct purpose of the method is to obtain the diagnosis or health status of the subject from whom the sample is derived. It seems possible to argue for the eligibility of a method of detecting the presence of a bacterium or virus in a sample since it would not provide an individual diagnosis. As to the second criterion, methods will be deemed to have the immediate purpose of obtaining the diagnostic **4.25** results if the physical parameters acquired from a human body directly lead to the diagnosis on the basis of medical knowledge of the art.

**4.26** The Guidelines list the following methods as examples of methods of diagnosis which are excluded from patentability: X-ray diagnosis, ultrasonic diagnosis, gastrointestinal imaging diagnosis, endoscopic diagnosis, isotopic tracing diagnosis, infrared non-intruding diagnosis, method of evaluating the risk of suffering a disease, method for predicting the therapeutic efficacy for disease, gene screening diagnostic method and so on.

**4.27** If a method has both diagnostic and non-diagnostic applications, the claim will be deemed to lead on the diagnostic method and is not allowable. Under such circumstances, it is possible to restrict the claim to a non-diagnostic method in order for it to be patentable. It is advisable to clearly indicate the wording 'non-diagnostic method' since the amendment to restrict the subject matter may be objected on the ground of introducing new subject matter.

*(ii) Treatment of diseases*

**4.28** Medical treatments are excluded from patent subject matter. According to the Guidelines, this includes methods of treatment that are practiced on the human or animal body for surgery, therapy or prophylaxis.

**4.29** Methods practiced on the human or animal body without therapeutic purpose or without direct therapeutic purpose are not excluded from patentable subject matters under Article 25 Chinese Patent Act.

**4.30** The following methods are not excluded from patent protection because they are not deemed as being practiced on the human or animal body:

(1) methods for making artificial limbs or prosthesis, or in vivo measuring methods for making such artificial limbs or prosthesis;
(2) methods for slaughtering animals;
(3) methods for treatment of a dead human or animal body;
(4) methods for killing bacteria, viruses, lice or fleas on the exterior surface of a human or animal body.

**4.31** However, the following are examples that are not excluded from patent protection for having no therapeutic purpose:

(1) methods for modifying animal growth features through treatment of an animal by non-surgical methods;

(2) methods for pure cosmetology, that is, non-intruding or non-hurting cosmetology methods, including methods of deodorization, protection, decoration or modification for a non-therapeutic purpose practiced on such visible parts of human body as skin, hair, nails and teeth;
(3) methods for delivering oxygen, negatively charged oxygen or vapor into a non-pathological human or animal body to render pleasure, happiness and so on.

*(iii) Swiss-type claims*

The most effective way for rebutting a disease treatment or diagnosis objection is to change the format of the claims into 'Swiss-type' claims. In the Guidelines, the Swiss-type claim format is proposed for the second medical use of a known substance. Such claim is formulated by 'use of substance A for the production of a medicament for the treatment of disease X'. **4.32**

In practice, Swiss-type claims can be applied broadly. A medical indication can be formulated as a specific disease, for example, as in the following claim: **4.33**

> Use of anti-α2 macroglobulin antibody in the manufacture of a medicament for treating glaucoma in a mammal.

A medical indication could also be the cause of the disease or drug target, as in the following claim:

> Use of anti-α2 macroglobulin antibody in the production of a medicament for preventing retinal ganglion cell (RGC) death mediated by high intraocular pressure.

In essence, the patient is the target of a medical indication by a drug. Therefore, the patient can be defined with various features. This is especially important because modern medical practice puts much weight on individualized treatment. For example, the medical indication of 'breast cancer' is limited to those patients who are HER2 positive. **4.34**

> Use of an anti-VEGF antibody for the manufacture of a medicament for preventing or reducing metastasis in a patient suffering from relapsed HER2 positive breast cancer during or after treatment with an anti-HER2 antibody.

Most of the Chinese examiners understand the term 'production' in a Swiss-type claim as the production of the physical dosage form of the drug, such as tablets, capsules, injection solution and so on. Based on such understanding, those features which do not affect the actual production of the medicament do not have limiting effects on the claim and are thus not considered during the evaluation of the novelty and/or inventive step of the claim. Consequently, the **4.35** dosage and dosage regiments are considered as a matter to be decided or selected by the doctors and do not affect the production of the medicament per se. However, for a new drug, the dosage and dosage regiments are one of the most important aspects of the innovation to be patented. The dosage of the drug is determined by the innovator of the drug and not by the doctors who prescribe the drug. This is underscored by the definition of a drug or medicament in the regulatory law.

**4.36** According to the Chinese Drug Administration Act, a drug or medicament means a product intended for use in the prevention, treatment or diagnosis of human diseases, or intended to effect the purposive regulation of human physiological functions, for which indications or major functions, usage and *dosage* are prescribed. Therefore, the current interpretation of Swiss-type claims by SIPO is criticized as too narrow and as excluding too many pharmaceutical innovations and improvements from patent protection. In many cases, the successful treatment of a disease is based on a novel dosage regimen of a known drug.[2] Before such invention, selecting the claimed dosing regimen for the improved treatment is not in the range of ordinary choices a doctor has, as the doctor is supposed to follow the approved existing dosing regimen. The reasonable interpretation of 'production of a medicament' should be the production of the known medicament or substance *into* the claimed new medicament that may be defined with indication, usage and/or dosage in consistency with the Chinese Drug Administration Act. However, the *Cubist* decision rendered by the Supreme People's Court at the end of 2013 denied this broad interpretation of the term 'production of a medicament'.[3] This will direct the practitioners as far as possible to shift their efforts to other claim formats, such as pharmaceutical kits for the protection of drug-administration based inventions.

**4.37** Although not explicitly regulated by the Guidelines, in practice, Swiss-type claims are also applicable to the diagnosis, for example, the use of substance A in the production of a medicament/agent for the diagnosis of disease X. The steps of diagnosis can be set forth in such use claims as in the following example.

> Use of anti-$\alpha$2 macroglobulin antibody in the production of an agent for testing for chronic ocular degeneration in a patient, wherein said testing comprises:

2 *Merck v. Patent Reexamination Board*, Beijing No. 1 Intermediate Court's Judgment No. 399 in 2008.

3 *Cubist Pharmaceuticals v. Patent Reexamination Board and Xiaohong*, Supreme People's Court's Judgment No. (2012) ZXZ75.

(1) measuring the expression level of α2 macroglobulin in the aqueous humor of the patient; and
(2) comparing the expression level to that of α2 macroglobulin in individuals with normal ocular function, wherein a higher expression level of α2 macroglobulin and/or a lower expression level of α2 macroglobulin as compared to the expression level of α2 macroglobulin in individuals with normal ocular function indicates that the patient has chronic ocular degeneration.

Swiss-type claims can even be used for a screening method, as in the following example: **4.38**

Use of anti-α2 macroglobulin antibody in the production of an agent for identifying an intraocular pressure-regulated early gene (IRPEG), wherein the identifying comprises:

(a) determining whether expression of a gene is altered by ocular hypertension, wherein expression of the gene is not altered by retinal ganglion cell (RGC) damage;
(b) determining whether expression of the gene is altered early after the onset of ocular hypertension;
(c) determining whether the altered expression of the gene is sustained after onset of ocular hypertension or glaucoma; and
(d) determining whether expression of the gene remains altered after ocular hypertension is reduced.

Although Swiss-type claims are very useful in patent practice, it is not always possible during the patent examination to change a claim for disease treatment or diagnosis into a Swiss-type claim. One reason is that the technology per se does not rely on the use of a certain substance for a treatment or diagnosis. Another reason is that the examiner will raise new matter objections in case of a conversion of the original method claim into a use claim. Therefore, it is advisable to include Swiss-type claims or corresponding embodiments in the specification when drafting a patent application. However, against the background of the recent *Cubist* decision,[4] pure diagnostic procedure features might be considered as non-limiting and the patentability of such claims may thus have to be established on the new finding of the relationship between the agent and the medical disease to be diagnosed. **4.39**

### *(c) Plant or animal varieties*

Article 25(1) Chinese Patent Act excludes the possibility of patenting plant and animal varieties. In practice, the term 'plant and animal variety' is interpreted as plant and animal in general, irrespective of their scientific classification. **4.40**

4 See above note 3.

**4.41** Article 25(2) Chinese Patent Act stipulates that processes for producing animals and plants may be patented in accordance with the provisions of the patent law. However, the Guidelines define such processes as 'not including essentially biological processes'. A process does not form an 'essentially biological process' if the technical intervention by man in the process plays a significant part in determining or controlling the result or effect that the invention intends to achieve. A method for producing a milk cow which is characterized by a high milk production due to the exposure of the cow to radiation during feeding is thus patentable.

**4.42** Embryonic stem cells of animals are excluded from patentability under Article 25(1) Chinese Patent Act.

**4.43** Adult human or animal stem cells, methods for their production or use, as well as methods for producing or using animal embryonic stem cells are not excluded from patentability.

**4.44** Microorganisms as defined by the Guidelines include bacteria, actinomycetes, fungi, viruses, protozoa, algae, and so on. A microorganism is neither a plant nor an animal. Therefore, it is not excluded from patentability under Article 25(1) Chinese Patent Act. An isolated or substantially pure culture of a microorganism is patentable.

**4.45** It has long been accepted in China that plant and animal cells shall not be excluded from patentability. For example, transgenic plant or animal cells are potentially patentable. However, in recent years, Chinese examiners have increasingly objected to the patentability of plant cells. Such objections are almost regularly raised if the patent specification indicates that a certain cell of the plant can be used for the regeneration of the plant. According to SIPO, if a plant cell is capable of developing into a whole plant according to the specification or prior art, it will be deemed as a plant reproductive material. Some examiners even go as far as to reject patent applications regarding the protection of a plant cell as a category asserting that a plant cell has the potential to develop into a whole plant. However, such rejection of applications pertaining to plant cells seems to contradict the provisions of the Guidelines. They provide that a plant according to the Chinese Patent Act refers to a life form which synthesizes carbohydrate and protein from inorganic substances, such as water, carbon dioxide and inorganic salts through photosynthesis, and which is usually immovable.[5] The Guidelines further provide that a single plant and its reproductive materials (such as seeds), which synthesize carbohydrate and

5 Part II, Chapter 1, Section 4.4.

protein from inorganic substances, such as water, carbon dioxide and mineral salts through photosynthesis, belong to the category of 'plant variety' as defined above.[6] Consequently, they are excluded from patentability. However, the Guidelines also provide that

> if a cell, a tissue and an organ of a plant do not possess the above-mentioned characteristics, they cannot be qualified as 'plant varieties'.

A plant cell is qualified as plant variety and thus excluded from patentability under Article 25(1) No. 4 Chinese Patent Law if it can be qualified as a reproductive material. The Guidelines provide that a plant or its reproductive material has the capability of photosynthesis. A cell which cannot live on inorganic materials through photosynthesis does not meet the definition of a plant. The 'above-mentioned characteristics' as provided in the above-mentioned provision of the Guidelines refer to photosynthetic ability. However, the process of regeneration from a cell is a complicated process involving the utilization of organic carbon sources and plant hormones, which is far beyond photosynthesis. Therefore, a new generation of a plant from a cell does not necessarily mean that such a cell forms reproductive material. Additionally, reproductive material of a specific plant has a clear meaning for a person skilled in the art: this person knows exactly which parts of a certain plant are reproductive and which are not. Therefore, a cell is generally not considered as a reproductive material by a person skilled in the art. **4.46**

Some examiners follow the first line of argument, others do not. Obviously, a consistent and reasonable practice on this issue depends on future decisions of the Patent Reexamination Board or even of the courts on appeal cases. **4.47**

## C. SUPPORT OF THE CLAIMS BY THE DESCRIPTION

Article 26(3) Chinese Patent Act provides that the description of a patent application shall disclose the invention in a clear and sufficient manner so that a person skilled in the art can carry out the invention. Article 26(4) Chinese Patent Act provides that the claims have to be supported by the description. These two grounds can be used interchangeably. However, Article 26(3) Chinese Patent Act is applied if the description fails to sufficiently disclose a single embodiment of the claimed invention. Let us hereinafter refer to the requirement under Article 26(3) as the 'enablement requirement' and to the requirement under Article 26(4) as the 'support requirement', respectively **4.48**

6 Part II, Chapter 10, Section 9.1.2.3.

objections due to non-compliance with these provisions as 'non-enablement objection' and 'lack-of-support objection'.

**4.49** First of all, compliance with the requirements as to enablement and support is determined on grounds of the contents disclosed in the description as filed. No supplemental data or example should be relied on to establish the compliance with these requirements. Therefore, it is very important to disclose the supporting examples and data for the technical effects on which the inventive step of the invention is based. This practice is quite different from the practice in Europe and the US where post-filing data are more flexibly accepted. Therefore, practitioners from these jurisdictions are well-advised to include the necessary data or working examples in their PCT applications which are entering the national phase in China.

**4.50** The Guidelines set forth some rules on the determination of the support for claims by the description. These rules can be summarized as follows:

- The Guidelines require that the claims be supported by the description not only formally but also as to substance. The claims are supported by the description as to substance if every technical solution described in the claims is directly available or can be generalized from the information given in the description.[7]
- Generally, claims are generalizations from one or more particular examples. However, when determining compliance with the support requirement, the whole content of the description rather than merely particular examples must be considered. Examiners are required to assess the reasonableness of the generalizations and then the support of the claims by the description in light of the relevant prior art.
- From the specific examples given in the Guidelines as to the determination of support, it can be seen that the scope of a claim is reasonable and thus regarded as being supported by the description if it is predictable that the subject matter of the invention can be carried out over the whole scope of the claim.

**4.51** The following elements are usually considered determining the predictability:

(1) the number of examples versus the scope of the claim;
(2) the clarification of the general relationship between the examples and other claimed embodiments;

7 *Eli Lilly v. Patent Reexamination Board*, Supreme People's Court's Judgment No.3 in 2009.

(3) the routine methods of experimentation or analysis available in the relevant art.

Additionally, the Guidelines allow the adoption of functional features only if either the features cannot be defined by structures or functional features are more appropriate than structural ones. Furthermore, the examples given in the description should disclose that the function can be achieved by different means or that a person skilled in the art can easily realise that the function can also be achieved by alternative means in addition to the one described in the example. **4.52**

Based on the above-mentioned provisions in the law and regulations, the following arguments against the objection due to lack of support are possible. **4.53**

(1) When the lack-of-support objection targets non-distinguishing features of the invention, it is helpful to explain which features are new and which are in common with the prior art. For the non-distinguishing features, the requirement of support by the working examples is lower and possibly met by relying on supporting documents about prior art knowledge. For example, an invention relates to the conjugate of a specific antigen with a VLP (virus-like particle) of an RNA bacterophage to achieve increased immunogenicity against the antigen. The examiner raises a lack-of-support objection with regard to the feature of the RNA bacterophage, which is based on the fact that only one RNA bacterophage is used in the working examples while there are many different RNA bacterophages known in the art. The argument would be that many VLPs of RNA bacterophages are known in the state of the art. Furthermore, it is also known as demonstrated by the supporting documents that the VLPs of these different bacterophages share a highly conservative spatial structure. Therefore, based on the technical information disclosed in the description and the prior art knowledge, a person skilled in the art would be able to reasonably appreciate the same or similar technical effect over the whole scope of VLPs of RAN bacterophages.

(2) It is important to argue from the technical point of view as to the predictability of the technical effect of the invention over the entire scope of the claim. For example, an invention relating to a genus compound may be rejected for lack of support from the description, by arguing that the latter only provides one working example. A valid counter-argument could be that the chemical radicals in the genus claim are actually bio-equivalents of the group pertaining to the verified compound and therefore the same technical effect is predictable over the whole scope of the claim.

(3) Since the examiners are required to assess compliance with the support requirement in the light of the relevant prior art, it can be argued that the examiners' objections should be based on either the well-known general knowledge in the relevant art or cited prior art document(s). Since the examiners rarely cite references to support their lack-of-support objections, it is also possible to rebut such objections with the argument that their allegations lack factual basis.

**4.54** However, it is rather unusual in examination practice that examiners substantiate their view by *prima facie* evidence. Therefore, it may occur that unsubstantiated objections from examiners may result in subsequent reductions of the scope of the claim. What aggravates the situation is that even in the case of granted patents, a long-established rule that the burden of proof regarding non-compliance with the lack-of-support requirement in the course of post-grant invalidation shall be with the petitioner has been ignored or even abolished by a series of decisions of the Patent Reexamination Board (PRB) of SIPO. A series of patents were declared invalid by the PRB because the claims lacked support from the description in several cases between *Ajinomoto v Changchun Dahe*. The claims used the genus name Escherichia bacteria while the working examples only used the species E. coli. Most of these cases are now on appeal before the courts.

**4.55** To ensure meaningful claim scopes and a relative stability of granted patents or at least to prevent a granted patent from being invalidated rather arbitrarily, a clear rule about the determination of compliance with the support requirements seems to be necessary. The following rules from the EPO Guidelines for Patent Examination and case law of the EPO Boards of Appeal could serve as a source of inspiration:

> As a general rule, a claim should be regarded as supported by the description unless there are well-founded reasons for believing that the skilled man would be unable, on the basis of the information given in the application as filed, to extend the particular teaching of the description to the whole of the field claimed by using routine methods of experimentation or analysis. … The examiner should raise an objection of lack of support only if he has well-founded reasons. … Where objection is raised, the reasons should, where possible, be supported specifically by a published document. (EPO Guidelines for Patent Examination, Part F, Chapter IV, 6.3)
>
> However, as long as there were no concrete grounds for believing that the invention could not be carried out within the whole range claimed, there was no reason for not allowing more broadly based claims in an application (T 242/92 and T 484/92).

In opposition proceedings the opponent bore the burden of proving that the invention could not be carried out within the whole range claimed (T 456/91, T 418/91 and T 548/91).

The subsequent parts of this chapter will discuss the enablement and support requirements in connection with chemical compound inventions and antibody inventions. 4.56

## 1. Chemical compound[8]

The description has to disclose the identification, preparation and use and/or effect of a compound so as to meet the requirement of sufficient disclosure. 4.57

### *(a) Identification of a compound*

As for the invention of a specific compound, the description has to disclose the chemical name, structural formula or molecular formula of the compound and the physicochemical data sufficient for identifying the compound, such as melting point, NMR, IR, UV, MS and XRPD data.[9] 4.58

As for the invention of a compound having a general formula, the description must disclose the general formula, including the definition of substituent(s) in the formula. Furthermore, if a specific compound falls under the general formula, it must meet the above requirements on sufficient disclosure of the invention of a specific compound. 4.59

In some cases, however, the qualitative or quantitative test data demonstrating the use and/or the effect of the compound can serve as a basis for the identification of the compound. This may be the case, for example, if the description fails to disclose the physicochemical data for identifying a compound but discloses the method for preparing the compound, and the qualitative or quantitative test data demonstrate the use and/or the effect of the compound. Under such circumstances – if the examiner concludes that the preparation method would necessarily result in the target compound – the test data regarding the use and/or the effect of the compound can serve as a basis for identifying the compound, and thus the description will be considered to meet the requirement on sufficient disclosure even in the absence of the physicochemical data for identifying the compound. 4.60

8 Guidelines, Part II, Chapter 10, Section 3.1.

9 NMR stands for Nuclear Magnetic Resonance spectroscopy; IR for Infrared spectroscopy; UV for ultraviolet spectroscopy; MS for mass spectroscopy; and XRPD for X-ray powder diffraction.

*(b) Preparation of a compound*

**4.61** In order to meet the requirement of sufficient disclosure, the description has to disclose at least one method for the preparation of a compound so that a person skilled in the art can obtain the compound according to the preparation method.

**4.62** As for the compound of a general formula, in addition to the preparation route of the compound, at least one preparation example is usually required to be disclosed in the description to meet the requirement on sufficient disclosure.

**4.63** As for the claimed specific compound, in principle, the description has to disclose the preparation example of the compound.

*(c) Use and/or effect of a compound*

**4.64** In order to meet the requirement of sufficient disclosure, the description has to disclose a sufficient amount of qualitative or quantitative test data to convince a person skilled in the art that the compound has the use and/or can achieve the effect as outlined in the description, unless the person skilled in the art is able, on the basis of the prior art, to predict that the compound has said use and/or can achieve said effect.

**4.65** Hereby, the description must clarify which specific compound(s) is/are used in the test. A general description of the tested compound as, for example, 'any one of the compounds according to the present invention', so that it is unclear to a person skilled in the art which specific compound(s) is/are used in the test, would not be considered as meeting the requirement of sufficient disclosure.

**4.66** The specific method and condition for the test has to be clearly disclosed in the description. It should also be noted that a test conclusion with the wording 'the above test has demonstrated that the compound according to the present invention has said use and effect' will not be considered as qualitative or quantitative test data required for sufficient disclosure. However, it is acceptable to disclose the test results by a range of data, for example, 'the compounds of the preparation examples were shown to have a $IC_{50}$ from xx to xx nM'.

2. Crystalline of a compound[10]

**4.67** In addition to the requirements with regard to the disclosure of a compound, it is necessary to disclose at least one feature in a manner which is sufficient for

10 Reexamination Decisions Nos. FS36005 and FS38859.

identifying the crystalline of the compound, which can be the cell parameters and space group of the crystalline; the XRPD pattern or data of the crystalline; or the solid-state NMR spectroscopy or data. If there are different methods for determining the characteristic in the prior art and such different methods lead to different results, the description has to explicitly disclose the method including the condition for determining the characteristic. If a special method is used for determining the characteristic, the special method has to be described in detail so that a person skilled in the art can carry it out.

In principle, it is not allowed to generalize a claim in a manner that it covers a crystalline form other than the one actually prepared in the working example which pertains to such claim. In other words, it is only permitted to claim the specific crystalline form actually prepared in the working example. **4.68**

If a claim defines a specific crystalline form with the XRPD data thereof, it is not necessary to include the diffraction peak intensity in the claim. However, for the claim to be supported by the description, generally all the diffraction peak positions of the specific crystalline form disclosed in the description have to be recited in the claim. If the applicant wants to pursue a crystalline claim defined only with the characteristic peaks, it is necessary to show why these characteristic peaks are sufficient to represent the crystalline form. Alternatively, the characteristic peaks of XRPD can be used together with other parameters to define the crystalline form to exclude the possibility that other crystalline form is covered by the claim. **4.69**

### 3. Antibody patents[11]

In recent years, therapeutic antibodies have become a major issue in the biopharmaceutical industry. However, patenting such antibody inventions in China may face various challenges. **4.70**

#### *(a) Enablement*

The enablement requirement is decisive with regard to the extent of disclosure by the patent specification in relation to an invention. In Chinese practice, assessment as to compliance with the enablement requirement is the examination of the sufficiency of disclosure of the claimed invention. **4.71**

The sufficient disclosure requirement can vary significantly from industry to industry depending on the invention at stake. However, the basic requirement is **4.72**

11 Guidelines, Part II, Chapter 10, Sections 9.2 and 9.3.

that the specification has to teach a person skilled in the art in how to prepare the claimed product and how to use this product.

**4.73** Years ago, when the sequences of an antibody had not been well identified, an antibody was in most cases described as a product secreted from a certain hybridoma. There was no further disclosure of the structure of the antibody, although various binding and biological properties could have been determined and disclosed accordingly in a patent specification. The hybridoma technology has in almost all cases been qualified as non-reproducible. Therefore, it was almost impossible to disclose the invention sufficiently by a written description, in a manner such that a person skilled in the art would have been able to obtain the claimed antibody. In any case, the deposit of the hybridoma with an International Deposit Institute under the Budapest Treaty before the earliest priority date and provision of the deposit information in due time with SIPO was necessary to sufficiently disclose antibody inventions.

**4.74** Nowadays, most antibodies are disclosed not only by their original means of production, such as hybridoma or transgenic animal, but also by their sequences of the variable regions of the heavy chain and the light chain of the obtained antibody. With the developed recombinant DNA technology and the availability of established antibody expression systems in the art, most of the examiners in China no longer raise objections to sufficiency of disclosure of the antibody in connection with its production. However, some examiners are still trying to challenge the sufficiency of disclosure in the absence of a deposit of hybridoma for producing the claimed antibody. In this regard, a recent decision of the Patent Reexamination Board clarified that the disclosure of the full sequences of the variable regions of an antibody is sufficient to enable a person skilled in the art to obtain the antibody.[12] Furthermore, it held that although the working examples made the antibodies of the invention through hybridoma technology, this technology is not the only way to produce an antibody.

**4.75** In fact, prior to the application, it was known in the art to express and produce monoclonal antibodies in host cells by recombinant DNA technology and gene transfer methods. Since the applicant has disclosed the sequences of the variable regions of the heavy chain and light chain and their coding DNA sequences, a person skilled in the art will be able to synthesize said sequences by standard molecular biological technology, such as PCR amplification and site-directed mutagenesis. By inserting the coding sequences of the variable regions into suitable vectors, the full sequences of the antibody of any isotype can be obtained. Since the vector has carried the coding sequences of the

12 Reexamination Decision No. 51777, March 2013.

constant regions of the desired isotype which allow operable linking of between $V_H$ and $C_H$ and between $V_L$ and $C_L$ respectively, the transformation of host cells by the vectors will allow expression of the desired antibody into the host cells or secretion into the culture media, which can be isolated by standard protein purification technology. Therefore, a disclosure of the amino acid sequences and nucleotide sequences of the variable regions of the heavy chain and light chain of the antibody enables a person skilled in the art to obtain the antibody by recombinant expression in host cells, independent of the hybridoma technology as originally used in the working examples.

Based on current practice and the above case, it is advisable to provide general guidance in the specification as to the method of obtaining the claimed antibody through recombinant expression technology, such as the vectors, host cells and method of transformation and expression, and so on, preferably supported by literature. **4.76**

Although the sufficiency of disclosure of the production of an antibody is now less problematic, it is necessary to disclose the biological experimental data in connection with any property on which the inventive step of the antibody will be established. This is interrelated with allowable claim scope and inventiveness issues as discussed below. **4.77**

### *(b) Inventiveness*

An antibody is specifically directed against an antigen. Therefore, if the antigen is novel and inventive, an antibody against this antigen will also be deemed as novel and inventive. However, nowadays the majority of antibody applications are related to antigen targets which are known to be important in a particular pathology. The Guidelines provide the following concerning the inventiveness of a monoclonal antibody: **4.78**

> If an antigen is known and it is clearly known that the antigen has immunogenicity (for example, said antigen clearly has immunogenicity because a polyclonal antibody of the antigen is known or the antigen is a polypeptide with a large molecular weight), the invention of a monoclonal antibody of the antigen does not involve an inventive step. However, if the invention is further defined by other features, and hence has unexpected technical effects, the invention of that monoclonal antibody involves an inventive step.[13]

13 Guidelines, Part II, Chapter 10, Section 9.4.2.1 (5).

Therefore, the inventiveness of an antibody against a known antigen is basically dependent on the unexpected technical effects provided by the claimed antibody. The issue then is how to determine whether an effect is unexpected or not.

**4.79** The Guidelines set forth the criteria for an unexpected technical effect as follows:

> An invention produces an unexpected technical effect means that, as compared with the prior art, the technical effect of the invention represents a 'qualitative' change, that is, a new performance; or represents a 'quantitative' change which is unexpected. Such a qualitative or quantitative change cannot be expected or inferred by the person skilled in the art in advance. If an invention produces an unexpected effect, it means that the invention represents notable progress on the one hand, and it also means that the technical solution of the invention is non-obvious and thus has prominent substantive features on the other hand. Therefore the invention involves an inventive step.[14]

Therefore, it is necessary to disclose those properties of the claimed antibody which are not foreseeable from the known information about the relevant antigen and any existing antibody against it. The properties can be the affinity of binding to the antigen, the selective of the binding, the $IC_{50}$ in inhibiting an adverse effect, and so on.

**4.80** It should be noted that the properties for establishing the inventive step and their supporting experimental data should be disclosed in the specification as filed. Otherwise, the examiner will raise insufficiency objections or simply refuse to rely on the relevant technical effect to evaluate the inventiveness of the invention. This practice is quite different from that in other major jurisdictions, such as the US and Europe, which allow the submission of post-filing data to show the workability of the invention or to support the disclosed technical effects.

**4.81** According to EPO practice, experimental results or other data may be contained in applications as filed or may be supplied during the course of the examination procedure. The post-filing data may serve as evidence that an application meets the requirements of 'inventive step', 'industrial applicability' or 'sufficient disclosure', although it is evident that the application must meet these requirements on the filing/priority date. Such evidence may be provided to substantiate previously merely alleged but unsupported statements or effects foreshadowed in the application as originally filed but will not be taken into account if they concern a new effect not mentioned in the application as originally filed.

14 Guidelines, Part II, Chapter 4, Section 5.3.

In contrast to EPO's practice, the practice in China since 2006 does *not allow* the filing of post-filing experimental data as evidence to meet the requirements of 'sufficient disclosure' or 'support of claims' by description. This practice might be changed according to SIPO's latest briefing on patent examination which was issued in December 2013.[15] The key information of the SIPO's new briefing is that post-filing data should be considered during examination if it belongs to evidence. Although this is a positive signal, the contents of the briefing are far from being clear. The best interpretation suggests that post-filing experimental data can be submitted as evidence to support the credibility of the statements made by the applicant in the specification if the technical solution and its technical effects per se have been disclosed in the specification. This approach would be more or less consistent with the EPO practice. However, for the time being it is still unclear as to what extent SIPO will consider post-filing experimental data. Furthermore, the briefing leaves open whether such late filed experimental data can be considered by the examiner – in case the examiner raises the issue of insufficient disclosure or of lack of inventive step due to missing supporting data filed with the application – even if the examiner did not initially moan that there is a lack of information (that is to say, data) when filing the application. In other words, the examiner did not issue a so-called 'lack-of-enablement rejection'. Therefore, it is important to consider the different Chinese practice in the course of drafting the patent specification, at least in case of PCT applications designating China. It is necessary to explain in detail the inventiveness of the invention and add all necessary experimental data to the specification to support the inventive step. 4.82

One may argue that one cannot know all prior art documents at the time of filing, and that it is also not practical to provide the comparative data in relation to all prior art documents. Therefore, it is not necessary to disclose the comparative data in the specification, even though it is advisable to do so. 4.83

During the examination, when the examiner cites specific prior art documents, it is allowable to provide comparative data to show that the technical effect disclosed in the specification is unexpected in comparison with the cited prior art. Such 'post-filing' data can be submitted for demonstrating the 'unexpected' nature of the relevant technical effect that has already been disclosed and verified by experimental data in the specification. 4.84

Finally, it has proven helpful to provide relevant prior art information or a summary thereof in the specification to reflect the level of the prior art 4.85

15 Notice on the implementation of relevant provisions of the Patent Law, Patent Regulations and Patent Examination Guidelines in Patent Examination, 17 October 2013, circulated within SIPO.

knowledge at the filing date. For example, the normal range of antibody affinity for binding to the same or similar antigen in the prior art may be described in the specification. Without such background information, the examiner may not consider the affinity disclosed in connection with the claimed antibody as 'high' enough and raise lack-of-inventiveness objections. In practice, information disclosed in the specification is more convincing for the examiners than information submitted at a later date, especially in post-grant proceedings.

*(c) Allowable scope of claims*

**4.86** If an antigen is novel and inventive, it is allowable to claim, as a genus, an antibody that binds to the antigen.

**4.87** As mentioned in the above observations on inventiveness, antibodies directed to a known antigen have to be defined with more features in addition to 'binding to' the antigen, usually by the sequences of the antibody. It is generally understood in the art that the antigen-binding property and, in turn, the associated biological effects of the antibody are substantially determined by the 'Complementarity Determining Regions' (CDRs) in the variable regions of the heavy chain and light chain of an antibody. The current practice is that at least the sequences of the six CDRs of an antibody should be included in the claim so that it is supported by the specific antibody having the same CDRs as verified in the working examples. Of course, antibody claims defined with the full sequences of the heavy chain variable region and the light chain variable region are also allowable.

**4.88** The most important CDR is CDR3 of the heavy chain of the antibody. Therefore, some applicants have tried to pursue antibody claims defined with the sequences of only heavy chain CDR3. Only very few of these attempts have been successful. In extremely exceptional cases, claims are allowed to define an antibody by means of functional languages only, such as values of binding parameters and IC.

**4.89** The Chinese government has significantly subsidized research and development in the pharmaceutical and biotechnological sector. When prosecuting patent applications in these areas, domestic patent applicants face the same challenges as foreign applicants. Hopefully, SIPO will adopt a more patentee-friendly attitude in future, perhaps also due to an increase in lawsuits challenging its decisions, as well as an increased use of the patent system by domestic stakeholders.

## D. REGULATORY ISSUES

### 1. 'Safe harbour' for regulatory submissions

4.90 The amendments to the Chinese Patent Act which entered into effect on 1 October 2009 explicitly introduced a regulatory submission exception which is similar to the Bolar exception in the US and Europe.

Article 69 No. 5 Chinese Patent Act:

> None of the following shall be deemed an infringement of the patent right:
>
> ...
>
> (5) where one makes, uses or imports a patented drug or patented medical device for the purpose of providing information necessary for administrative approval, or any other person manufactures or imports the patented drug or patented medical device solely for him to provide such information.

4.91 Article 69 No. 5 Chinese Patent Act is designed to allow pre-clinical trials, clinical trials and validation of manufacturing process of a patented drug (that is, the use of a patented drug for providing information necessary for administrative approval) in China before the relevant patent expires so that the generic drug is available to the public earlier. In order to do the pre-clinical, clinical tests and process validation, the use of samples of the patented drug is necessary. Therefore, Article 69 No. 5 Chinese Patent Act also allows the production or importation of the patented drug for use in pre-clinical and/or clinical tests in China.

### 2. Data exclusivity

4.92 In order to comply with the relevant provisions under the TRIPS Agreement (Article 39.3), China amended its Implementing Regulations to the Drug Administrative Act in 2001 and set up a legal basis for the protection of undisclosed data submitted for drug approval.[16]

---

16 R. 35 of the Regulation reads as follows:

> The State provides protection for undisclosed experimental data and other data created and submitted by a manufacturer or distributor applying for approval of manufacturing or distributing a drug containing a new chemical entity. No one shall put the undisclosed experimental data and other data into unjustified commercial use.
>
> For a period of six years after the issuance of the approval to manufacture or distribute a drug containing a new chemical entity to the manufacturer or distributor, the drug administration authority shall not allow other applicants' requests for approval of the manufacturing or distribution of the drug which contains the new chemical entity by using the data as described in the preceding paragraph without authorization by the

**4.93** Data exclusivity is more than confidentiality protection. Within the six-year term, any approval of the same drug to a subsequent applicant should not rely on data under such exclusive protection. There are different opinions with regard to the question as to whether China actually provides exclusivity for data submitted for regulatory approval, even though confidentiality protection is clearly available. According to the current interpretation by the SFDA (the China State Food and Drug Administration), a new chemical entity means that no drug containing the subject chemical entity has ever been launched *anywhere in the world* when the drug registration request is submitted to the SFDA. As the majority of drugs marketed by multinational companies have been launched in the mature markets before importing them to China, data exclusivity is not applicable to these drugs according to SFDA's interpretation.

### 3. Market exclusivity – monitoring period for new drugs

**4.94** A monitoring period for a new drug approved for manufacture is set by the SFDA, in order to closely monitor the safety of the drug. During the monitoring period, the drug manufacturer has to investigate the manufacturing processes, quality, stability, therapeutic effect and adverse reactions, and so on of the new drug, and report annually to the drug regulatory authority. Any critical quality problem, serious or unexpected adverse reaction to a new drug under monitoring will also be closely observed by relevant drug institutions and has to be reported to the drug regulatory authority.

**4.95** The monitoring period scheme provides a certain market monopoly over the drug under monitoring by the manufacturer thereof because the SFDA will not accept and approve a generic application for the production or import of the same drug.

**4.96** According to Rule 34 Chinese Implementing Regulations to the Drug Administrative Act, a monitoring period of up to five years may be set for new drugs.[17] Within this period, other companies will not be permitted to manufacture or import the same drugs. It becomes clear from this provision that the monitoring

---

applicant who has obtained the approval, unless such data are created by applicants themselves.

The drug administration authority shall not disclose the data described in the first paragraph unless 1) such disclosure is necessary to safeguard the public interest; or 2) measures have been taken to assure that the data are not put into unjustified commercial use.

17 R. 34 Chinese Implementing Regulations to the Drug Administrative Act:

The drug regulatory department under the State Council may, in conformity with the need to protect the public health, set a monitoring period of not more than five years for a new drug produced by a drug manufacturer; and no approval shall be given to any other entity to produce or import the drug during such monitoring period.

period is only applicable to new drugs approved for manufacturing in China. There is no monitoring period for imported drugs. Furthermore, once a drug is imported, it will no longer be qualified as a new drug. Also, there will be no monitoring period for a drug manufactured in China if the same drug has been approved for importation into China before the approval for manufacture. In the latter case, generic applications can be filed with the SFDA for marketing approval of the generic drug.

After the start of the monitoring period, no new application for approval of the same drug will be accepted and those applications (if any) already accepted (before the start of the monitoring period) but not yet approved for clinical trial will be rejected. However, if the manufacturer granted with a monitoring period fails to produce the drug within two years from the approval date, the SFDA may approve another manufacturer's application and reset the monitoring period for the drug. **4.97**

After the expiration of the monitoring period, generic applications in relation to the same drug will be accepted for approval. **4.98**

In sum, the monitoring period can be regarded as an additional monopoly for pharmaceutical companies in the Chinese market. The right timing with regard to the application for manufacture or import of a drug is crucial for procuring such a monopoly. **4.99**

### 4. Patent linkage

Although formal patent linkage between drug approval and patent right protection is not available in China, Rule 18 Provisions for Drug Registration requires an applicant for drug approval to disclose information about the patent protection status of the drug at issue and to declare that the drug at issue does not infringe upon patent rights of third parties.[18] The Provisions for Drug Registration further provide[19] that if a drug is covered by a third party's patent, **4.100**

---

18 R. 18 Provisions for Drug Registration:

The applicant shall indicate its own patents as well as the patents of others granted in China in relation to the drug which is subject matter of the application or the dosage, production process and indication of the drug as well as the status of patent ownership. Where a relevant Chinese patent is owned by a third party, the applicant shall provide a declaration of non-infringement of such patent. The Drug Administrative Authority shall publish the applicant's indication or declaration on its website. If a patent right dispute occurs during the drug registration, it shall be resolved according to patent law and regulations.

19 R. 19 Provisions for Drug Registration:

In case of a drug for which a third party has obtained patent right in China, the applicant may apply for registration of such drug within two years prior to the patent expiration. The SFDA shall review the an application for a generic version of the drug may only be filed within two years prior to the patent expiration, and that no drug approval shall be granted before the patent expiration.

**4.101** In spite of these provisions, the SFDA is, in general, not an effective forum to enforce a patent right because the agency does not have the necessary resources for the determination of patent infringement and will in most cases be satisfied with a declaration of non-infringement by the applicant.

**4.102** Having said this, it is advisable for an applicant for drug registration to exercise due diligence in this area. Article 83 Chinese Drug Administration Act prohibits anyone from obtaining drug approval by providing false certificates or by other fraudulent means. Rule 13 Provisions for Drug Registration stipulates that the applicant shall be responsible for the authenticity of all documents submitted. Applicants are obliged to deal with the SFDA in a truthful manner. If the applicant knows or should have known that the drug at issue is related to a third party's patent, it is not right in law to make a non-infringement declaration. Otherwise, he or she risks a violation of the Drug Administrative Act. If the applicant has conducted a reasonable patent search in relation to the relevant drug at stake and found no barring patent of a third party, the applicant would be safe to make the non-infringement declaration.

---

application according to this Regulation and, after expiration of the patent, issue a drug approval number, Imported Drug License or Drug Product License, provided that the application meets the requirements.

# 5

# BIOTECHNOLOGICAL, CHEMICAL AND PHARMACEUTICAL INVENTIONS II: SUPPORT AND EXPERIMENTAL DATA

**Toby Mak**



The basic principles of patentability in China are similar to the rest of the world. However, support requirements in China have undergone significant changes in the last ten years, resulting in a relatively low predictability of prosecution of patent applications, in particular of applications in the areas of chemistry, pharmaceutics and biotechnology. This chapter will discuss the specific requirements for protection in these areas and how to rid oneself of obstacles to patent grant. **5.01**

## A. BACKGROUND OF THE CHANGES TO SUPPORT REQUIREMENTS

Before 2004, support requirements in China were in line with those in the majority of patent regimes. Specifically, sufficient description and experimental data were required to allow a person skilled in the art to practice the invention. Back then, the requirements were not as stringent as today, which will be explained below. In fact, before 2004, experimental data for one single compound covered by a Markush-type claim[1] was sufficient to support such claim. **5.02**

1 A Markush-type claim is a listing of specified alternatives of a group in a patent claim and is used as an alternative to define genus of related molecule solely by function.

The now obsolete Examination Guidelines of 2001 did not allow further addition of unpublished data to the specification after the application date, but the applicant could use such data to convince the examiner to accept novelty, inventiveness, and/or utility of the invention when responding to an office action.

**5.03** All this changed drastically in 2004 when Pfizer's Chinese Viagra patent CN ZL94192386.X (hereinafter '386') was declared invalid by the Patent Re-examination Board of SIPO. The validity of this Chinese patent had been challenged by eight Chinese companies. Specifically, '386' had only one single claim directed to a single compound,[2] as Pfizer chose this compound during prosecution of the application due to various documents challenging the patentability of other compounds. However, the description of '386' did not contain any experimental data for this particular compound. Interestingly, experimental data proving that '386' worked as claimed were contained in another earlier published document. In any event, the Re-examination Board declared '386' invalid for lack of reason for the choice of exactly this single compound out of other compounds, as such choice was not supported by experimental data.

**5.04** Since this invalidation, SIPO had required that every single compound covered by a claim be supported by experimental data. Furthermore, SIPO henceforth refused to accept unpublished data after the application date when responding to an office action.

**5.05** Things changed again in 2007, when the Re-examination Board's decision was overturned by the Beijing Higher People's Court. Since then, the test whether an invention is supported by the specification aims at answering the question 'whether a person skilled in the art can reasonably expect the invention to work', which appears to be a more appropriate approach. The following sections will discuss the current support requirements in more detail.

**5.06** However, the pre-2007 approach adopted by SIPO still seems to influence some examiners.

---

2 (5-[2-ethoxy-5-(4-methyl-1-piperazinylsulphonyl)-phenyl]-1-methyl-3-n-propyl-1,6-dihydro-7H-pyrazolo[4,3-d]pyrimidin-7-one, the active ingredient of Viagra).

## B. PRESENT GENERAL PRINCIPLES AND SPECIFICS OF SUPPORT REQUIREMENTS

As stated above, the current principle governing support requirements in China is 'a skilled person can reasonably expect the invention to work'.[3] 5.07

The following are the specific requirements of the Examination Guidelines with regard to claims directed to chemical compound and claims directed to chemical compositions: 5.08

- for chemical compound/composition that cannot be clearly described by structure/components, proper chemical/physical parameters and/or manufacturing process must be indicated;
- at least one method of preparing the compound/composition, including disclosure of raw materials, procedures, conditions, and if involved, specially adapted equipment used for such method;
- use and/or technical effect of the compound/composition must be provided;
- if based on prior art a person skilled in the art is unable to predict that the use and/or technical effect indicated in the specification can be carried out, sufficient qualitative or quantitative experimental data should be provided to convince the skilled person that the invention will work as claimed;
- for new pharmaceutical compound/composition, other than the specific medical use or pharmacological action, its effective amount and means of application should be described. Again, if, based on prior art, a person skilled in the art is unable to predict that the medical use or pharmacological action indicated in the specification can actually be carried out, sufficient qualitative or quantitative experimental data should be provided to convince the skilled person that the invention will work as claimed;
- for parameters showing the effect of the invention, methods for measuring such parameters should be specified if prior art provides for more than one measuring method which could produce different results. Of course, if a special method is used to measure such parameters, detailed explanations should be provided.

For claims pertaining to chemical compounds, the requirements of the Examination Guidelines are as follows: 5.09

3 Examination Guidelines, Part II, Chapter 10.

(1) details of the compound shall be provided in a way that a person skilled in the art can identify the compound, including its chemical name and structural formula;
(2) parameters of those chemical/physical properties which pertain to the solution of the technical problem shall be provided. For example, if the compound has an improved tensile strength as compared to solutions pertaining to prior art, the details of such tensile strength shall be indicated;
(3) for polymeric compounds, other than those details already required under (1) above, the molecular weight distribution as well as the arrangement state of the repeating unit (for example, homopolymeric, copolymeric, block-polymeric or graft-polymeric) shall be described. If such description does not suffice to specify the polymeric compound satisfactorily, additional parameters such as crystallinity, density, glass transition temperature must be indicated.

**5.10** For claims pertaining to chemical compositions, the Examination Guidelines require that:

- the components of the composition shall be identified individually, and their respective chemical and/or physical properties, ranges of selection and content, and effects on the property of the composition shall be described.

**5.11** For claims pertaining to chemical processes, the Examination Guidelines require that:

- raw materials, procedures, conditions and, if involved, specially adapted equipment must be specified;
- the effect of the process on the target substance must be described; and
- raw materials used in the process must be specified in a way that a person skilled in the art can obtain them. For example, the components, property, preparing method, or source of such raw materials must be indicated.

## C. POST-FILING UNPUBLISHED EXPERIMENTAL DATA NOT CONSIDERED AS SUPPORT

**5.12** In sharp contrast to the obsolete Examination Guidelines (2001), the present Guidelines (2010) explicitly stipulate that unpublished experiments and experimental data submitted after the filing date (or priority date, if priority is claimed) will not be considered.[4]

Even though the present Guidelines (2010) specify that the above stipulation shall be applied when considering sufficiency of disclosure only, in practice, many examiners do not even consider experimental data published after the filing date when examining the application as to novelty or inventiveness. This practice has also been adopted by many re-examination decisions.[5] **5.13**

## D. PRIOR ART CONSIDERED AS SUPPORT

Unlike post-filing unpublished data, prior art will be considered as support and for examination of other patentability requirements. Of course, it must be proven that such prior art has been published before the filing date (or priority date, if priority is claimed). This practice is also applied by many Re-examination Decisions.[6] **5.14**

## E. GENERALIZATION OF NUMERIC RANGES MAY BE CONSIDERED AS SUPPORT

With regard to a claim pertaining to a composition which provides ranges of various different components, with a description providing one set of experimental data related to one specific composition which falls within such ranges, Re-examination Decision FS6571 (for CN application no. 03113290.1) implies that the generalization of ranges of the components may be considered as support. Specifically, the Board allowed such generalization on the basis that 'there is no reason to doubt that the ranges in claim 1 cannot be practiced'. **5.15**

## F. IMPORTANCE OF DISCLOSING DETAILS OF MEASURING METHODS

If a parameter is vital to working an invention or distinguishing it from the prior art, special care should be taken when describing the method for measuring such parameter in the description. Specifically, the conditions of the measuring **5.16**

4 Section 3.4 (2), Chapter 10, Part II of the Chinese Patent Examination Guidelines.

5 For example, FS6509 (for CN application no. 97196561.7) and FS5904 (for CN application no. 99125308.6); decisions available on the website of the Patent Re-examination Board at http://www.sipo-reexam.gov.cn/reexam_out/searchdoc/search.jsp.

6 e.g., FS6076 (for CN application no. 01113524.7) and in FS6087 (for CN application no. 00112732.2).

methods should be provided in the very detail, for example temperature, pressure, concentration and/or contents of components of measurement media and so on. As stated above, if there are several known measuring methods which can produce different results, those methods which are actually used should be specified, preferably with direct reference to textbooks or international standards. Reference to unpublished industrial manuals such as the operation manual for a piece of equipment should be avoided, as in practice, the SIPO will regard such reference as insufficient.

## G. FURTHER ADVICE ON HOW TO MITIGATE SUPPORT REQUIREMENTS

**5.17** As stated above, an invention is sufficiently supported if 'the person skilled in the art can reasonably expect the invention to work'. In any event, applicants should bear in mind that any data submitted after filing will be ignored according to the present Guidelines (2010). Therefore, experimental data must already be contained in the specification at the filing date.

**5.18** Experimental data are still required in most cases but their submission is no longer required for each and every compound covered by claims pertaining to chemical compounds. For example, for a compound with various substitute groups of alkyl, alkenyl, aryl, nitro, amino, sulfono and so on, with various numbers of carbon atoms, the most promising approach is to provide, for instance, experimental data for alkyl, aryl, nitro and amino groups (of course, the experimental data should show that the compounds show similar activities), as these data can show that the compound works as claimed, even if it is for a compound with various substitute groups which would bring different physical and/or chemical properties to the compound.

**5.19** In contrast, a suboptimal approach would be to only provide experimental data for compounds with $C_1$-$C_6$ alkyl group. In such a case, Chinese examiners are likely to require to narrow the claim to cover only compounds with alkyl group on the basis that the skilled person could not expect that a compound with substituted groups other than alkyl group would work. An even worse approach would be to provide experimental data for only one compound with a specific substituted group. In such case, a Chinese examiner would require to narrow the claim to cover only this specific compound.

**5.20** However, the above mentioned, most optimal approach may be hard to realize if the claim at issue is related to biomaterials, in particular protein and related materials such as DNA/RNA fragments, which involve three-dimensional conformation structures. For applications involving such material, Chinese examiners almost regularly issue objections against proteins covered by a broad claim (for example, in the form of a functional claim such as 'protein having affinity to substance X', or similarity statements such as 'protein having artificially introduced amino acids') while experimental data is provided for only a limited number of proteins covered by such claims. The examiner would arrive at the conclusion that, as the function of biomaterials cannot be predicted due to the fact that their three-dimensional conformation structures will drastically change in light of such broad limitation, a person skilled in the art will not be able to predict that the resulting proteins would behave in a biologically similar manner. Such objections are difficult to deal with unless data showing proteins with different three-dimensional conformational structure have similar behavior/activities. In short, the more experimental data cover various different species the better.

# 6

# SOFTWARE-RELATED INVENTIONS

**Li Yonghong***



## A. INTRODUCTION

**6.01** The Patent Act of the People's Republic of China (hereinafter 'Patent Act') entered into effect in 1985. Within less than 30 years, rapid development in computer technology has raised a number of questions with regard to software-implemented inventions. In China, as there is not yet much case law on software patents, the majority of concerns lie in the area of patent prosecution, in particular with respect to eligibility for protection, inventiveness of claims which contain technical as well as non-technical features and specific claim forms which are based on flow diagrams of computer programs. As the corresponding provisions are still in the course of improvement and examiners are still accumulating experience in this area, the present system can hardly be regarded as mature and so the following explanations will concentrate on the above three issues.

* The views expressed in this article represent those of the author and should not be attributed to the State Intellectual Property Office of the People's Republic of China (SIPO).

## B. ELIGIBILITY FOR PATENT PROTECTION

### 1. Legal provisions

As to the question of whether a software-related invention is patentable, Article 2(2)[1] which defines the term 'invention' and Article 25[2] which excludes certain subject matter from patentability, are the most relevant provisions. Article 2(2) refers to 'technical solutions' as subject matter eligible for protection; Article 25(1) No 2 excludes rules and methods for intellectual activities from protection. 6.02

Whereas the Patent Act remains silent on software-related inventions, the SIPO Examination Guidelines (hereinafter 'Guidelines') provide more detailed provisions on this issue. 6.03

First of all, they provide a definition of 'technical solution', as an 'aggregation of technical means applying the laws of nature to solve a technical problem'.[3] Secondly, they define 'rules and methods for intellectual activities' as 'rules and methods governing people's thinking, expression, judgment and memorization'.[4] 6.04

Moreover, Part II of the Guidelines includes a whole chapter (Chapter 9) about the 'examination of invention applications relating to computer programs' (that is, software-related inventions), which further interprets the concepts of 'technical solution' and 'rules and methods for intellectual activities' with regard to computer technology. 6.05

### 2. Analysis of some concepts

#### *(a) Technical solution*

Even though many applications related to computer programs are excluded from patent protection as both 'rules and methods for mental activities' (Article 25) or 'non-technical' (Article 2(2)), the threshold of the former is considerably lower than the threshold of the latter. 6.06

---

1 'The term "invention" refers to a new technical solution put forward for a product, method or the improvement thereof.'

2 'For any of the following, no patent right shall be granted: (1) scientific discoveries; (2) rules and methods for mental activities; (3) methods for the diagnosis or for the treatment of diseases; (4) animal and plant varieties;(5) substances obtained by means of nuclear transformation; (6) two dimensional designs of images, colours, or combinations of the two that mainly serve as indicators.'

3 Examination Guidelines, Part II, Chapter 1, 2.

4 Examination Guidelines, Part II, Chapter 1, 4.2.

**6.07** The Guidelines, Part II, Chapter 9, 2.(2), stipulate in greater detail that 'if all the contents of a claim include not only rules and methods for mental activities but also technical features, [ … ] the claim as a whole is not rules and methods for mental activities, and shall not be excluded from patentability'.

**6.08** According to this provision, the majority of invention applications relating to computer programs should not fall under non-patentable rules and methods for mental activities pursuant to Article 25(1) No 2, as almost all solutions in the area of computer software contain also 'technical' features such as storages, CPU, and so on.

**6.09** However, Part II, Chapter 9, 2.(2) (fourth paragraph) also stipulates that 'if the solution of an invention application relating to computer programs involves the execution of computer programs not in order to solve technical problems, or does not reflect technical means in conformity with the laws of nature by computers running programs to control and process external objects, or the effect obtained is not restrained by the laws of nature, the solution is not a technical solution as provided for in Article 2 and is not the subject matter of patent protection'.

**6.10** Therefore, a claim which includes technical features may not be excluded from patent protection just because it pertains to 'rules and methods for mental activity' pursuant to Article 25(1) No 2 Patent Act, as long as it includes 'technical' subject matter. Only if the technicality requirement pursuant to Article 2 Patent Act is not met, in a manner that the technical solution does not aim at solving a genuinely 'technical' problem posed by the restraints of the laws of nature, the computer program at issue is not eligible for protection. Therefore, the crucial question for examiners is whether the claimed subject matter pertains to a 'technical solution' pursuant to Article 2 Patent Act.

**6.11** What actually constitutes 'technical' subject matter? According to the Guidelines,[5] a solution is only 'technical' if it comprises three elements. Apart from the two elements 'technical means' to be resorted to and 'technical problems' to be solved by the invention,[6] the Guidelines stipulate a third element, namely 'technical effect' to be produced by the invention.[7]

**6.12** 'Technical' is one of the most commonly used terms in the patent field. In fact, it marks a critical dividing line between patentable and non-patentable subject

5 Examination Guidelines, Part II, Chapter 9, 2.

6 Examination Guidelines, Part II, Chapter 1, 2.

7 Examination Guidelines, Part II, Chapter 9, 2.

matter. Nevertheless, legislators are reluctant to define it. Some disputes already arose due to different understandings of it. The EPO Boards of Appeals, for instance, pointed out:

> It may very well be that, as put forward by the appellant, the meaning of the term 'technical' or 'technical character' is not particularly clear. In the Board's view, the fact that the exact meaning of a term may be disputed does in itself not necessarily constitute a good reason for not using that term as a criterion, certainly not in the absence of a better term.[8]

This view is understandable. On the one hand, a legal definition of 'technical' would be desirable to limit the range of patentable inventions whereas, on the other hand, the public policy that would underlie such definition depends on many complex and dynamic factors. Therefore, legislators rather tend towards leaving a certain leeway so as to provide the determination of patentable subject matter with sufficient flexibility to adapt to the development of technology. **6.13**

China's legislature refrained from defining the term 'technical'. However, there seems to be a common understanding which is also reflected by the Guidelines that a solution is 'technical' if it is 'restrained by the laws of nature'. In this author's opinion, such definition makes sense, especially with regard to solutions which include rules and methods for intellectual activity. **6.14**

### *(b) Rules and methods for intellectual activities and laws of nature*

Even though the exclusion of 'rules and methods for intellectual activity' from patent protection is a common worldwide practice, the understanding of this term varies from country to country. For instance, pursuant to the EPC, mathematical methods are a category on their own and therefore different from rules and methods for intellectual activities, whereas according to the SIPO Guidelines, mathematical methods pertain to the category 'rules and methods for intellectual activity'. **6.15**

In this author's opinion, the public policy to exclude abstract ideas such as mathematical methods is different from the policy behind excluding concrete rules and methods for intellectual activities such as game rules or commercial rules. **6.16**

#### *(i) Abstract intellectual concepts*

As to the reason why abstract intellectual concepts shall be excluded from patent protection, the US Supreme Courts has stated as follows: **6.17**

8 T-931/95.

> Phenomena of nature, though just discovered, mental processes, and abstract intellectual concepts are not patentable, as they are the basic tools of scientific and technological work.[9]

**6.18** It should be noted that abstract intellectual concepts such as mathematical theories, just like natural phenomena, can be 'technical' and even become basic tools for further technical activity. Therefore, testing their conformity with the laws of nature may not suffice to exclude them from patent protection. The real reason for excluding such abstract intellectual concepts from protection is that they form basic tools for research, and that their monopolization may jeopardize further research and development. Consequently, their exclusion from protection is grounded in the necessity to find a balance between the interests of patent holders and the general public.

**6.19** In the very old *O'Reilly v Morse* decision,[10] the US Supreme Court rendered a landmark decision which also reflects the present Chinese understanding of abstract concepts. One of the disputed claims had been worded as follows:

> Eighth: I do not propose to limit myself to the specific machinery or parts of machinery described in the foregoing specification and claims; the essence of my invention being the use of the motive power of the electric or galvanic current, which I call electromagnetism, however developed for marking or printing intelligible characters, signs, or letters, at any distances, being a new application of that power of which I claim to be the first inventor or discoverer.

**6.20** With regard to this claim, the Supreme Court opined as follows:

> It is impossible to misunderstand the extent of this claim. He claims the exclusive right to every improvement where the motive power is the electric or galvanic current, and the result is the marking or printing intelligible characters, signs, or letters at a distance. If this claim can be maintained, it matters not what process or machinery does accomplish the result. For aught that we now know some future inventor, in the onward march of science, may discover a mode of writing or printing at a distance by means of the electric or galvanic current, without using any part of the process or combination set forth by the plaintiff in specification. His invention may be less complicated or less liable to get out of order or less expensive in construction, and in its operation. But yet if it is covered by this patent the inventor could not use it, nor the public have the benefit of it without the permission of this patentee.

Therefore, abstract concepts which cover a too broad subject matter to be supported by limiting embodiments should be excluded from patentability.

9 409 U.S., at 67.
10 56 U.S. 62 (1853).

*(ii) Concrete intellectual rules*

Concrete intellectual rules such as game rules or rules pertaining to business organization, however, are different from abstract intellectual concepts as basic tools of scientific or technical work. Therefore, the reasons to exclude them from patent protection must be different from the reasons for the exclusion of abstract concepts. Or, in other words, the exclusion of a rule for a game and the exclusion of a mathematical method must be based on different public policy considerations. **6.21**

If we compare, for instance, a concrete intellectual rule that teaches us a specific method of selling cups with a technical solution such as a method of making cups, the differences are as follows. **6.22**

First, any method of making cups is restrained by the laws of nature, in that the inventor must select from a range of limited materials, means or structures. In contrast, methods of selling cups are almost unrestrained by the laws of nature but creative arrangements are made on grounds of the mental assessment of consumer behavior, human weakness, and so on, which pertain to the areas of psychology or sociology. Of course, psychology or sociology are also grounded on certain rules, statistical methods, and so on but such rules are more open to changes or refinement than the laws of nature. Therefore, their effect is hardly restraining but they rather serve as reference material. **6.23**

Second, any method of making cups has a certain objective effect which can be confirmed experimentally or by theoretical deduction, without having to put the product on the market. In contrast, the effect of a method of selling cups can hardly be demonstrated without having put the cups on the market. **6.24**

These two differences between truly 'technical' solutions and intellectual rules are crucial with regard to maintaining a balance between the right holder's and the public interest. **6.25**

The founders of the patent system never had large numbers of patents as the main purpose of the patent system in mind. As *Thomas Jefferson* has stated: **6.26**

> If nature has made any one thing less susceptible than all others of exclusive property, it is the action of the thinking power called an idea, which an individual may exclusively possess as long as he keeps it to himself; but the moment it is divulged, it forces itself into the possession of every one, and the receiver cannot dispossess himself of it. Its peculiar character, too, is that no one possesses the less, because every other possesses the whole of it. He, who receives an idea from me, receives instruction himself without lessening mine; as he who lights his taper at mine, receives light without darkening me. That ideas should freely spread from one to another over the globe, for the moral and

> mutual instruction of man, and improvement of his condition, seems to have been peculiarly and benevolently designed by nature, when she made them, like fire, expansible over all space, without lessening their density in any point, and like the air in which we breathe, move, and have our physical being, incapable of confinement or exclusive appropriation. Inventions then cannot, in nature, be a subject of property. Society may give an exclusive right to the profits arising from them, as an encouragement to men to pursue ideas which may produce utility, but this may or may not be done, according to the will and convenience of the society, without claim or complaint from anybody.

**6.27** Because patent systems throughout the world were established to serve society, limiting too many patents in worthless solutions is as important as encouraging inventors. Without reasonable limitations, patents will end up as obstacles to innovation, comparable to a real-world scenario in which each section of a road would be owned by a different owner and each owner would have to be asked for permission before entering his section. Therefore, there is good reason to limit patentable subject matter, for example, by requiring an inventive step.

**6.28** In contrast to copyright, a patent is a very strong right of high exclusivity which also excludes those who use the same technical solution without having had reason to know about the existence of such patent. In order to balance public and private interests, the costs of obtaining patent information so as to escape liability for infringement should also be taken into account. Too many patents in trivial solutions would burden the public with excessive search costs and prohibit other, more meaningful, activities. The inventive step requirement, for instance, has been developed to limit patents to such technical solutions which meet certain quality expectations.

**6.29** The legislature and SIPO have endeavored to enhance the objective comprehensibility of the inventive step requirement, so as to contribute to the transparency and predictability of the patentability requirements. With growing experience over a long period, certain principles and methods have been established. Now, with regard to truly 'technical' solutions, the question whether an invention can be easily comprehended by an ordinarily skilled artisan, as required by the inventive step requirement, can be comparably easily answered, especially with regard to inventions which form combinations or selections of subject matter pertaining to prior art. This is because the restraints of the laws of nature facilitate the identification of subject matter which is not only new but also remarkably different from existing technical solutions, in that it could not be easily conceived by a skilled artisan at the application date. In case of technical solutions, such non-predictability can be quite easily proven or rebutted, either experimentally or by theoretical deduction, so that a judgment as to whether the inventive step requirement is met can be made on the basis of objective evidence.

In contrast, such proof is very difficult with regard to intellectual rules which can cross one's mind without any restraint, and the effect of which can hardly be identified before actually operating them in practice. Therefore, assessing the patentability of mere intellectual rules is extremely challenging for patent examiners. Actually, it requires them to make a judgment as to patentability without being able to assess how such rule will actually be worked in practice. **6.30**

Moreover, a rule for a concrete intellectual activity is often the result of instantaneous inspiration and enjoys popularity for a short period. For example, over a certain period of time, a business method may have developed which, however, is hardly recorded in well-classified documentation. Such absence of documentation renders the assessment of the inventive step incorporated in business methods, which, in addition, is likely to appear as pertaining to the state of the art in the eyes of many consumers, extremely difficult. Therefore, in this author's opinion, the exclusion of concrete rules for mental activities from patent protection primarily lies in the difficulty of assessing their inventiveness. **6.31**

In any case, the close link between the examination of the exceptions to patentability and the criteria of novelty and inventive step is an interesting issue. Many patent systems have qualified the technical contribution to the prior art as part of the examination of exceptions to patentability. However, in the meantime the opinion prevails that the patentability criteria of novelty and inventive step are better qualified to determine the level of the technical contribution the invention at stake achieves vis-à-vis the state of the art. This is not least reflected in China's 'the three elements of technical solution' approach and the EPO's case law regarding the patentability of computer implemented inventions which provides that the claims have to be examined from the point of view of what may be called 'the further technical effect', which, if present, could lead to the subject matter not being excluded under Article 52(2) and (3) EPC 1973.[11] **6.32**

As the assessment of 'technical' or 'non-technical' relies on the analysis of the causality between a means which intends to solve a problem and the problem itself, and as 'problem' means a concept that has to be reflected against a certain background (more about this under C.2), the term 'technical' inherently forms the inseparable link between the criteria for patent eligibility with regard to the inventive step requirement, irrespective of whether 'technical contribution' is **6.33**

11 T 1173/97 (*OJ EPO* 1999, 609) and T 935/97.

only tested in the course of patent eligibility examination or also within the inventive step examination. In fact, the consequences in both cases might not be different.

**6.34** Actually, it should be noted that even though still examined within the framework of general patent eligibility, Chinese examiners increasingly apply the criterion of 'technical contribution' also in the course of inventive step examination.

## C. ASSESSMENT OF THE INVENTIVE STEP

### 1. Relevant provisions of the Patent Act and of the Examination Guidelines

**6.35** Pursuant to Article 22 of the Patent Act, 'inventive step' means that the invention, as compared with the prior art before the date of filing, has prominent substantive features and represents a notable progress.

**6.36** Even though this provision is a bit different from the corresponding provisions in other countries, the principles of examination set forth in the Guidelines are quite similar to the practice of the EPO.

**6.37** The Guidelines provide in greater detail that:

> When assessing whether or not an invention involves an inventive step, the examiner shall consider not only the technical solution itself, but also the technical field to which the invention pertains, the technical problem solved and the technical effects produced by the invention. The invention shall be considered as a whole.[12]

### 2. Analysis of some concepts

#### *(a) Claim as a whole*

**6.38** With regard to claims which comprise both technical and non-technical features, the above requirement that the examiner shall consider the invention 'as a whole' is very important.

**6.39** In practice, the expression 'as a whole' is, in this author's opinion, too often understood as focusing on the completeness of all features. Examiners are used to list all features and to compare each of them one by one with corresponding

12 Examination Guidelines, Part II, Chapter 4, 3.1.

features pertaining to the prior art. However, a different meaning of 'as a whole' should be considered as well, namely 'integrity' which understands the claimed subject matter as an integral solution.

In other words, understanding a claim 'as a whole' does not mean to merely understand it as an aggregation of all its features, but such understanding should also include those links which make it an integral technical solution. What would be such a link? In order to identify it, some terms should be clarified, such as technical means, technical problems and technical effects. **6.40**

### *(b) Technical means and technical features*

The concept of 'technical means' is closely linked with the concept of 'technical features', and both are often confused with each other. The Guidelines, however, contain a provision which describes their relationship: 'Usually, technical means are embodied as technical features.'[13] In other words, technical means are combined with technical features. **6.41**

Even though this definition explains the relationship between technical features and technical means, it does not clarify the substantial difference between them. Therefore, some confusion may arise. For example, is a technical feature equal to a technical means if such means includes only one technical feature? Is it possible for a technical means to include technical features and non-technical features? **6.42**

Neither the law nor the Guidelines or judicial reviews of patent office decisions provide a definite answer to this question. Also this author cannot offer a definite answer. **6.43**

In her view, the substantial difference between the two concepts lies in their association with certain purposes. When people talk about a 'feature' of something, they only make a description of it without need of considering its purpose. In contrast, 'means' is usually perceived as a tool in order to achieve a specific purpose. The same object, a stick, for instance, can have objective features such as long, solid, flexible, and so on, but be used as all kinds of means to achieve different purposes. **6.44**

If we look at it from this point of view, 'technical feature' appears to be a statistical concept rather than an exact one. If we turn back to our example of a stick, we find that it can be classified as a technical feature because it is normally used to support an activity or to perform other functions in conformity with the **6.45**

13 Examination Guidelines Part II, Chapter 1, 2.

law of nature. However, it can also serve as a mere ornament, and therefore has a non-technical purpose and consequently serves as a non-technical means. In the latter case, an object which can be described by its technical features is nevertheless used as a non-technical means.

**6.46** That is, the link between features and means is the purpose of the object at issue. Even if a technical means includes only one technical feature, both means and feature are not yet identical. The key question is: at which purpose does the technical solution aim?

**6.47** In patent applications, 'purpose' is usually expressed as 'problem'. Therefore, whenever we talk about a technical means, we should also think about the problem to be solved by the invention.

*(c) Technical problems*

**6.48** In patent examination practice, many disputes arise around the question as to whether the problem to be solved by the invention is of a technical or non-technical nature.

**6.49** Thus, the first question is whether such problem can be identified by resorting to the claim only, without considering other information. This author has her doubts. 'Problem' is a relative concept. The perception of 'problem' depends on the persons involved, on the time of its occurrence and on the state of technology. For instance, prior to the above-mentioned invention of Mr. Morse, long-distance communication was a problem to be solved whereas nowadays it is no longer a problem. That is, it is hard to talk about a problem to be solved without simultaneously considering the state of the art at the time when it occurred.

**6.50** As known, the specification within a patent application mentions such technological background, as far as it is understood by the applicant. Sometimes, examiners reject claims just because they do not solve the technical problem in the light of the technological background as mentioned in the specification. In fact, in the area of computer programs, the validity of claims is quite frequently questioned for this reason.

**6.51** In most cases, problems to be solved should be assessed by the objective background of prior art, which is more likely to be found through examination as to inventive step than through examining whether the invention is not excluded from patentability.

6.52 Another question is whether the assessment of the technical character of the problem should be carried out independently of the assessment of the technical character of the means. Again, this author has doubts. As mentioned above, 'technical' should be understood as subject to the restraints of the laws of nature. Or, more exactly, only where the causality between the means and the problem to be solved is restrained by the laws of nature, both means and problem can be regarded as technical. For example, if a stick is used to support something, the problem pertaining to the technical solution, namely the need for support, is also in conformity with the laws of nature. In this case, the problem as well as the means and the effect are technical. If, however, the stick is used as an ornament, the problem to be solved, for example, of decorating a room, is based on aesthetic feelings which are not restrained by the laws of nature. In such case, neither the problem nor the means are technical.

6.53 The clarification of these concepts may contribute to solving some debates with respect to the examination of inventions related to computer programs. For example, let us think of a claim that describes a computer which is used for playing a new game and includes certain features such as storage, monitor, CPU, and so on, each of them being linked with other, exchangeable features pertaining to information such as the rules of a new software or the playing rules for a new computer game which is used in combination with the same storage, monitor, CPU, and so on. The question arises whether the problem to be solved by such solution is either technical or depends on the aim of the invention, in particular on whether the invention aims at providing a new computer structure or whether it simply aims at introducing a gaming rule or a new form of applying the computer. The answer to this question depends on how the features of the invention are linked with each other, and on the prior art.

## D. FORMS OF CLAIMS

6.54 Different kinds of claims have different forms. According to the Guidelines, the claims of an invention application relating to computer programs may be drafted as a process claim or a product claim, that is, apparatus claim. The claim shall be supported by the description.[14]

6.55 Hereby, an apparatus claim which is only based on the flow of a computer program disclosed in the description is likely to be rejected. The more appropriate form of claim for such invention would be a process claim. On the other

14 Examination Guidelines, Part II, Chapter 9, 5.2.

hand, the applicant may fear that a process claim might not suffice to protect the invention effectively. One likely concern could be that the process patent can only be enforced against infringing users. With regard to inventions related to computer programs, this would mean that the patent holder can only proceed against the users of the computer device by which the program is carried out, not against the manufacturers or distributors of such device.

**6.56** Such problem arises from the contradiction between the traditional understanding of a process patent and the special essence of a process which consists of running a computer program. Traditionally, a process is executed at the initiative of someone, so that these persons, respectively the enterprises they represent, can be held liable for infringement. In case of computer programs, however, the process is automatically executed by computers as soon as the program is loaded into the computer. During such process, the intervention by someone may be limited to only pushing one button. Patent holders normally do not want to sue such operator. Instead they prefer holding liable the manufacturers of the device which is necessary to execute the process.

**6.57** In order to accommodate the interest of patent holders in getting hold of the manufacturers, SIPO has introduced a computer program specific form of claims which resorts to the computer program flow. Such new form, as stipulated by the Guidelines since their revision in 2006, reads as follows:

> If an apparatus claim is drafted on the basis of computer program flow completely and according to the way completely identical with and corresponding to each step in the said computer program flow, or according to the way completely identical with and corresponding to the process claim reflection the said computer program flow, i.e., each component in the apparatus claim completely corresponds to each step in the said computer program flow or each step in the said process claim, then each component in the apparatus claim shall be regarded as function modules which are required to be built to realize each step in the said computer program flow or each step in the said method. The apparatus claim defined by such a group of function modules shall be regarded as the function module architecture to realize the said solution mainly on the basis of computer program flow described in the specification rather than entity devices to realize the said solution mainly through hardware.[15]

**6.58** At first, patent applicants welcomed such new form of claims, for it provided the possibility of drafting an apparatus claim only based on a computer program flow, without having to fear rejection for lack of support by the solution disclosed in the specification. The new claim form facilitated the prosecution of the manufacturers of the apparatus. However, the draft of such claims, in

---

15 Examination Guidelines, Part II, Chapter 9, 5.2.

particular adherence to the several 'completeness' requirements of the above provision, turned out to be quite difficult.

SIPO is presently in the course of reviewing these requirements, so as to lessen the burden on applicants. Hereby, it considers that as the complexity of computer programs increases, the more difficult it becomes to describe them in hardware terms. In fact, more and more solutions tend to be solely based on the computer program flow rather than on hardware. Therefore, it can be expected that such claims will be accepted even if they are not described through hardware. **6.59**

## E. CONCLUSION

Regulations on the examination of patent applications relating to computer programs, as well as examination practice are under constant but careful improvement. As far as the current legal framework is concerned, Chinese practice appears to be quite conservative as compared to other legislations. However, improvements in this area have to keep pace with simultaneous improvements in many other areas, so as to align the whole patent system with the national technological development objectives. **6.60**

# 7

# EMPLOYEE INVENTIONS

**Ma Qian and Berrit Roth**



## A. INTRODUCTION

**7.01** More than 90 per cent of all patent filings in Germany are based on inventions made by employees.[1] Similar numbers can be expected for China, even though until 2008, the number of private inventions was still higher than the number of service inventions.[2] Individual inventors working in their small private laboratories are on the decrease. Nowadays, expensive resources provided by an employer or the expertise of a working group are required to achieve groundbreaking patentable inventions.

1 Kurt Bartenbach and Franz-Eugen Volz, *Arbeitnehmererfindungen, Praxisleitfaden mit Mustertexten*, 5. Auflage 2010, marginal note 1.

2 Yuanshi Bu, *Patentrecht und Technologietransfer in China*, Verlag C.H. Beck/Helbing Lichtenhahn Verlag, München et al. 2010, 37.

## B. GENERAL LEGAL FRAMEWORK FOR EMPLOYEE INVENTIONS

The Chinese Patent Act primarily regulates employee inventions.[3] Further regulations concerning employee inventions can be found in the Rules for the Implementation of the Patent Act of the People's Republic of China ('Implementing Regulations')[4] and in the Several Opinions on Further Strengthening the Protection of Service Inventor's Legal Interests and Promoting IPR ('Intellectual Property Rights') Implementation (Opinions)[5] which were published on 26 November 2012 by the State Intellectual Property Office (SIPO) and 12 other authorities. Furthermore, different Chinese municipalities' guidelines, for example, the Shanghai Implementing Measures on the Ownership of and Remuneration for Employee Inventions (Shanghai Measures)[6] must be considered. Likewise, the Shanghai Higher People's Court issued Guidelines on the Adjudication of Disputes Involving Rewards and Remuneration for the Inventors or Designers of Service Invention Creations (Shanghai Guidelines) on 25 June 2013. As the Shanghai Measures and the Shanghai Guidelines provide important and useful provisions and play an exemplary role for other municipalities' guidelines they will be cited later on in this chapter. It should be noted, though, that they are not legally binding and will not be considered outside Shanghai.[7] [8] 7.02

3 中华人民共和国专利法 (Zhonghua renmin gongheguo zhuanli fa), adopted at the 4th Meeting of the Standing Committee of the Sixth National People's Congress on 12 March 1984, amended for the first time in accordance with the Decision of the Standing Committee of the Seventh National People's Congress on Amending the Patent Law of the People's Republic of China at its 27th Meeting on 4 September 1992, amended for the second time in accordance with the Decision of the Standing Committee of the Ninth National People's Congress on Amending the Patent Law of the People's Republic of China adopted at its 17th Meeting on 25 August 2000, and amended for the third time in accordance with the Decision of the Standing Committee of the Eleventh National People's Congress on Amending the Patent Law of the People's Republic of China at its 6th Meeting on 27 December 2008.

4 中华人民共和国专利法实施细则 (Zhonghua renmin gongheguo zhuanli fa shishi xize), promulgated by Decree No.306 of the State Council of the People's Republic of China on 15 June 2001, and revised according to the Decision of the State Council on Amending the Rules for the Implementation of the Patent Law of the People's Republic of China promulgated on 28 December 2002.

5 关于印发《关于进一步加强职务发明人合法权益保护促进知识产权运用实施的若干意见》的通知 (guanyu yinfa 《guanyu jin yi bu jiaqiang zhiwu famingren hefa quanyi baohu cujin zhishi chanquan yunyong shishi de ruogan yijian》 de tongzhi, http://www.sipo.gov.cn/tz/gz/201301/t20130105_782351.html.

6 上海市发明创造的权利归属与职务奖酬实施办法 (Shanghai shi faming chuangzhao de quanli guishu yu zhiwujiangchou shishi banfa); Promulgated by Decree No. (2007) 30 of the Intellectual Property Bureau of the Shanghai Municipality on 29 April 2007.

7 See Albert Chen, 'How Should Chinese Businesses Pay Remuneration for Inventions Created by Their Employees?', *Bridge IP Law Commentary*, 07 January 2013.

8 China has a number of organizations with legislative power. Apart from the actual legislature, the Chinese National People's Congress and its Standing Committee, the Chinese Supreme People's Court may act not only as a judicative organ but also as legislator, by enacting provisions, providing written answers to lower courts, and by enacting Supreme People's Court interpretations, which are an important source of law. Unfortunately, so far neither the Patent Law nor the available Interpretations enacted by the Supreme People's Court contain any provisions on service inventions. Nevertheless, it should be noted that the Supreme People's Court's rulings and courts rulings in general are quite significant within China's legislative infrastructure.

**7.03** Furthermore, on 30 December 2013, SIPO published a Provisions of Service Inventions (Draft Provisions) after taking public opinions and expertise suggestions into consideration. This new draft will be submitted to the State Council soon for final examination. It is unclear whether courts and authorities already consider the Draft Provisions in spite of their draft form. We address the Draft Provisions only where they add further information to our observations.

## 1. Definition of employee invention

**7.04** The definition of 'employee invention' is very important since the law concerning employee inventions has to find a compromise between the two principles that all inventions made in the course of employment shall belong to the employer, and that all other inventions made outside an employment relationship shall belong to their inventor.[9]

**7.05** In China, the regulations concerning service inventions do not contain the terms 'employee' or 'worker'. The Chinese wording of Article 6 Chinese Patent Act only refers to 'service inventions' (*zhiwu faming chuangzao*) and 'inventor' (*famingren*).

**7.06** Thus, it is controversial whether or not the Chinese Patent Act distinguishes between service inventions and non-service inventions in a way that such distinction would depend on whether the invention has actually been made by an employee. It rather seems that the Chinese Patent Act defines the term 'service invention' on the basis of the situation and conditions that lead to the invention, and not on the status of the inventor-entity (*danwei*) relationship.

**7.07** Furthermore, the term 'employee' is not defined in Chinese law. Neither the Chinese Labour Contract Act nor the Chinese Labour Act provide for such definition. In fact, the exact difference between labour contracts and service contracts is rather unclear.[10] That is why we consider the situation in and the conditions under which the invention has been made to be the factors which decide whether a service or a non-service invention is at issue. Article 6 Chinese Patent Act and Rule 12 Implementing Regulations list the typical situations and conditions under which the invention must be defined as a service invention. Whether such a situation or such conditions respectively are present must be examined on a case-by-case basis.[11]

---

9 Joseph Straus, 'Rechtsvergleichende Bemerkungen zum Begriff des Arbeitnehmererfinders', **1984** *GRUR Int.* 402.

10 Guang Li and Roman Frik, 'Das neue Arbeitsvertragsgesetz Chinas', **2008** *NZA* 86.

11 This case-by-case-approach also applies to the concept of joint inventors. In China, the concept of joint inventions is generally accepted but only generally regulated. Art. 8 Chinese Patent Act states that for an

## 2. Definition of service invention

Typically for the matter of service inventions, the respective laws and regulations differentiate between service inventions and non-service inventions. The terminology might be different internationally, but in essence most countries acknowledge such a differentiation. The same applies to the Chinese Patent Act. **7.08**

A service invention under Chinese law is an invention made by a person while executing the tasks of the entity for which he or she works. Alternatively, it is an invention made while taking advantage of the material and technical means of the entity (Article 6(1) Chinese Patent Act). In addition to this definition, Rule 12 Implementing Regulations defines a service invention as any invention of the employee, created: **7.09**

(1) in the course of performing his duty;
(2) in execution of any task, other than his own duty, which was entrusted to him by the entity to which he belongs; or
(3) within one year of his retirement, resignation or termination of employment or personnel relationship with the entity in which he was previously employed, where the invention relates to his own duty or the other task entrusted to him by the entity in which he was previously employed.

A difficult, but relevant situation occurs when inventions are made outside working hours, but are based on the experience made on the job. It must be decided, if these inventions belong to the inventor or to the entity. With reference to Article 6(1) Chinese Patent Act and Rule 12 Implementing Regulations this question must be decided on a case-by-case basis. If the inventor uses only his/her experience and no other means of the entity, there is strong evidence that the invention belongs only to the inventor. **7.10**

---

invention jointly made by two or more entities or individuals, the right to apply for a patent remains with the entities or individuals which jointly made the invention. Although this regulation does not apply directly to employee inventions, it gives us a hint with regard to the Chinese understanding of inventions made through joint work. The regulation of aspects of jointly made inventions in the employee handbook or in the employment agreement is recommended, such as the reward and remuneration of the joint inventors. A corresponding agreement should be concluded before the invention is made, especially if the employees are supposed to receive different amounts of remuneration based on their respective contributions.

## C. RIGHTS AND DUTIES

7.11 Chinese law statutes specify the rights and duties of the employer and employee as being contradictory to each other.

### 1. Rights and duties of employers

7.12 German law provides for a number of specific rights and duties of the employer on which the Chinese Patent Act remains silent, such as the employer's right to be informed by the employee of the service invention pursuant to Article 5 Act on Employee's Inventions (ArbEG) or the duty of the employer to observe secrecy concerning the subject of the invention towards third parties. Article 6(1) 2nd sentence Chinese Patent Act is instead based on the assumption that the employer will, in any event, file the patent application for a service invention. Furthermore, pursuant to the wording of Rules 76, 77 and 78 Implementing Regulations, the obligation to pay a reward and remuneration only arises if a patent or respective industrial property right is granted to the employer. Therefore, it seems to be possible to avoid such payments simply by not filing a patent application. It should be noted, however, that such an approach bears the risk of novelty loss if the invention is made public, so it cannot be recommended. Moreover, in the case of a subsequent lawsuit concerning remuneration claims, Chinese courts could regard such moves as deceitful and grant the employee a right to reward and remuneration anyway.

7.13 Concerning non-service inventions, Chinese law does not give the employer any specific right to be notified by the employee. Thus, Milner and Robley, for instance, recommend that in China 'employers should make sure that all employment contracts contain clear disclosure obligations requiring an employee to notify the employer of all inventions (and other works) created in the course of employment ...'. They also recommend requesting a list of inventions created by the employee prior to his employment to avoid any disputes over whether or not such inventions were created during his employment.[12]

7.14 It must be noted, however, that the situation may change. The third chapter of the 'Draft Provisions' deals with the employer's right to be informed by the inventor of any invention of any relation to the entity[13] and the employer's duty

12 Gordon Milner and Claire Elizabeth Robley, 'Employees' Rights to Inventions and Rewards under the Revised Patent Law', *Association of Corporate Counsel*, 30 April 2010.

13 The Draft Provisions are quite detailed on this matter. According to R.10 Draft Provisions the inventor must inform the entity within two months of the invention and joint inventors must give the respective information

to either file for a patent or to release a service invention to be a free invention, so that the inventor may file a patent application.[14]

## 2. Rights and duties of employees (including remuneration)

The employee who has made a service invention is entitled to be named as the inventor in any patent obtained by the employer. Rule 8 'Draft Provisions' also stresses this right. 7.15

A very important and, in practice, most complex right of the employee is the right to remuneration. 7.16

### (a) General

Article 16 Chinese Patent Act provides that the entity to whom a patent is granted shall grant the inventor or designer of the service invention a reward and, after exploitation of the patented invention, shall pay the inventor or designer a reasonable remuneration on the basis of the scope of use of the invention, as well as the economic benefits yielded from the invention. The employee is, thus, entitled to a one-off reward upon patent grant and to a subsequent reasonable remuneration after the exploitation of the patent. 7.17

### (b) 'Reasonable remuneration'

Pursuant to Rule 76 Implementing Regulations, the employing entity and the employee can either agree about the amount of both reward and remuneration by contract or the entity can regulate these amounts in its internal rules which, however, need to provide at least the regulatory minimum level of compensation. 7.18

### (i) Rewards

In the absence of both contractual agreement and internal rules, the entity shall, within three months from the date of the announcement of the grant of the patent right, pay to the inventor or creator of a service invention a fixed money reward. According to Rule 77 Implementing Regulations, such sum shall not be less than RMB 3,000 ($485, €365) in the case of inventions and not be less than RMB 1,000 ($161, €121) in the case of utility models or designs. Even though the law does not set any limits to this fixed money award paid upon grant of a patent, utility model or design right that can be agreed upon by contract, the 7.19

together. R.11 Draft Provisions contains detailed requirements concerning the written information form. R. 12 Draft Provisions concerns the dispute if the invention is a service or non-service invention.

14 See R.15 Draft Provisions.

prevailing view is that the standards of Rule 77 should also apply to contractually regulated amounts, that is, a contract shall not regulate a remuneration less than RMB 3,000 in case of inventions or RMB 1,000 in case of utility models or designs. On the other hand Item 8 Shanghai Guidelines states that 'if an inventor or designer claims a bonus in an amount exceeding RMB 3,000 or RMB 1,000, any portion claimed which exceeds RMB 3,000 or RMB 1,000 respectively shall not be upheld'. According to the Shanghai Higher People's Court 'while the employer is obligated to pay the statutory minimum standard for a Service Invention-Creation, it is not legally obligated to pay bonuses or remuneration on top of the statutory minimum standard'.[15]

*(ii) Remuneration for the use of the patent*

**7.20** With regard to the reasonable remuneration to be paid for the exploitation of the patent, Rule 78 Implementing Regulations states that where the parties have not entered into a contract and where no rules and regulations concerning the amounts exist, the entity shall, within the duration of the patent right, award the employee not less than 2 per cent per year from the profits of exploitation of the invention or utility model, or not less than 0.2 per cent from the profits of exploitation of the design. By making reference to the said percentages the entity may also award a lump sum of money as a one-time remuneration for the exploitation of the patent. In case of a contract regulating the exploitation of the patent right during its duration, corresponding percentages must be agreed upon.

**7.21** Finally, pursuant to Rule 78 Implementing Regulations, the employee is entitled to 10 per cent of any exploitation fee agreed upon by the employing entity and any other entity or individual.

**7.22** Even in cases in which a mere proposal of the employee inventor has resulted in a service invention, the entity to which the patent is granted shall award the respective employee a remuneration on reasonable terms.[16]

**7.23** In sum, the formulation of a reward and remuneration calculation system either in a so-called employee handbook that provides for special provisions concerning all employees or in the respective employment agreement is recommended. A general provision in the employment agreement, such as 'the employee's salary includes a component for invention reward and remuneration' will probably not be upheld by the Chinese courts.[17]

---

15 It.9(3) Shanghai Guidelines.

16 R.77(2) Implementing Regulations.

17 Xia Yu and Matthew Murphy, 'Employee Inventor Rights Under the New Chinese Patent Regulations', *MMLC Group*, 29 July 2010.

In contrast to the Chinese Patent Act, the Implementing Regulations and the Opinions, which do not contain detailed regulations concerning a reward and remuneration agreement between the employer and the employee, the Shanghai Guidelines provide for several such regulations. According to Item 3 Shanghai Guidelines, 'the standards for rewards and remuneration for Service Invention-Creations may be agreed upon by an employer and an inventor or designer through consultations, or specific in the rules and regulations formulated by the employer in accordance with law'. Pursuant to Item 4(1) Shanghai Guidelines 'the terms of an agreement shall not only be limited to specifying the amount of such rewards and remuneration, but shall also include the form in which the rewards and remuneration are to be given'. Therefore Item 4(2) Shanghai Guidelines states that, 'in addition to monetary form, rewards and remuneration may be given in the form of shares, options, promotions, raises, paid leave and so forth'. Most relevant is Item 4(3) Shanghai Guidelines, since it regulates that the requirements specified in the Patent Act to give reasonable remuneration shall be satisfied. If this is not the case, according to the Shanghai Higher People's Court reasonable rewards and remuneration shall be determined based on the specific circumstances of the case, rather than directly applying the statutory standard for rewards and remuneration.[18] **7.24**

In addition to the national Implementing Regulations, Rule 8 Opinions stipulates higher remuneration standards for service inventions made within state-owned institutions or within facilities of the Chinese army. In the case of use of the service invention by state-owned institutions or the army, the amount of the remuneration shall be, at least, 3 per cent of the business income resulting from the use of the respective service invention. If the respective service invention is licensed or transferred to another entity, the remuneration shall amount to at least 20 per cent of the licensing or transfer fee. It should, however, be noted that Rule 8 Opinions only applies in cases in which no agreement or internal regulations exist. **7.25**

Furthermore, the Shanghai Measures regulate special calculation measurements. Most notably, the Shanghai Measures provide for higher remuneration levels than the Implementing Regulations. Where the entity uses the employee invention itself, it has to pay at least 5 per cent of its profits after tax for the exploitation of inventions or utility model patents and at least 1 per cent of its profits after tax for the exploitation of design patents. If the entity licenses or transfers the employee invention to a third party, it has to pay at least 30 per cent **7.26**

18 It.6(4) Shanghai Guidelines.

of its profits after tax from the licensing fee or the transfer fee[19] to the inventor. The relationship between Rule 8 Opinions and the Shanghai Measures is not yet clear, however.[20] Moreover, it is critical that the Shanghai Guidelines of the Shanghai Higher People's Court of June 2013 do not refer to the Shanghai Measures, but only to the Implementing Regulations. Concerning the calculation measurements set out in Rule 78 Implementing Regulations, the Shanghai Guidelines state in Item 9 that where the percentage claimed by an inventor or designer is higher than the statutory minimum standards, the courts shall not uphold such claim. Since the employer is not legally obligated to pay remuneration on top of the statutory minimum standard, any higher amount requires a respective agreement between the employer and employee.

**7.27** Last but not least, the Draft Provisions[21] provide for even higher remuneration levels than the Shanghai Measures. Moreover, they provide for specific rules for cases in which the service invention is not used by the employing entity but by a third party. It remains unclear, however, how these Draft Provisions will impact on remuneration in future.

### *(c) Questions related to the quality of a service invention*

**7.28** The available provisions remain silent on the question of whether or not the amount of money awarded or the remuneration can be varied according to the quality of the service invention.[22] It seems that the minimum requirements regarding the payments to be made to the employee inventor remain the same, irrespective of how useful and valuable the service invention is. It might be argued that the explicit sums to be awarded according to Rule 77 Implementing Regulations and the explicit percentages according to Rule 78 Implementing Regulations facilitate the calculation of a reasonable remuneration to the employee. Such clear guidance may have its advantages, especially because the remuneration for service inventions in Chinese firms is not yet as firmly established as in German firms. Furthermore, the Chinese government has a large interest in increasing the numbers of patent filings and thus seeks to support service inventions. Last but not least, as the remuneration pursuant to Rule 78 Implementing Regulations links the remuneration amount to the profits made from the exploitation of the invention, the market objectively determines the value of the service invention. Thus, even though the question of quality is not directly dealt with by the Implementing Regulations, it is, nonetheless, important for the final calculation of the remuneration.

---

19 See Albert Chen, above note 7.

20 See Albert Chen, above note 7.

21 See R. 21, 22 and 23 Draft Provisions.

22 According to R.22 Draft Provisions the importance and impact of the service invention shall be considered while calculating the remuneration.

Another question arises in cases in which no patent application for the service invention has been filed or, even if an application has been filed, but no patent has been granted. Where the respective invention may be summarized under the Law of the People's Republic of China on Promoting the Transformation of Scientific and Technological Achievements, the employing entity has to grant the inventing employee some kind of remuneration.[23] Unfortunately, there is no statutory definition of the term 'scientific or technological achievement made by employees'. Since this law seeks to improve China's scientific and technological as well as its patent situation, the respective remuneration provision is likely to refer to the definition of the service invention as provided by the Chinese Patent Act and its Implementing Regulations.[24] **7.29**

### *(d) Burden of proof with regard to the profit made from the invention*

When calculating the reasonable remuneration for a service invention after exploitation, the reference profits are those after tax (at least according to the Shanghai Measures). According to a reported ruling of the Guangdong Dongguan Intermediate People's Court, which was held by the Guangdong Higher People's Court, the employing entity bears the burden of proof concerning the specific amount of the profits after tax.[25] **7.30**

### *(e) Right to information*

Neither the Patent Act nor the Implementing Regulations state that the employee is entitled to information given by the employer concerning his service invention in order to enable him or her to calculate the amount of reward and remuneration by him- or herself. However, it seems likely that the Chinese courts would grant such a right on the basis of fairness in contracts. Notably, if the employee invention has been exploited, transferred or licensed, the Shanghai Measures recognize such an inventor's right to information. According to Rule 12 Shanghai Measures, the unit shall notify the inventor of the scope of use within three months after the utilization of the invention has started, or within 30 days after the transfer of the invention or after the execution of a licence agreement with a third party.[26] **7.31**

### *(f) Time of the remuneration payment*

Until recently, the available rules remained silent on the time of the remuneration payment. However, Rule 10 Opinions now regulates two different dates. If the remuneration is to be paid in cash, it shall be paid within three months after **7.32**

23 Yuanshi Bu, above note 2, 40.

24 Yuanshi Bu, above note 2, 40.

25 Albert Chen, 'Who has the Burden of Proving "Profit After Tax" When Calculating Remuneration for a Patented Invention?', *Bridge IP Law Commentary*, 4 February 2013.

26 Albert Chen, above note 7.

each accounting year. If the remuneration is to be paid in shares, the payment shall be divided in accordance with the laws, regulations and the share issue system set up by the articles of association of the company.

#### *(g) Waiver agreement*

**7.33** In Chinese contract law, the principle of 'fairness in all contracts'[27] has a long tradition. Therefore, an employee's waiver of the right to be remunerated is likely to be held invalid by Chinese courts and cannot be recommended.

## D. UNIVERSITY INVENTIONS

**7.34** Inventions made by professors or other personnel of universities and public research institutes are of special interest, as many groundbreaking inventions emerge from co-operation between private companies and public research institutes.

**7.35** In contrast to Germany, where professors enjoyed the so-called 'Professor's privilege' until 2001,[28] China has never had a specific regime regarding university inventions.

**7.36** However, several specific regulations with regard to inventions made in higher academic and scientific institutions can be found in the Opinions and the Shanghai Measures. Rule 5 Opinions obliges higher academic and scientific institutions, which have been established by the state (that is, private entities are not included) to 'provide notice to the inventor one month prior to the decision to abandon exclusive rights in the patent or other intellectual property right'.[29] If the inventor seeks to own any rights in the patent or other intellectual property right, he or she may start respective negotiations with the academic and scientific institutions. These institutions must support these negotiations actively.[30] Furthermore, the Shanghai Measures provide for a specific remuneration calculation scheme with regard to licensing and transfer of employee inventions by higher academic and scientific institutions. The remuneration should amount to at least 50 per cent of the revenue gained from the licence or transfer.[31]

---

27 White and Williams, LLP, 17 June 2010.

28 Nowadays all inventions made by professors, lecturers and other academics are subject to the regular rules unless sec. 42 ArbEG provides differently. In particular, there is no special scheme for defining a service and a non-service invention.

29 Albert Chen, above note 7.

30 R. 5 Opinions.

31 Albert Chen, above note 7.

## E. INVENTIONS MADE WITHIN GROUPS OR HOLDINGS

One question of practical relevance concerns the transfer of patents from a company to its so-called parent company. Such transfer might occur against payment or a licence fee; however, realistically more often than not the patent right will be transferred for free. 7.37

Even though it is possible to establish a so-called China Holding Company (CHC) with at least USD$30 million as start-up capital, such CHC is not a widespread legal company form in China.[32] Instead, it is more common to establish corporate structures with parallel subsidiary companies outside the legal framework governing CHCs. 7.38

As far as the remuneration for service inventions in such corporate structures is concerned, several situations can be imagined. 7.39

First, the inventing employee is employed by the subsidiary company and the service invention is registered by the subsidiary company. In this case, only the subsidiary company can be defined as the inventor's employer and sole owner of the patent right deriving from the service invention. That also means that only the subsidiary company must pay remuneration to the employee. Even if the patent right has been filed by the parent company and the patent right has been transferred to the subsidiary company later, the subsidiary company alone is liable for remuneration.[33] 7.40

A second situation would be that the subsidiary company as employer has filed the application and afterwards transfers the granted patent to its parent company in exchange for a licence fee. In such a case, it is again the subsidiary company as the immediate employer who must pay remuneration to the employee; however, the licence revenue will impact on the calculation of the remuneration. 7.41

One of the possibly most likely situations would be where the subsidiary company, as the employer, has filed the application for the patent but transfers it to its parent company for free. According to Chen, in such a case the employee is entitled to remuneration either from his/her employer or from the parent company.[34] Such a granting of choice is, however, not convincing, especially if 7.42

32 Jan Becker and Thomas Loose, 'China: Neue Entwicklungen zu Holdinggesellschaften', 2006 *IStR-LB* 1, 2.

33 See Albert Chen, 'Shall Parent Company Make the Payment for Subsidiary Employee's Invention for Hire?', *Bridge IP Law Commentary*, 1 February 2013.

34 See Albert Chen, above note 33.

the parent company rightfully believes that the employee has already been remunerated. With reference to the respective German law only the employing entity should be liable to pay remuneration to the inventing employee.[35]

**7.43** A final, but nevertheless problematic situation would be where the rights to the invention will be transferred by the subsidiary company prior to the patent application. Chen points out that until now there have not been any court cases dealing with such a situation. But he proposes that the inventor 'can claim a reward or appropriate remuneration from both the employer or the affiliated company of the employer who enjoys the patent right and exploits it'.[36] It remains to be seen how in the future such situations will be determined by the courts.

## F. DISPUTE RESOLUTION

**7.44** Employee inventions potentially give rise to two forms of disputes. First, the employer and the employee can disagree about the character of the invention at issue, whether it forms a service invention, as asserted by the employer, or a non-service invention, as asserted by the employee. The second type of dispute is normally related to the rewards and remuneration.

**7.45** The Chinese Patent Act does not provide for specific rules concerning these two types of disputes.[37] However, pursuant to Rule 85 Implementing Regulations, the patent administration authority is competent to decide on:

(1) any dispute about the ownership of the right to apply for a patent [...] and
(2) any dispute about the reward and remuneration to the inventor or creator of a Service Invention-Creation.

**7.46** In addition to these administrative authorities, the Supreme People's Court[38] has clarified that China's People's Courts are also competent to decide in such matters. The parties can therefore choose between administrative and judicial dispute resolution. However, after appealing to the administrative authorities the parties can still appeal to the courts, but after appealing to the courts they may no longer appeal to the administrative authorities.

---

35 See in detail Anja Bartenbach-Fock, *Arbeitnehmererfindungen im Konzern*, 2007, 12 et seq.

36 See Albert Chen, above note 33.

37 As already mentioned, R. 12 Draft Provisions refer to the first type of disputes but it is not yet clear whether they will become binding law in their present form.

38 Lin Ma and Ziyuan Xiao, 'Die Zuständigkeit für Patentrechtsstreitigkeiten', **2006** *GRUR Int.* 28, 31.

Item 16 Shanghai Guidelines refers to this Supreme People's Court's provision when it clarifies that disputes relating to rewards and remuneration for the inventor or designer of a Service Invention-Creation shall be classified as patent disputes and shall be within the jurisdiction of those People's Courts having jurisdiction over patent disputes. **7.47**

For German and other foreign companies, the question arises as to whether it is possible to include an arbitration clause in the labour contract with the employee. However, until now there are no regulations concerning arbitration in the Chinese Patent Act and its Implementing Regulations. The latter only mentions 'negotiations' between the employer and the employee and mediation by the patent administrations. *Argumento e contrario* is, therefore, that it is not permissible to nominate an arbitration court in the labour contract concerning patent affairs. However, Rule 40 of the Draft Provisions would be the first provision which would contain arbitration rules. Thus, in the future parties might have the option to agree on arbitration proceedings, although the details are still unclear. **7.48**

## G. SUGGESTIONS FOR IMPROVEMENT

A first suggestion would be to include the current Implementing Regulations, the Opinions and further municipality-level guidelines, such as the Shanghai Measures in a new Patent Act reform in such a way that provisions which are no longer operable will be repealed. Currently the legal situation is often unclear. In particular, the development of different region-specific rules raises concerns, for example, with regard to the differences between the Shanghai Measures or other municipality regulations and the Opinions. In case of a comprehensive reform, former regulations should be repealed in order to clarify and simplify the application of the provisions on service inventions. **7.49**

Second, the definition of employer and employee in contrast to the definition of a worker should be clarified by law and court rulings. **7.50**

Third, an answer to the question of whether arbitration in disputes regarding service inventions shall be permitted must be found. That Rule 40 of the mentioned Draft Provisions already permits arbitration is a welcome development. **7.51**

As a final suggestion, employers should be careful when drafting employment and remuneration agreements. The employment agreement, in particular, should include the duty of the employee to inform the employer of any **7.52** invention made in the course of employment, so as to provide the employer with the opportunity to examine whether such invention actually forms a service invention. The Draft Provisions already mention this issue, but the present provisions do not regulate such legal obligation.[39]

39 Yuanshi Bu, above note 2, 38.

# 8

# EXCEPTIONS AND LIMITATIONS

**Christopher Bailey and Lucy Wang**



## A. INTRODUCTION

Exceptions and limitations in patent law, combined with exclusions on patentable subject matter, both provide policy makers with the means to balance the incentive of the patent monopoly with the interests of the public and the desire to promote the dissemination of technology. The increasing harmonization of patent law internationally around patentable subject matter and the need to include new forms of technology means that in many countries, outright exclusions to patentability are becoming increasingly narrow. Exceptions and limitations to infringement, provided that they fall within the broad prescriptions of TRIPS,[1] remain as a flexible policy tool for countries to maintain this balance. As noted in Chapter 1, in the third amendment to its Patent Law,[2] China has clearly set its priorities in favour of dissemination of technology in crafting its catalogue of exceptions, most explicitly in relation to patented drugs. While China's stated ambition is to become a global innovation leader, the **8.01**

1 Article 30 TRIPS allows member states to impose limitations provided that they do not 'unreasonably conflict with a normal exploitation of the patent and do not unreasonably prejudice the legitimate interests of the patent owner, taking account of the legitimate interests of third parties'.

2 Patent Law of the People's Republic of China (2008).

codification of a so-called 'naked Bolar' exemption for regulatory approval and the introduction of international exhaustion, demonstrates that it still prioritizes its needs in terms of a developing country.

**8.02** Those who followed the many rounds of drafting of the third amendment of the Patent Law[3] will know that the exceptions in the current law are in fact very much watered down from earlier versions which intended to create some very significant limitations to patentees' rights. The current law then should be seen in the context of having already scaled back. In particular, earlier drafts looked to impose a series of escalating limits on the patentee's rights to claim compensation from an infringer the longer they delayed taking action, and would eventually deny patentees their rights to enforce their patent at all after a period of inaction. These provisions met vocal objections during the periods available for public commentary on the draft, including warnings that these provisions may have even been in conflict with TRIPS, and were fortunately dropped from the final amended law.

## B. OVERVIEW OF EXCEPTIONS AND LIMITATIONS

**8.03** The exceptions and limitations that have survived into the Patent Law 2008 amendment can be summarized in the following simple terms:

- In Article 68 Chinese Patent Act, a statutory limitation of two years to claim compensation from the date of discovering infringement.
- In Article 69 Chinese Patent Act, an exclusive catalogue of exceptions to infringement:
  (1) A provision for post-sale exhaustion, including where the patented product is 'imported', which introduced international exhaustion into Chinese patent law.
  (2) A provision that exempts from infringement any product or process which has been used by the alleged infringer prior to the date of the patent application.
  (3) An exception for patents incorporated into land, sea or aircraft that are temporarily transiting through China.
  (4) An exception for working the patent solely for the purpose of conducting scientific research and experiments.

3 For an excellent summary of the drafting history, see 'Third Revision of China's Patent Law. Legal Texts and documents on the drafting process 2006–2008, published by the EU-China IPR2 office, found at http://ipr2.org/document-centre/document.php?id=308.

(5) An exception for working the patent for the purposes of regulatory approval, or, as it is commonly known, the 'Bolar' exemption.

- In Article 62 Chinese Patent Act, provision for a 'prior art defence' where the alleged infringer can furnish prior art against the asserted patent. It should be noted that while this is strictly speaking a defence to infringement and not a limitation to patent rights, this provision and the above exemptions are commonly grouped together and referred to as 'defences' to infringement. We therefore cover it briefly in this chapter, noting that the interplay between infringement and invalidity is covered in Chapter 14 of this book.

There are further provisions which are worth mentioning here, although they are not the focus of this chapter: **8.04**

- Article 70 Chinese Patent Act, exempts from damages a user or seller who commits the acts unknowingly. Since the patentee may still prevent the seller or user from continuing their conduct, the fundamental right to exclude is not affected, and we therefore have not made it a focus of this chapter.
- Articles 48 to 58 Chinese Patent Act set out the regime for compulsory licensing, also a form of limitation on patent monopoly rights.

In addition to the provisions of the patent law, exceptions and limitations are further interpreted in certain judicial opinions and interpretations, chiefly in the 'Interpretations of the Supreme People's Court On Several Issues Concerning Adjudicating Patent Infringement Disputes (2010)' (SPC Interpretations). Articles 14 and 15 SPC Interpretations relate to determination of prior art and prior use rights respectively. This and other judicial pronouncements will be covered in more detail in the relevant sections. **8.05**

## C. CASE LAW

The following sections will review each of the exceptions and limitations in more detail, and provide some case examples. **8.06**

A word of caution must always be applied in relation to case law in China. As noted elsewhere in this book, China is a civil law jurisdiction and the Chinese courts do not have a system of binding precedent, even for decisions of the higher courts, although higher court decisions are persuasive and interpretations of the Supreme People's Court, are treated as having the same status as legislation. Decisions with almost identical legal and factual background may be decided differently by different courts, and lawyers in China do not extensively cite cases in their arguments.[4] Judgments are brief and may not fully present all the facts and arguments, as they are written to provide a decision to the parties in suit, not to contribute to a public body of law. Those with a common law training who try to trace a line of reasoning between cases are likely to be left bemused. To determine how legislation is interpreted in practice involves compiling a mosaic of cases that cite the same grounds and seeing how the preponderance of decisions lie.

**8.07** A further hindrance to research of case law in China is the lack of systematic publication of decisions by the courts. Only a fraction of decisions made are published, and those that are may be subject to selection bias, based on what individual courts feel are in some respect worthy of publication, rather than representing the universe of case law.

**8.08** Our review here relies on the CIELA database,[5] which compiles data on virtually all published intellectual property civil decisions dating back to 1 January 2006, currently totalling over 23,000. We are grateful to Aria Tian, our colleague and researcher for the CIELA database for assisting us in compiling the cases cited here.

## D. ARTICLE 68 CHINESE PATENT ACT – STATUTORY LIMITATION

**8.09** As noted above, earlier drafts of the amended law attempted to impose escalating levels of limitations on a patentee's remedies, but fortunately the law as enacted reverted to a more simple formula.

**8.10** Article 68 Chinese Patent Act provides that the time limit for instituting legal proceedings for an act of patent infringement is two years from the date on which the patentee knew or ought to have known about the infringing act.

**8.11** It also provides that the two-year period may also include recovery of royalties for the period between a patent application being published and its eventual grant, counting back two years from the date that they knew or ought to have known of the infringing act after the grant, or starting from the date of grant if they were aware of the infringement before the date of grant.

---

4 For a more detailed explanation of how case law operates in China, see Douglas Clark, *Patent Litigation in China*, Oxford: Oxford University Press 2011, 10–11.

5 See www.ciela.cn. Actual copies of decisions are not published on this website but obtained from the archives of this database.

8.12 For an act which is continuing, the patentee retains the right to obtain an injunction, and it is only the right to claim damages that is subject to limitation of two years from the date of filing of the case.

8.13 The rules on limitations are also governed by the 'General Principles of Civil Law (1986)'[6] and 'Provisions of the Supreme People's Court on Certain Issues Concerning the Application of the Statute of Limitations to Civil Case Trials (2008)'[7] (SPC Provisions on Limitations), the latter giving detailed guidance for example on what acts constitute effective notice and suspension of the limitation period.

8.14 Thus a lawsuit will be dismissed if the infringement claim is filed after the expiry of the two-year period[8]. However, courts will not actively dismiss cases that exceed the limitation, and it is incumbent on the defendant to advance the claim. Likewise, recourse to the limitation must be made at first instance, and the defendant is barred from asserting the defence at appeal if they did not do so both at first instance and as a ground for appeal.[9]

8.15 The countdown on the limitation period is stopped not only through filing of a civil lawsuit, but through serving effective notice, or through other forms of dispute resolution, such as an application for arbitration or a complaint to a government agency.[10] China also provides for administrative as well as judicial *fora* for enforcement, and administrative enforcement is a commonly sought alternative to court litigation. Thus in *Qiao Chang Lin v Qingdao Ji'er Engineering Adhesives Co. Ltd*,[11] the plaintiff became aware of the infringing act through the defendants' publication of the patented product in a magazine in August 2007, while the suit in relation to that act was filed in May 2010. However, the court held that since the patentee had previously submitted an infringement complaint to the Shandong Provincial Intellectual Property Office (the administrative body for enforcement of patents) in July 2009, the infringement action was considered to have commenced from that date, and the statutory limitation had not expired.

6 The English version referred to can be found at http://en.chinacourt.org/public/detail.php?id=2696.

7 The English version referred to can be found at http://www.lawinfochina.com/display.aspx?lib=law&id=7057&CGid=.

8 General Principles of Civil Law (1986), Art.138.

9 *Fugui v Zhang Wenling*, Cao Yanpeng, Jilin Higher People's Court Judgment No. 80 (2007).

10 SPC Provisions on Limitations (2008) Arts. 10, 13, 14 & 18.

11 *Qiao Chang Lin v Qingdao Ji'er Engineering Adhesives Co. Ltd*, Shandong Intermediate People's Court, Judgment No. 80 (2010).

**8.16** In CIELA, there are only three cases on record where the issue of statutory limitation has been litigated. This perhaps reflects the fact that the rule operates fairly clearly. In all three cases, the statutory limitation defence was not upheld.

### E. ARTICLE 69(1) CHINESE PATENT ACT – EXHAUSTION OF RIGHTS

**8.17** Article 69(1) Chinese Patent Act provides that where the sale of a patent product or products directly obtained from a patented process is made by the patentee or under the authorization of the patentee, any other person may use, offer to sell, sell or import that product.

**8.18** While exhaustion of rights after first sale is universal in patent law, in a number of jurisdictions the law applies only to domestic acts and does not permit importation of patented products sold with the patentee's authorization elsewhere. The issue of 'international exhaustion' is a contentious one at the international level. It is not surprising therefore that in the public comments received during the drafting process, there was considerable objection to the introduction of international exhaustion into Article 69(1) Chinese Patent Act. As was clear from the comments of the State Intellectual Property Office,[12] this was introduced ostensibly for the purpose of obtaining access to low-priced medicines, and this rationale for international exhaustion is common amongst developing countries.

**8.19** In practice, the amendment does not appear to have a great deal of impact to date. We have found no reported cases filed under Article 69(1) Chinese Patent Act that involve imported products. Given that companies regularly protest about the complexities of import approval for drugs and medical devices into China, there is little sign that international exhaustion has opened the floodgates to cheap parallel imported drugs. Likewise, there may be few sectors in which the price of patented products in China is significantly higher than those in other countries to make parallel import into China an attractive prospect. The vast majority of patent infringement suits in China are between domestic entities and it is only companies operating internationally that are likely to bring suit over cases of patented products imported into China. However, it is inevitable that in time this limitation will have an increasing effect in reducing the value of exclusive licences and giving users in China the advantage of international price arbitrage.

---

12 'Third Revision of China's Patent Law. Legal Texts and documents on the drafting process 2006–2008', above note 3.

The CIELA database contains just four published cases citing this article, all of which relate to domestic resale of products or components incorporating patented subject matter. In two of those cases,[13] the defendants were unsuccessful in claiming that the patentee's rights had been exhausted, because in both cases, they were not simply re-selling the patented product, but were re-using the patented product incorporated in a product of their own. In the case of *Santai County Luhu Wine Factory v Sichuan Province Mianyang City Fenggu Spirits Co. Ltd*, the defendant was re-filling the plaintiff's patented spirits bottle and selling the resulting product – a graphic illustration that in Chinese patent law one is not permitted to put new wine in old bottles! **8.20**

In the two published cases where the defence was successful, the facts clearly demonstrate that the alleged infringing products were sold under the authorization of the patentee, and there is nothing in these cases that challenges the substance of the law. **8.21**

## F. ARTICLE 69(2) CHINESE PATENT ACT – PRIOR USE

Article 69(2) Chinese Patent Act states that it is not an infringement if any person, prior to the patent application date, has already made identical products or used an identical process, or made necessary preparations for making or using it, and continues to use it within the original scope only after grant of the patent. **8.22**

The Article 15 SPC Interpretations give further elucidation to this provision, stating that 'necessary preparations' should be adduced where the defendant has already completed the main technical drawings or documents, or the raw materials and equipment for implementing the patented subject matter have been obtained. **8.23**

The term 'original scope' means the existing manufacturing scale or the manufacturing scale which could be obtained based on the existing preparations for manufacturing before the date of application. **8.24**

Finally, this provision adds that a prior user may not subsequently transfer or assign their right to another entity except where the prior user and their product or process in question are simultaneously transferred or assigned to a successor. **8.25**

13 *Santai County Luhu Wine Factory v Sichuan Province Mianyang City Fenggu Spirits Co. Ltd*, Sichuan Higher People's Court Judgment No. 20 (2010) and *Li Min v Yang San*, utility model infringement case, Sichuan Higher People's Court Judgment No. 114 (2010).

**8.26** The 'prior use' defence is not unique to China, and its intention is generally to remedy the unfairness that results in cases of simultaneous invention by two parties where one party obtains the patent right and could thereby exclude the other. At the same time, the prior user's rights must be strictly limited in scope and scale to prevent total erosion of the patentee's rights. Balancing these interests can be legally complex.

**8.27** Where the patentee has obtained the patent right through improper means, or has obtained a patent on subject matter which is not novel, their right of ownership of the patent is invalid *ab initio*. Hence the 'prior use' right is quite different in nature to the prior art defence, although a *bona fide* prior user, by publication or sale of a product covered by a subsequent patent would logically have destroyed the novelty of that application, and so the issues may be combined. The prior art defence is discussed further below.

**8.28** Article 69(2)'s 'prior use' limitation has seen a relatively high number of cases in China – over 41 cases citing either Article 69(1) Chinese Patent Act or Item 15 SPC Interpretation. This is perhaps owing to the fact that, as well as being a strictly first-to-file jurisdiction, pre-emptive (and improper) registration of others' inventions is relatively common in China, where business partners or employees may part ways having developed a new product or process. The proliferation of low quality patents, especially design and utility model patents that are not subject to examination, and which are nothing more than claims over existing inventions, is a well-documented issue in China.[14] Ownership disputes can be tricky to resolve, and given that patent validity and ownership disputes must be brought to a separate forum – the Patent Review Board and its appellate courts – the prior use defence, and its relative the prior art defence, are the most immediate responses a defendant can make in the face of an infringement suit.

**8.29** The criteria for establishing the prior use limitation have thus been tested in a range of cases in the court.

**8.30** Firstly, as in other jurisdictions, valid prior use is based on the prerequisite that the claimed prior user has acquired the technology in good faith, and the exemption does not apply where the defendant violated a non-disclosure

14 For a detailed study on patent quality in China, see Dan Prud'homme, *Dulling the Cutting-Edge: How Patent-Related Policies and Practices Hamper Innovation in China*, August 2012, available at www.european-chamber.com.cn.

agreement or stole confidential information to enable their prior use.[15] Obviously in cases where a defendant is alleged to have illegitimately acquired the technology prior to the patent application, the patentee may also be claiming trade secret infringement, and it is worth noting that Chinese courts, in *prima facie* cases of trade secret theft, have shifted the burden of evidence to the alleged infringer to prove that the subject matter was independently created.

The courts appear to be strict in their application of Item15 SPC Interpretation in determining what constitutes evidence of effective implementation, or necessary preparations for use of the technology prior to the application date. This might include evidence of design drawings and commissioning of moulds,[16] or preparations for approval of a drug.[17] However, a purchase order for the patented product, in the absence of any other evidence of production or sale, is not sufficient proof.[18] There appears to be little scope for the courts to make presumptions, as the case of *Xiao Zongli v Longyan City Wanteng Vehicle Manufacturing Co et al.* shows,[19] even though the defendant was able to show that it had obtained an industry certification for its product in August 2007, the court did not support the claim that they must have made effective preparations for its production before the patentee's application date of January 2007. **8.31**

As noted above, to remain within the exemption, the prior user is also restricted to using the technology only within the scope of their original use. However, the restriction relates only to the manufacture, and does not impose any restriction on the way that the defendant sells the product.[20] Furthermore, the burden of proof that the original user has exceeded the original scope of use must be adduced by the patentee plaintiff.[21] **8.32**

---

15 *Guangxi Wuzhou Pharmaceutical (Group) Holding Co. Ltd v Shaanxi Yong Shou Pharmaceutical Co Ltd*, Nanning Intermediate People's Court Judgment No. 240 (2010).

16 *Sun Zhengqun v Pan Jiahong*, Shanghai Higher People's Court Judgment No. 21 (2011).

17 *Chengdu Zhonghui Pharmaceutical Co. Ltd v Changchun Haiwai Pharmaceutical Group et al.*, Beijing No. 2 Intermediate People's Court Judgment No. 21063 (2009).

18 *Guangdong Lianbang Furniture Group Company v Yancheng City Chaoyang Real Wood Furniture Factory*, Beijing No.1 Intermediate People's Court Judgment No. 15559 (2010).

19 *Xiao Zongli v Longyan City Wanteng Vehicle Manufacturing Co et al.*, Fuzhou Intermediate People's Court Judgment No. 1878 (2009).

20 *[Unnamed] Qiu v Shenzhen City [Unnamed] Investment Co. Ltd*, Shenzhen Intermediate People's Court Judgment No. 158 (2010).

21 *Han Xiuping v Shenzhen City Quanli Leather Products Co. Ltd*, Beijing Higher People's Court Appeal Judgment No. 2233 (2012).

**8.33** The prior use defence is only available to the person making the product or process, not a seller. A seller would only be able to rely on the prior art defence if they can show that the same subject matter had been publicly disclosed.[22]

**8.34** As noted above, the prior user is not permitted to license that use to others, and the issue of transfer and succession of the prior right also appears to be applied strictly. In the case of *He Guoying v Dazu County Guo Hao Machinery Factory*[23] the technology was developed by a partnership of three people, including the eventual patentee, and preparations were made by that partnership to produce the machinery which was the subject matter of the later patent. The partnership terminated and one of the partners continued the venture exploiting the technology under the entity 'Guo Hao'; however, 'Guo Hao' was not in existence before the date of filing of the patent and no direct succession of the technology from the partnership to 'Guo Hao' could be shown.

**8.35** The CIELA database records testify to the fact that the prior use exception is strictly interpreted and in more than two-thirds of the cases (27 out of 41) the defendant's use of this exception failed. The successful cases are where the evidence for production or effective preparation for production of the technology at issue was abundantly clear, a typical case being *Chengdu Zhonghui Pharmaceutical Co. Ltd v Changchun Haiwai Pharmaceutical Group et al.*,[24] where the defendant had obtained regulatory approval for a drug which was the subject of the dispute. Such approval involved inspection of facilities, deposit and testing of samples and other evidence of extensive preparations to manufacture. Like most of the other cases citing this provision, there was a relationship between the parties to the dispute, in this case, a prior technology transfer agreement.

**8.36** Clearly the prior use defence performs a different function from the prior art defence and is accordingly more restrictive. Where a defendant is able to produce valid, datable prior art that falls clearly within the scope of the plaintiff's patent, it would be preferable to use the prior art defence, as this would provide objective *prima facie* evidence of the patent's lack of novelty. The prior art defence, unlike the prior use defence, imposes no burden of evidence on the defendant to show how and when they used the technology at issue; nor would it impose any restriction on their use of that technology after the defence

---

22 *Shaoguan City Shengji Trade Co Ltd v Tang Lichang*, Guangdong Higher People's Court Appeal Judgments No. 39 & No. 40 (2011).

23 *He Guoying v Dazu County Guo Hao Machinery Factory*, Chongqing No.1 Intermediate People's Court Judgment No. 289 (2010).

24 *Chengdu Zhonghui Pharmaceutical Co. Ltd v Changchun Haiwai Pharmaceutical Group et al.*, Beijing No. 2 Intermediate People's Court Judgment No. 21063 (2009).

has been successfully applied. However, not all alleged prior use can furnish valid prior art, as we note below.

## G. ARTICLE 69(3) CHINESE PATENT ACT – TEMPORARY TRANSIT

Article 69(3) Chinese Patent Act provides that a foreign means of transport which temporarily passes through the territory of China which uses the patent for its own needs, in its devices and installations, and which belongs to a member state of any agreement or international treaty, does not infringe. **8.37**

This exemption has long been part of China's patent law, as it is required in Article 5*ter* of the Paris Convention 1967, and its necessity in preventing patent injunctions from throwing international transportation links into chaos is obvious. In line with the Paris Convention terms, China's exemption is limited to patented devices which are used or installed on the means of transport, and this does not include items being carried as freight. Unlike some other countries, the exemption in China does not extend, in the case of aircraft, to parts stored within the territory for means of repair. **8.38**

The agreements or treaties mentioned in the provision are not defined, but presumably include the Paris Convention, and would therefore apply to all WTO member states. **8.39**

There are no reported cases in China that cite this provision. **8.40**

## H. ARTICLE 69(4) CHINESE PATENT ACT – SCIENTIFIC RESEARCH AND EXPERIMENTS

This provision provides that use of a patent solely for scientific research and experimentation does not infringe. **8.41**

Also relevant is Article 11 Chinese Patent Act which grants the patentee the right to exclude others from using the patent 'for production or business purposes', which is an implied exclusion for private use. **8.42**

It is important to note that the wording of this exception has remained virtually unchanged from China's 1984 Patent Act, through its 1992 and 2000 amendments, to the present 2008 amendment. **8.43**

**8.44** The research and experimental use limitation is universal in patent law, serving an important purpose of giving others scope to develop new inventions from the patented subject matter, but its boundaries can be contentious, as experimental use may be a precursor to unauthorized exploitation of a patent. The application of this exemption in other jurisdictions has thus often been tied to two tests, which is whether the use is genuinely for the purpose of experimentation, and whether the use is for a commercial purpose. The interaction of these two tests can be problematic, given that research, even by universities and not-for-profit institutions may often have ultimately a commercial purpose. In the US, the breadth of the commercial purpose test has made even university research an infringing act.[25]

**8.45** The research and experimentation exemption also commonly distinguishes between research *on* a patented invention and research *with* a patented invention (for example, using patented testing or diagnostic equipment). This means that where a patented invention is used as a tool for experimenting on a different invention, its use infringes. Thus the research exemption is normally restricted to research and experimentation on the patented invention for the purpose of improving on it.

**8.46** In many countries the research and experimentation exemption has been litigated most often around the issue of drug discovery and clinical trials, although many patent regimes now contain specific exemptions for use of patents in regulatory approvals, and so this issue is now separate from more generalized research and experimentation, including in China.

**8.47** In China, the use of the word 'solely' emphasizes that the exemption is strictly limited to scientific research and experiment. An early interpretation of this exemption was in Item 98 Opinions of the Beijing Higher People's Court on Several Issues relating to the Establishment of Patent Infringement (Trial Implementation) 2001[26] (Beijing Patent Trial Opinions). While only a regional higher court opinion, the Beijing Patent Trial Opinions have established long-standing principles in including that research 'on' or research 'with' a patented invention are to be distinguished. The 'Beijing Patent Trial Opinions' also advise that the exemption should apply where the purpose is to 'study, test or improve' the invention so as to develop a new technology. Conversely, if the use of patented technology is not for the purpose of improving that technology and the result is not related to that technology, infringement is established.

25 *Madey v Duke University*, 307 F.3d 1351 (Fed. Cir. 2002).

26 Authors have used own translation from the original.

While there is no subsequent legislation on this issue, academic commentators[27] have argued that, from a public policy perspective given China's developing nation status, the research and experimentation exemption should remain broad, and that the test should simply be whether the research and experimentation is directed at validating, studying or improving the patented subject matter. It has also been proposed that the commercial purpose, and whether the entity carrying out the research is a commercial entity or an institution, is not a reliable test for the exemption, given that many universities and research institutions may be carrying out research for a commercial purpose.[28] Indeed, the above 'Beijing Patent Trial Opinions' make no mention of the application of 'commercial purpose' to the issue of infringement, and prior to the introduction of the 'Bolar' exemption in China, it was held that clinical trials fell outside of Article 11's 'commercial purpose'[29] prerequisite for infringement. **8.48**

The long-standing doctrine that the research and experimentation exemption does not constitute a commercial purpose means that China has avoided entangling the two issues. The apparent dearth of litigation in this area perhaps suggests that the exclusion may indeed be operating as a clear, blanket rule. **8.49**

The CIELA database contains only two cases that apply this clause, and in both the defence failed[30] because the use was clearly beyond experimentation and involved sale of the patented products. **8.50**

In both legal and practical terms, the lack of damage to the plaintiff arising from experimental use by a university or not-for-profit research institution is likely to deter any actions being launched in the first place, not to mention that research on patented inventions may result in dependent inventions which increase the value of the first patent. It is worth noting, however, that according to research, patent applicants in China academic institutions account for 16 per cent of all patent applications, compared with 4 per cent in the US and 1 per cent in **8.51**

---

27 Fan Xiaobo and Meng Fanxing, 'Research on Patent Infringement Through Experimental Use', 23 March 2012, found at http://www.fengxiaoqingip.com/ipluntan/lwxd-zl/20120323/8179.html.

28 Fan Xiaobo and Meng Fanxing, above note 27.

29 See *Sankyo Corporation v Wansheng Pharmaceutical Co. Ltd*, Beijing No.1 Intermediate Court Judgment No. 04314 (2006); prior to that in 2003, the Supreme People's Court issued the draft judicial interpretation, the Provisions on Several Issues Relating to Trial of Cases of Dispute From Patent Infringement, which in It. 84(2), advised that use for the purpose of a clinical trial would fall under Art. 63, paragraph one (4) of the Chinese Patent Act, which was the experimental use exemption article of the then current patent law. This draft, however, was never issued.

30 *Lu Zhengming v Shanghai Engineering Taocheng Holding Co*; Wuxi City Environmental Waste Engineering and Testing Plant Appeal Judgment, Shanghai Higher People's Court Appeal Judgment (1991) and *Nanjing Yiheng Pharmaceutical Co v Nanjing Kanghai Pharmaceutical Co*, Jiangsu Higher People's Court Appeal Judgment No. 0027 (2010).

Japan.[31] It is also common in China for universities to be contracted by companies to do commissioned research. Given that universities are a major part of the commercial research landscape in China, it will be interesting to see if the research and experimentation exception as applied to universities is tested in the courts in the near future.

### I. ARTICLE 69(5) CHINESE PATENT ACT – REGULATORY APPROVAL

**8.52** Article 69(5) Chinese Patent Act provides that it is not an infringement if any person makes, uses or imports a patented drug or a patented medical apparatus for the purpose of providing the information needed for administrative approval.

**8.53** The regulatory exemption for the purposes of drug approval, nicknamed the 'Bolar' exemption,[32] which was introduced into the Patent Law 2008 amendment met with vocal opposition, especially from foreign commentators, as there was no compensating patent term extension (or Supplementary Protection Certificates as in Europe) allowing for recovery of the patent term lost during the drug approval process. Thus it is termed a 'naked' Bolar exemption. The drafters of China's 2008 amendment were unequivocal in stating that their aim was to make low-cost generics available as soon as the patent term was ended, and cited both TRIPS, and the absence of patent term extension in other countries, as justification for China's stance.

**8.54** Despite the protests, however, the appearance of the 'Bolar' exemption in the 2008 amendment was no more than statutory consecration of an earlier judicial practice which started from a 2006 Beijing No.1 Intermediate Court decision, *Sankyo Corporation v Wansheng Pharmaceutical Co*[33] which did not recognize patent infringement of a drug where the defendant's use, including production and clinical trial, is clearly for the purposes of regulatory approval and not for the purpose of commercial sale. Five subsequent cases in the same court[34] provided the same result.

**8.55** This exemption in Chinese patent law, however, contains some differences from those of other countries. It does not explicitly state whether a sale or offer to sell

---

31 Eve Zhou and Bob Stembridge, 'Patented in China, The Present and Future State of Innovation In China', Thomson Reuters, found at ip-science.thomsonreuters.com/m/ppt/WorldIPTodayChina.ppt.

32 After the US case *Roche Products v Bolar Pharmaceutical*, 733 F.2d 858 (Fed. Cir. 1984).

33 *Sankyo Corporation v Wansheng Pharmaceutical Co. Ltd*, above note 29.

34 Including the high profile case of *Eli Lilly v Gan Li Pharmaceutical Co. Ltd*, Beijing No. 1 Higher People's Court Judgment No. 1844 (2007).

may infringe, although the wording of the statute, and the above-cited case law on clinical trials prior to the 2008 amendment suggests that sale would fall outside of the exemption and thus it may be narrower than US law. On the other hand, the fact that the provision refers simply to a 'patented drug' or 'patented medical apparatus' suggests a broader exemption than that in operation, say, in the EU, as China's exemption may extend to new drugs and not be strictly limited to generics.

While there is no corresponding regime for patent extension or term restoration in China, a form of 'patent linkage' operates. Under Rule 2 Administrative Regulations on Registration of Pharmaceuticals, the State Food and Drug Administration can accept applications for approval of a drug that uses a third party patent within two years of the expiry date of that patent. Hence the exemption is subject to a time limitation and, particularly for new drugs that will require safety and efficacy tests, a new drug is very unlikely to appear quickly after the expiry of the patented drug on which it is based. **8.56**

Since the pre-2008 amendment cases cited above, there are no reported lawsuits involving Article 69(5) Chinese Patent Act, and therefore the boundaries of the exemption have not been tested by case law. **8.57**

## J. ARTICLE 62 CHINESE PATENT ACT – PRIOR ART DEFENCE

Article 62 Chinese Patent Act provides that, during a patent infringement dispute, no infringement will be found if the alleged infringer has evidence proving that his technology or design belongs to an existing technology or design. **8.58**

This is further elucidated by Item 14 SPC Interpretations, which states that Article 62 Chinese Patent Act applies where the technical characteristics of the alleged infringing subject matter are identical or without substantial difference to the corresponding differences to a prior art technical scheme (or a prior design, in the respect of designs). **8.59**

This provision is colloquially called the 'prior art defence', as the standard for establishing 'existing' technology or design is the same as for proving the existence of prior art. Its introduction into the 2008 amendment was also merely statutory confirmation of an existing judicial practice on prior art evidence. The 2008 amendment and the 'SPC Interpretations', however, confirm that the prior art defence applies both to literal and equivalent infringement. **8.60**

**8.61** A defence to infringement on the basis of prior art implies that the patent being asserted in fact lacks validity and hence this provision is not strictly speaking an exemption or limitation on otherwise legitimate patent rights, unlike the other articles discussed in this chapter. However, as mentioned earlier, the prior art defence in Article 62 Chinese Patent Act shares some similarity with the prior use limitation in Article 69(2) Chinese Patent Act. Both issues relate to whether the patent holder is truly the first inventor, both are likely to require a detailed evidential examination before determining infringement, and the evidence furnished may apply to both provisions. Both provisions are therefore more often litigated compared with the other limitations which, as we have seen, largely operate as clear rules that will deter an infringement claim *ex ante*. This observation is apparent from the CIELA database, where there are 45 cases citing the 'prior use' limitation (Article 69(2) Chinese Patent Act or Item 15 SPC Interpretations) and 56 based on the prior art defence (citing Article 62 Chinese Patent Act or Item 14 SPC Interpretations). This compared with just 17 published cases dealing with all of the other limitations and exceptions covered in this chapter.

**8.62** The CIELA data also tells us that, like the prior use limitation, the prior art defence more often than not fails – out of the 56 cases, only 11 were successful. Under China's bifurcated system where issues of validity and infringement are tried separately, the court has no jurisdiction to rule on validity, so Article 62 Chinese Patent Law is intended to function as a knockout defence for cases where the prior art is so clear that the court can make a *prima facie* determination that the patent is likely invalid. A review of the cases shows that defendants have encountered all the usual difficulties that accompany showing prior art: that the claimed prior art technical scheme was not proven to have been disclosed to the public, that the prior art could not be accurately dated, or that the claimed prior art is a composition of references and not a single item.

## K. CONCLUSIONS

**8.63** We can conclude that the exceptions and limitations in operation in China's patent law are, for the most part, continuations of previous versions of the law, or codifying established judicial practice, and therefore, operate as settled rules, attracting somewhat relatively little controversy. The truly 'new' limitation of international exhaustion is also consistent with a gradual rolling back of strict territorial exhaustion regimes, although its effects on the domestic market are, for the time being at least, minimal. The only exception which is regularly litigated, the prior use exception and the related prior art defence, are symptomatic of the recent era in China where patent volumes have exploded, but patent quality has lagged, and disputes over the ownership of inventions that are similar or identical, particularly unexamined design and utility model patents, are rife. As patent quality gradually rises, litigation claims and costs increase, and the financial stakes become higher, we expect to see patentees and users challenging the boundaries of the research exception, the Bolar exemption and international exhaustion, over the coming years.

## BIBLIOGRAPHY

### Chinese

Chen Qing, 'The International Application and Development of Patent Exhaustion', *Hebei Legal Studies*, 2012, Vol.1, 133–8.

Fan Xiaobo and Meng Fanxing, 'Research on Patent Infringement Through Experimental Use', *Fengxiaoqingip* (2012).

Fei Yanling, Yangchao, 'Discussing Patent Exhaustion Principles – Using the Example of the 2004 DVD Patent Royalties Case', *Ha'erbin Industrial University Journal*, 2007, Vol.2, 73–6.

Feng Kefa, 'Three Current Problems in Patent Infringement Lawsuit Time Limits', *Contemporary Economics*, 2011, Vol.5, 31–3.

Hu Xiaoxiao, 'The Pros and Cons in China's Patent Research Exemption Regime', *Guizhou Social Science* 2010, Vol.5, 122–5.

Liang Yinxiang, Wang Wuping and Han Jiebo, 'An Analysis of IPR Parallel Imports in the Context of the Financial Crisis', *Innovation*, 2010, Vol.3, 94–7.

Lou Duhe, 'The Development and Application of the Bolar Exemption Provisions in Pharmaceutical Patents', *China Invention and Patents*, 2011, Vol 7, 80–2.

Ou Xiuping, 'An Exploration of Issues in Patent Infringement Decisions', *Sino-Foreign Civil And Commercial Arbitration Net* (2012).

Sun Mingfei and Huang Jun, 'The Determination of "Similar Products" in the Prior Use Defence – A Scientific and Legal Analysis of a Patent Infringement Case', *Science and Law*, 2010, Vol.1, 65–9.

Wang Linghong, 'An Analysis of the Prior Use Right Regime', *Electronics and IPR*, 2010, Vol.11, 92–4.

Yang Hongjun and Zhao Jiabing, 'Researching Patent Exhaustion Principles', *Public Policy and Law*, 2011, Vol.7, 11–13.

Yi Xintian, 'Detailed Commentary on China's Patent Law', (3rd edn.) Intellectual Property Publishing House, 2011.

Zhang Xiaodu, 'Time Limits in Patent Infringement Suits', *China Invention and Patents 2008*, Vol.5, 69–71.

Zhang Xuejun, 'Application of the Prior Use Defence in Patent Trials', *People's Jurisprudence*, 2008, Vol.22, 100–06.

Zhao Chengqiu, 'Parallel Import As A Limitation On Rights', Academia, 2003, Vol.4, 195–9.

Zhou Huishan and Qu Sanqiang, 'An Analysis of the Landscape for Patents on Research Tools – The Regime for Patent Experimental Exceptions', *Intellectual Property*, 2011, Vol.6, 9–17.

### English

'Third Revision of China's Patent Law. Legal Texts and documents on the drafting process 2006–2008' *EU-China IPR* 2, 2010.

Anderson, Robert, 'Exceptions to infringement', Ch.4 in Fysh, Roughton, Cook and Spence, (eds) *The Modern Law of Patents*, London: Butterworths, 2005.

Clark, Douglas, *Patent Litigation in China*, Oxford: Oxford University Press, 2011.

Prud'homme, Dan, *Dulling the Cutting Edge: How Patent-Related Policies and Practices Hamper Innovation in China*, European Chamber of Commerce in China, 2011.

Wu Yuhe and Xiong Yanfeng, *Comparison of Practice in Relation to 'Bolar Exception' in China and United States*, China Patent Agents HK Ltd Article, 2008.

Zhou, Eve and Bob Stembridge, 'Patented in China, The Present and Future State of Innovation In China', Thomson Reuters, 2010.

# Part C

# PATENT APPLICATION AND EXAMINATION PROCEDURE

# 9

# PATENT EXAMINATION: A GENERAL OUTLINE

**Deng Ming**



## A. PATENT APPLICATION IN CHINA

### 1. First-to-file principle

China applies the first-to-file principle. If two or more persons make an invention independently of each other, the right to the patent shall belong to the person whose patent application was filed first. For this purpose, the date of filing is the priority date for applications claiming priority. This principle is actually embodied in the definition of the prior art in Article 22 Chinese Patent Act. The first-filed application forms part of the prior art for a later-filed **9.01** application for the same subject-matter, thereby taking away the novelty claims of the latter.

**9.02** The first-to-file principle imposes an administrative burden on the inventor who has to file the application as soon as possible, so as to forestall the application for the same subject-matter by a competitor. Moreover, it renders the patent system less complex and provides a higher degree of legal certainty than a patent system based on the first-to-invent principle. Moreover, as it incites inventors to quickly disclose their new invention-creations, it is favourable to present China which promotes and encourages innovative activity and its early disclosure. On the other hand, a right of prior use under Article 69(2) Chinese Patent Act can be considered as a balance of interest for those who have made an invention but have not filed a patent application. It provides that 'where, before the date of filing of the application for the patent, any person who has already made the identical product, used the identical process, or made necessary preparations for its making or using, continues to make or use it within the original scope only' does not infringe upon the patent.

## 2. Filing of a patent application

**9.03** A Chinese patent application must be filed with the State Intellectual Property Office (SIPO). It can be delivered personally, by post or in electronic form. Upon receipt of the application, SIPO promptly carries out an examination of the documents of the application to determine whether the application conforms with the formal requirements of the Chinese Patent Act. If SIPO finds that the application is in conformity with the relevant provisions, it will, without delay, issue a notification (Notification of Acceptance) to the applicant stating the date of filing and the application number, as well as the filing fees to be paid. If the application is not in conformity with the formal requirements, it will not be accepted. The date of filing should be the date at which SIPO has received the application or the mailing date indicated on the postmark if the application has been sent by post. Among the requirements for acceptance of a patent application, foreign applicants should pay particular attention to the requirements with regard to representation and language.

**9.04** A Chinese patent application shall be filed in Chinese, which is a prerequisite for obtaining a filing date. It is impossible to file a Chinese patent application in a foreign language and to submit the Chinese translation of the application after the date of filing. Exceptionally, it is possible to file a PCT application with SIPO either in Chinese or in English, and to submit the Chinese translation when entering into the Chinese national phase (*Mak*, Chapter 10). If the Chinese application is filed in accordance with the Paris Convention, the

Chinese translation of the foreign application, which gives rise to the right of priority, but not the foreign application, will be regarded as authentic in all proceedings before SIPO and in all procedures related to patent enforcement in China.[1] For this reason, translation accuracy is always a major issue for Chinese applications filed by foreigners. It is not unknown that even technical translators experience substantial difficulties when translating complex terms in a patent specification. To ensure accurate translation of an application, it is recommended that a professional translator or a Chinese patent attorney makes the translation, and that the Chinese patent attorney who is in charge of the application reviews the claims carefully in the light of the description and drawings and finalizes the translation.

In general, applicants are not required to be represented in the course of proceedings in SIPO. Exceptionally, foreign applicants and the applicants of Hong Kong, Macau and Taiwan, who have no habitual residence or place of business in mainland China, will appoint a legally incorporated patent agency to act as their agent to file a patent application and to deal with other patent matters.[2] This requirement also applies to foreign applicants who file a patent application as the first applicant jointly with a Chinese applicant from mainland China. Choosing a Chinese IP firm as a reliable co-operation partner is an important issue for foreign enterprises. **9.05**

At present, more than 900 agencies in China are registered to represent foreign applicants. In reality, however, foreign and domestic applicants still do not entrust their cases evenly to all these agencies. Statistics show that more than half of the patent applications published in 2010 had been dealt with by the top 50 agencies in China.[3] It can therefore be estimated that significantly more than 50 per cent of patent prosecution cases initiated by foreigners are entrusted to the top 50. That is, most of the existing Chinese patent agencies have only small market shares in the representation business. It seems that many of these agencies still need time to convince the domestic and international clients of the reliability, quality and capacity of their services. **9.06**

### 3. Divisional applications[4, 5]

An applicant may submit one or more divisional applications on his own volition (voluntary division) or at the request of the examiner to overcome an **9.07**

1 Examination Guidelines, Part II, Chapter 8, 5.2.1.
2 Article 19(1) Chinese Patent Act.
3 Wang Zhe and Zhu Xinyu, [2011] **1** *China Invention & Patent* 26.
4 Examination Guidelines, Part I, Chapter 1, 5.1.
5 Examination Guidelines, Part II, Chapter 6, 3.

objection that the application lacks unity (mandatory division). A voluntary divisional application may be filed for economic reasons, for example, to focus on an independent claim on a product or a method which will be interesting for the Chinese market.

**9.08** Divisional applications accepted by SIPO are deemed to have been filed on the date of filing of the initial application and shall enjoy the same rights of priority. A divisional application is regarded as a new Chinese application and its further prosecution proceeds, in principle, independent from that of the initial application. It may be examined by another examiner than the one who examines the parent application. As the applicant has the same opportunities to voluntarily amend the divisional application as he has with regard to a usual application, he may file the divisional application by just submitting the specification of the parent application first, and make voluntary amendments to the filed divisional application later. That is, the requirements for filing a normal patent application are the same as the requirements pertaining to a divisional application. There are, however, the following additional requirements with regard to divisional applications:

- a divisional application may be filed only in respect of subject-matter which does not extend beyond the content of the initial application;
- an applicant may not divide a patent application by filing a divisional application for a utility model patent, and vice versa;
- the applicant of a divisional application must be the same individual or entity which has filed the initial application. Otherwise, a document certifying the change of the applicant must be submitted; the inventor of a divisional application must be the same person or belong to those persons who have made the invention which is the subject-matter of the initial application.

**9.09** A divisional application can be filed so long as the initial application is pending. In case of grant or rejection of the initial application, the applicant can still file a divisional application at the latest up to the expiration of two months after receiving the notification of grant or until the expiration of three months after receipt of the decision to reject the application. In the case of a rejected initial application which is pending in the re-examination procedure at the Patent Re-examination Board (PRB) or is under review by a court, the applicant can still file a divisional application. In practice, it often occurs that the applicants file a divisional application within three months after receiving PRB's rejection of the initial application, without filing a lawsuit with the court to challenge the decision of PRB in respect of the initial application. Although the divisional applications filed within these three months are accepted by SIPO, no corresponding legal basis or provision for doing this can be found.

An applicant may also voluntarily file a divisional application which is based on another divisional application where the initial application is pending or within two months after receiving the grant notifications or within three months after receiving the decision to reject the initial application. If the initial application is no longer pending, the applicant may file a divisional application based on an earlier divisional application only in cases in which the examiner has raised a lack of unity objection against the earlier divisional application. **9.10**

### 4. Double patenting

Article 9 Chinese Patent Act provides that for any identical invention, only one patent right shall be granted, which bans double patenting in China. Where two applications relating to the same or overlapping subject-matter and filed at the same date meet substantive requirements of patentability, the issue of double patenting may arise. A double patenting problem can only arise if claims in two or more applications or patents seek the same extent of patent protection. The Examination Guidelines[6] provide for the following means to avoid the problem of double patenting with different applicants or only one applicant. **9.11**

In the case of different applicants, the examiner will raise a double patenting objection against both applications. Therein, the applicants will be required to amend their applications in such a manner that the applications do not claim the same subject-matter, or they will be advised to solve the question of who shall be entitled to file a patent application through negotiations. If the double patenting objection cannot be overcome by the amendments or if the applicants fail to reach an agreement, both applications will be rejected. It is interesting to note that this situation is handled differently under the EPC, where each applicant must be allowed to proceed as though the other did not exist.[7] **9.12**

If only one applicant is involved, the examiner shall notify him or her to choose only one of the applications for grant or to amend both applications so as to overcome the double patenting objection. If the applicant does not make such choice or if the amendments fail to overcome the double patenting objection, both applications will be rejected. **9.13**

6 Examination Guidelines, Part II, Chapter 3, 6.

7 Guidelines for Examination in the European Patent Office (EPO) 2012, G-IV, 5.4.

**9.14** In accordance with Article 9(1) Chinese Patent Act, an applicant may, on the same day, file applications for both patent and utility model relating to any identical invention-creation with a corresponding indication that the two applications are being filed. In order to avoid the problem of double patenting in this specific situation, the examiner will, if the utility model patent, which should be granted within three to ten months of the date of filing, is valid, before granting the invention patent, require the applicant to do the following:[8]

- abandon the utility model patent to give way to the grant of the invention patent; or
- abandon the invention patent application to uphold the utility model patent; or
- amend the invention patent application in a manner that it no longer claims the same subject-matter as the utility model patent.

## B. PROCEDURE UNTIL GRANT

### 1. Preliminary examination and publication of patent applications

**9.15** After the application has been accorded a date of filing, SIPO carries out a preliminary examination to make the application ready for publication. If neither a defect pertaining to formalities nor an obvious defect as to the substance of the application (for example, subject-matter excluded from patentability, lack of unity) is found, or if defects which have been found have been eliminated, or an objection raised by the examiner due to the obvious substantial defect has been overcome by the applicant, the application will pass the preliminary examination. Otherwise, if the applicant has failed to rectify the defect or to overcome the objection, the application will be rejected.

**9.16** After the application has passed the preliminary examination, SIPO will issue a notification (Notification of Passing Preliminary Examination) of such passing and inform the applicant of the text of the application which will be published. During the preliminary examination, SIPO does not yet carry out a search, which differs from the practice of EPO where the search report is drawn up simultaneously with the formalities examination.

**9.17** According to Article 34 Chinese Patent Act, SIPO shall publish the application as soon as possible:

---

8 Examination Guidelines, Part II, Chapter 3, 6.2.2.

- after the expiry of 18 months from the date of filing or, if priority has been claimed, from the date of priority; or
- at the request of the applicant, prior to the expiry of the 18-month period.

The application will not be published if it has been finally rejected, withdrawn or deemed withdrawn before the completion of the preparation for publication. If the applicant withdraws his application after such preparation, the application may still be published.[9] In contrast to European practice where the technical preparation for publication is deemed to have been completed at the end of the last day of a period of five weeks before the expiry of said 18-month period, SIPO does not officially announce the exact date of such completion. Based on this author's practical experience, the applicant is well-advised to withdraw his or her application before the expiry of 15 months from the date of filing or, if priority has been claimed, from the date of priority, to ensure that publication will not be made. **9.18**

The publication of an application has two effects which are very similar to the corresponding effects created by the publication of a European patent application. First, it creates a prior right effect, that is, a novelty-destroying effect on all applications filed after the filing date of the published application, including those which have been filed before or on the date of publication. Another effect of the publication is the provisional protection provided by Article 13 Chinese Patent Act from the date of publication. **9.19**

## 2. Request for substantive examination and voluntary amendments

According to Article 35 Chinese Patent Act, the applicant shall file the request for substantive examination within three years from the date of filing or, if priority has been claimed, from the date of priority. Under the EPC, the corresponding period is determined by the publication of the search report, that is, from the filing of the application up to the six months after the date of publication of the search report. This means, in a normal case, that the search report of EPO is published together with the application and the time period within which an applicant shall file the request for substantive examination with EPO is 12 months shorter than with SIPO. If the applicant fails to meet the time limit for filing a request for examination without justified reason, the application shall be deemed to have been withdrawn. SIPO may, at its own initiative, proceed to examine applications even after the applicant has failed to request substantive examination. Such a situation may arise, for instance, if an **9.20**

9 Treaty and Law Department of SIPO, Explanation of the newly amended Patent Act.

application is deemed to be of great significance for the interest of the State or to the public interest.

9.21 In accordance with Rule 51(1) Implementing Regulations to the Patent Act, the applicant has only two occasions for voluntary amendments to the application, namely:

- at the date of filing a request for substantive examination; and
- within three months after receiving the notification from SIPO that the application has entered substantive examination (Notification of Entering the Substantive Examination Stage of the Application).

9.22 During the substantive examination, the applicant is no longer allowed to make voluntary amendments. He may, in response to the Office Action, only make amendments to overcome objections raised by the examiner. In contrast, the previous EPO practice has permitted voluntary amendments also on the occasion of responding to the first Office Action. However, in recent years, EPO has restricted opportunities to make voluntary amendments to the response to the search opinion, in order to speed up the proceedings.

### 3. The first Office Action[10]

9.23 The substantive examination shall be carried out based on the application documents as initially filed by the applicant, or as amended upon the requirements of the preliminary examination department of SIPO, or as voluntarily amended by the applicant under Rule 51(1) Implementing Regulations. Before issuing the first Office Action, the Chinese examiner proceeds as follows:

#### *(a) Understand the invention well by reading the application documents*

9.24 As a basic requirement of SIPO on all the Chinese examiners, the examiner will carefully read the application documents, to understand, in particular, the technical problem to be solved, the technical solution employed to solve the problem, and the technical effect produced by the solution. The examiner will identify all essential features of the solution, especially those differing from the prior art. Considering the positive feedback that this author has heard from many European patent professionals with respect to the quality of the Office Actions issued by SIPO, it seems to the author that many Chinese examiners do meet the above-mentioned basic requirement of SIPO.

10 Examination Guidelines, Part II, Chapter 8, 4.

*(b) Carry out a search*[11]

As a very important step of the substantive examination, the search has the purpose of identifying documents from the prior art which are closely related to the subject-matter of the application, to assess the novelty and inventive step of the related invention, and to identify conflicting applications which are prejudicial to the novelty of the application at issue. Exceptionally, if the subject-matter of the application is excluded from patentability, is not industrially applicable or is not set forth in a sufficiently clear and complete manner to enable a skilled artisan to comprehend it, the examiner does not have to carry out a search. **9.25**

*(c) Examine and eventually handle the unity problem*[12]

Lack of unity may be noticed before or after prior art has been investigated. If the application obviously lacks unity, the examiner can directly raise the corresponding lack of unity objection without having to carry out a search. If the lack of unity relates to independent claims, the examiner may proceed with the examination in different ways, depending on the specific situation: **9.26**

- If the first independent claim and the dependent claims thereof, that is, the first group of the claims, have a prospect of being granted and if there is a lack of unity between them and other independent claims, the examiner will not carry out a search and examination of these other independent claims. He or she will only make observations with regard to the first group of the claims, and invite the applicant to delete or to amend the other claims to overcome the objection of lack of unity.
- If the first group of claims does not have a prospect of being granted, and if there is lack of unity between them and other independent claims, the examiner has two options to proceed with the examination. He or she may either issue the first Office Action which indicates that the first group of the claims does not have a prospect of being granted and that the application lacks unity, or continue examination by carrying out a search and examination with regard to the other claims. The latter option is frequently applied if the technical field in which the search will be carried out is very close to or largely overlapping with the technical field to which the first group of claims pertains.

The above-mentioned possibilities to proceed also apply to the situation in which the dependent claims lack unity after the fall of the relevant independent claim due to lack of novelty or inventive step.

11 Examination Guidelines, Part II, Chapter 8, 4.5.
12 Examination Guidelines, Part II, Chapter 8, 4.4.

*(d) Verify the right of priority*[13]

**9.27** The verification will be carried out unless all reference documents have been published before the priority date of the application.

- If an application claims priority over an earlier application, the examiner shall verify that (a) the subject-matter of the later application is disclosed in the earlier application, (b) the earlier application is the first application which discloses the subject-matter claimed by the later application, and (c) the date of filing of the later application is within 12 months of that of the earlier application.
- If partial priority is claimed, the examiner will verify the priority only of those claims for which priority is claimed.
- If multiple priorities are claimed, the examiner will verify that each claim is actually entitled to the priority claimed respectively, and that the application meets the requirement of unity.
- The priority dates of certain reference documents shall be verified to determine whether these documents can be used to assess the novelty and inventive step of the application, whether they should be considered as conflicting applications or whether they should be taken into account to avoid double patenting.

If the claimed priority right is found to be invalid, the examiner will continue the examination based on the effective date, that is the newly determined priority date or the filing date of the application.

*(e) Carry out a comprehensive examination as to formality and substance*[14]

**9.28** Before issuing the first Office Action, the examiner will examine whether the application is in conformity with all the provisions of the Patent Act and the Implementing Regulations as to formality and substance, which can be summarized as follows:

- Examination of general issues, such as:
  - whether the subject-matter of the invention shall be excluded from patentability;
  - whether a request for confidentiality examination (*Luginbuehl*, Chapter 11) was approved if the applicant did the first filing abroad and if the examiner sees a reason to doubt that the invention disclosed in the application was completed in China, for example, in

13 Examination Guidelines, Part II, Chapter 8, 4.6.

14 Examination Guidelines, Part II, Chapter 8, 4.7.

a case where the inventor is a Chinese national having his habitual residence or place of business in China;
- whether the applicant has submitted the Registration Form for Indicating Source of Genetic Resources in case of applications pertaining to biological material which require indication of direct and original source of such material, unless the applicant states the reason for not indicating.

- Examination of the claims in the following order of steps:[15]
  - assess the novelty and inventive step of the independent claims;
  - assess the novelty and inventive step of the dependent claims, which, however, is only necessary if the result of the last step of assessing the independent claims is negative.

It should be emphasized that SIPO adopts the absolute novelty standard to assess the novelty of a claim as EPO does, and that both SIPO and EPO use the same approach to assess the inventive step of patent application for invention, namely the problem and solution approach consisting of three stages. If the examiner cannot assess the novelty and inventive step due to defects in the claims, he may continue such assessment later, after the applicant has eliminated the defects, or he may carry on with the assessment based on his understanding of the description and the drawings. Only if the last two steps of assessment produce positive results, the examiner may continue with the examination as to the following:

- whether all the claims are supported by the description and the drawings, and whether the claims define the scope of protection sought in a clear and concise manner;
- whether an independent claim provides a complete technical solution which contains all the essential features necessary to solve the problem;
- whether a dependent claim, which refers to a preceding claim and limits it by additional features, fulfils the formality requirements. Based on Rule 22(2) Implementing Regulations, a multiple dependent claim which refers to various other claims, shall not serve as a basis for any further multiple dependent claims;
- whether the terms used in the claims are the standard scientific and technical terms as officially determined, and whether they are consistent with those used in the description.

15 Examination Guidelines, Part II, Chapter 8, 4.7.1.

It has to be noted that only two basic kinds of claims, that is the product claim and the process claim, are allowed in China. Other kinds of claims such as 'computer program' or 'software product' are not admissible.

- Examination of the description and the abstract, focusing on the following items:
  - whether the description sets forth the invention in a clear and complete manner to enable the skilled person in the art to put the invention into practice, and whether the technical solutions described in the description are able to solve the technical problem of the invention and to achieve the anticipated effect;
  - whether the technical solutions described in the 'Contents of the Invention' section of the description are consistent with those outlined in the claims, and whether the protection scope of each claim is supported by the description;
  - whether the description uses standard terminology and possesses clarity as required by Rule 17 Implementing Regulations, and, if applicable, whether the drawings are in conformity with Rule 18 Implementing Regulations.

*(f) Handle the third-party observations, if they are available*[16]

**9.29** According to Rule 48 Implementing Regulations, any person may, from the date of publication of a patent application till the date of announcing the grant of the patent right, submit to SIPO his observations on the application which is not in conformity with the provisions of the Patent Act. Since such observations help to avoid the grant of invalid patents, the examiner shall take them into consideration in the course of substantive examination and shall include them in the application file. Filing the third-party observations is an easily accessible route to avoid the grant of a patent, because there are no official fees to be paid for doing it.

**9.30** According to this author's experience, the third party, before filing his observations, should consider the following:

- the examiner will more likely consider the observations if they are submitted before the examiner completes most of the examination work and if they are supported by strong evidence, particularly that which cannot easily be obtained by the examiner;

16 Examination Guidelines, Part II, Chapter 8, 4.9.

- the applicant may match the claims to overcome the examiner's objections based on the evidence filed by the third party, so that this evidence can hardly be used later in the invalidation procedure;
- SIPO will not send communications in the procedure to the third party who submitted the observations.

By the way, it should be mentioned that the observations may be filed anonymously. Due to this reason, it is possible in practice for a foreigner or a person from Hong Kong, Macau or Taiwan, who has no habitual residence or place of business in mainland China, to file his observations himself, instead of through his representative as required by Article 19(1) Chinese Patent Act.

In order to speed up the examination procedure, the number of Office Actions should be kept as low as possible. For this purpose, the first Office Action should cover all comprehensive observations of the examiner, and refer not only to substantive but also to formal matters. However, occasionally in the past some examiners raised the formality issues after the first Office Action. Based on the experiences of the author, SIPO needs about 12 months to issue a first Office Action after entry into substantive examination. **9.31**

The time limit for the applicant to submit a response to the first Office Action is four months,[17] which may be extended once by one or two months upon request of the applicant and upon payment of a fee for the extension before the expiry of the time limit. **9.32**

## 4. Examination after the first Office Action

After issuing the first Office Action, the examiner continues with the examination. He or she will consider the applicant's response to the issued Office Action and examine whether the observations and evidence submitted by the applicant are suitable to overcome the objections of the Office Action. If the applicant has made an amendment to the application in the course of responding to the Office Action, the examiner will carefully check whether the amendment extends beyond the contents of the application as filed. SIPO adopts the stringent requirement of amendments that the contents of the application as filed means the contents which are described in or can be directly and unambiguously determined from the initial application.[18] In practice, some examiners interpret this requirement to the extent that they only accept the amendments to which a literal correspondence can be found in the description. **9.33**

---

17 Examination Guidelines, Part II, Chapter 8, 4.10.

18 Examination Guidelines, Part II, Chapter 8, 5.2.

**9.34** The strict amendment requirements of SIPO have been criticized by the patent community in China. Recently, a decision[19] was handed down by the SPC in the case *Seiko-Epson v PRB* in which the court took a more liberal stance than the PRB. Regarding a patentee's amendment during prosecution which changed the term 'semiconductor storage device' to 'storage device', the SPC held that the original disclosure of the specification does not only include the textual content of the original application but also any information that can be directly and clearly 'inferred' from the original application by an ordinarily skilled artisan. On this basis, amendments are permissible. Hereby, the court overturned the PRB decision. Many commentators in China hope that this case ('the Ink Cartridge case') will prompt SIPO to liberalize its amendment requirements.

**9.35** In the further examination proceedings, the examiner may handle various situations that may arise as follows:

- The examiner will issue a further Office Action if:
  - a supplementary search brings to light prior art documents which are more relevant than the first search to the evaluation of the patentability of the application;
  - claims which do not meet the requirements of the Patent Act and its Implementing Regulations and which have remained unnoticed in the last Office Action have been identified;
  - after the applicant has submitted observations or amendments, the necessity of new observations arises;
  - defects which may result from the amendments made by the applicant or which had been mentioned in the last Office Action but have not been eliminated by the applicant are found;
  - the examiner intends to reject the application but has not clarified the facts, grounds or evidence upon which the rejection is based in his or her last Office Action.

The specified time limit for responding to such further Office Action is two months. It can be extended once by one or two months upon the request of the applicant.

- The examiner will decide to reject the application if the applicant fails to eliminate the defects referred to by the last Office Action.
- The examiner will issue the notification of grant (Notification to Grant Patent Right) if the applicant's response to the last Office Action renders

19 (2010) IP Administrative Ruling No. 53 of the Supreme People's Court.

the application compliant with the requirements of the Patent Act and the Implementing Regulations.

At the date of or after the submission of the response to the first Office Action, the examiner may arrange an interview upon request of the applicant or at his or her own initiative, so as to accelerate examination proceedings. The examiner may also reject the applicant's request for an interview if he or she considers the interview unnecessary. The interview can be arranged by a corresponding notification or by telephone and should be recorded in the application file. Where a patent agency is appointed by the applicant, the applicant may participate in the interview together with his patent agent. Usually, the matters discussed, the conclusions reached, and the amendments agreed upon should be included in the Record of Interview which is provided by SIPO. The examiner and the applicant may also discuss problems pertaining to the application on the phone. However, such communication by phone should only be made in case of minor issues such as formal questions which are unlikely to cause misunderstandings.[20] **9.36**

On condition that the principle of examination under request and the principle of hearing are followed, SIPO encourages the examiners to follow the principle of procedural economy, by requiring them to close an application case as soon as possible. To reach this goal, the examiners usually indicate all open issues in the first Office Action and invite the applicant to respond to all raised issues in due time. Such procedural economy has contributed to the current examining cycle of 22.6 months on average.[21] According to this author's experience, the average number of the Office Actions per application for which a patent could be granted, is only slightly over two. **9.37**

After SIPO has issued the notification of grant, the applicant should fulfil the formality issues within two months from the receipt of the notification. Afterwards, SIPO will grant the patent right, issue the patent certificate and announce the grant of the patent right. **9.38**

20 Examination Guidelines, Part II, Chapter 8, 4.12.
21 Annual Report of SIPO 2012.

## C. RE-EXAMINATION PROCEDURE

### 1. Request for re-examination

**9.39** If an application is rejected after substantive examination, the applicant may, within three months from the date of receipt of the rejection decision, file a request for re-examination with PRB of SIPO. In recent years, the number of re-examination requests has sharply increased; 17,230 requests in 2012 shows an increase of 33.8 per cent compared to the preceding year.[22]

**9.40** The request should outline the reasons for the re-examination and include the relevant evidence where necessary. The petitioner may amend the application at the time of submitting the request, responding to the notification of re-examination or the oral proceedings. Any amendment must, however, be limited to eliminating the defects indicated by the rejection decision or by the collegiate panel carrying out the re-examination. If the request is considered admissible after the formality examination, PRB will notify the applicant that it has accepted the request. Otherwise, the request will be deemed not to have been made or the applicant will be instructed to correct the request within 15 days from receipt of the notification.[23]

### 2. Interlocutory examination[24]

**9.41** After accepting the request for re-examination, PRB will transfer it to the substantive examination department which decided to reject the application. The substantive examination department normally needs one month for interlocutory examination as to whether:

(1) the request for re-examination is admissible and whether the decision of rejection shall be revoked;
(2) the amendments submitted by the applicant have eliminated the defects which gave rise to the rejection, so that the rejection shall be revoked;
(3) the observations and amendments submitted by the applicant are not sufficient to give reason to such revocation, so that the rejection will be upheld.

---

22 Annual Report of SIPO 2012.
23 Examination Guidelines, Part IV, Chapter 2, 2.
24 Examination Guidelines, Part IV, Chapter 2, 3.

If the interlocutory examination arrives at conclusion (1) or (2), PRB will not carry out a re-examination but it will immediately decide to revoke the rejection. 9.42

If the examination arrives at conclusion (3), PRB will form a collegiate panel to carry out a re-examination. The collegiate panel normally consists of three members, but in special cases, for example, if the outcome is expected to have a great impact on China or its foreign relations, if it involves important legal issues or if it has significant economic implications, it can be extended to five members.[25] The establishment of a collegiate panel follows the general principle which is laid down in Rule 37 Implementing Regulations, namely that any party is entitled to have its case objectively decided by impartial examiners. 9.43

### 3. Collegiate examination

The panel may carry out the examination in written form, by oral proceedings, or in a combination thereof. It shall issue at least one Notification of Re-examination where it: 9.44

- intends to uphold the rejection; or
- requires the applicant to make specific amendments, so that the panel can revoke the rejection; or
- requires the applicant to submit further evidence and explanations; or
- finds new grounds or evidence for the rejection.

The applicant shall respond to the Notification of Re-examination in written form within one month after receipt. Otherwise, the request for re-examination will be deemed to have been withdrawn. 9.45

Upon receipt of the applicant's response, the panel shall make a re-examination decision to uphold or to revoke the original rejection decision. In 2012, PRB concluded 11,363 re-examination cases. The current average duration of re-examination procedures is 12.5 months.[26] 9.46

If it revokes the rejection, PRB shall remit the relevant dossier to the previous examination department which will continue the examination. The examination department must follow the re-examination decision of PRB; it may not decide contrary to PRB's findings on the same facts and evidence. 9.47

25 Examination Guidelines, Part IV, Chapter 1, 3.

26 Annual Report of SIPO 2012.

9.48 If the applicant is not satisfied with the re-examination decision of PRB, he or she may, within three months from the date of receipt of the final Notification of Re-examination, initiate an administrative lawsuit in the People's Court No. 1 of the City of Beijing which is in charge of handling judicial reviews of re-examination decisions in the first instance. If the applicant is unsatisfied with the ruling made by the first instance court, he or she may appeal to the Higher People's Court of the City of Beijing.

## D. INVALIDATION PROCEDURE

### 1. Filing the request for invalidation[27]

9.49 China's Patent Act does not provide for an opposition procedure after grant in the same way as, for instance, EPO. The only way to challenge granted patents is to file a request with PRB for an invalidation procedure, which is characterized in that (1) it is a patent office procedure and (2) the official fees for it are quite moderate. In 2012, PRB received 2,941 invalidation cases altogether, which included 602 invention patent, 1,318 utility model and 1,021 design invalidation cases. The statistics show that the number of Chinese invention patents which have gone through an invalidation procedure is much lower than the number of European patents which are opposed (more than 2,000 per year), considering the huge number of invention patents granted in China per year (for example, 217,000 in 2012).[28]

9.50 According to Article 45 Chinese Patent Act, after the date of the announcement of grant, any entity or individual who considers that the grant of the patent right is not in conformity with the relevant provisions of the Chinese Patent Act may file a request with PRB to declare the patent right invalid. Hereby, the term 'any entity or individual' can be construed as anybody who is eligible to institute a civil action, which means that the circle of parties entitled to the invalidation request is actually unlimited. This is obviously due to the reason that patent invalidation is not only in the interest of parties which are in some way connected to the patent in question but also in the interest of the public. Correspondingly, SIPO also accepts straw men as petitioners for invalidation, which is similar to the practice of EPO where straw men are accepted as opponents.

---

27 Examination Guidelines, Part IV, Chapter 3, 3.2.

28 Annual Report of SIPO 2012.

Compared to the status of opponents before EPO, the SIPO provides for some specific requirements for petitioners for invalidation. For instance, it admits invalidation requests by patentees in respect of their own patents as long as a partial invalidation is intended and only evidence, which shall be limited to the publications, is submitted, whereas EPO considers any opposition filed by the patentee himself inadmissible. This difference between SIPO and EPO is logically understandable, because EPO allows the patentee to file a request for limitation or revocation of his or her patent under EPC Article 105a-b, but there is no such provision provided in the Chinese Patent Act and the Implementing Regulations thereof. Furthermore, SIPO also does not accept invalidation requests which are filed jointly by several petitioners unless they are joint patentees of the patent to be invalidated, whereas EPO allows several opponents to file an opposition jointly, so that they only have to jointly pay one opposition fee. Even though PRB does not accept invalidation requests which are jointly filed by several petitioners, it may hear different cases in combination in order to increase the efficiency of the examination and to relieve the burden of proof of the parties. 9.51

## 2. Formality examination[29]

As soon as PRB receives a request for invalidation, it examines the request as to formalities, that is, as to whether the subject-matter of the request actually is a granted patent, whether the petitioner is eligible to file a request, whether the desired extent of invalidation is clearly substantiated and supported by relevant evidence, whether the respective fees have been paid and whether a qualified representative has been appointed in cases in which the petitioner is a foreigner. 9.52

The grounds for invalidation are exhaustively regulated in Rule 65(2) Implementing Regulations. They are very similar to the grounds for opposition before EPO: non-conformity with the substantive patentability requirements, insufficient disclosure and extension of protection to subject-matter beyond the content of the application as filed. In contrast to opposition grounds admitted by EPO, however, SIPO considers several additional grounds for invalidation, namely lack of clarity or non-conciseness or lack of support, double patenting with the same priority date, and non-conformity with the provisions on confidentiality examination for inventions made in China. Based on the author's experiences, lack of clarity, non-conciseness, and lack of support are the grounds which have been used in many invalidation procedures in China. This is mainly due to the fact that many patents granted over ten years ago and many utility model patents, which have never been substantively examined, indeed 9.53

29 Examination Guidelines, Part IV, Chapter 3, 3.3.

contain such problems. With quality improvement of the drafting or the translation of the applications, as well as of the substantive examination, the number of the invalidation requests based on those grounds should decrease.

**9.54** Under the principle of *res judicata*, after a decision on a request for invalidation of a patent has been made, PRB will not accept any new request for invalidation of the same patent which is based on the same grounds and evidence.

**9.55** In general, if the request is found to be not in conformity with the requirements, PRB shall issue a corresponding notification (Notification to Make Rectification) which invites the petitioner to eliminate corrigible defects within 15 days from receipt, or notify the petitioner that the request is inadmissible. If the request is found to conform to the rules, PRB will notify the petitioner that the request has been admitted and transfer copies of such request and of the relevant documents to the patentee. The patentee shall respond within one month from the date of receipt of the notification.

**9.56** Under certain circumstances, PRB may, after carrying out the formality examination, issue other kinds of notification. If, for instance, another invalidation procedure with respect to the same patent is already pending and if PRB considers that the examination of the new request should be examined on grounds of the results of the decision of the pending procedure, it shall notify the new petitioner as well as the patentee that the request will not be examined until the decision with regard to the pending procedure is made. Where an admissible request for invalidation relates to a patent infringement case, PRB may, at the request of the infringement court, submit a 'Notification of Examination Status of Request for Invalidation' to the court. The same court will then, upon termination of the invalidation procedure, receive another 'Notification of Termination of Examination at Request for Invalidation' from PRB.

## 3. Collegiate examination[30]

### *(a) Extent of examination*

**9.57** PRB usually limits its examination to the extent of the invalidation request and considers only the grounds and evidence submitted by the parties concerned. It is not obliged to carry out a comprehensive examination with regard to the validity of the patent.

30 Examination Guidelines, Part IV, Chapter 3, 4.

However, PRB may carry out further examination at its own initiative with respect to any ground for invalidation which has not been invoked by the petitioner but may nevertheless prejudice the maintenance of the patent. For example: 9.58

- where the grounds raised by the petitioner are obviously not supported by the submitted evidence, PRB may inform the petitioner about this problem and either invite him or her to amend the request or change the grounds *ex officio* to more suitable ones;
- where the subject-matter of the patent is obviously excluded from patent protection, PRB may introduce a corresponding ground to the invalidation procedure;
- where a patent has a defect which remained unmentioned by the petitioner but which inhibits the examination on the grounds raised by the petitioner, PRB may add those grounds which correspond to the defect;
- where the petitioner files a request to invalidate certain claims which are related to others with respect to the ground for such request, PRB may examine all concerned claims with regard to such ground;
- PRB may determine *ex officio* whether a technical means belongs to common knowledge of the art and may introduce the relevant evidence, for example, a technical dictionary, manual or textbook, into the examination.

Usually, after filing the request for invalidation, the petitioner has only one month to submit additional grounds for invalidation which must be substantiated and accompanied by the corresponding evidence. Afterwards, the petitioner and the patentee may only be allowed to submit grounds and evidence as required by PRB within a specified time limit. The above time limits do also apply to submitting Chinese translations of evidence in foreign languages. Exceptionally, the parties may present common knowledge – material (for example, technical dictionaries or manuals) or complementary material such as notarizations as evidence until closure of the oral proceedings. 9.59

### *(b) Evidence requirements*[31]

Where a party submits evidence in a foreign language, he or she shall also submit the Chinese translation thereof. If a translation of only a part of the evidence is submitted, the other non-translated parts may not be used as evidence, unless the translation of these parts is subsequently submitted at the request of PRB. If the opposite party objects to the translation, he or she may, within a certain time limit, submit another translation by him or herself. If the 9.60

31 Examination Guidelines, Part IV, Chapter 8, 2.2.

parties disagree about the correctness of a translation, PRB may entrust a translator or a professional translation agency to translate the evidence wholly or in part. In this case, each party shall bear 50 per cent of the translation fee. If a party refuses to pay the fee, it will be deemed to have acknowledged that the translation submitted by the other party is correct.

**9.61** Normally, any evidence originating from abroad shall be notarized by a notary organ in the respective country and then be verified by the Chinese embassy or consulate in that country. This requirement also applies to evidence originating from Hong Kong, Macau and Taiwan. However, it does not apply to evidence which can be obtained through public channels in mainland China or the authenticity of which can be sufficiently supported by other evidence or is acknowledged by the opposite party.

**9.62** In practice, the evidence of patent documents, articles in scientific journals, reference books or any other document which has been recorded by an authority forms the strongest evidence. In contrast, it is much more difficult to obtain recognition of witness testimonies or evidence proving prior use such as internal user manuals, email communications and advertisements which have not been officially recorded in the course of patent invalidation and infringement procedures.

### *(c) Requirements with respect to amendments*[32]

**9.63** In principle, any amendment to the patent shall be limited to the claims and meet the following requirements:

(1) the title of the subject-matter of a claim may not be changed;
(2) the scope of protection may not be extended beyond the scope of the granted patent;
(3) the amendment may not go beyond the scope of the disclosure contained in the initial description and claims;
(4) technical features disclosed in the description may not afterwards be incorporated into the claims.

**9.64** Requirements (2) and (3) above are the same as the requirements contained in Articles 123(2) and (3) EPC. Counterparts to the strict requirements (1) and (4), however, cannot be found in the EPO provisions; European patent professionals should pay particular attention to these when drafting Chinese patent applications, especially when applying for claims.

32 Examination Guidelines, Part IV, Chapter 3, 4.6.

Furthermore, subject to the above requirements, the manner of amendment is generally limited to three permitted types, that is, deleting one or more claims, combining claims, and deleting one or several technical solutions which are defined in parallel in one claim. The combination of claims means that two or more claims, which depend on the same independent claim and have no dependent relation with each other, may be combined to form a new claim, and the new claim should contain the technical features of all the dependent claims thus combined. Such combination may only be made in response to the request for invalidation, so as to overcome the objections based on the grounds for invalidation submitted by the petitioner or raised by PRB. **9.65**

In a recent decision handed down by the SPC in case *Simcere v PRB*,[33] the SPC applied a more liberal approach than the very strict requirement (4) above. In this case, the patentee sought to amend the claimed range from '1:10–30' to a specific ratio of '1:30' during an invalidation action, which was rejected by PRB under the requirement (4). The SPC held that the amendment does not go beyond the scope of the original specification because a composition of 1mg:30mg is disclosed in one of the embodiments as the preferred ratio and that it is unreasonable to disallow the amendment simply on the basis that it does not belong to one of the three permitted types of amendment as set out in the Examination Guidelines. Although the SPC found that PRB had interpreted the provision on amendment too strictly, it is still unknown if SIPO will amend the Examination Guidelines regarding the requirement (4). **9.66**

In light of these comparably strict requirements, it is recommended that applicants should consider possible fallbacks already at the stage of claim drafting and to protect subject-matter which has only been disclosed in the description by filing a divisional application during the examination procedure. **9.67**

### (d) *Method of examination*

Similar to re-examination cases, invalidation cases are examined by a collegiate panel. The composition of a collegiate panel responsible for an invalidation procedure does not differ from a panel in charge of re-examination, as outlined at 9.43. In addition to the general principles of establishing collegiate panels as mentioned before, some specific limitations apply to the establishment of a panel in charge of invalidation. If, after PRB has decided to uphold a patent right fully or partially, the same petitioner files a new request for invalidating the same patent on different grounds or on the basis of different evidence, members of the panel which has made the previous decision shall not participate in the new invalidation procedure. Where an examination decision has **9.68**

33 (2011) IP Administrative Ruling No. 17 of the Supreme People's Court.

been overturned by an effective court judgment, the new examination shall, in general, be carried out by a newly composed panel.[34]

**9.69** At the early stage of an invalidation procedure, the panel always carries the examination out in writing. Usually, PRB transfers the relevant documents to the parties and requires them to submit their responses within one month after receipt of the documents. If a party fails to respond in due time, it shall be deemed to have been aware of the content of the documents and to have no objection to facts, grounds and evidence contained therein. Where a party's response is deficient or if PRB introduces other invalidation grounds and evidence at its own initiative, PRB may submit a 'Notification of Examination on Request for Invalidation' to both parties. The parties shall respond within one month from receipt of the notification. If a party fails to respond, it shall be deemed to have been aware of the facts, grounds and evidence mentioned in the notification and to have no objections to them.

**9.70** At a later stage of the invalidation procedure, PRB may, at the request of the parties or if the necessity arises from the examination, invite the parties to an oral hearing by issuing a 'Notification of Oral Proceedings'. The oral proceedings which aim at accelerating the invalidation procedure and at providing the parties with the opportunity to communicate their observations before the panel are quite similar to the oral opposition proceedings in EPO.

**9.71** Based on the results of the examination, PRB decides to either revoke the patent wholly or in part *ex tunc* or to uphold the validity of the patent. In recent years, PRB has accelerated the invalidation procedures. It currently takes 6.5 months on average to make a decision as to validity,[35] which is much shorter than the average duration of opposition proceedings in EPO.

### *(e) Termination of an invalidation procedure*

**9.72** Before PRB decides on the request for invalidation, the invalidation procedure may be terminated if the invalidation request is withdrawn or deemed to be withdrawn. However, even if a request has been withdrawn or is deemed to be withdrawn, PRB may continue the examination at its own initiative if it thinks that the patent can still be invalidated wholly or in part based on the examination performed by it so far. Therefore, if both parties agree to terminate the invalidation procedure before a decision as to validity has been made, the petitioner should withdraw his or her invalidation request in a sufficiently clear manner at latest one week before the scheduled date of the oral hearing.

34 Examination Guidelines, Part IV, Chapter 1, 3.

35 Annual Report of SIPO 2012.

PRB's decisions as to validity can, within three months from the receipt of the decision, still be challenged by instituting an administrative case in the Intermediate People's Court No.1 of the City of Beijing, which is also the first instance court dealing with the invalidation cases. If within these three months no party proceeds in court, the decision of PRB becomes effective and the invalidation procedure will be terminated. Otherwise, the invalidation procedure will be continued in court, with PRB as defendant and the party other than the appellant as the third party. The first instance decision of the court can be appealed in the Higher People's Court of the City of Beijing. If the final court decision upholds the PRB decision, the invalidation procedure will come to an end. Otherwise, the court will remit the case to PRB for further examination. According to this author's experience, a first instance decision is made after approximately 6 months, whereas a second instance ruling can be expected after approximately 10 months. It is also interesting to note that from 2009 to 2011, 20 per cent of the invalidation decisions made by PRB were challenged in court and 8 per cent of them were overturned by a court judgment.[36] 9.73

Finally, it should be noted that the official fee for an invalidation procedure at PRB or for a court appeal is much lower than the opposition, limitation or revocation fee raised by EPO. 9.74

## E. GENERAL PROCEDURAL MATTERS

### 1. Time limit[37]

Similar to EPO, SIPO distinguishes between two types of periods. To the first type belong periods of legally determined durations. Most of the time limits of this type are calculated from a fixed date, for example, the 20-year patent term from the filing date or the 12-month period for claiming priority from the first filing date. The second type are those periods which are specified by the examiner in various notifications under the Patent Act and the Implementing Regulations thereof, for example, time limits notified to the applicant to make a response to an Office Action, or to submit a Chinese translation of the certificate on the transfer of the priority right. All these specified time limits are calculated from a fictitious receipt of notification, that is, from the 15th day following the date of issuing the notification by SIPO. It is interesting to note that EPO calculates a specified time limit in the same way but starting from the 9.75

36 Explanations of SIPO on the draft amendments to the Chinese Patent Law for comment released in January 2013.

37 Examination Guidelines, Part V, Chapter 7.

tenth day following dispatch of the notification from EPO.[38] Moreover, for a notification or decision delivered by post, if the applicant can prove that the actual date of receipt is later than the fictitious date of receipt, the actual date of receipt shall be considered. The latter is applied by both EPO and SIPO.[39]

**9.76** Only the time limits specified by SIPO may be extended upon an applicant's request which must state justified reasons and be accompanied by a fee for requesting the extension. Such extensions shall not exceed two months and, in general, may be extended only once.[40] It should be noted, however, that in the course of invalidation proceedings, the time limit specified by the Patent Re-examination Board may not be extended.[41]

### 2. Restoration of rights[42]

**9.77** The legal basis for restoring a right which has been lost due to non-observance of a time limit is given in Rule 6 of the Implementing Regulations. On the one hand, paragraphs (1) and (2) of Rule 6 provide for two remedies for non-observance of time limits which will be further outlined below. On the other hand, Rule 6(5) rules out restoration of rights which are lost due to non-observance of the following periods: the six-month grace period for non-prejudicial disclosures under Article 24 of Chinese Patent Act, the 12-month priority period, the 20-year patent term and the two-year limitation for instituting infringement proceedings (statute of limitation). If the restoration of rights has been successful, the legal consequences of the failure to observe the time limit shall be deemed not to have ensued.

**9.78** Based on Rule 6(2) Implementing Rules to the Patent Act, where a time limit is not observed by a party concerned by any justified reason except *force majeure*, resulting in loss of a right, the party may, within two months from receipt of the relevant notification, request SIPO to restore the right. Although the requester is required to state justified reasons for the request, there is no strict limitation to possible reasons. In practice, such a request is easily granted if the prescribed fee is paid and the delayed act is completed by the requester. Therefore, the remedy of Rule 6(2) is very similar to the further processing of the European patent application under Article 121 and Rule 135 EPC, which allow further processing of a European application merely upon payment of the prescribed fee and completion of the delayed act, without even requiring the applicant to

38 R. 126(2) EPC.
39 Examination Guidelines, Part V, Chapter 7, 2.
40 Examination Guidelines, Part V, Chapter 7, 4.
41 R. 71 of the Implementing Regulations.
42 Examination Guidelines, Part V, Chapter 7, 6.

state a reason. Without doubt, the restoration of rights under Rule 6(2) is a reliable remedy for the applicant.

9.79 In accordance with Rule 6(1) Implementing Regulations, where the time limit is not observed because of *force majeure* resulting in loss of rights, the party concerned may, within two months from removal of the cause of non-compliance and at latest within two years immediately following the expiry of the unobserved period, request SIPO to restore its rights. The European counterparts to the restoration of rights regulation in Rule 6(1) are the re-establishment of rights provisions under Article 122 and Rule 136 EPC. However, the European provisions differ from the Chinese ones in several respects. Two of these differences will be briefly outlined. First, the second period given in Rule 6(1) Implementing Regulations is two years instead of only one year as provided by Rule 136(1) EPC. Moreover, in the case of non-compliance with the 12-month period for claiming priority, it is impossible to rely on Rule 6(1) Implementing Regulations to restore the right of claiming right of priority. In contrast, Rule 136(1) EPC allows the re-establishment of the right within two months from the removal of the cause of non-compliance with the period and within two months from the expiry of the 12-month period. Similar to the prerequisites for the re-establishment of rights under the EPC, the restoration of rights under Rule 6(1) Implementing Regulations requires that the requester has exercised all due care, which must be proven convincingly. Such proof requirement enhances the uncertainty as to whether the requested remedy will be granted.

### 3. Suspension of procedures[43]

9.80 The suspension of the SIPO procedures during entitlement proceedings aims at securing the rights of a concerned party and allows it to prove its entitlement to the patent application or the patent before an administrative authority or a court. Rules 86(1) and 87 of the Implementing Regulations specify the conditions to be met for suspension of the procedures, which are as follows:

(1) a third party, as the requester, provides evidence to SIPO proving that the dispute over the entitlement to the patent application or the patent in which it is involved has been accepted by an administrative authority or a court; or

43 Examination Guidelines, Part V, Chapter 7, 7.

(2) a third party or a court, as the requester, requests SIPO to suspend the administrative procedures so as to enable the execution of the court-approved property preservation measures targeted at the entitlement to the patent application or the patent right.

**9.81** Under condition (1), the duration of suspension shall generally not exceed one year. If no decision on the entitlement dispute can be made by the administrative authority or the court within this year, the requester may request an extension of the suspension period once. Such extension shall not exceed six months. Under condition (2), the duration of the suspension shall normally be six months. Afterwards, if the court orders continuation of the property preservation, it shall notify SIPO to extend the suspension by a further six months.

**9.82** Under these two conditions, a variety of procedures may be suspended, including:

- preliminary examination, substantive examination, re-examination, grant of a patent and invalidation procedure;
- deeming a patent application to be withdrawn, abandoning a patent and terminating a patent due to non-payment of annual fee;
- withdrawal of a patent application, abandonment of a patent, change of the name of the applicant or patentee, transfer of right to apply for a patent or transfer of a patent, and registration of the pledge of a patent.

**9.83** Comparing the practices of SIPO and EPO in respect of suspending the procedures reveals the following differences:

- The proceedings for grant before the publication of the European patent application shall not be stayed (Rule14(1) EPC); SIPO does not provide for such restriction.
- After grant, SIPO may suspend any procedure (for example, the procedure of invalidation, of patent right transfer, of registering the pledge of the patent), whereas EPO may only suspend the opposition proceedings (Rule 78 EPC).
- If, upon a final decision of an administrative authority or a court pursuant to which a party other than the applicant shall be entitled to the grant of the patent, the EPC gives such other party more choices with regard to possible remedies than the corresponding Chinese provisions. Under Article 61 EPC, such other party may prosecute the application as its own application in lieu of the applicant, file a new application with respect to the same invention, or request that the application be refused. A provision

which would correspond to Article 61 EPC is not available in China. The relevant Chinese provisions only mention that the suspended procedure shall be resumed (Rule 86(3) Implementing Regulations) after the change of the owner of the relevant right in accordance with the final decision.

It is also interesting to note that the EPC provides for another category of staying proceedings to which no counterpart can be found in the Chinese provisions, namely the interruption of proceedings under Rule 142 EPC, which aims at providing a remedy for failed time limits due to the medical and financial hardship of the applicant, the patentee and his or her professional representative. The remedy can make non-observance of time limits to be regarded as not having occurred and interrupt the time periods, which start anew or continue to run after resumption of the proceedings. Obviously, such remedy is favourable for applicants and patentees. In contrast, its lack in China appears to be inconsistent with the current Chinese policy of encouraging Chinese individuals and entities to file more patent applications and to own more patents. **9.84**

### 4. Inspection of files[44]

By virtue of Rule 118(1) Implementing Regulations, any person may, upon approval by SIPO, consult or copy the files of the published applications for patents, utility models and designs as well as the relevant registers, and may request SIPO to issue a copy of extracts from the patent register. Under the general principle that applications which have not yet been published shall not be made available for inspection, SIPO has established the following principles, procedures and limitations for the inspection of files: **9.85**

If an application has been published but the grant of the patent is not yet announced, the contents in the file which may be inspected by anyone are limited to those available until the date of the publication, that is, the application documents, formality documents directly related to the application, publication documents, notifications and decisions sent by SIPO to the applicant during the preliminary examination and the text of the observations submitted by the applicant in response to the notifications issued before the publication. **9.86**

If the grant of a patent, utility model or design patent has been announced, the contents in the file which may be inspected by anyone extend to the application documents, the formality documents directly relating to the application, the **9.87**

44 Examination Guidelines, Part V, Chapter 4, 5.

pamphlet of the patent certificate, the patent register, the patent evaluation report (if available), the notifications and decisions issued by the Patent Office or the PRB, and the text of the observations submitted by the applicant in response to the notifications. Hereby, the notifications and decisions issued by the PRB in the re-examination or invalidation proceedings and the observations of the parties concerned in response thereto may be inspected by any party only after these proceedings have been closed. Otherwise, if the re-examination or invalidation proceeding are still ongoing, inspections can be carried out only for special reasons after approval of the responsible department of SIPO.

**9.88** In addition, public access to the contents of a file will be denied if:

- the contents concern the interests of the State or are kept in the file only for internal operation or management needs of SIPO;
- access to these contents may cause damage to the legitimate interest of the concerned party or may involve privacy or trade secrets, and so on;
- the contents are related to a re-examination or invalidation procedure which has been terminated because the request for re-examination or invalidation has been deemed not to have been filed, has not been accepted, has been withdrawn by the requester himself or has been deemed to have been withdrawn;
- access is sought to contents which are related to the substantive examination of applications which have been finally rejected.

**9.89** Currently, files of Chinese patent applications and patents are mainly inspected with the help of copies of these files. The procedures are as follows:

- the requester files a written request and pays the prescribed fees,
- a staff member of SIPO retrieves the file from the department where the file is kept, where applicable, lays aside those documents to which access is prohibited, and notifies the requester to agree upon date and location of inspection,
- the requester inspects the documents at the date and location agreed upon and obtains a paper copy of the documents as required.

**9.90** Application files which, in the past, had only been available in paper form are increasingly made available on the internet. Recently, SIPO has made substantial progress in further enhancing its web presence (http://cpquery.sipo.gov.cn) towards enabling the inspection of files. The site can be used without request and is free of charge. At present, it provides the public with the following information pertaining to applications filed after 10 February 2010:

- general information including the bibliographic data;
- information pertaining to examination, including:
  - description, drawing(s), claim(s) and abstract;
  - intermediate documents, for example, the request for substantive examination, certificate of assignment of the priority right;
  - notifications and Office Actions.

However, the observations submitted by the applicants in response to the notifications and Office Actions cannot be found under the item 'examination information' on the website.

As SIPO intends to continuously and intensively develop this website with user interfaces in different foreign languages, it can be expected that this system will be used by increasing numbers of domestic and foreign users in the near future. **9.91**

# 10

# PCT APPLICATIONS

**Toby Mak**



## A. INTRODUCTION

**10.01** Examination of a PCT application upon entry into the Chinese national phase is very similar to the examination of a non-PCT application. However, there are some practical points to observe, and knowing these can ease prosecution in the Chinese national phase ('PCT-CN entry') and enable the applicant to obtain better patent protection at reduced costs.

## B. MINIMUM REQUIREMENTS FOR PCT-CN ENTRY

It is important to note the minimum requirements for effecting the PCT-CN entry. In order to successfully enter the Chinese national phase, the following three requirements must be fulfilled: 10.02

1. A written statement in Chinese stating that the applicant desires to enter the Chinese national phase indicating the PCT application number and the type of protection sought by such entry. Specifically, this written declaration must indicate whether the applicant seeks invention patent or utility model protection. This requirement is typically fulfilled by completing a proper application form.
2. Payment of application fee, publication fee, and restoration fee (this will be explained later) if necessary.
3. The specification in Chinese, including description and claims.

If any one of the above is not satisfied, the Chinese SIPO will deem the international application not to have entered the Chinese national phase.

The following should be observed: 10.03

- The applicant must indicate whether invention patent or utility model protection is sought. If the type of protection sought is not indicated, if a type of protection outside invention patent or utility model protection is indicated (for example design protection) or if both invention patent and utility model protection are indicated, the SIPO will treat the application as not having entered the national phase.
- Application fee and publication fee (and restoration fee, if necessary) must be paid at the date of PCT-CN entry. This is noteworthy as, by contrast, for a non-PCT application it is possible to delay payment of these fees to two months from the application date.
- A Chinese specification must be submitted when entering the Chinese national phase. A specification in another language would preclude the PCT-CN entry. This is different, for example, from the Japanese practice, where it is possible to submit a specification in another language first and to later hand in a Japanese specification within a month from the entry into the Japanese national phase.
- The deadline for entering the Chinese national phase is 30 months from the earliest priority date, or the PCT application date if no priority is claimed during the international phase. However, it is possible to effectively extend this deadline by two months by paying a fee, utilizing the two

months restoration period to which applicants are legally entitled. Therefore, the restoration period can also be used to delay submission of the Chinese specification by two months.

## C. PREFERENCE OF INVENTION PATENT OVER UTILITY MODEL IN THE COURSE OF PCT-CN ENTRY

**10.04** Even though the applicant can opt for utility model protection in the course of PCT-CN entry, such a choice is not advisable. This is because the purpose of pursuing a Chinese utility model is to obtain early protection after a quick preliminary examination. However, if the applicant uses the full international 30-month period, utility model protection through PCT would be granted at the latest after a period of 40 to 48 months from the earliest priority date. This would run counter to the purpose of seeking utility model instead of invention patent protection.

**10.05** Therefore, as typical PCT-CN entries aim at invention patent protection, the following observations will focus on prosecuting PCT-CN entries as Chinese invention patent applications.

## D. FURTHER REQUIREMENTS RELATED TO PCT-CN ENTRY

**10.06** Apart from the above requirements, the following is also required in the course of a PCT-CN entry:

(a) The written declaration (that is, the application form) shall include the title of the invention, the address of the applicant(s), name of the inventor, and all of these shall correspond with the indications made in the PCT application.

(b) Chinese translations of the PCT abstract, figures, and figure accompanying the abstract if these were submitted in another language during the international phase. If the PCT figures are accompanied by text in a non-Chinese language, such text must also be translated into Chinese.

(c) If the applicant has changed during the international phase, in particular due to an assignment of the application right or due to a merger of the applicant with another firm, documents showing the new applicant's rights to the application shall be submitted. However, if only the name of the applicant has changed and such change has been recorded during the international phase (form PCT/IB/306), additional documents do not have to be submitted unless the Chinese Examiner specifically asks for them.

(d) Additional fees other than the application fee and the publication fee, including fees for claiming priority, excess claims (in excess of 10), and excess pages (in excess of 30).

If any of the above requirements are not fulfilled, the SIPO will issue a notification requesting correction of the respective defects. If the applicant fails to respond to such notice by correcting the defects in due time, SIPO will treat the national application as having been withdrawn. If the above minimum and further requirements are fulfilled, the Chinese SIPO will issue a notification stating the corresponding Chinese application number and the date of entry into the Chinese national phase. It is advisable to resolve the above issues when entering the national phase, as delays may result in the application being deemed to have been withdrawn. **10.07**

## E. ADDITIONAL REQUIREMENTS REGARDING PCT-CN ENTRY

Failure to meet the requirements under (b) has the consequence that SIPO will treat the application as not having entered the national phase, whereas failure to meet the requirements under (d) would result in the PCT-CN entry being deemed to be withdrawn after entry into national phase. Therefore, it is vital to fulfil these requirements. **10.08**

In contrast, the requirements outlined below are less strict. Failure to meet them would not result in the application being deemed to not have entered the national phase or to have been withdrawn. Only those parts of the application to which the respective requirements are related will become ineffective. **10.09**

If applicable, the following additional materials may have to be submitted to SIPO: **10.10**

(1) Declaration that a non-prejudicial disclosure of the invention has occurred; materials supporting such declaration should be submitted within two months from the date of entry into the Chinese national phase.

(2) Information and details of the deposition of biological samples, for example genetically modified bacteria, to be submitted within four months from the date of entry into the Chinese national phase.

(3) Where the completion of the invention involves the use of genetic

material, a declaration indicating the source and/or origin of such genetic material should be submitted at the Chinese national phase entry.

**10.11** As mentioned above, failure to fulfil any of the above requirements will not result in deeming the PCT-CN entry to have been withdrawn, but only those parts of the application to which these requirements are related will become ineffective.

## F. EFFECT OF PRIORITY DOCUMENTS SUBMITTED DURING THE PCT INTERNATIONAL PHASE

**10.12** A priority document submitted during the international phase in due time will also support the respective priority claim in China and it should not be necessary to submit another priority document in the course of entering the Chinese national phase unless the Chinese Examiner specifically requests so.

## G. BAN ON THE RESTORATION OF PRIORITY CLAIMS

**10.13** In certain countries, for example, the United Kingdom, it is possible to restore the priority claim even if the PCT application has been filed after 12 months from the earliest priority date. However, according to Article 6 Implementing Regulations to the Chinese Patent Law ('Implementing Regulations'), such practice is not allowed in China. Therefore, even if a priority claim has been restored during the international phase, such restoration will not be recognized in China.

## H. ISSUES TO BE OBSERVED WITH RESPECT TO EARLY ENTRY INTO NATIONAL PHASE

**10.14** It is possible to enter the Chinese national phase well before the expiry of the 30-month period for the international phase. However, if the aim of such early entry is to seek early grant, it should be noted that a special request under Article 23(2) PCT should be submitted. Otherwise, the early PCT-CN entry will be put in abeyance until expiry of the 30-month deadline, which will, as a matter of course, also delay the grant of the patent.

Furthermore, if the International Bureau has not transmitted the PCT application to SIPO at the time of such early PCT-CN entries, it is necessary to submit a certified copy of the PCT application as filed with the International Bureau. 10.15

## I. PROCEDURES AND FLOWS INVOLVED IN THE PROSECUTION OF PCT-CN ENTRY

The general flowchart is shown as below (Figure 10.1): 10.16

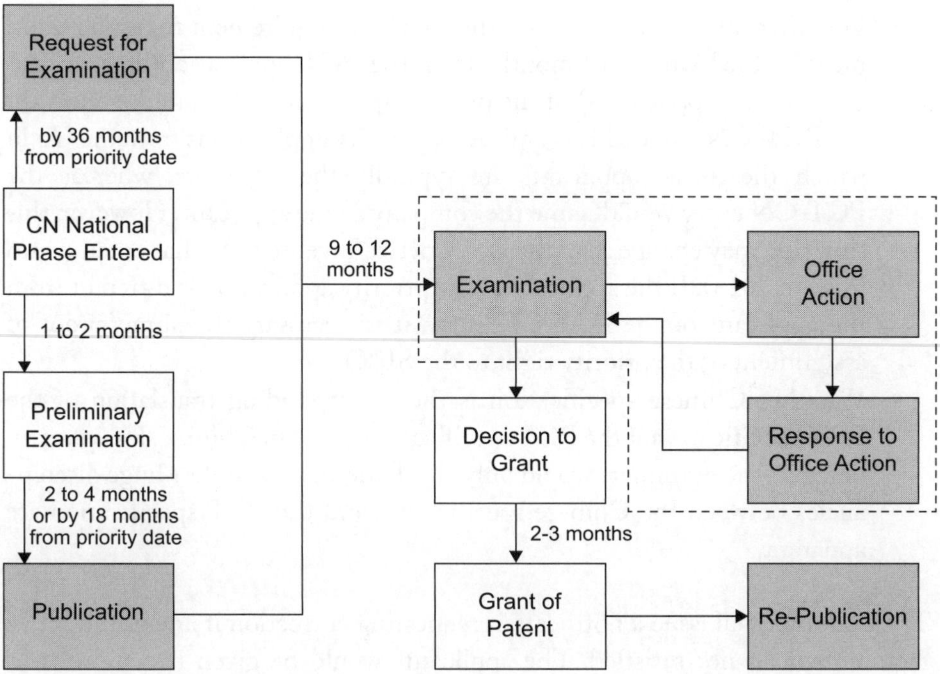


*Figure 10.1 CN Invention patent application: Flowchart for PCT national phase entry*

It should be noted that the procedures of re-examination are not contained in the above Figure 10.1. Specifically, when an invention patent application is rejected by the examiner during the substantive examination stage, for the application to continue, the applicant has to file a request for re-examination. This, however, is a separate process, so that the procedures involved are not included in Figure 10.1. 10.17

As noted above, once a PCT application has entered the Chinese national phase, it will go through preliminary examination which can last between one 10.18

or two months. During this period, the examiner checks whether the formalities mentioned under (b) and (d) above are met; in particular:

- Whether the correct type of protection to be sought is indicated. As mentioned, the applicant may opt for invention or for utility model protection.
- For foreign applicants, whether a Chinese patent firm has been appointed, and a proper Power of Attorney has been submitted.
- Whether the name and address of the applicant are property indicated.
- Whether the specification has been submitted in Chinese, using simplified Chinese characters.
- Whether the priority claim satisfies the legal requirement that such claim must be filed within 12 months from the PCT application date; and/or whether the applicant(s) of the priority application(s) is/are the one(s) of the PCT-CN entry (this is typical for priority applications from the US in which the initial applicants are typically the inventors, whereas the PCT-CN entry would name the company as the applicant. However, this situation may change after the US America Inventors Act has entered into force in 2013). If the applicant of the priority application is different from the applicant of the PCT-CN entry, it is necessary to submit proof of assignment of the priority right to the SIPO.
- Whether Chinese specification is the corresponding translation of the PCT specification if the PCT specification is not in Chinese. However, in practice, the examiners would only check the abstract unless huge discrepancies between the Chinese specification and the PCT specification are apparent.

**10.19** The examiner will issue a notification requesting correction if any of the above requirements is not satisfied. The applicants would be given two months to correct the defects. Failure to respond to the notification properly and in due time will result in the refusal of the application.

**10.20** After the preliminary examination is finished and all formality requirements have been satisfied, the application will be arranged for publication as soon as possible. This is because a Chinese application should be published shortly after 18 months from the earliest priority date and the PCT-CN entry typically occurs after this 18-month publication period.

## J. OPPORTUNITIES FOR VOLUNTARY AMENDMENT

A Request for Examination of a non-PCT application must be filed within three years (36 months) from the earliest priority date. Otherwise, the Chinese invention patent application would be deemed to have been withdrawn. Apparently, the deadline for filing the Request for Examination (36 months from the earliest priority date) expires shortly after the 30-month deadline for entering the Chinese national phase entry. Typically, various notices will be issued by SIPO within the remaining six months if the applicant has made full use of the 30-months period, which include the following: **10.21**

- Notice of confirmation of entry into the Chinese national phase (including a Chinese patent application number).
- Notice that preliminary examination has been passed.
- If necessary, notice that defects found in the course of preliminary examination have been corrected.
- Notice of publication.

It is generally advisable to reduce the number of communications as much as possible during this six-month period, so as to avoid any matters being inadvertently overlooked. Therefore, it is advisable to file a request for examination in the course of PCT-CN entry, otherwise it may be overlooked by mistake. The filing of such a request for examination at the date of entering the national phase does not cause any harm to the applicant. In particular, it will not affect the chances of filing voluntary amendments to the Chinese application. **10.22**

In case of invention patent applications entering the national phase, the applicant has only two chances to voluntarily amend the patent application as follows: **10.23**

(1) During the filing of the request for examination.
(2) Within a three-month period after receipt of the notice that the application has entered substantive examination.

These chances to voluntarily amend the application should be treated seriously for the following two reasons: **10.24**

(a) After grant, during invalidation proceedings, the patentee can amend the claims only in two specific ways which do not allow him to extend the original scope of the claims. He can only delete existing claims, or he can combine dependent claims with those claims they immediately depend upon. That is, if a feature is described only in the description but not included in the claims as granted, the patentee is not allowed to add this feature to the claims in the course of invalidation proceedings, even though such an additional feature could improve the chances of the claim being upheld.

(b) When responding to an Office Action, the Chinese Patent Examination Guidelines stipulate that an examiner shall reject addition of any claims, irrespective of whether such claims are dependent or independent (Part II, Chapter 8, 5.2.1.3 Patent Examination Guidelines).

**10.25** These restrictions on post-grant amendments have been challenged by the Supreme People's Court in *Shanghai Jiahua Technology Inc. v The Chinese Patent Re-examination Board*. The court opined that such restrictions would be overly restrictive. Nevertheless, the above restrictions still pertain to the current practice of SIPO, so that applicants are well-advised to take them into account and to make wise use of the two pre-grant amendment chances. Otherwise, if the applicant misses the opportunity to add important claims to the pending application, he may afterwards find it difficult to defend his patent in the course of an invalidity attack.

**10.26** However, procedurally, the notification of entry into substantive examination will only be issued after filing the request for examination, as such notice will only be issued after publication of the invention patent application *and* filing of the request for examination. This is highlighted by the flowchart in Figure 10.2.

**10.27** As shown in Figure 10.2, even though a request for examination is filed upon entry into the national phase, the applicant still has a chance to file voluntary amendments within the three-months period.

**10.28** If, in case of an international application entering China's national phase, filing the request for examination is submitted within 36 months from the earliest priority date, the applicant will have two chances to submit voluntary amendments within a very short period of time, usually within two to three months. Apparently, such timing is not very useful.

## K. PCT SPECIFICATION AS ORIGINAL DISCLOSURE AND OPPORTUNITIES TO CORRECT TRANSLATION ERRORS

**10.29** The major distinction between PCT-CN entry and an original Chinese patent application is that the specification as filed in the PCT application is considered

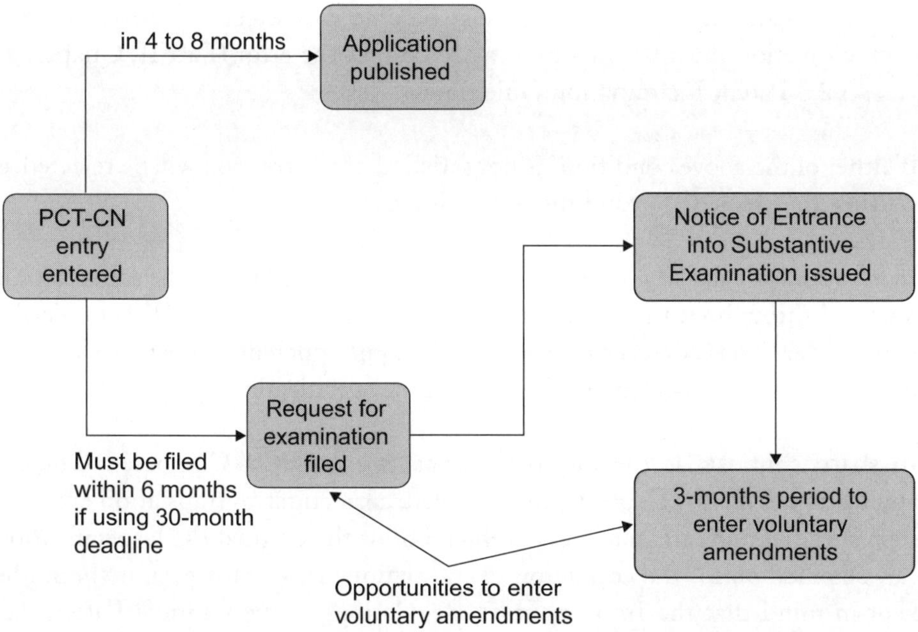


*Figure 10.2 Timeline of opportunities to enter voluntary amendments*

to be the original disclosure when the PCT application enters China. For example, if the original PCT application is in English, the original disclosure is also considered to be this English version when the application enters China's national phase.

By contrast, in case of a non-PCT application, the original disclosure is the Chinese specification as filed with SIPO. Any other documents filed in other languages than Chinese do not form part of the original disclosure, for example, the certified priority document, specification, and/or other written materials in other languages. **10.30**

One consequence of this difference is that translation errors in the Chinese specification pertaining to non-PCT applications are much more difficult to correct than errors in specifications pertaining to PCT-CN based Chinese applications, unless such errors could be corrected solely on grounds of the Chinese specification. Corrections to Chinese specifications share many similarities with the European practice. That is, valid corrections have to meet the following two conditions: **10.31**

(1) The error is apparent to a person skilled in the art.

(2) A person skilled in the art must be able to correct the error, and the correction must be the only way to correct the error (Part II, Chapter 8, 5.2.3 Patent Examination Guidelines).

If either of the above conditions is not satisfied, the correction will be rejected as causing an extension beyond the initial disclosure.

**10.32** In many cases, translation errors tend to be systematic. That is, the same error is repeated throughout the specification. In such cases, condition (1) is especially hard to meet because the error would not become apparent to a person skilled in the art, due to its repeated use throughout the specification.

**10.33** In sharp contrast, as the original disclosure of a PCT-CN based Chinese application is the PCT specification as filed, corrections to translation errors in such specifications are much less problematic as the original PCT specification can be relied on for the correction of translation errors. However, it should be kept in mind that the Implementing Regulations to the Chinese Patent Act provide only two opportunities for voluntary corrections.

**10.34** As the Chinese Patent Examination Guidelines stipulate that the applicant shall only respond to objections raised by the examiner when reacting to an Office Action, technically, translation errors cannot be corrected voluntarily when responding to an Office Action, unless the examiner's objection is directly related to such translation error. The examiner could then reject such corrections as not responding to the objections raised. However, in practice, some examiners may allow such voluntary corrections when responding to an Office Action, even if the Office Action was not related to the error.

## L. CONSEQUENCES OF TRANSLATION ERRORS AFTER PATENT GRANT

**10.35** According to Rule 117 Implementing Regulations to the Chinese Patent Act, in case of translation errors in a Chinese patent granted on grounds of a PCT application which extend the scope of protection beyond the scope of the claim in the original language, the protection scope of the respective claim shall be reduced to the scope which is represented by the claim in the original language application. In the reverse situation where the scope of the claim in Chinese is narrower than the scope of the claim in the original language, the protection scope of the Chinese claim shall be determined to be the scope as granted by the Chinese patent.

10.36 In short, if there is any difference between the scope of the claim of the Chinese patent and the claim in the original language of a PCT-CN entry, the narrower scope prevails.

## M. BASIS OF EXCESS CLAIM FEES, AND SUGGESTION TO REDUCE SUCH FEES

10.37 The basis of calculating excess claim fees during the PCT-CN entry is the number of claims published in the PCT publication. Reducing the number of claims during the PCT-CN entry will *not* result in reduced excess claim fees. In light of the above observations regarding the non-permissibility of adding new claims during the prosecution of the Chinese application, there is also *no* reason to reduce the number of claims during the PCT-CN entry, as a reduction of claims will only weaken the later patent, for example, in case of an invalidation attack. More importantly, such reduction would not have any effect on the excess claim fees. Therefore, reducing the number of claims in the course of PCT-CN entry is not recommended.

10.38 Therefore, avoiding or limiting excess claim fees should be considered far in advance of a PCT-CN entry, initially at the stage of filing the PCT application, at which the applicant may limit the number of claims to 10, which would then be published in the PCT publication. Other claims could be included in the PCT specification, for example, in the form of so-called consistory clauses in the description, to form a basis for additional claims. After entering the Chinese national phase, these new claims could then be added at the above-mentioned two opportunities for voluntary pre-grant amendments. Surprisingly, the SIPO does not raise excess claim fees for such voluntary amendments. Therefore, this is a useful technique to limit the excess claim fees to be paid in China. Unfortunately, such technique can only be used in China but not in the course of entries into US and European national phases.

## N. HANDLING OF INVENTIONS LACKING UNITY

10.39 During searches carried out in the course of the International Searches, the PCT examiner may consider that some claims do not conform with the unity requirement, and request excess fees for searches related to the additional subject matter. If the applicant does not pay such excess fees, a search on said additional subject matter will not be carried out.

**10.40** When entering the Chinese national phase, if SIPO finds that the opinion of the PCT examiner as to unity is correct (which it would do in most cases), it will request the applicant to pay the fees for restoring the unity of the application within a prescribed period. If the fees are not paid in due time, the subject matter which has remained unsearched during the International Searches will be considered to have been withdrawn.

## O. HANDLING OF AMENDMENTS MADE DURING THE INTERNATIONAL PHASE

**10.41** It is possible to amend a PCT application during the international phase under Articles 19 or 41 PCT.

**10.42** Amendments filed under Article 19 PCT are restricted to amendments to the claims only, which are generally filed in response to the issuance of the International Search Report (ISR), and/or the Written Opinion of the International Search Authority (ISA). The deadline for submitting such amendments is either 16 months from the priority date or two months from the date of issuance of the ISR, whichever is later. If the ISR is issued in due time according to Rule 42 Regulations of the PCT, that is, three months from the date of receipt of such copy by the International Searching Authority or nine months from the priority date, whichever expires later, this means that the deadline for submitting amendments under Article 19 PCT would be 16 months from the priority date at the latest. If this is the case, such amendments pursuant to Article 19 PCT will be published during the international phase.

**10.43** Amendments made in accordance with Article 41 PCT are submitted under Chapter 2 of the PCT in the course of the International Preliminary Examination. In recent years, requests for International Preliminary Examination have become rare, as they are no longer necessary to extend the deadline for entering various national phases to at least 30 months from the priority date. In any event, amendments filed under Article 41 PCT could be much more extensive. Specifically, amendments under Article 41 PCT can be related to the claims, description, and drawings. In contrast to amendments under Article 19 PCT, amendments under Article 41 PCT will not be published during the international phase.

**10.44** It is important to note that whatever amendments are made during the international phase, they will *not* be published by the Chinese SIPO after entering the Chinese national phase. More specifically, the Chinese publication will correspond with the specification, including the claims, as published in the

PCT A1 or A2 publication. For the applicant, this has the commercially disadvantageous consequence that such amendments, which for example may be aiming at capturing specific types of infringement, would not be able to result in compensation if infringements covered by such amendments occurred during the period between publication and grant of the Chinese patent.

# 11

# CONFIDENTIALITY EXAMINATION

**Stefan Luginbuehl**[1]



## A. INTRODUCTION

**11.01** The revised Patent Act introduced in 2009 the so-called 'confidentiality examination' for any inventions made in China[2] (including Hong Kong and Macau) and for which patent protection is sought outside of China.

**11.02** The confidentiality examination consists of a mandatory screening and disclosure of the inventions made in China to SIPO and other related ministries for each relevant technology sector. It thus aims at examining which technologies are researched in China and who applies for patents. Furthermore, it avoids an uncontrolled outflow of inventions made in China.[3]

**11.03** A request for confidentiality examination has to be filed with SIPO prior to filing an application abroad. If the applicant does not file a request for a confidentiality examination and directly applies for a patent outside of China in relation to an invention made in China, no patent will be granted to the applicant for the territory of China,[4] as any subsequent patent application in China will be refused on the grounds of lack of patentability.[5] Furthermore,

1 Any views expressed in this chapter are those of the author and do not necessarily reflect the views of the European Patent Office.

2 There is no confidentiality examination for designs.

3 Cf. also Peter Ganea, 'China's Amended Legal Regime on Patents for Inventions and Utility Models', [2010] 5 *JIPLP* 650, 653.

4 Art. 20(4) Chinese Patent Act.

5 Art. 20(5) Chinese Patent Act.

third parties can invoke non-compliance with this procedure as a ground for invalidation,[6] and administrative and criminal proceedings may be initiated.[7]

The fact that confidentiality examination would have shown the applicant to be perfectly entitled to have filed a patent application abroad is irrelevant. No remedy is granted in the law for accidental oversight. **11.04**

If an invention is qualified as important for national security or other vital state interests, filing a patent application abroad in relation to such invention will be prohibited. **11.05**

It is no surprise that European[8] and other companies had great concerns as R&D centres in China, technology co-operation projects and other business models employing or using Chinese inventors had to deal with another layer of government control before they would be able to use inventions made in China abroad by filing for patent protection outside China. Furthermore, stakeholders feared that the confidentiality examination would be used to manipulate and initiate invalidation attacks against patents held by European companies for inventions partially researched in China. However, five years after its introduction it seems that these concerns have not materialized. **11.06**

## B. GENERAL REMARKS ON THE PROCEDURE

Article 20(1) Chinese Patent Act, which previously only applied to Chinese entities and individuals who had to file first in China before being allowed to file abroad, requires *any* entity or individual intending to file a patent application abroad for an invention made in China to apply first to SIPO for a prior confidentiality examination. Consequently, a request for a confidentiality examination has to be filed irrespective of whether a Chinese or foreign applicant wants to protect abroad an invention made in China. Furthermore, it should be noted that the request for a confidentiality examination has to be filed irrespective of whether a patent application was or will be filed in China, and irrespective of the field of technology. **11.07**

Applicants who would like to protect their inventions first in China and then abroad can file the request for confidentiality examination together with the Chinese patent application. However, it is also possible to first file the request **11.08**

6 Art. 45 Chinese Patent Act; R. 65 Implementing Regulations to the Chinese Patent Act.

7 Art. 71 Chinese Patent Act.

8 See the IPR Chapter of the EUCCC Position Paper 2009/2010.

for confidentiality examination and later the Chinese patent application. In any case it must be ensured that the request is filed before the patent application is filed abroad.

**11.09** If an international application is filed first with SIPO, then no separate request for confidentiality examination is necessary. In this case, SIPO conducts the confidentiality examination *ex officio*.[9]

## C. DETAILS OF THE PROCEDURE

**11.10** Rule 8 Implementing Regulations to the Chinese Patent Act provides that confidentiality examination is required for any invention for which patent protection is sought abroad and for which a substantial part of the technical solution was made in China.

**11.11** The patent law does not provide any clarification as to what an invention 'made in China' means. Rule 8(1) Implementing Regulations to the Chinese Patent Act provides that Article 20(1) Chinese Patent Act refers to those inventions for which a substantial content of the technical solution was completed in China. The Implementing Regulations or Patent Examination Guidelines do not contain further rules on what should be regarded as 'substantial content'. However, it seems that the geographical position of the inventor is seen as the decisive factor. Nevertheless, it is not entirely clear how this system is applied to inventions where one part was researched in China, but other parts were researched abroad by other team members. Inventions jointly made in China by Chinese and non-Chinese co-inventors are subject to be regarded as 'made in China'.[10] The burden of proof of whether or not an invention has been made in China will in principle lie with applicants for invalidation or SIPO. However, according to informal information from SIPO if one of the inventors named in the invention has a Chinese name, this will be seen as sufficient initial evidence and shift the burden of proof to the applicant or patent holder, who then in turn will have to prove that the Chinese inventor was not on Chinese soil when he completed the invention.

**11.12** The request for a confidentiality examination must include a detailed description of the technical solution offered by the invention if no national patent

9 R. 8(3) Implementing Regulations to the Chinese Patent Act.

10 Cf. Eve Y. Zhou and Bob Stembridge, 'Patented in China – The Present and Future State of Innovation in China', Thomson Reuters 2010, 18.

application has been filed. The guidelines for examination clarify that explanatory remarks on the technical solution must correspond to those in the planned foreign application.[11] In theory, the requester can choose whether he would like to file an isolated description of the technical solution or a full patent application in Chinese with SIPO. In practice, SIPO requires a full patent application in Chinese.

As mentioned earlier, in the case of an international application filed with SIPO it is not necessary to file a separate request for confidentiality examination as SIPO in such a case conducts the confidentiality examination *ex officio*. **11.13**

Once the request for confidentiality examination has been filed, SIPO first examines whether the invention is likely to involve national security or other 'substantial interests' requiring confidentiality.[12] Even five years after the introduction it is still quite unclear what kind of interests qualify as 'substantial'.[13] **11.14**

If the applicant does not receive a notification from SIPO within four months from the date of submitting the request, he can apply for a patent abroad. In practice, SIPO has issued the notices (positive and negative notifications) in general within less than four weeks.[14] If SIPO is of the opinion that the request needs further examination, it informs the applicant accordingly in writing. If the applicant does not then receive notification of SIPO's final decision on the request within six months from the date of submitting the request, again he can apply for a patent abroad.[15] **11.15**

Since the introduction of the confidentiality examination SIPO has reportedly examined more than 50,000 requests for confidentiality examination and obviously less than 10 applications were denied a filing outside of China. Nevertheless, the primary goal of keeping a clear overview of what is invented in China should have been reached. **11.16**

11 Part V. Chapter 5, 6.1.1 Filing the request, Patent Examination Guidelines.

12 Art. 4 Chinese Patent Act in conjunction with R. 9(1) Implementing Regulations to the Chinese Patent Act.

13 Cf. also Richard Bird, 'Pace of Patent Law Reform Reflects Economic Explosion', *Intellectual Property Magazine*, May 2010, 31, 33.

14 Information provided at the EU-China IP Working Group on patents, held in Beijing on 24 June 2010.

15 R. 9(2) Implementing Regulations to the Chinese Patent Act.

[illegible]

[illegible] SIPO [illegible]

[illegible] 11.14

[illegible] 11.15

[illegible] SIPO [illegible]

[illegible] made a patent request.

[illegible] SIPO [illegible] 11.16

[illegible]

# Part D

# ENFORCEMENT

# 12

# DUAL ENFORCEMENT SYSTEM

**Cao Jingjing**



## A. INTRODUCTION

Western companies which are doing or are planning to do business in China are interested in the opportunities offered by the Chinese market. According to the *Business Confidence Survey 2012* which has been newly released by the European Chamber, the responding European companies were, almost without exception, optimistic about their sector's growth prospects in China. They believe that the importance of China in their companies' overall global strategy will further increase.[1] However, in spite of encouraging developments over the past years resulting from both the improved performance by courts in major cities and increased awareness of the intellectual property issues amongst the public, uncertainty arising from the regulatory environment for the protection of intellectual property rights still forms a significant obstacle. In 2012 70 per cent **12.01**

1 European Chamber, 'European Business in China – Business Confidence Survey 2012', published at http://www.europeanchamber.com.cn/upload/media/media/14/European_Chamber_Business_Confidence_Survey_2012_EN%5B559%5D.pdf.

of the respondents still rated China's enforcement of intellectual property rights and relevant regulations as inadequate or very inadequate.[2]

**12.02** A few years ago, China was frequently criticized for implementing intellectual property laws only for the sake of gaining favorable trading partnerships with Western countries through various international agreements.[3] Some commentators attributed the failure to curb piracy and counterfeiting in China to the lack of political will on the part of Chinese policymakers.[4] Recently, however, such criticism has become silent. Commentators even identified a political will to guarantee robust enforcement.

**12.03** In March 2011, the Eleventh Session of the Fourth National People's Congress of China discussed and passed 'The national economic and social development of the Twelfth Five Year Plan Outline' and announced the goals of transforming, upgrading and enhancing the core competitiveness of industries. The cultivation and development of strategic emerging industries, the promotion of energy production and the innovation of energy utilization are at the head of China's list.[5]

**12.04** It is therefore no wonder that some American scholars warn that 'while business bumps along in the United States, the sleeping giant of the twentieth century is now wide awake and threatens to outpace the U.S. in innovation and patenting in the twenty-first century'.[6]

**12.05** Robust enforcement of the available IP rights is one important element of China's innovation oriented industrial policy. In China, both civil courts and administration authorities are competent to deal with patent infringement cases.[7] This chapter will provide an overview of this dual system of the enforcement of intellectual property rights in China.

---

2 Ibid.

3 Jennifer A. Crane, 'Riding the Tiger: A Comparison of Intellectual Property Rights in the United States and the People's Republic of China', [2008] **7** *Chi.-Kent J. Intell. Prop.* 95, 97; Scott J. Palmer, 'An Identity Crisis: Regime Legitimacy and the Politics of Intellectual Property Rights in China', [2001] **8** *Ind.J. Global Legal Stud.* 449, 450.

4 Peter K. Yu, 'Still Dissatisfied after All These Years: Intellectual Property, Post-WTO China, and the Avoidable Cycle of Futility', [2005] **34** *Ga. J. Int'l & Comp. l.* 143, 155.

5 See Chapters 10 and 11 of 'The national economic and social development of the Twelfth Five Year Plan Outline' published on http://www.gov.cn/2011lh/content_1825838.htm.

6 Wayne C. Jaeschke, Zhun Lu and Paul Crawford, 'Comparison of Chinese and U.S. Patent Reform Legislation: Which, if Either, Got it Right?', [2012] **11** *J. Marshall Rev. Intell. Prop. L.* 567, 569.

7 Thomas Pattloch, 'The Enforcement of Patent Rights in China', in Christopher Heath and Laurence Petit (eds), *Patent Enforcement Worldwide. Writings in Honour of Dieter Stauder,* Oxford: Hart Publishing, 2nd edn., 2005, 285–320, at 285; Stefan Luginbuehl and Thomas Pattloch, 'The Awakening of the Chinese Patent Dragon – the Revised Chinese Patent Act 2009', [2011] **42** *IIC* 130, 142; Tilman Mueller-Stoy, 'Patent Litigation in the People's Republic of China', [2007] **38** *IIC*, 520, 538.

## B. JUDICIAL ENFORCEMENT OF PATENTS

China provides for a bifurcated enforcement system. A patentee can choose to take an infringement case to a People's Court or he can go through a patent-specific administrative procedure. 12.06

### 1. China's court system and jurisdiction over patent infringement cases

The Chinese civil court system consists of the Supreme People's Court (SPC), the special People's Court and the local People's Court at three levels, including 3,117 Basic People's Courts, 409 Intermediate People's Courts and 32 Higher People's Courts in total.[8] 12.07

The SPC is the highest judicial organ of China. It supervises the case law of the local People's Courts at various levels.[9] 12.08

The Higher People's Courts are set up at the level of provinces, autonomous regions and municipalities directly under the central government, for instance, Beijing, Shanghai, Tianjin or Chongqing.[10] The Intermediate People's Courts are established at the level of provinces, autonomous region and municipalities directly under the central government or under the jurisdiction of a province or autonomous region, or at the level of autonomous prefectures.[11] Basic People's Courts are county-level People's Courts and municipal People's Courts, People's Courts of autonomous counties and People's Courts of municipal districts.[12] 12.09

The Higher People's Court is authorized to supervise, both from the administrative and the judicial perspective, the People's Court at lower levels including the Intermediate People's Courts and the Basic People's Courts within the same province. The interpretations and implementing guidelines released by a People's Court at a higher level bind the People's Courts at lower levels within the same province. 12.10

8 Article 1 Organic Law of the People's Courts; Zhipei Jiang, 'Patent Litigation in China', [2000] **9** *Fed. Circuit B. J.* 481; Cheng Yong-Shun, 'Judicial Protection of Intellectual Property in China', [1998] **9** *Duke J. Comp. & Int'l L.* 271; Douglas Clark, 'Intellectual Property Litigation in China', *China B. Rev.* November–December 2004, 25, 27; Lin Yasong and Marco T. Connor, 'An Overview of the Judicial Protection of Patents in China', [2008] **3** *JIPLP* 2008, 163, 166.

9 Art. 28 Organic Law of the People's Courts.

10 Art. 25 Organic Law of the People's Courts.

11 Art. 22 Organic Law of the People's Courts.

12 Art. 17 Organic Law of the People's Courts.

**12.11** Unlike case law under the common law system, decisions of a People's Court at a higher level do not have a binding effect on the courts at lower level. In practice, however, decisions previously rendered by a court at a higher level are cited by attorneys as references in their writs submitted to the same court or a court at lower level.

**12.12** The Basic/Higher People's Courts adopt the system whereby the second instance is the last instance. If the SPC finds a definite error in a legally effective judgment or order of a People's Court at any level, it has the authority to review the case itself or to cancel the decision and remand it back for retrial. The same applies to any Higher People's Court which finds such an error in a legally effective judgment or order of a People's Court at a lower level.

**12.13** As there are no specialized intellectual property courts, the judicial enforcement of patents falls under the jurisdiction of the ordinary civil courts.[13] Patent cases are handled by SPC-appointed Intermediate People's Courts in the first instance. As an exception, if the value in dispute is extraordinarily high, a Higher People's Court will handle the patent infringement cases in the first instance.[14] According to Articles 22 and 29 of *Civil Procedures Act* and Item 5 of *SPC's Certain Provisions on Issues Concerning Application of Law in the Trial of Patent Disputes*,[15] a patent infringement lawsuit shall be brought to the People's Court of the place where the defendant's domicile is located or where the patent infringement has been carried out.

### 2. Statistics on the judicial enforcement of patents

**12.14** Since the enactment of the third amendment to the Patent Act in 2008, the number of patent-related civil disputes accepted by the People's Courts in the first instance has significantly increased. In 2008, 4,074 civil patent cases have been accepted in the first instance. In 2009, the courts have accepted 4,422 first instance cases, which indicate an increase of 8.54 per cent over the previous year. The year 2011 showed an increase of 30.82 per cent (5,785 new cases). According to the latest statistics, the increase in 2012 amounted to 35.16 per cent (7,819 new cases).[16]

---

13 According to Item 1(4) Certain Provisions of the Supreme People's Court on Issues Concerning Application of Law in Trying Cases Involving Patent Disputes (*Fashi* [2001] No. 21, released on 22 June 2001), People's Courts shall accept inter alia disputes over infringement of patent rights.

14 For example, patent infringement cases will be heard by the Higher People's Court in Beijing if the disputed value is higher than 100 million Yuan, R. 3(1) Regulations on the Trial Jurisdiction of People's Courts at Varied Levels in Beijing over Intellectual Property Civil Cases at the First Instance.

15 *Fashi* [2001] No. 21, released on 22 June 2001.

16 Annual Reports 2008–2011 issued by the State Intellectual Property Office.

The propensity towards litigating has increased. However, it should be noted that the number of foreign related cases is still relatively small. For example, in 2009, among 30,626 intellectual property civil cases in the first instance, only 1,361 cases were foreign related,[17] which corresponds to a relatively small percentage of 4.5. In 2011 the portion of foreign related cases even decreased to 2.3 per cent. In 2012, the local People's Courts handled 58,201 civil intellectual property related cases altogether in the first instance, of which merely 121 cases were foreign related.[18] **12.15**

Such a decrease in foreign related litigation may to some extent be attributed to the fact that more foreign right owners choose to grant licences to their subsidiaries in China and authorize them to enforce these rights in court. On the other hand, remaining concerns about local protectionism, the lack of firsthand knowledge about the enforcement procedures and doubts about the efficiency of the execution of court decisions may also deter foreign right owners from pursuing their rights in court. **12.16**

As regards the patent infringement proceedings see the contribution of *Pfaffenzeller*, Chapter 13. **12.17**

## C. ADMINISTRATIVE ENFORCEMENT OF PATENTS

After the third amendment to the Patent Act, the focus of administrative protection shifted from administrative handling of patent infringement disputes to administrative investigation and handling of illegal acts related to patents. Patent administration authorities have transformed from quasi-court-like entities which handled civil disputes for a transitional period[19] to purely administrative entities with competencies limited to protecting the public and the market order against illegal acts.[20] **12.18**

### 1. The competencies of local patent administration authorities

Patent administration authorities include the Patent Administration Department under the State Council, that is, the State Intellectual Property Office (SIPO), and the local patent administration authorities. **12.19**

17 With regard to foreign related cases, only figures with regard to all kinds of intellectual property were available.

18 Judicial Protection of Intellectual Property Rights by Chinese Courts 2011. Available at http://www.court.gov.cn/xwzx/tt/201204/t20120419_176081.htm.

19 Tang Zongshun, *Interpretation of Patent Act*, Beijing: Intellectual Property Publishing House, 2002, 32.

20 Meng Hongzhi, 'Study on New Development of Administrative Protection of Intellectual Property Rights', Beijing, 2011, 115.

**12.20** According to Article 3 of the Chinese Patent Act, SIPO is responsible for the administration of patent work nationwide, for accepting and examining patent applications and for granting patent rights. The local patent administration authorities instead are competent to deal with patent infringement cases, including the determination of possible infringements and, where an infringement is determined, to order injunctions. However, as mentioned above, they are not authorized to award damages. Furthermore, the competence of local patent administration authorities to investigate evidence has been limited to the cases of 'passing-off' (that is, passing off another person's patent as one's own) and 'patent counterfeiting' (that is, advertising with a non-existent patent). Thus, the competences of local patent administration authorities in infringement cases are not strong.[21]

**12.21** According to Article 64 of the Chinese Patent Act, when investigating and handling 'passing-off' and 'patent counterfeiting' cases, the patent administration authorities may, based on existing evidence, make enquiries of the relevant parties, and carry out further investigation, including, inter alia, on-the-spot inspection of places where the alleged illegal acts have been carried out, examining and photocopying relevant contracts, invoices, account books and other material, and inspecting the products pertaining to the infringing act. Products which infringe the counterfeited patent can be sealed up or detained.

**12.22** On 14 October 2011, ten ministries and commissions including SIPO jointly released the *12th Five-Year Plan for Development of National IPR issues* ('IP Five Years Plan'), which proposes to 'enhance the construction of the administrative enforcement system of intellectual property'. That is, the plan reiterates the importance of enhancing administrative protection. It also provides for specific measures such as completing the administrative enforcement and service systems with regard to patents, trademarks, copyrights, agricultures and forestry at province and county levels, establishing a network of law enforcement and rights protection, as well as increasing the number and the qualification of law enforcement personnel.

## 2. Administrative patent infringement procedures

### *(a) Request for administrative measures*

**12.23** Only patent owners or 'interested parties', that is, licensees, are entitled to request administrative measures against infringement.[22] In case of sole licenses

21 Stefan Luginbuehl and Thomas Pattloch, above note 7,130.

22 R. 8, Measures for the Enforcement of Patent Administrative Law, promulgated by SIPO on 29 December 2010.

or exclusive licenses, the licensee may proceed independently. In case of non-exclusive licenses, the consent of the patent owner is required.

The written request shall clearly outline the facts of the case. It must indicate the name and address of the respondent(s), type of infringement, analysis on the scope of the patent and the infringement of the patent, quantity of infringing products and other relevant information. Such information must be supported by evidence. In addition, evidence on the identity of the requester, the validity of the patent and a power of attorney shall be submitted in case the requester wants to be represented by a lawyer. **12.24**

Evidence on the validity of the patent includes copies of patent certificates, receipts of the latest payment of renewal fees or the duplicate of the patent register. In addition, if a utility model or design patent is at issue, the requesting party shall also submit a search report issued by SIPO on the validity of the claimed right. If the utility model patent or design patent has been granted after 1 October 2009,[23] an evaluation report issued by SIPO shall be submitted. For utility model or design patents granted before 1 October 2009, only search reports are available. In such search reports, only copies of reference documents will be provided without any comments made by SIPO. For utility model and design patents granted after 1 October 2009, the so-called 'evaluation reports' instead of search reports are available. The evaluation report does not only include copies of the reference documents but also a comparison made by SIPO between the searched utility model/design patent and the closest prior art. **12.25**

If the requester is a foreign company, its incorporation certificate and the power of attorney have to be notarized by a public notary and legalized by the Chinese embassy or Chinese consulate in the state of the seat of the requester. **12.26**

### *(b) Collection of evidence*

Rule 8 Measures on Administrative Patent Enforcement promulgated by SIPO on 29 December 2010 (SIPO Measures) requires that the subject matter of a request for administrative measures has to be specific and be supported by facts and reasons. In order to fulfill this requirement, it is necessary for right owners to collect evidence on the infringement before filing the request. **12.27**

First of all, the identity of the infringer(s) shall be determined. The status of the infringer, for example, whether it is a company with limited liability or a partnership, can have a significant impact on the further proceedings as the partners of a partnership are personally liable for patent infringement, whereas **12.28**

23 The effective date of the amended Patent Act.

in the case of a limited company, the decision of the authority will only bind such company but not its shareholders.[24]

**12.29** Furthermore, in a case of joint infringement, it is important to investigate the connection between the infringers, for example, who has manufactured the infringing parts, who has assembled them and who has been in charge of distribution? Even though not explicitly required by administrative provisions, right owners are well advised to collect evidence under the supervision of public notaries and to obtain a notarization report so as to prevent the respondent from challenging the authenticity of the evidence.

**12.30** Furthermore, in the course of handling a patent infringement dispute, if the requester is unable to collect evidence on his own, he may request the patent administration authorities to investigate and collect relevant evidence.[25]

**12.31** The patent administration authorities may consult and copy contracts, account books and other relevant documents, question the parties and witnesses and conduct on-site inspection. If a patent for a manufacturing process is at issue, the patent administration authorities may require the respondent to carry out an on-site demonstration proving that the process he uses is not infringing.

**12.32** In addition, the patent administration authorities may confiscate samples of the infringing products. They will keep the original samples and can, upon request of the applicant, provide the applicant with pictures of the collected samples for verification.

### *(c) Details of the procedures*

**12.33** The patent administration authorities shall initiate the case[26] and inform the requesting party within five days from the date of the filing about the acceptance of the request. If the request does not meet the legal requirements, the patent administration authority shall, within five working days, inform the requesting party that the request has been rejected and explain the reasons.[27]

**12.34** Upon acceptance, a copy of the request shall be delivered to the respondent within five working days. The respondent may then submit a written response

24 China's new Company Law of 2005 allows veil piercing only in exceptional cases – see Knut Benjamin Pißler, *Der Haftungsdurchgriff im chinesischen Gesellschaftsrecht, in: Unternehmen, Markt und Verantwortung – Festschrift für Klaus J. Hopt zum 70. Geburtstag am 24. August 2010*. Berlin: De Gruyter, 2010, 3217.

25 R. 35 SIPO Measures.

26 The so-called '立案程序' (li an cheng xu), a special procedure of placing a case on file for investigation.

27 R. 11 SIPO Measures.

within 15 days. The patent administration authority has five working days to forward the response to the requester.

Furthermore, when handling a patent infringement dispute, the patent administrative authority may decide *ex officio* whether an oral hearing should be conducted. If the patent administrative authority decides to conduct such hearing while the requester refuses to participate without justified reasons or leaves without permission, the request shall be regarded as withdrawn. If the respondent behaves in such manner, he or she shall be deemed to have been absent.[28] **12.35**

During the oral hearing, the patent administration authorities usually mediate between the parties. Historically, Chinese culture views litigation as a 'failure of community and a reflection of disharmony'. Therefore, mediation is a preferential form of resolving a dispute. If the parties cannot reach a settlement at this stage, the mediation will be continued after the oral hearing. **12.36**

The duration of such administrative proceedings has been determined as four months in normal cases. It can be extended by another month if the case is especially complicated.[29] **12.37**

### *(d) Outcome of the administrative procedure*

There are three possible outcomes of an administrative enforcement procedure. **12.38**

First, the parties settle their case privately and the requester withdraws its request for administrative enforcement. **12.39**

Second, a settlement is reached through administrative mediation. In such case, the authority will prepare an agreement text and attach its official seal to it. The execution of the mediation agreement can be supervised by the authority upon request by the party. **12.40**

Third, the parties cannot reach an agreement, so that the patent administration authority has to issue a written decision. Such decision shall determine whether the patent right was infringed and stipulate the grounds. It should be noted that in a case of repeat infringement by the same infringer, the patent administrative authority may decide to order immediate cessation from the infringing act just on grounds of a previous infringement decision rendered by a People's Court. In its decision, the administrator does not have to carry out an analysis on the **12.41**

28 R. 14 SIPO Measures.

29 R. 19, Measures for the Enforcement of Patent Administrative Law.

infringement again, that is, it is not necessary to compare the technical features of the patent claims and the infringing products again.

*(e) Statistical data on the administrative enforcement of patents*

**12.42** According to a report published by SIPO,[30] China's State Council has launched a nationwide special campaign against IPR infringements and production and sales of counterfeited and forged commodities – the 'Special Campaign' – which lasted from October 2010 to June 2011. The Special Campaign primarily targeted manufacturing hubs, commodity distribution centers, key regions in which IP infringement turned out to be rampant, and production and sales of counterfeited and forged commodities.

**12.43** During the implementation of the Special Campaign, IP administrations across China have dramatically improved patent enforcement. From October 2010 to June 2011, the nationwide patent administration authorities have spent about 167,000 personnel hours on enforcement, and 2,572 patent cases were settled in total. About 2.3 million goods were inspected and more than 80,000 patent infringing goods were seized; 1,092 cross-region enforcement actions and 665 cross-authorities enforcement actions were launched.

**12.44** Apart from the Special Campaign, statistics on regular enforcement from 2010 to 2011 show that in 2011, the local patent administration authorities have handled 3,017 patent cases which represent an increase of 65 per cent over the previous year.

**12.45** However, if we ignore the short-term effect arising from the Special Campaign, statistics show that the amount of the administrative enforcement cases accepted by the patent authorities has continuously decreased until 2009, from 1,597 cases in 2005 to 937 in 2009.

**12.46** Furthermore, the data also indicate that from the total of 4,242 patent infringement cases accepted by the authorities between 2006 and 2009, only 230 cases involved foreign patentees, which corresponds to 5.42 per cent of the total amount of cases.[31]

**12.47** According to some scholars, the decrease in administrative enforcement can be partly traced back to the fact that administrative patent enforcement had

30 China's Intellectual Property Protection in 2011, published by SIPO at http://www.sipo.gov.cn/yw/2012/201204/t20120425_679211.html.

31 Deng Jianzhi, 'Study on the Efficiency of Patent Administrative Enforcement in China', [2012] **2** *China Soft Science* 80, 83.

originally been intended as a transitional arrangement, due to the specific historical conditions of China. According to this view, it had played an important role at the initial stage of establishing an intellectual property system, at a time when the judicial system was not yet fully matured. However, in the course of perfecting China's intellectual property system, as judicial enforcement became stronger, administrative mediation and arbitration is increasingly perceived as having accomplished its historical mission.[32] A further reason may be the subsequent weakening of the local patent administration authorities' power to investigate and handle patent infringement in the course of the preceding two amendments to the Patent Act.[33] For instance, in contrast to previous versions of the Patent Act, in the present version the authorities are no longer entitled to determine damages in administrative proceedings. The responsible authorities are only allowed to mediate on the damages question if so requested by the parties.[34]

In addition, China's Intellectual Property Statistical Yearbook[35] of 2011 indicates that patent enforcement cases are unevenly distributed throughout the country. Up to 2011, patent administrations in 31 regions had handled 14,777 patent infringement cases and 16,914 cases of 'patent counterfeiting' and 2,024 other patent-related disputes. Among these, 3,247 patent infringement cases and 1,232 patent counterfeiting cases were handled in Guangdong Province, which corresponds to 22 per cent and 7.2 per cent respectively of the total amount of cases. In some other provinces such as Zhejiang (1,701 patent infringement cases and 172 patent counterfeiting cases), Shandong Province (1,604 patent infringement cases and 4,013 counterfeiting cases) and Jiangsu Province (788 patent infringement cases and 1,151 counterfeiting cases) patents are also frequently enforced by administrations. The majority of these provinces are located in the coastal area where economic development is especially fast. **12.48**

Thus it should be noted that different provinces seem to have specialized in certain categories of administrative cases. For example, Zhejiang Province is characterized by a relatively high number of small and medium-size private enterprises and a correspondingly high number of intellectual property infringement cases. Whereas until 2011, the patent administration authorities **12.49**

32 Zhang Li and Xu Liming, 'The Administrative Mediation of Patent Infringement Issues, Right or Wrong?', [2010] *Administration and Law*, July 84, 85.

33 Another reason for strengthening the civil litigation system was to meet the requirements laid down in TRIPs. See Thomas Pattloch in Christopher Heath and Laurence Petit (eds), *Patent Enforcement Worldwide. Writings in Honour of Dieter Stauder*, Oxford: Hart Publishing, 2nd edn. 2005, 285 in this regard.

34 Xu Xiaojun, Li Jianmin and Wu Jian, 'Proposals on Amendment of Patent Act and Thoughts on Enhancing Patent Administrative Enforcement', [2012] **5** *Today's Technology* 21.

35 Published by SIPO, Beijing: 2012, 47–50.

of Zhejiang Province have handled 1,701 cases regarding patent infringement disputes, only 172 cases involved so-called patent counterfeiting. The share of counterfeiting cases is therefore significantly lower than in other provinces with a high number of IP cases such as Guangdong, Shandong or Jiangsu.

**12.50** In contrast, in some provinces where economic development proceeds at a relatively slow pace such as Hebei, Inner Mongolia, Anhui, Guizhou, Shaanxi or Xinjiang, the local patent administration authorities seem to have specialized in investigating and handling patent counterfeiting cases. The number of patent counterfeiting cases investigated and handled by local patent administrations until 2011 in each of these provinces or regions amounts to 700 to 800, which is far more than the number of counterfeiting cases, for example, in Zhejiang.

### 3. Problems of administrative enforcement

#### *(a) Local protectionism*

**12.51** Local patent administration authorities are established by the government of the respective locality. They have competence over patent enforcement within their administrative regions.

**12.52** Scholars and foreign investors criticize that central legislation and enforcement by local authorities are the weakest elements of China's intellectual property system. Even where patent infringement disputes are brought to local authorities, the officials may not remain as independent as they are expected to be.[36] For instance, they usually pressurize the parties to resolve their dispute by settlement. The 'attitude of the particular parties' and partially the attitude of the provincial judges towards local interests may impact the effectiveness of intellectual property rights enforcement.[37]

#### *(b) Lack of unified rules on the jurisdiction of local patent administration authorities*

**12.53** In practice, the administrative provisions in each province differ in regulating the question of which authority shall be competent to deal with enforcement. The following examples may support this:

- According to Rule 3 of the Patent Protection Ordinance of Liaoning Province, the patent administration at county level shall be competent to enforce patents within its jurisdiction.

36 Jennifer A. Crane, above note 3, 115–116.
37 Jennifer A. Crane, above note 3, 115–116.

- According to Rule 3 of the Patent Protection Ordinance of Henan Province, only the patent administration authority established by the People's Government at city level shall be competent to enforce patents, whereas the authorities at county level shall assist their superior authorities in enforcement work.
- According to Rule 31 of the Patent Protection Ordinance of Shandong Province, the patent administration authority established by the People's Government at city level shall have the right to handle patent infringement disputes, and the patent administration authority at county level shall be responsible for investigating and handling counterfeiting and passing-off cases.
- According to Rule 16 of the Patent Protection Ordinance of Yunnan Province, the patent administration authority established by the People's Government at city level shall have the right to handle patent infringement disputes, and the patent administration authority at county level shall be responsible for investigating and handling patent counterfeiting and passing-off cases and may also mediate infringement disputes.
- According to the provisions of the Patent Protection Ordinance of Hebei Province, the patent administration authority established by the People's Government at city level may authorize the patent administration authority at county level to handle patent infringement disputes and carry out administrative punishment.

### *(c) Lack of cross-regional co-operation*

Unlike courts, the patent administration authorities can only accept a request if the respondent is located or if the infringing act is carried out within their local jurisdiction. For example, if the infringing good is produced in Province A and sold in Province B, the patent owner can request the patent administration authorities of Province A only to prosecute manufacturing, not the distribution. **12.54**

In order to solve the enforcement problems regarding cross-region patent infringement, 27 intellectual property authorities in such provinces and cities as Jiangsu Province, Zhejiang Province and Shanghai Municipality signed the 'Coordination Agreement on Patent-related Administrative Enforcement by the Intellectual Property Office System in Yangtze River Delta Area' in September 2005. It provides that local intellectual property offices at all levels may request their superior intellectual property offices, including SIPO, to organize cross-regional enforcement measures to prosecute infringement or counterfeiting cases of significant economic impact. **12.55**

## D. SUMMARY

**12.56** Some scholars provide multiple reasons for the establishment, existence and development of the patent-related administrative protection system, inter alia, that it has the advantage of being more convenient, more efficient and cheaper as compared to court enforcement. Moreover, one characteristic of the patent administration authorities is that they can crack down on illegal acts *ex officio*, whereas judicial enforcement follows the 'no trial without a complainant' principle. Patents are different from some other civil rights, as they are strongly connected to the interest of the public. For example, patent counterfeiting and passing-off do not only harm the private rights of the patent owner but also cause damage to the interests of the public.[38] Furthermore, administrative enforcement comprises faster and cheaper procedures and lower requirements regarding the burden of proof.

**12.57** However, administrative enforcement also has disadvantages, in particular, the available remedies do not include compensation but only administrative fines. Therefore, depending on the individual case, the deterring effect of administrative enforcement on infringers may be lower than that of a civil court decision.

**12.58** The parallel competencies of courts and of special administration authorities to deal with patent infringement are a special feature of the Chinese patent enforcement system. The question of which route shall be followed cannot be definitely answered. The answer depends on the individual case. Each route has its advantages and disadvantages. Therefore, patent owners should carry out a strategic analysis of the different possibilities before initiating enforcement measures.

---

38 Deng Jianzhi, 'The Road of Development of Patent Administrative Protection in China', [2012] **3** *Intellectual Property* 68, 74; Li Gang, 'Discussion about the Patent Administrative Enforcement System', [2012] **2** *Intellectual Property Work* 15; Ji Yu and Li Jianmin, 'Discussion about the System of Administrative Enforcement of Patent Infringement Disputes and its Improvements', [2011] **7** *Intellectual Property* 97, 97–98.

# 13

# PATENT INFRINGEMENT PROCEDURES AND REMEDIES

**Oliver Pfaffenzeller**



## A. INTRODUCTION

Patent litigation has taken root in China. China has emerged as the country with the largest number of patent litigation cases.[1] The vast majority of these cases are contended between Chinese parties. Even if one takes into account that Chinese statistics count local subsidiaries of western companies, as well as Taiwanese and Hong Kong companies among local litigation parties, the large number demonstrates that Chinese companies embrace patent rights[2] as a strategic asset to be leveraged against competitors. This development is heavily fostered by Chinese authorities on different levels (*Luginbuehl*, Chapter 1). **13.01**

1 7,819 patent litigation cases in 2011, roughly twice as many as in the United States, **492** *Nature*, 323 (20 December 2012).

2 In this chapter the terms 'patents' or 'patent rights' refer to all intellectual property rights governed by Chinese patent law, that is, invention patents, utility models, and design patents. 'Patents' in the more narrow sense are referred to as 'invention patents'.

**13.02** So far, the focus of western companies has been whether and how own patent rights can be enforced in China. The emphasis on the enforcement of patent rights has been closely linked to the danger of technology being copied or 'pirated' by Chinese companies. The future, however, is likely to increasingly shift the role of western companies to the defendant's side. Chinese companies are generating vast numbers of patents. In particular, the moderate inventive step requirement for utility models extends the space for patent protection in China vis-à-vis other countries and provides rising local players with an edge over their internationally established competitors. In view of this trend, the defendant's role deserves good coverage, too.

**13.03** Even after the second amendment to the Chinese Patent Act in 2001 the enforceability of Chinese patent rights was still put into doubt by many commentators.[3] Meanwhile, such criticism has largely abated. China has made major strides in strengthening patent protection. The proclaimed strategy,[4] as well as recent development in patent law[5] indicate that further improvements to the patent owner's position are to be expected.

**13.04** The breathtaking evolution of the Chinese patent system should not shroud one's perception of persisting caveats. A study on the strength of intellectual property enforcement regimes by the law firm Taylor Wessing found China to rank only 22nd among 24 countries in the field of patents.[6] Remedies often fall behind one's expectations. But there is good news, too. Civil patent litigation appears to be a legal area in which foreign or foreign invested companies face little discrimination. A study carried out by the law firm China Patent Agent (CPA) found that local and foreign companies have achieved virtually identical success rates as claimants in patent litigation.[7] An investigation of court practice published in the International Review of Intellectual Property and Competition Law (IIC)[8] indicates that intellectual property litigants are treated more fairly in China than parties in other areas of law. In view of the multifarious difficulties and challenges for business in China, the enforcement of patent rights seems by comparison a well-established and comparatively reliable procedure once litigation is well prepared and the rules are followed.

---

3 See, for example, Michael A. Kock, 'Die Durchsetzung von Schutzrechten in der VR China' *VPP-Rdbr.* 4/2004, 124.

4 See strategy paper 关于进一步做好打击侵犯知识产权和制善假冒伪劣商品工作的意见.

5 See section M.

6 TaylorWessing, Global IP Index 2011, http://www.taylorwessing.com/ipindex/index.php.

7 [2009] **4** *China Patents & Trademarks* 12.

8 Rongjie Lan, 'Are Intellectual Property Litigants Treated Fairer in China's Courts? An Empirical Study of Two Courts', [2012] **43** *IIC* 751.

## B. LEGAL MATERIALS

13.05 The Chinese Patent Act contains little procedural law for infringement procedures in its seventh Chapter on 'Protection of Patent Rights'. The course of action in civil infringement litigation is mainly governed by the Chinese Civil Procedures Act. In addition to the laws, there are a host of subordinate regulations which further define or complement codified law. Such regulations are enacted on various levels of China's rule-making hierarchy.

13.06 The highest level in the rule-making hierarchy is the Standing Committee of the National People's Congress (全国人民代表大会常务委员会) which enacts the laws of China.[9] A level below are the implementing regulations or supplementary regulations issued by the State Council (国务院), which are also binding for China's People's Courts, in spite of the fact that they are enacted by an administrative authority. Of special importance for procedural law are the regulations issued by the Supreme People's Court, a further level below. These third level regulations are binding for all subordinate courts. Below this level, Higher People's Courts also enact their own regulations. The regulations issued by the Supreme People's Court play a major role in fixing important procedural details. The list below comprises a number of legal sources on which this contribution relies. This list, however, is by far not exhaustive with respect to those regulations which are relevant for procedural law.

## C. LAWS RELATING TO PATENT INFRINGEMENT

13.07 Laws:

- Patent Act of the People's Republic of China (中华人民共和国专利法), 3rd amendment, effective 1 October 2009.
- Civil Procedures Act of the People's Republic of China (中华人民共和国民事诉讼法), effective 1 January 2013.

13.08 Provisions enacted by the Supreme People's Court:

- Several Provisions of the Supreme People's Court on Issues Relating to Application of Law to Adjudication of Cases of Patent Disputes

9 Diverse English translations of Chinese legal documents are available. However, as some of them reflect the Chinese meaning only inaccurately, the names of legal resources and some important legal terms will be added in Chinese.

(最高人民法院关于审理专利纠纷案件适用法律问题的若干规定), effective 1 July 2001 (hereinafter '2001 Judicial Interpretation').

- Several Provisions of the Supreme People's Court for the Application of Law to Pre-trial Cessation of Infringement of Patent Right (最高人民法院关于对诉前停止侵犯专利权行为适用法律问题的若干规定, effective 1 July 2001 (hereinafter 'Injunction Interpretation').
- Several Provisions of the Supreme People's Court on Evidence in Civil Litigation (最高人民法院关于民事诉讼证据的若干规定), effective 1 April 2002 (hereinafter 'Evidence Interpretation').
- Interpretation of the Supreme People's Court on Several Issues concerning the Application of Law in the Trial of Patent Infringement Dispute Cases (最高人民法院关于审理侵犯专利权纠纷案件应用法律若干问题的解释), effective 1 January 2010 (hereinafter '2010 Judicial Interpretation').[10]
- Supreme People's Court Opinion on Certain Issues with respect to Intellectual Property Judicial Adjudication Under the Current Economic Situation (最高人民法院关于当前经济形势下知识产权审判服务大局若干问题的意见), effective 21 April 2009 (hereinafter 'Opinion on Economic Situation').

**13.09** There are excellent recent monographs available in German language: a book on patent law written by Bu Yuanshi,[11] an introduction to Chinese law by the same author,[12] and a book on the enforcement of patent rights in China by Cao Jingjing.[13] A superb resource in the English language is a book on patent litigation in China by Douglas Clark.[14] One standard work on Chinese patent law is Yin Xintian's 中国专利法详解[15] (Detailed Explanation of the Patent Law of China). Its last version also covers the recent amendments. The evolution of some procedural aspects is set out in 专利纠纷与处理[16] (Patent Disputes and Handling). The system of defenses in Chinese patent litigation is broadly discussed in 侵犯专利权抗议事由[17] (Defenses in Patent Infringement Cases). A good but now outdated article about the enforcement of intellectual

---

10 2010 Judicial Interpretation complements and in parts supersedes 2001 Judicial Interpretation.

11 *Patentrecht und Technologietransfer in China*, Munich: C.H. Beck/Helbing Lichtenhahn, 2010 (hereinafter 'Bu, *Patentrecht*').

12 *Einführung in das Recht Chinas*. JuS Schriftenreihe, Band 191. Munich: C.H. Beck Verlag, 2009 (hereinafter 'Bu, *Einführung*').

13 *Die Durchsetzung von Patenten in China*, Cologne: Heymanns, 2010 (hereinafter 'Cao, *Durchsetzung*').

14 *Patent Litigation in China*, Oxford: Oxford University Press, 2011 (hereinafter 'Clark, *Patent Litigation*').

15 中国专利法详解/尹新天.- 北京: 知识产权出版社, 2011.1 (hereinafter, 'Yin').

16 专利纠纷与处理/程永顺.- 北京: 知识产权出版社. 第2版, 2011.7.

17 侵犯专利权抗议事由.- 北京: 知识产权出版社, 2011.5.

property rights was published in IIC in 2001.[18] Recent developments in litigation are outlined by Zhou Cui in IIC.[19]

## D. INITIATION OF PATENT INFRINGEMENT PROCEEDINGS

The legal basis for initiating patent infringement proceedings is a granted patent right. An injunction to cease from infringement will require the patent right to be in force. In contrast, an expired patent right may still be used to collect damages that have not come under the statute of limitations (*Bailey and Wang*, Chapter 8). There is no obligation to concentrate the assertion of multiple patent rights against the same act of infringement into one lawsuit. The plaintiff may opt to go for just one lawsuit to assert multiple patent rights infringed by the same act of infringement.[20] Some courts even tend to separate cases where multiple patents are asserted together.[21] **13.10**

The patent register is constituent with respect to patent ownership.[22] Some international companies follow a strategy pursuant to which patent rights are held by a single legal entity, which may be the parent company or a legal entity established for managing and exploiting patent rights. Sometimes, patent rights are held by such entity in trust for a subsidiary, which has a contractual claim to ownership. According to Article 60 Chinese Patent Act, the capacity to sue extends to the registered patent owner and parties with a legal interest (利害关系人).[23] The general term 'legal interest' does not accurately account for the fact that in reality the capacity to sue needs to be directly derived from the registered patent owner. An exclusive license suffices to bestow capacity to sue on the licensee, whereas a sole license even requires the patent owner to abstain from civil litigation.[24] A normal license will usually not suffice to be eligible to file an infringement action unless an explicit contractual authorization is given by the patent owner[25] or the licensee sues together with the patent owner.[26] **13.11**

18 Liu Xiaohai, 'Enforcement of Intellectual Property Rights in the People's Republic of China', [2001] **32** *IIC* 2001 141.

19 Cui Zhou, 'Recent Developments in Litigation Involving Intellectual Property in China', [2012] **43** *IIC* 21.

20 Art. 140 Chinese Chinese Civil Procedures Act; in this respect Chinese patent law is different from German patent law ('Klagekonzentration' according to Art. 145 German Patent Act).

21 Oral communication by lawyers from China Patent Agent.

22 Yuanshi Bu, 'Die Rolle des Registers im Rechtsverkehr mit Immaterialgüterrechten in China', **2009** *GRUR Int.* 986.

23 The capacity to sue does not depend on nationality, see Art. 5 Chinese Civil Procedures Act.

24 It. 1 Injunction Interpretation.

25 Yin, 670 on Art. 60 Chinese Patent Act.

26 Cao, *Durchsetzung*, 116.

**13.12** Patent co-owners do not have the authority to sue individually unless contractually authorized by an agreement among the co-owners. License income from successful litigation against infringers will be shared among the co-owners in the absence of prevailing contractual stipulations (so implied by Article 15 Chinese Patent Act).[27] The legal provisions on the distribution of license revenues and on co-ownership give priority to contractual agreements. In general, it is strongly recommended to conclude contracts governing all rights regarding the inventions, patent applications and patents, preferably prior to collaborations and at the latest upon the generation of an invention.

**13.13** Article 60 Chinese Patent Act provides for consultation (协商), legal relief (司法救济), and administrative relief (行政救济) as measures of conflict resolution. Consultation or pre-suit negotiation tends to be of little avail except in cases where the parties have some pre-existing relationship (collaboration partners, seller-customer relationship and so on). Administrative relief means that specialized patent administrations take action (*Cao*, Chapter 12). Administrative actions may be helpful to stop infringement or to coerce the infringer into a settlement. In spite of the envisaged enhancement of power of patent administration authorities by a possible future amendment to the Chinese Patent Act,[28] civil litigation appears to be the most appropriate path for dealing with the infringement of technical patent rights, that is, invention patents and utility models, unless the infringement amounts to blatant product piracy.[29]

**13.14** The jurisdiction on patent infringement cases in the first instance lies with designated Intermediate People's Courts (*Cao*, Chapter 12).[30] Exceptionally, Higher People's Courts have jurisdiction in the first instance if the value in litigation exceeds 200 million RMB or if both the value in litigation exceeds 100 million RMB and either the residence of one of the parties lies outside the area of the court's jurisdiction or the case is related to a foreign country, Hong Kong, Macau, or Taiwan.[31] Recently, the Supreme Court announced an amendment to Item 2 of the 2001 Judicial Interpretation, pursuant to which the Basic People's Courts may also be designated as competent courts to accept

27 Yin, 672.

28 See section M.

29 Cao, *Durchsetzung*, 206.

30 It. 2 2001 Judicial Interpretation; see also Lin Ma and Zhiyuan Xiao, 'Die Zuständigkeit für Patentstreitigkeiten in China', [2006] *GRUR Int.* 28.

31 Notice of the Supreme People's Court on Adjusting the Standards for the Jurisdiction of Local People's Courts at Different Levels over Intellectual Property Rights Civil Cases of the First Instance (最高人民法院关于调整地方各级人民法院管辖第一审知识产权民事案件标准的通知), effective 1 February 2010.

patent cases in the first instance.[32] However, in view of the complexity of patent litigation, the SPC can be expected to make such designation only in exceptional cases.

Territorial jurisdiction depends on both the place of infringement and the seat of the infringer.[33] That is, the plaintiff can normally choose between two different courts with territorial responsibility.[34] A joint suit against manufacturer and seller is the standard strategy to avoid jurisdiction of the court at the location where the infringer has his business and where the danger of local protectionism is correspondingly high. If manufacturer and seller are sued together, the place where the infringing sale takes place defines the territorial responsibility, irrespective of whether manufacturer and seller are identical or not.[35] **13.15**

According to Article 6 Chinese Civil Procedures Act, courts are independent of administrative bodies, social institutions and individual persons. In particular, administrative proceedings according to Article 60 Chinese Patent Act will not prejudice civil court proceedings. This independence of civil courts does not, however, amount to a full separation of powers.[36] **13.16**

A standard preparation of a lawsuit is a notarized purchase of an infringing product at a location where an appropriate court has jurisdiction, as the infringing sale gives responsibility to the jurisdiction of the court at the location where such sale has taken place.[37] Accordingly, seller and manufacturer can be jointly sued in this court. Popular venues are the Intermediate People's Courts of Beijing and Shanghai.[38] **13.17**

The 2010 Judicial Interpretation resolved a longer discussion as to whether and under what circumstances infringers shall be entitled to influence the choice of venue.[39] According to Item 18 of the 2010 Judicial Interpretation, a warning letter will trigger a deadline of one month after receipt of such letter or of two months after dispatch. Upon expiry of whichever expires first, the alleged **13.18**

---

32 最高人民法院关于修改《最高人民法院关于审理专利纠纷案件适用法律问题的若干规定》的决定，法释（2013）9号.

33 It. 5 2001 Judicial Interpretation.

34 Art. 35 Chinese Civil Procedures Act.

35 It. 6 2001 Judicial Interpretation.

36 Bu, *Einführung*, 25.

37 Obviously, any infringing act according to Art. 11 Chinese Patent Act can be prosecuted; the reason why most litigants resort to infringing sale is the necessity to get hold of notarized evidence, which generally is more difficult to obtain for other acts of infringement.

38 Statistics on the performance of Chinese courts can be found at www.ciela.cn.

39 See 专利纠纷与处理.

infringer may file an action for declaration on non-infringement. The court where this lawsuit has been filed would also be in charge of the infringement proceedings. Filing actions for declaration on non-infringement is especially favorable for allegedly infringing manufacturers, as it puts them in the position to avert litigation at the location where the product is sold and to shift the battleground to the court at the location where they have their domicile.

**13.19** Finally, it should be noted that a published patent application will give rise to a claim for compensation payments from a third party using the invention. Such compensation, however, can only be claimed after the patent has been granted.[40]

## E. THE COURSE OF PATENT INFRINGEMENT PROCEEDINGS

**13.20** This section outlines the various stations of patent infringement proceedings in front of a civil court.[41] The proceedings are governed by the recently amended Chinese Civil Procedures Act (in force since the beginning of 2013) and its supplementary regulations.

**13.21** Civil litigation is initiated by a complaint with the competent court. Pursuant to Article 119 Chinese Civil Procedures Act, the complaint shall meet the following conditions:

(i) the plaintiff has a legal interest;
(ii) the defendant is clearly identified;
(iii) there is a specific claim for relief and reasons and facts are provided;
(iv) the court has jurisdiction over the case.

**13.22** If the complaint complies with the above conditions, the court shall accept (受理) the case. A duly filed case has to be placed on file for investigation and prosecution (立案) within seven days. In reality, getting a case on file for investigation and prosecution is a difficult and time-consuming procedure. It requires compliance with the conditions to file a lawsuit (起诉条件). For instance, the complaint must meet the requirements of Article 121 Chinese Civil Procedures Act. That is, it must provide details about the plaintiff and the defendant as well as information on evidence. Without evidence, the court may

40 Yin, 176; the author sees an analogy to conciliation procedures which, according to R. 85 of the Implementing Regulations to the Patent Act (专利法实施细则), can also only be carried out after grant.

41 A concise description of the patent litigation procedure is provided by Xiaolin Dang in China 2012, special issue 'Intellectual Property Focus' published by *Managing Intellectual Property*.

dismiss the case for lack of merit.[42] A list of evidence should generally be sufficient to avoid this situation.[43] If the patent in suit is a utility model or design, a search report or patent evaluation report established by the State Intellectual Property Office (SIPO) is to be provided.[44] The requirement in Article 121 Chinese Civil Procedures Act pursuant to which information about the defendant has to be provided in the very detail, for example, due registration of a company, can become a formidable obstacle to getting the case accepted. Foreign companies need to have the required documents, such as the power of attorney and the company's identity certificate, notarized and legalized.[45] If the conditions to file a lawsuit are not met, the court issues a decision (裁定). This decision can be appealed.[46]

If it is hard to get the case accepted by a civil court, the complainant may opt for the administrative route. The acceptance criteria posed by the 'patent administration authorities'[47] (*Cao*, Chapter 12) are tentatively lower. An administrative action can be brought against the infringer according to Article 60 Patent Act. Parties which are not satisfied with the administrative decision can appeal in the competent civil court.[48] For the plaintiff, such appeal can have the advantage that the case is finally accepted by a court, which may not have happened if he had filed the complaint directly in court without taking the administrative route.[49] **13.23**

As far as representation is concerned,[50] unless explicitly specified, the power of attorney does not include the authorization to accept, relinquish, or modify the claim, to reach a settlement, or to bring in a counterclaim or an appeal.[51] Foreign parties have to appoint a representative[52] to whom communications may be served.[53] A Chinese company may also be represented by an employee.[54] **13.24**

42 Tilman Müller-Stoy, 'Patent Litigation in the People's Republic of China', [2007] **38** *IIC* 529
43 Tilman Müller-Stoy, above note 42, 531.
44 It. 8 of the 2001 Judicial Interpretation; a patent evaluation report according to Art. 61 Chinese Patent Act must be established for applications filed after the third amendment of the patent law came into force on 1 October 2009.
45 Notarisation and Legalisation Practices in China, EU-China IPR 2, 2011.
46 Art. 123 Chinese Civil Procedures Act Chinese Civil Procedures Act and Art. 154 Chinese Civil Procedures Act.
47 As defined in R. 79 Implementing Regulations to the Chinese Patent Act.
48 Art. 60 Chinese Patent Act; the deadline for filing the appeal is 15 days.
49 The author would like to thank Grace Li from the patent law firm Deheng for this idea.
50 Art. 53 Chinese Civil Procedures Act.
51 Art. 59 Chinese Civil Procedures Act.
52 Art. 263 Chinese Civil Procedures Act.
53 Art. 267(4) Chinese Civil Procedures Act.
54 Art. 58(2) Chinese Civil Procedures Act.

**13.25** After the case has been placed on file for investigation and prosecution (立案), the complaint will be sent to the defendant within five days. The defendant may reply within 15 days[55] from receipt.[56] Foreign defendants are given an extended deadline of 30 days.[57] Posting a reply before the end of this period is generally sufficient to meet the deadline.[58] With the exception of court decisions, the court may use fax and email as means of communication, provided that the parties give their consent.[59] If the party is an organization, communications will be sent to its appointed representative.[60] The defendant may refrain from filing a response without consequences for the course or outcome of the lawsuit.[61] Nevertheless, some commentators state that a response is advisable.[62]

**13.26** In his reply, the defendant may challenge the court's competence to hear the case by filing a corresponding petition.[63] In such case, the court will make a decision on jurisdiction which can be independently appealed.[64] If the petition is successful, the case will be transferred to the responsible court.[65] The period for replying is also the due occasion for requesting the Patent Re-examination Board (PRB) to stay the case (*Heide*, Chapter 14).[66]

**13.27** A separate step of patent litigation consists of the exchange of evidence (证据交换).[67] In most patent litigation cases the court will arrange a pre-trial hearing for both parties to cross-examine the exchanged evidence (互相质证).[68] The dates for the exchange of evidence are agreed upon by the parties or determined by the court.[69] Usually, only up to two dates will be admitted for such exchange of evidence. Exceptions may be allowed in especially complicated cases.[70] In the course of such exchange, the parties have the opportunity to check the authenticity of the opponent's evidence (质证) and

---

55 Chinese Civil Procedures Act deadlines expiring on a holiday are extended to the first day after the holiday; Chinese Civil Procedures Act deadlines are deemed to be kept if the relevant document is posted before the expiry of the respective deadline (see Art. 82 Chinese Civil Procedures Act).

56 Art. 125 Chinese Civil Procedures Act.

57 Art. 268 Chinese Civil Procedures Act.

58 Art. 82 Chinese Civil Procedures Act.

59 Art. 87 Chinese Civil Procedures Act.

60 Art. 91 Chinese Civil Procedures Act.

61 Art. 125 Chinese Civil Procedures Act.

62 Tilman Müller-Stoy, above note 42, 530.

63 Art. 127 Chinese Civil Procedures Act.

64 Art. 154 Chinese Civil Procedures Act.

65 Art. 36 Chinese Civil Procedures Act.

66 See Items 10 and 11 of 2001 Judicial Interpretation.

67 It. 37 Evidence Interpretation.

68 Art. 68 Chinese Civil Procedures Act.

69 Art. 38 Evidence Interpretation.

70 Art. 40 Evidence Interpretation.

raise objections to pieces of evidence.[71] As a rule, the opposite party can request the party producing evidence to furnish originals, except if there are valid reasons why the originals cannot be furnished.[72] The court will also examine the authenticity of the provided material (查证属实) so as to decide whether it can be admitted as evidence.[73]

During the evidence exchange phase, which is normally determined to be one month, new evidence may be provided.[74] The court may extend such phase, however, if the evidence is hard to obtain.[75] After the expiration of the deadline, new evidence can only be presented in exceptional cases.[76] Exceptions can be granted if the evidence has come into existence after the expiration of the deadline for the exchange of evidence, or if there are objective reasons why the evidence could not be produced in time.[77] **13.28**

In the trial phase, upon closure of the evidence exchange, the court will arrange a formal oral hearing. Non-compliance of a plaintiff with a summons to attend an oral hearing may result in a dismissal of the action.[78] If instead the defendant does not appear, the case may be decided in his absence.[79] The hearing typically consists of the following parts: **13.29**

- opening statements with brief presentations by plaintiff and defendant;
- court investigation (法庭调查) with focus on facts (claims and supporting evidence);[80]
- court debate with arguments from plaintiff and defendant;
- closing statements by the parties.

Typically, the trial is conducted in the course of one or two public[81] hearings, whereby each hearing would not last longer than one day.[82]

71 Art. 47 Chinese Civil Procedures Act. A ruling based on evidence which has not been made available to the opponent is a ground for retrial (see section H.2).

72 It. 49 Evidence Interpretation; originals can be requested as documentary evidence (书证), material evidence (物证), and audiovisual material (视听资料).

73 Arts. 63 and 67 of the Chinese Civil Procedures Act, It. 39 Evidence Interpretation, which uses the term '记录在卷', that is, record on file, for admitted evidence.

74 Tilman Müller-Stoy, above note 42, 531; Xiaolin Dang in China 2012 IP Focus special issue of Intellectual Property Focus, *MIP*.

75 Art. 65 Chinese Civil Procedures Act.

76 Tilman Müller-Stoy, above note 42, 531.

77 Item 41 Evidence Interpretation in connection with Art. 139 Chinese Civil Procedures Act.

78 Art. 143 Chinese Civil Procedures Act.

79 Art. 144 Chinese Civil Procedures Act.

80 Detailed procedure in Art.138 Chinese Civil Procedures Act.

81 Art.134 Chinese Civil Procedures Act.

82 Tilman Müller-Stoy, above note 42, 531.

**13.30** Mediation (调解) by the court plays a major role in patent litigation. Typically, Chinese courts assume a quite active part in mediation, more active than in many western countries. Mediation can take place before the court trial.[83] Also in the course of the trial, the court will ask the parties whether they are ready to settle. Upon successful mediation, a conciliation agreement (调解书) will be drawn up and become effective upon signature by both parties.[84] Such conciliation agreement is enforceable even if a party rejects its postal delivery.[85]

**13.31** Usually, a written decision is issued within four to six weeks after the trial hearing.[86] Courts normally deliver it via judicial express. Court decisions are open to the public and can be searched unless they contain state secrets, business secrets or private information.[87] The court has to conclude the case within six months.[88] This period can be extended by another six months if justified. Further extensions require the approval from a Higher People's Court.[89] These deadlines, however, are not applicable to cases which involve foreign parties.[90]

**13.32** It is possible to change the asserted patent claims until the end of the trial.[91] During the trial, an asserted claim may turn out to be unenforceable due to a prior art defense (*Bailey and Wang*, Chapter 8; *Heide*, Chapter 14) or unable to withstand an invalidation procedure (*Heide*, Chapter 14). Under these circumstances, a change of asserted claim(s) may be advisable.[92]

## F. EVIDENCE

**13.33** Adducing evidence is key to successful litigation. Chinese courts are generally stricter than courts in other countries with regard to evidence standards. Painstaking evidence preparation is required to stay clear of problems. A failure to have evidence admitted contributed to Schneider's notorious setback in the

83 Art. 133(2) Chinese Civil Procedures Act.
84 Art. 97 Chinese Civil Procedures Act.
85 Bu, *Einführung*, 292.
86 Tilman Müller-Stoy, above note 42, 532.
87 Arts. 148 and 156 Chinese Civil Procedures Act.
88 Art. 149 Chinese Civil Procedures Act.
89 Art. 149 Chinese Civil Procedures Act.
90 Art. 270 Chinese Civil Procedures Act – strictly speaking for cases relating to foreign matters. A foreign party would be sufficient to make the cut. For more details see Bu, *Einführung*, 310.
91 Art. 51 Chinese Civil Procedures Act and It. 1 of the 2010 Judicial Interpretation.
92 According to It. 1 of the 2010 Judicial Interpretation the right owner may change the claim which he asserts before the end of the submissions of the first instance trial.

*Chint v Schneider* case.[93] Here, Schneider failed to invalidate all claims of the utility model asserted against its Tianjin subsidiary in invalidation proceedings, partly because the authenticity (真实性) of Schneider's evidence on prior public use was not acknowledged.[94]

In order to provide valid evidence, a number of rules must be observed.[95] The evidence regulations of the Chinese Civil Procedures Act merely constitute a raw basis. Most detailed regulations are contained in the Evidence Interpretation and some other provisions issued by the Supreme People's Court. **13.34**

According to the Chinese Civil Procedures Act, the following categories of evidence are acceptable:[96] **13.35**

- Statements of the parties (当事人的陈述)
- Documentary evidence (书证)
- Material evidence (物证)
- Audiovisual material (视听资料)
- Electronic data (电子数据)[97]
- Testimony of witnesses (证人证言)
- Conclusions of expert witnesses (鉴定意见)
- Transcripts of inspection and examination (勘验笔录)

As a central tenet of procedural law, the burden of proving a fact lies with the party that adduced the fact.[98] That is, each party needs to prove those facts which favor its case. **13.36**

According to Article 65 Chinese Civil Procedures Act, evidence is to be presented as early as possible. The amended Chinese Civil Procedures Act explicitly introduced the possibility to request an extension of the deadline for exchange of evidence, which would be accepted if justified. **13.37**

If, for objective reasons, evidence is not within reach of one of the parties, a request can be filed that the court may obtain such evidence of its own account.[99] **13.38**

---

93 专利名案解读 (Interpretation of Famous Patent Cases): 16 起典型专利纠纷案例评析, 知识产权书版社, case no. 7 – patent infringement case between Schneider's Tianjin JV and Chint.

94 专利名案解读(2) (Interpretation of Famous Patent Cases, No. 2): 20 起典型专利纠纷案例评析, 知识产权书版社, case no. 5 – invalidation case between Schneider and Chint.

95 Excellent account of procedural law related to evidence is provided by Cao, *Durchsetzung* and Bu, *Einführung*.

96 Art. 63 Chinese Civil Procedures Act.

97 New in Chinese Civil Procedures Act from 2013.

98 It. 2 Evidence Interpretation.

99 It. 3 Evidence Interpretation.

**13.39** If an invention patent for a new manufacturing process is asserted, the burden of proof can be reversed. In such case, a manufacturer of an identical product can be requested to prove that he uses a different manufacturing process (*Ganea*, Chapter 16).[100]

**13.40** Facts admitted by the opponent are not required to be supported by evidence. An admission can be retracted with the consent of the other party or if the statement has been obtained under duress or made by mistake. The party is held responsible for its representative's statements, that is, facts admitted by a representative are treated in the same way as admissions by the party itself.[101] Counter-evidence can be produced to render erroneous admissions moot.[102]

**13.41** Generally known facts, facts known to the court and laws of nature do not need to be proven. The same is true with regard to facts set out in a court judgment, in an effective arbitration ruling or in an effective notarized document. The assumption of the correctness of these facts, however, can be challenged by evidence to the contrary.[103]

**13.42** As mentioned, evidence must be provided in original form (original documents or objects). Exceptionally, duplicates or copies which are identical with the original evidence can be accepted if the original evidence is difficult to obtain.[104]

**13.43** Evidence collected outside China must be notarized (in the country of origin) and legalized (that is, confirmed by the Chinese representation in that country). This requirement does not have to be observed by residents of countries with which China has concluded bilateral treaties that regulate different procedures.[105] However, China has not yet concluded such treaty with the majority of western countries, so that litigants from these countries have to shoulder this additional burden. Typically, such requirements play a special role when it comes to proving prior public use outside China, either for supporting a prior use defense or as evidence in invalidation proceedings (*Bailey and Wang*, Chapter 8; *Heide*, Chapter 14). In addition, documents in foreign languages have to be translated into Chinese.[106]

---

100 It. 4(1) Evidence Interpretation and Art. 61 Chinese Patent Act.

101 It. 8 Evidence Interpretation.

102 It. 74 Evidence Interpretation; counter-evidence can also be used to disprove already admitted evidence.

103 It. 9 Evidence Interpretation.

104 It. 10 Evidence Interpretation.

105 It. 11 Evidence Interpretation.

106 It. 12 Evidence Interpretation.

Collection of evidence (调查收集证据) by the court can be requested,[107] for example, if the evidence in point cannot be obtained by the requesting party or such parties' attorney for objective reasons, for example, because such evidence pertains to a trade or business secret held by the opponent.[108] Such request must be filed within seven days before the expiry of the evidence deadline (举证期限).[109] **13.44**

Pursuant to Article 81 Chinese Civil Procedures Act, the same deadline (that is, seven days before the end of the evidence deadline) is determined with regard to requests for preservation of evidence (保全证据).[110] **13.45**

The deadline for producing evidence will not be shorter than 30 days if set by the court, but it may also be agreed upon between the parties.[111] The deadline can be extended upon request if a party finds it difficult to provide evidence in due time.[112] **13.46**

Failure to provide evidence within the deadline is considered to be a waiver of the right to produce evidence. Evidence submitted after the end of the deadline is not considered in the evidence cross examination (互相质证) unless the other party agrees to include it.[113] **13.47**

Extensions of and amendments to the plaintiff's claims are, in principle, possible until the end of the deadline for evidence presentation. The same holds true with regard to countersuits to be tried in conjunction with the patent infringement suit. Exceptionally, such moves can be made after the expiry of the deadline, for example, if new facts are to be taken into account.[114] Moreover, the deadline does not apply to a change of the asserted patent claims (see footnote 92). **13.48**

Evidence obtained under violation of the opponent's rights or under breach of law is not admissible.[115] There is a grey zone with regard to what is still acceptable to get hold of evidence; for instance, devious ways that are not tantamount to a blatant breach of law may still make the cut. In particular, an infringement of patent right is often not provable by a product purchase if the **13.49**

107 It. 16 Evidence Interpretation.
108 It. 17 Evidence Interpretation.
109 It. 19 Evidence Interpretation.
110 It. 23 Evidence Interpretation.
111 It. 33 Evidence Interpretation.
112 It. 36 Evidence Interpretation.
113 It. 34 Evidence Interpretation.
114 It. 35 Evidence Interpretation.
115 It. 68 Evidence Interpretation.

infringing technology is implemented in a system of larger scale, for example, a factory or a plant. The patent owner would need to substantiate the probability of a patent infringement for filing a successful request that the court collect further evidence. The substantiation material may only be accessible under sounding out the grey zone area of the respective court.

**13.50** The court then assesses the evidence provided. If evidence is found to be non-conclusive, the party which adduced the evidence has to bear the consequences.[116] Notarization is a major factor in the course of evidence consideration.[117] Upon an unfounded refusal by one of the parties to present certain evidence the court can assume the correctness of facts the other party claims to be proven by such evidence.[118] As discussed in section M, future patent law may provide stronger ammunition against infringers who withhold evidence on unlawful gains.

## G. REMEDIES

**13.51** Relevant legal statues for remedies are found in Article 134 of the General Principles of the Civil Law of the People's Republic of China,[119] Article 15 of the Chinese Tort Act,[120] and the Chinese Patent Act.[121] As *lex specialis*, the regulations of the Chinese Patent Act prevail over the other regulations. It is undisputed that patent owners are at least entitled to two remedies, namely cessation from infringement and payment of damages. The availability of further remedies is more contentious and will be discussed at the end of this section.

### 1. Cessation from infringement

**13.52** Cessation from infringement translates into an injunction to abstain from infringement during the duration of the patent.[122] Cessation can be ordered irrespective of whether the defendant has acted intentionally or negligently.[123] A cessation order can be enforced until the expiration of two years from the

116 It. 73 Evidence Interpretation.

117 It. 77(2) Evidence Interpretation.

118 It. 75 Evidence Interpretation.

119 中华人民共和国民法通则, effective 1 January 1987.

120 中华人民共和国侵权责任法, effective 1 July 2010.

121 Patent infringement per se is not a criminal act, that is, there is no criminal liability unless the infringement is connected with a criminal act such as counterfeiting. See Lin Ma and Junjie Zheng, 'Patent Criminal Enforcement in the People's Republic of China', [2010] **41** *IIC* 7.

122 It. 23 of 2001 Judicial Interpretation.

123 Bu, *Patentrecht*, 118.

decision, which is the deadline for enforcing a civil court decision.[124] Consequently, the injunction to abstain from infringement during the duration of the patent is not necessarily enforceable during the entire duration of patent. Instigation of another law suit would be required after the enforcement deadline. The proposed changes to the patent law (see section M) propose more severe sanctions for repeated infringement, that is, would provide deterrence to resume patent infringement after expiry of the enforcement deadline but before the end of the patent's duration.

In general, patent owners can rely on this remedy. There are, however, caveats. Traditionally, western players have been wary of compulsory licenses. Chinese patent law comprises a body of regulations on compulsory licenses (Articles 48–58 Patent Act) which have been strengthened in the course of the 2009 amendment to the Chinese Patent Act and supplemented by implementing regulations.[125] Recently, the discussion about compulsory licenses has abated in spite of the fact that some developing countries resort to this instrument. There are two reasons why China is unlikely to make frequent use of compulsory licenses. First, there is no precedent of China granting compulsory licenses, a record China is keenly aware of and which is used to stave off criticism. Second, a decision of the Supreme Court has paved the way to a less conspicuous mode of dealing with situations in which an injunction would contravene a preponderant public interest.[126] The decision shall be briefly presented here because it may set a trend for the future of IP protection in China.[127] **13.53**

In December 2009, the Supreme People's Court made the final judgment in the case of *Wuhan Jingyuan Engineering Co. Ltd. (Wuhan Jingyuan) v Huayang Electric Industry Co. Ltd.* (Huayang Electric) *and Fuji Water Co., Ltd.* (Fuji Water). The Japanese defendant Fuji Water sold a sea water type flue-gas desulfurization system to the Chinese defendant Huayang Electric. Huayang Electric employed this system in the Houshi Thermal Plant in Fujian Province, which is operated by Huayang Electric. The Fujian Higher People's Court and, in the final instance, the Supreme People's Court found the system to infringe the patent 'a method of using sea water for desulfurization of flue-gas and aeration device' of the Chinese plaintiff Wuhan Jingyuan. **13.54**

The Fujian Higher People's Court as well as the Supreme People's Court denied an injunction against the operation of the Houshi Thermal Plant to Wuhan **13.55**

124 Art. 239 Chinese Civil Procedures Act.

125 Measures for Compulsory License for Patent Exploitation (专利实施强制许可办法), effective 1 May 2012.

126 Anti-monopoly measures are a possible exception where a compulsory license is a more likely resort – see *Pattloch*, Chapter 17.

127 Legal Affairs Department of CPA, [2010] **2** *China Patents & Trademarks* 9.

Jingyuan because 'the flue-gas desulfurization system has been installed in the power plant of Huayang Electric and put into operation, and ordering cessation from the infringement would have a major impact on the local public interests, with full consideration of the interests of the patentee and those of the general public'.

**13.56** Two earlier decisions made by lower instance courts also denied injunctions as a remedy in similar cases. The rationale behind such denial has been explained by Cao Jianming, Vice-President of the Supreme People's Court, in a speech given in February 2008 and therefore prior to the Wuhan Jingyuan ruling. He held that 'where an infringement goes on when a first-instance decision is made, the court should generally order the infringement to be ceased'. However, he also opined that 'a reasonable balance should be kept between the interests of the parties and those of the general public according to the specific circumstances of a case. If permanent injunction is likely to knock the parties' interests greatly out of balance or contravenes the public interest, or if it is practically impossible to cease the infringement, the court could weigh upon the interests according to the specific circumstances of a case, and may not give order to cease from infringement where it is possible to take substituting measures, such as [...] monetary compensation.'[128] This reasoning is confirmed by the Opinion on Economic Situation.[129]

**13.57** Invoking the public interest is in line with the international trend. It also corresponds with trends that can be observed in the USA, for example, in connection with the *eBay* decision[130] or the discussion about limitations to the entitlement of so-called non-practicing entities (NPEs) to grant and execute injunctions. It is to be expected that permanent injunctions are more likely to be denied in technical fields, in which the public interest is evident, such as green technologies and medical technologies. On the other hand, it would be almost impossible to deny an injunction for a design patent on such grounds.

**13.58** The statement of Cao Jianming goes beyond the mere invocation of public interests. It indicates that the question whether a permanent injunction should be issued shall be subject to a balance of interests between the parties. The example given, that is, cases 'in which it is practically impossible to cease the infringement' seem to refer to the previously mentioned lower instance cases where cessation would have resulted in tearing down a building. There is a certain likelihood, however, that the 'balance of interests' argument could also

128 Legal Affairs Department of CPA, [2010] **2** *China Patents & Trademarks* 15.

129 Item 15 Opinion on Economic Situation.

130 *eBay Inc. v MercExchange*, L.L.C., 547 U.S. 388 (2006).

be invoked in favor of the defendant in less extreme cases, for example, if the plaintiff's behavior unwarrantedly added to the burden an injunction would impose on the defendant. For instance, forfeiture is a legal concept indigenous to many patent systems.[131] The run-up to the 2009 patent law amendment has seen several attempts to incorporate such forfeiture into the Chinese patent system. In an early draft version, a new Article 72 Chinese Patent Act intended to provide for a possible forfeiture of the patent if the plaintiff, without justification, did not initiate litigation within three years after obtaining knowledge about the infringement. Even though this regulation did not become law, experts believe that an unwarranted delay can become a valid defense in patent litigation.[132] Hence, protracting legal action in order to accumulate high amounts of damage payments may tip the balance in favor of the defendant against the issuance of an injunction.[133]

In contrast, an Intermediate People's Court's decision of 2006 which qualified the use of a patented fastener for the construction of a museum building as non-commercial use should remain an exception.[134] In similar future cases, the public interest may instead be invoked, in analogy to the precedent set by the *Wuhan Jingyuan* decision. **13.59**

## 2. Damages

Article 65 Chinese Patent Act provides for four different methods of damage calculation: **13.60**

(a) compensation of suffered damage;
(b) return of unlawful gains;
(c) payment of an appropriate multiple of a license fee;
(d) statutory damages.

According to the wording of the provision, calculation on grounds of unlawful gains is only allowed if calculation based on actual damages is impossible, and so forth, so that the plaintiff cannot choose the method of calculation. In practice, however, a choice of the calculation method is often accepted.[135] **13.61**

---

131 The US patent system uses the term 'laches'.

132 See discussion of forfeiture defense (专利懈怠抗议) in 侵犯专利权抗议事由.

133 Also see Item 15 Opinion on Economic Situation, where temporary acquiescence in infringement is mentioned as a criterion in assessing whether to grant an injunction.

134 *Fischerwerke Arthur Fischer GmbH & Co. KG v Shanghai Luming, Shenyang Kaixing and Shanxi Museum*; see the discussion in 侵犯专利权抗议事由 which also refers to a contrary decision in a similar case (use of patented garbage press by public services).

135 Bu, *Patentrecht*, 123.

**13.62** Item 20 of the 2001 Judicial Interpretation outlines calculation according to the actual damage in greater detail, namely as lost sales calculated by the number of products that were not sold due to the infringement, multiplied by an appropriate profit per product. If it is difficult to estimate the additional sales that would have been made in the absence of infringement, the lost profit can also be determined by multiplying the number of sold infringing products by an appropriate profit.

**13.63** The second method multiplies the number of sold infringing products by the infringer's profit per sale. According to Item 20 of the 2001 Judicial Interpretation, the business profit should be the basis for the calculation, unless the infringer solely concentrates on patent infringing business. In this case, the sales profit may be taken as the calculation basis.

**13.64** Item 16 of the 2010 Judicial Interpretation further refined the instructions with regard to this calculation method. Some commentators hold that such refinement is at least partly due to the disputed calculation of damages in the *Chint v Schneider* case in which the infringer's profit was estimated to be one-third of the total turnover, and the full profit was taken to be the damages to be paid to Chint.[136]

**13.65** In its 2010 Judicial Interpretation, the Supreme People's Court also clarifies that the infringer's gains from infringement are limited to the profit earned by the infringement of a patent right, that is, causality is required. Profits that arose from non-infringing activity have to be discounted. If the infringement is related to a part of a product, the relevance of this part for the whole product is to be taken as the basis to calculate damages. It can be expected that such blatant over-calculation of damages as in the above cited *Chint v Schneider* case are unlikely to recur after the Supreme People's Court's clarifications.

**13.66** According to Item 21 2001 Judicial Interpretation, calculation in license analogy is subsidiary to the two above-mentioned methods. That is, the plaintiff can only opt for it if calculation by the other two methods is not possible. The court may calculate the damages as one to three times the license fee to be paid for a hypothetical license of the patent in suit. Multiple damages were rarely awarded in the past, a tendency that may change with the impending fourth amendment (see section M).

**13.67** Finally, the court can impose a statutory damage between 10,000 and one million RMB if calculation by the other methods has failed. In spite of the fact

136 *CPA newsletter* 1/2010.

that this method forms the last resort if calculation by all other means has failed, a study carried out by China Patent Agents revealed that in 99 per cent of patent infringement cases, the courts actually imposed statutory damages.[137] Apparently, the information which is necessary to calculate by the other three methods is hard to obtain. The envisaged fourth amendment may partly eliminate some of the deficits of the present calculation practice.

According to Article 65 Chinese Patent Act, damages also include the reasonable expenses incurred by the claimant. These reasonable expenses cover both expenditures to prove the infringement (purchases of infringing products, notary costs, travel expenses and so on) and attorney fees. While the amount spent for the purchase of the infringing product is regularly recovered[138] the compensation awarded for attorney fees typically falls far short of covering the real costs.[139] **13.68**

In contrast to the order to cease the infringement, Article 106 of the General Principles of the Civil Law of the People's Republic of China (中华人民共和国民法通则, effective 1987)[140] provides that damages are subject to an element of fault (过错). **13.69**

The element of fault as a prerequisite for damage claims becomes apparent in Article 70 Patent Act, pursuant to which no damages shall be imposed if a patented product is used, offered for sale or sold without knowledge of the absence of the patentee's authorization and if the product has been obtained from a legal source. This article aims at exempting distributors who unknowingly infringe upon a patent from liability for damages.[141] In contrast, manufacturers of infringing products cannot invoke ignorance as an excuse, that is, the manufacturer is expected to apply a stricter duty of care than the distributor. **13.70**

It should be noted that Article 70 Chinese Patent Act does not mention manufacturing and, notably, importation as actions which are exempted from damage liability. **13.71**

---

137 [2009] **4** *China Patents & Trademarks* 12.

138 For instance, in the famous Neoplan case (see http://legalweekly.cn/index.php/Index/article/id/752), the price of 930,000 RMB paid for a design infringing bus was recovered in the first instance.

139 Bu, *Patentrecht*, 124.

140 Prerequisites for a damage claim are unlawfulness of the defendant's act, existence of an actual damage suffered by the claimant, a causal link between damage and infringement, and fault at side of the defendant (see Cao, *Durchsetzung*, 63). The following observations, however, will center on the element of fault as the most critical prerequisite.

141 Before the second amendment, the acts pursuant to Art. 70 Chinese Patent Act were not considered to constitute patent infringement, that is, an injunction would not have been granted either.

**13.72** As ignorance or 'not knowing' (不知道) is a precondition to escape damage claims, the infringer can no longer rely on this exception once he has learned about the patent's existence. Yin argues that negligence or 'should know' (应当知道) should be a sufficient prerequisite to deny the application of the exemption.[142]

**13.73** In any case, a warning letter informing the infringer about the infringing act would trigger liability for damages from the moment of its receipt.

**13.74** In practice, there are a number of cases in which infringers were exempted from liability with reference to Article 70 Patent Act. For instance, in the first instance decision of the *Neoplan* case, no damages were imposed on the second defendant who bought the bus from an allegedly legal source.

### 3. Further remedies

**13.75** The list of remedies in Article 15 Chinese Tort Act raises the question of whether further remedies in addition to the above ones are also available.

**13.76** One remedy that is discussed in the literature is an apology to be delivered by the infringer. This remedy goes back to item 7 and item 8 of Article 15 Chinese Tort Act, that is, apology and removal of the adverse effect and restitution of reputation. An official apology was sometimes delivered as part of a sentence or a settlement. According to a 2005 statement of the Supreme Court, however, apology shall no longer be used as a remedy in patent litigation.[143]

**13.77** Of more practical relevance seems to be the question of whether courts can order the destruction of apparatus, and so on, for the production of infringing products. A statement made by the Supreme People's Court in 2009 clarified that such destruction can be ordered as an optional remedy subject to the consideration of the interests of the parties and of the public.[144] The Opinion on Economic Situation confirms the availability of this remedy, which, however, is to be used prudently.[145]

---

142 Yin, 840.

143 Yin, 661.

144 最高人民法院关于当前经济形势下知识产权审判服务大局若干问题的意见, no. 15, see also Yin, 664.

145 lt. 15 Opinion on Economic Situation.

## H. APPEAL AND RETRIAL

It goes without saying that a first instance decision on patent infringement can be appealed. As an appeal can be filed only for a limited time after the first instance decision, it is no longer a suitable resort to remove the court decision after expiry of the deadline for appeal. A different remedy is needed if, for instance, new evidence appears at a later time which allows for a successful invalidation suit. In patent litigation, the invalidation of the patent in suit would reshuffle cards. Hence, a second legal means is provided to remedy the situation in such cases. This legal means is the retrial procedure. **13.78**

### 1. Appeal (上诉)

The second instance court shall review facts as well as the application of the law by the first instance court.[146] Higher People's Courts have jurisdiction to handle patent cases, that is, the second instance court will be the responsible Higher People's Court or the Supreme Court.[147] A decision may be made without a trial if no new facts or evidence need to be taken into account.[148] In practice, a decision without trial is rather the exception.[149] **13.79**

The deadline for appealing a decision is 15 days from receipt of a judgment (判决) and 10 days from receipt of a ruling (裁定). The appeal is to be filed with the next instance court.[150] Parties without residence in China enjoy an extended deadline of 30 days for both judgments and rulings.[151] **13.80**

A notice of appeal is to be filed within the prescribed deadline, which has to include details on the appellant, his representative (if applicable), and the first instance case (first instance court, case identification number, case brief). In addition, the appellant shall make a request and provide the reasons thereof.[152] Copies for the court and the respondent have to be provided.[153] **13.81**

If the notice of appeal is directly filed with the second instance court, it will be submitted to the first instance court within five days.[154] The first instance court then has five days to send the notice of appeal to the respondent. Receipt by the **13.82**

146 Art. 168 Chinese Civil Procedures Act.
147 See section D.
148 Art. 169 Chinese Civil Procedures Act.
149 Bu, *Einführung*, 300.
150 Art. 164 Chinese Civil Procedures Act.
151 Art. 269 Chinese Civil Procedures Act.
152 Art. 165 Chinese Civil Procedures Act.
153 Art. 166 Chinese Civil Procedures Act.
154 Art. 166 Chinese Civil Procedures Act.

respondent triggers a deadline of 15 days (30 days for a party with no residence in China[155]) for the respondent to reply. Failure to reply has no effect on the handling of the appeal. Within five days after receipt of the respondent's reply, the first instance court shall submit the case files to the second instance court.[156]

**13.83** The second instance court may sustain, change or rescind the first instance decision. The case may be remanded once to the first instance if the first instance decision is found deficient with respect to facts or legal reasoning. The case may not be remanded again in a second appeal.[157]

**13.84** In dealing with a first instance ruling (裁定) the second instance court has also to issue a ruling (裁定).[158]

**13.85** The second instance court can make an attempt to mediate. If a settlement is reached, the court will issue a judgment to rescind the first instance decision.[159]

**13.86** Withdrawal of the appeal is subject to the second instance court's approval.[160]

**13.87** The second instance is the last appellate instance.[161] The court has three months to review first instance judgments and 30 days to review first instance rulings (裁定).[162] An extension of these deadlines must be approved by the court. Such constraints are not applied to foreign-related cases.[163]

**13.88** Unlike other court systems, Chinese courts do not execute a patent judgment before it takes legal effect.[164] If necessary, the claimant has to go the second instance's distance before the infringing products can be removed and damages can be collected. There are no provisions which would entitle the defendant to damage claims if the plaintiff has lost the case. In contrast, damage claims do arise if interim measures were not justified.[165]

---

155 Art. 269 Chinese Civil Procedures Act.
156 Art. 167 Chinese Civil Procedures Act.
157 Art. 170 Chinese Civil Procedures Act.
158 Art. 171 Chinese Civil Procedures Act.
159 Art. 172 Chinese Civil Procedures Act.
160 Art. 173 Chinese Civil Procedures Act.
161 Art. 175 Chinese Civil Procedures Act.
162 Art. 176 Chinese Civil Procedures Act.
163 Art. 270 Chinese Civil Procedures Act.
164 For instance, first instance judgments of German court can be executed while an appeal is still pending ('vorläufige Vollstreckbarkeit'). See discussion in Tilman Müller-Stoy, above note 42, 532.
165 See section K.

### 2. Retrial (再审)

A second path to have a court decision revisited is the retrial procedure. Article 199 Chinese Civil Procedures Act opens the path for retrial of erroneous judgments and rulings by civil courts. Retrial is requested with the next instance court. During the retrial procedure, the execution of the retried decision will be suspended.[166] A retrial is admissible for a number of reasons enumerated in Article 200 Chinese Civil Procedures Act. 13.89

Many of these reasons are related to evidence. A retrial is in order if there is new evidence that is conclusive enough to overrule the original judgment or ruling, or if major evidence used in the original judgment or ruling is found to be insufficient, forged or not cross-examined (质证). Also, if a party to a lawsuit has been unable to obtain the evidence necessary for adjudicating the case for material reasons and has applied to the people's court for investigation and collection of such evidence in writing but the court has failed to do so, retrial may be admitted. 13.90

Also a mistaken or erroneous application of law can become a reason for a retrial. In general, if there was an error in the application of the law in the original judgment or ruling the path to retrial is open. More specific are reasons related to incorrect trial organization or adjudicators who should have withdrawn from the case. The violation of the right to be heard (literally, right to debate or 辩论权利) and an erroneous judgment made in the absence of a party which has not been served with a summons are further deficiencies which justify a retrial. 13.91

Further reasons for a retrial are related to the scope and foundation of the court decision. For instance, if valid claims were omitted or the court awarded more than claimed in the original judgment or ruling, the case may be retried. Here, it is important to note that if the legal document on which the original judgment or ruling has been based is cancelled or revised, the case is open to retrial, too. This can happen, for instance, if the patent in suit has lost its effect *ex tunc*, for example, through invalidation. 13.92

According to Article 47 Chinese Patent Act, an invalidation of a patent would generally have no retroactive effect on paid damages or license or assignment fees (*Heide*, Chapter 14). 13.93

166 Art. 206 Chinese Civil Procedures Act.

**13.94** A settlement can also be retried if the applicant can substantiate that the settlement has been reached through coercion or in an otherwise unlawful manner.[167]

**13.95** The deadline for applying for retrial is six months from the entry into effect of the disputed judgment or ruling.[168] This deadline does not apply to cases in which a retrial is requested due to new evidence, cancellation or revision of a document or involvement of forgery, bribery or fraud. For these latter situations, the deadline of six months starts from the date at which the reasons for retrial have become or should have become known to the requesting party. For instance, in the retrial of a judgment that has been made on grounds of a patent that has been invalidated afterwards, the six months will be counted from the date of invalidation.

**13.96** Within three months, the retrial court has to make a judgment (裁定) which either revises the original judgment or ruling, or rejects the retrial request.[169] The deadline is not applicable if the litigation is foreign-related.

**13.97** A party to the retrial may file a complaint (抗诉) with a responsible people's procuratorate[170] (人民检察院) if:[171]

- the retrial request is rejected
- a judgment is not issued in due time
- the retrial judgment is obviously flawed.

**13.98** The Supreme Court has the authority to carry out a retrial *ex officio* whereby it exercises its surveillance function, or to order a subordinate court to carry out such retrial if it finds the original court decision (judgment or ruling) to be flawed.[172]

---

167 Art. 201 Chinese Civil Procedures Act.

168 Art. 205 Chinese Civil Procedures Act

169 Art. 204 Chinese Civil Procedures Act.

170 The people's procuratorates in China are state organs of legal supervision. Their organization corresponds to that of the people's courts. They exercise their own authority according to law, independent from interference from any administrative organ, civic organization, or individual.

171 Art. 209 Chinese Civil Procedures Act.

172 Art. 198 Chinese Civil Procedures Act.

## I. COSTS

Litigation involves costs. Some but not all costs can be recovered by the winning party.[173] **13.99**

Costs can be classified as internal and external costs. The internal costs correspond to in-house costs for preparing the material and providing support to the attorneys. Evidently, internal costs depend on which part of the work is done in-house. The amount of work which has to be borne in-house tends to increase with the size of the company. In the author's experience, for companies with in-house patent departments, internal costs can be as high as external costs. In the absence of an in-house patent department, it may be advisable for foreign companies to draw in additional expertise from patent attorneys who are based in their home countries. Experienced litigators are scarce in China. Typically, high-quality input and support are crucial because of limited resources at the Chinese end. **13.100**

External costs can be divided into court fees, attorney fees and further expenses for raising evidence. **13.101**

Court fees are due according to Article 118 Chinese Civil Procedures Act, which refers to supplementary rules on court fees. These rules are provided by the 'Methods for the payment of litigation fees' (诉讼费用交纳办法)[174] which have been published at the end of 2006 and have become effective on 1 April 2007. They also regulate the fees which have to be paid in connection with requests for preliminary injunctions.[175] [176] **13.102**

Rule 6 of these Methods lists three different types of fees, namely lawsuit handling fees (案件受理费), request fees (申请费), and expenses for persons involved in the lawsuit as witnesses, experts, translators, and so on. **13.103**

The lawsuit handling fee is due in first and second instance lawsuits,[177] as well as in retrial lawsuits[178] and has to be paid in advance.[179] The fee will be repaid if the lawsuit or the appeal is not accepted and hence not processed.[180] No fee **13.104**

---

173 See section G.
174 Hereinafter 'Fees Methods'.
175 See section K.1.
176 It. 18 Injunction Interpretation.
177 R. 7 Fees Methods.
178 See section H.2.
179 R. 20 and R. 23 Fees Methods.
180 R. 27 Fees Methods.

needs to be paid for an appeal against the decision to not accept a case.[181] A second instance modification of a court judgment and a retrial judgment which overturned the original decision retroactively affect (that is, change) the first instance order for payment of costs to the losing party to cover the costs of the winning party.[182]

**13.105** Request fees are to be paid in case of requests, for example, for the execution of a judgment or the preservation of evidence. Thus, in the event of the execution of a judgment, the respondent has to pay a fee as prescribed.[183] Request fees are to be paid together with the submission of the request or within a deadline set by the court.[184] After the court has conducted an investigation into the case details, the plaintiff can request the reduction of the value in dispute. In this case a request fee has to be paid, too.[185]

**13.106** According to Rule 13(3) Fees Methods, the handling fee for intellectual property litigation ranges between 500 and 1,000 RMB if no value in dispute can be established. Within this range, the precise amount is set by the local authority.[186]

**13.107** If a value in dispute can be established, Table 13.1 is applied.[187]

**13.108** For requesting protective measures (evidence preservation, property preservation), the fee depends on the value of the property subject to preservation. Up to a value of 1,000 RMB, a fee of 30 RMB has to be paid. If the value is between 1,000 and 100,000 RMB, a fee of 1 percent has to be paid. This percentage is reduced to 0.5 percent if the amount is higher than 100,000 RMB. The fee is capped at a maximum of 5,000 RMB.

---

181 R. 8 Fees Methods.

182 R. 30 and R. 32 Fees Methods.

183 R. 10 in connection with R. 38 Fees Methods.

184 R. 22 Fees Methods.

185 R. 35 Fees Methods.

186 R. 13(6) Fees Methods.

187 R. 13(1) Fees Methods, the highest damage award in Chinese patent litigation amounted to nearly 335 million RMB. This resulted in a handling fee of about 1,69 million RMB, which is still moderate by German standards. See 专利名案解读 / Interpretation of Famous Patent Cases, 16 起典型专利纠纷案例评析. 知识产权书版社, case no. 7 – patent infringement case between Schneider's Tianjin JV and Chint, 151, Sabine Rojahn and Anja Lunze, 'Die Streitwertfestsetzung im Patentrecht – Ein Mysterium?', **2012** *Mitt.* 533.

*Table 13.1 Fees according to value of the case*

| Value in litigation | Handling fee | Execution fee |
|---|---|---|
| 10.000 RMB or below | 50 RMB | 50 RMB |
| From 10,000 to 100,000 RMB | 2.5% | 1.5% |
| From 100,000 to 200,000 RMB | 2% | |
| From 200,000 to 500,000 RMB | 1.5% | |
| From 500,000 to 1 m RMB | 1% | 1% |
| From 1 m to 2 m RMB | 0.9% | |
| From 2 m to 5 m RMB | 0.8% | |
| From 5 m to 10 m RMB | 0.7% | 0.5% |
| From 10 m to 20 m RMB | 0.6% | 0.1% |
| Above 20 m RMB | 0.5% | |

If a settlement is reached or the complaint has been withdrawn, half of the handling fee will be due.[188] The plaintiff will bear such fee if he withdraws his complaint.[189] In the case of a settlement, the corresponding contract should ideally include the distribution of court fees. Otherwise, the court will decide about distribution.[190] 13.109

The handling fee for the second instance is also calculated according to the value in dispute. The fee should be paid in advance. If the appellant does not pay in advance, the court will notify him to pay within seven days from reception of the notice. 13.110

If the defendant raises a countersuit or if the court combines another lawsuit initiated by a third party with an ongoing lawsuit, the handling fee is halved for each of the combined lawsuits.[191] In patent litigation, a countersuit may be raised, for example, to collect damages for an interim injunction that turns out to have been unfounded. The deadline for the defendant to pay the fee for such countersuit is seven days after filing the complaint.[192] 13.111

In case of an adjustment of the value in dispute, for example, after preservation of evidence, the additional handling fee has to be paid within seven days from 13.112

188 R. 15 Fees Methods.
189 R. 34 Fees Methods.
190 R. 31 Fees Methods.
191 R. 18 Fees Methods.
192 R. 22 Fees Methods.

receipt of the notice by the court if the value has been found to be higher than anticipated, or the excess fee must be returned if the value has been found to be lower than expected.[193] Such return is due within 15 days after the end of the lawsuit.[194]

**13.113** The costs for the lawsuit are to be borne by the losing party. In case of partial success, the costs shall be distributed accordingly. If more than one party is involved on one side, the costs are shared according to the distribution of interests (利害关系) of the parties.[195]

**13.114** A party has to bear the additional costs it causes by presenting new evidence in the second instance trial or retrial if it had failed to do so without justified reason before the expiration of the deadline for the exchange of evidence.[196]

**13.115** Court orders related to the payment of costs do not constitute a ground for filing an appeal. However, a reassessment (复核) of the issued order for payment of costs can be requested if the decision in the main proceedings is not to be appealed.[197] Upon such a request the court would check the correctness of its cost allocation and issue a revised order of payment if the original was found to be defective.

**13.116** If amounts in foreign currencies are in dispute, the exchange rate at the date at which the first instance court has accepted the complaint shall be applied to calculate the corresponding amount in RMB. This exchange rate would also be used by the appeal court and the retrial court.[198]

**13.117** Expenditures for attorney fees are hard to specify. Typically, law firms charge on a per-hour basis. The hourly rates for good litigators are almost comparable to those paid in Germany. For complex civil patent litigation, less than six digit Euro amounts of attorney fees would rather be the exception. In practice, the attorney fees are only partly recovered by the winning party because courts normally do not award compensation for all expenditure incurred.

**13.118** In 2010, an attorney fee schedule for the city of Beijing was issued and put into trial use.[199] The schedule allows calculation of attorney fees per case, according

193 R. 21 and R. 22 Fees Methods.
194 R. 53 Fees Methods.
195 R. 29 Fees Methods.
196 R. 40 Fees Methods.
197 R. 43 Fees Methods.
198 R. 55 Fees Methods.
199 北京市律师诉讼代理服务收费政府指导价标准 (试行).

to the value in litigation and in the form of an hourly rate. It is also acceptable to agree upon a success fee in the form of a share of the awarded damages (mostly 30 percent). A progressive scheme is proposed for the calculation according to the value in litigation with 2 percent of the value in dispute if such amount exceeds 10 million RMB. In view of the moderate damages in typical patent litigation cases,[200] this progressive scheme is rarely applied. Rule 1(4) Fee schedule proposes an hourly range of 100–3,000 RMB, which can be exceeded in cases which are exceptionally complicated or in foreign-related cases. Attorney fees for patent litigation typically lie in the upper section of this range or beyond. The fee schedule works in favor of winning parties, as it can be used as a reference to claim more adequate reimbursement of attorney fees.

## J. INTERIM MEASURES

13.119 The volatile business environment many companies face when carrying on business in China is more challenging in terms of quick action and response than in the majority of other countries. Intellectual property rights enforcement is no exception. The risk of losing grip of infringers or suffering economic damage often requires immediate action. Chinese law provides for interim measures ('provisional measures' according to the terminology of the TRIPS Agreement[201]) which have gradually improved in the course of the evolution of intellectual property law and practice. The interim measures available are preliminary injunction (临时禁令), preservation of evidence (证据保全) and property preservation (财产保全).[202]

### 1. Preliminary injunction

13.120 Article 66 Chinese Patent Act provides the legal basis for the grant of an interim injunction. An ongoing or imminent act of infringement can be sanctioned by interim injunction in cases in which otherwise the patent owner or a party with legal interest may suffer irreparable damage. Hereby, the claimant has to provide a security. Otherwise, the court will not accept the request for an interim injunction.

200 See section G.2.

201 Art. 50 TRIPS Agreement.

202 A good account of interim measures in view of the TRIPS Agreement requirements is provided by Cui Zhou, 'Die einstweiligen Maßnahmen und Beweissicherungsmaßnahmen zum Schutz der Rechte des geistigen Eigentums und Art. 50 TRIPS in China', **2006** *GRUR Int.* 560.

**13.121** The court has to decide within 48 hours from the receipt of the request. Exceptionally, the deadline can be extended for another 48 hours. A preliminary injunction is to be executed immediately after grant. The defendant can object to the preliminary injunction once. Execution, however, will not be suspended during the handling of the objection.

**13.122** The claimant has to file a lawsuit within 15 days after the receipt of the notification that the request for interim injunction has been granted.[203] If the claimant fails to do so, the interim injunction will be dropped.[204]

**13.123** If the request for interim injunction turns out to be without justification, the claimant will be held liable to compensate the damage suffered by the defendant.

**13.124** The above provisions of Article 66 Chinese Patent Act are supplemented by Supreme Court provisions which govern the detailed implementation of interim injunction measures.

**13.125** The provisions on the entitlement to request interim injunctions are the same as the provisions on entitlement to file a regular infringement lawsuit which have already been covered in section D.[205] The request for a preliminary injunction has to be filed with a court with jurisdiction over the infringement case,[206] that is, with an intermediate court authorized to hear IP litigation matters which also has territorial jurisdiction over the case. It is possible to file the request simultaneously with an infringement lawsuit. In such case, the court will first decide about the request for a preliminary injunction.[207] The question whether the request can be made after the infringement lawsuit has already started is controversially debated.[208] In view of recent civil law amendments a preliminary injunction during infringement proceedings should be possible, however (see below).

**13.126** The request must be in written form and include contact information for the parties. Evidence has to be provided, as well as an explanation why the claimant

---

203 Yin, 750.

204 See also It. 12 Injunction Interpretation.

205 It. 1 Injunction Interpretation.

206 It. 2 Injunction Interpretation.

207 It. 17 Injunction Interpretation.

208 Affirmative: Yin, 745, negative: Bu, *Patentrecht*, 142.

fears irreparable damage.[209] The required evidence comprises documents which prove the ownership and effectiveness of the patent right to be enforced. Moreover, evidence about the current or imminent infringement has to be provided, as well as evidence that the putative infringement constitutes an infringing act. If the requesting party is different from the patent owner, the capacity to sue has to be proven by additional evidence (such as a license contract, a declaration or authorization by the patent owner, and so on).[210] Yin argues that the formal requirements as a whole are not substantially different from the requirements for filing a regular lawsuit except for some additional ones, such as the requirement as to proof that irreparable damage may ensue.[211]

It is important to note that requests related to utility models and design patents will only be accepted if accompanied by a document issued by SIPO, which allows an assessment of the stability of the utility model or design in question. For patents filed before 1 October 2009, such document consists of a search report, as regulated by Article 57 2001 Chinese Patent Act. For patents with a later filing date, Article 61 Chinese Patent Act instead requires an evaluation report to be issued by the Chinese Patent Office.[212] It is evident that a negative search report or negative evaluation report greatly reduces the success chances of a request for preliminary injunction. In analogy with Item 1 2010 Judicial Interpretation pursuant to which the plaintiff can change the claims on which he wants to base his infringement accusation before the end of the submissions of the first instance trial, the request for a preliminary injunction should be based on those claims which have not been weakened by the patent office's assessment. **13.127**

The court is bound to decide within the scope of the request.[213] A security has to be provided that may have the form of a monetary bond or a mortgage and should cover the potential damage suffered by the alleged infringer if afterwards the request turns out to have been unfounded.[214] The amount of such security may be increased by the court if it turns out to be insufficient in the further course of events. Upon a refusal to comply with such increase, the court will lift **13.128**

209 It. 3 Injunction Interpretation.

210 It. 4 Injunction Interpretation.

211 Yin, 746.

212 The Transitional Measures for the Implementation of the Amended Patent Law (No. 53)《施行修改后的专利法的过渡办法》（第53号） provide that the third amendment shall be applicable to patents filed on or after 1 October 2009.

213 It. 5 Injunction Interpretation.

214 It. 6 Injunction Interpretation.

the preliminary injunction.[215] In contrast, a countersecurity provided by the alleged infringer does not give reason to lifting the injunction.[216]

**13.129** The court's assessment as to whether an injunction is adequate follows a four-criteria scheme.[217] Hereby, the assessment of whether or not the patent right is in the process of being infringed or is going to be infringed is crucial. A second criterion is whether irreparable harm will be suffered by the requester if the infringement continues. These two first criteria are unevenly applied by the People's Courts. Bu[218] and Cao[219] give a more detailed account of these inconsistencies.[220] In practice, the outcome of such assessment seems to depend on where the respective court is located. The Intermediate People's Court of Shanghai seems to be comparatively responsive towards preliminary injunction requests.[221] A third criterion is the payment of the mandatory security. Finally, the injunction should not contravene the public interest. Evidently, in the case of preliminary injunction requests, the application of the last criterion should be somewhat stricter than recourse to public interest in the main proceedings. Accordingly, the gist of the *Fuji Water* decision[222] should also be applicable here.

**13.130** Whereas the correct yardstick for the assessment of the probability of infringement is disputed, the Supreme People's Court has provided guidance with regard to another aspect of infringement. In 2003, it has issued a statement in connection with an infringement case pursuant to which interim measures shall, in general, only be issued in a case of literal infringement.[223] The Opinion on Economic Situation provides that preliminary injunctions are suitable mainly in cases where the facts are relatively clear and the infringement easy to judge. Especially in patent infringement cases, if the alleged infringing activity does not constitute literal infringement and a relatively more complex comparison of technology is needed, preliminary injunctions should not be ordered.[224] Hence, the chances that a preliminary injunction will be granted are quite low if only equivalent infringement is at issue.

---

215 It. 7 Injunction Interpretation.

216 It. 8 Injunction Interpretation.

217 It. 11 Injunction Interpretation.

218 Bu, *Patentrecht*, 142.

219 Cao, *Durchsetzung*, 128.

220 The Chinese text uses the term 'damage difficult to redress' (难以弥补的损害) rather than 'irreparable damage' of the TRIPS agreement without real consequences for actual practice, however, see Bu, *Patentrecht*, 141.

221 Cao, *Durchsetzung*, 120; oral communication by CPA attorneys who have recently won three cases.

222 See section G.1.

223 Yin, 748 cites '最高人民法院关于美国伊莱利利公司与常州华生制药有限公司专利侵权纠纷案件指定管辖的通知', where the comment was made.

224 lt. 14 Opinion on Economic Situation.

The court has to make a decision within 48 hours if the request meets the formal requirements. Upon grant, the injunction is to be executed immediately. One party or both parties may but do not have to be summoned to clarify the facts. The decision has to be communicated to the claimant within five days at the latest.[225] 13.131

The decision can be opposed within a deadline of ten days. Filing an opposition, that is, a request for the court to reconsider its decision (复议), does not stall a granted injunction.[226] 13.132

Whereas a plaintiff's loss in a patent case initiated in good faith does not entail any liabilities, an erroneously requested preliminary injunction results in damage claims. If no infringement lawsuit is filed or if the lawsuit is lost,[227] damages arising from the preliminary injunction can be claimed either in a separate lawsuit or in the course of the infringement lawsuit.[228] Moreover, liability for damages arises in case of invalidation of the patent on which the preliminary injunction had been based (possibly after a retrial, see section H.2).[229] Yin argues that both direct and indirect damage has to be compensated, that is, not only damage due to products that could not be sold, but also further damages caused by such drop in sales, for example, the closure of factories.[230] 13.133

The preliminary injunction ends when a court decision has become effective (for example, if it is replaced by a permanent injunction). Alternatively, the court may grant the preliminary injunction for a certain period of time. In the latter case, an extension of the injunction period is possible.[231] The defendant may request termination of the preliminary injunction before the regular expiry if new evidence raises doubts about the justification of the preliminary injunction.[232] 13.134

In case of non-compliance with the injunction, the court has to resort to compulsory measures pursuant to Article 111(6) Chinese Civil Procedures Act. Corresponding sanctions can be the imposition of a fine or detention.[233] 13.135

---

225 It. 9 Injunction Interpretation.

226 It. 10 Injunction Interpretation, Jun, 748.

227 Yin, 751.

228 It. 13 Injunction Interpretation; Yin (p.750) points to the fact that the wording of Art. 66 Chinese Patent Act is to be interpreted in a way that failure to initiate a lawsuit shall not be excluded from damage liability.

229 Bu, *Patentrecht*, 139.

230 Yin, 751.

231 It. 14 Injunction Interpretation.

232 Yin, 749.

233 It. 15 Injunction Interpretation.

**13.136** In the beginning of 2013, an amended Civil Procedures Act came into effect. Its new Article 100 regulates an 'action preservation system' (行为保全制度). Action preservation means a court decision which orders a party to perform a certain act or prohibits it from performing a certain act. As a prerequisite for such order, the requester must evidence that irreparable damage is imminent.[234] Thus, Article 100 Chinese Civil Procedures Act provides a kind of fall-back recourse to obtain an interim injunction even if the Supreme Court's Injunction Interpretation was construed not to provide for preliminary injunctions during the trial phase. Therefore, there is good reason to assume that the likelihood of an acceptance of an interim injunction request in the trial phase has increased.

### 2. Preservation of evidence

**13.137** In the course of the third amendment, a separate Article 67 on evidence preservation has been added to the Chinese Patent Act.

**13.138** The Civil Procedures Act of 1991 already contained early provisions on preservation of evidence during civil lawsuits. The urgency to prevent destruction of evidence, however, raised the demand also for pre-trial preservation measures. Until recently, China's early civil procedures provisions did not contain such stipulations on pre-trial preservation. As early as 2001, however, the Supreme People's Court regulated a pre-trial evidence preservation procedure in its Opinions on Interim Injunctions ('Injunction Interpretation'). It allowed requests for the preservation of evidence to be performed simultaneously with the execution of pre-trial measures to cease the infringement.[235]

**13.139** The newly introduced Article 67 Chinese Patent Act regulates a separate pre-trial request to preserve evidence. One may also say that in this regard, the Chinese Patent Act of 2009 has hurried ahead the general development in civil procedures law, as a corresponding rule has found its way into the Chinese Civil Procedures Act only recently.[236]

**13.140** Pre-trial evidence preservation requires that evidence is in danger of being lost or difficult to obtain later if no immediate action is taken. The court may require the requester to provide a security. Just as in a case of requests for interim injunctions the court has to decide on the request within 48 hours, and the

234 Zhang Guangliang, 'Impact of New Chinese Civil Procedure Law on Interim Measures in IP Civil Litigation', [2013] **1** *China Patents & Trademarks* 10.

235 It. 16 Injunction Interpretation.

236 Art. 81 Chinese Civil Procedures Act.

evidence preservation will be lifted if the requester does not sue within 15 days from the start of the preservation measures.[237]

The requester does not only have to convince the court of the necessity to act rapidly but he also has to provide evidence that patent infringement is taking place or is likely to take place.[238] In view of the comparatively minor damage incurred by evidence preservation as opposed to interim injunctions, this requirement is likely to be applied less rigorously than in case of interim injunctions. 13.141

The court can require the defendant or his representative to be present during the evidence preservation procedure.[239] 13.142

### 3. Property preservation

Even though the procedure for property preservation resembles the above-mentioned interim procedures, the Chinese Patent Act does not contain corresponding provisions. One reason may be that pre-trial property preservation has already been regulated by the former Civil Procedures Code and continues to be regulated by the present Civil Procedures Code, so that a patent-specific provision was not deemed to be necessary. 13.143

Property preservation can be requested before[240] or during a lawsuit.[241] Again, the court has to make a ruling within 48 hours. The requester can be required to provide a security. Upon grant, the requester has to file a lawsuit or start an arbitration procedure within 30 days (formerly 15 days). If the requester fails to meet this requirement, the measures will be lifted. The defendant has to be informed without delay after the property preservation has been carried out.[242] If he provides a sufficient countersecurity, the property preservation will be lifted.[243] 13.144

Property preservation can be requested in connection with preliminary injunction or evidence preservation.[244] In view of the reported difficulties in collecting damages from infringers, property preservation appears to be an appropriate 13.145

237 Zhang Guangliang, above note 234, argues that this shorter deadline of 15 days is still applicable, in spite of the longer period of 30 days provided by Art.101 of the new Chinese Civil Procedures Act.
238 Bu, *Patentrecht*, 140.
239 It. 24 Evidence Interpretation.
240 Art. 101 Chinese Civil Procedures Act.
241 Art. 100 Chinese Civil Procedures Act.
242 Art. 103 Chinese Civil Procedures Act.
243 Art. 104 Chinese Civil Procedures Act.
244 It. 16 Injunction Interpretation.

measure to avoid trouble. A closer look, however, reveals some caveats. For instance, the value of the preserved property shall not exceed the value in dispute.[245] A realistic estimate of damage claims, however, is often difficult to draw up. In addition, an erroneous request for property preservation gives rise to damage claims.[246] Such damage claim does not only have to be feared if the case is lost or if the patent is invalidated, but may even arise after the plaintiff has won the case. This is because, as mentioned, the majority of plaintiffs are awarded statutory damages for lack of evidence regarding the actual damage suffered by the plaintiff. As statutory damages, however, are normally considerably lower than the actual damage,[247] successful property preservation request still bears the risk of grossly overestimating the damages which will be finally awarded. Such overestimation (which may particularly occur in pre-trial property preservation) could then be considered to be an error (错误) in the property preservation request which would give rise to damage claims by the defendant.

## K. CUSTOMS PROTECTION AND PROTECTIVE MEASURES DURING EXHIBITIONS

**13.146** The above section has outlined the pre-trial measures provided by Chinese law. Hereby, the term 'pre-trial' implies that a lawsuit will follow the measure. With the help of such a broad definition of pre-trial measures, two further types of measures can be considered to provide pre-trial leverage, namely customs protection measures and exhibition-specific measures. These measures can be invoked strategically to better enforce patent rights. On the other hand, the growing maturity of the Chinese intellectual property system also entails a more elaborate use of such measures by Chinese companies against western competitors.

### 1. Customs protection

**13.147** Chinese law provides for intellectual property specific regulations on customs protection which have been enacted in 1995 and amended in 2003[248] and 2010. The latest version of these Regulations of the People's Republic of China on Customs Protection of Intellectual Property Rights (中华人民共和国知识产权海关保护条例) became effective on 1 May 2010 (hereinafter 'Customs Protection Rules'). The Customs Protection Rules are

245 Art. 102 Chinese Civil Procedures Act.

246 Art. 105 Chinese Civil Procedures Act.

247 See section G.2.

248 On the 2003 amendment see Xiang Yu, 'The New Regulations Regarding Customs Protection of Intellectual Property Rights of the People's Republic of China', [2005] **36** *IIC* 835.

supplemented by implementing regulations, the Method of the General Administration of Customs of the People's Republic of China for the Implementation of the Regulations of the People's Republic of China on Customs Protection of Intellectual Property Rights (中华人民共和国海关关于<<中华人民共和国知识产权海关保护条例>>的实施办法), hereinafter cited as 'Customs Implementation Method'.

In contrast to many other countries, the regulations do not only prohibit the importation but also the exportation of infringing products.[249] **13.148**

Customs protection comes in two flavors: with and without prior registration. **13.149** As will be seen below, registration provides for some procedural advantages, in particular the *ex officio* monitoring of goods for infringement of registered patents.

Customs registration of a patent requires submission of the following information:[250] **13.150**

(1) the business name or name, place of registration or nationality, and so on of the owner of the intellectual property right;
(2) the description, contents and any other relevant information related to the intellectual property right;[251]
(3) the status quo regarding licenses;
(4) description, origin, customs at the port of entry or exit, importer or exporter, main features and prices, and so on of the goods in which the owner of the intellectual property lawfully exercises his right;
(5) the manufacturers, importers or exporters, customs at the port of entry or exit, main features and prices, and so on of the infringing goods, as far as known by the right owner.

The owner of the intellectual property right shall attach any evidentiary **13.151** documents which prove the details specified in the application for registration. In addition, a fee has to be paid.[252] A Chinese translation has to be submitted if the documents are written in a foreign language.[253] It should be noted that registration also requires an evaluation report established by SIPO according to

249 R. 3 and R. 4 Customs Protection Rules.
250 R. 7 Customs Protection Rules.
251 For a patent right, the title or designation, type, application date, and transfer of right have to be provided according to R.6(2) Customs Implementation Method.
252 R.32 Customs Protection Rules; there is no fee due for renewal or modification of the registration according to R.8 Customs Implementation Method.
253 R.7 Customs Implementation Method.

Article 61 Chinese Patent Act if the registered patent is a utility model or a design patent.[254] Even though customs authorities are not required to assess the validity of the registered patent, such document may convince the customs authority that the case for infringement is strong enough to detain the goods at issue (see below).

**13.152** A decision as to registration will be made within 30 days. The requester will be informed about the decision without delay.[255] It should be noted that only the right owner can request registration.[256] That is, an exclusive licensee who intends to resort to customs protection is well advised to include a stipulation in the license contract which obliges the licensor to go through the registration procedure.

**13.153** The registration is effective for a period of ten years and can be renewed for another ten years within six months before the expiration of the first registration period.[257] If the patent at issue has undergone changes, the registration has to be modified within 30 days from such change. Otherwise, the registration may be cancelled if the erroneous registration information has severe effects, for example, possible obstruction of the lawful business of a licensee whose goods may be detained because the license was not duly registered. Such cancellation may be effected by an interested third party or made by the customs authority at its own initiative.[258]

**13.154** Detention of allegedly infringing products requires a request for customs action.[259] Such request has to provide the following information:

(1) business name or name, place of registration or nationality, and so on of the owner of the intellectual property right;
(2) description, contents and any other relevant information related to the intellectual property right;
(3) business name of the consignee and consignor of the suspected infringing goods;
(4) descriptions, specifications, and so on of the suspected infringing goods;
(5) possible ports, time, means of transport, and so on related to the importation or exportation of the suspected infringing goods.

---

254 R.7(2) Customs Implementation Method.

255 R.8 Customs Protection Rules; upon refusal to register a right, registration can be requested again within one year, see R.13 Customs Implementation Method.

256 See R.8(2) Customs Protection Rules.

257 R. 10 Customs Protection Rules; if the registered right expires before the end of the ten years registration period, the registration will be cancelled, see R. 9 Customs Implementation Method.

258 R. 11 Customs Protection Rules.

259 R. 12 Customs Protection Rules.

Registration is not a precondition for a detention request but the registration number should be provided if available. The requester has to provide a security, which is meant to cover damage claims raised by the sender and recipient of the alleged goods if the detention turns out to have been unjustified.[260] In addition, a fee has to be paid for storage and handling of the request by customs authorities. This fee can be either included in the security or directly paid.[261] After a successful lawsuit, the fee will be reimbursed to the patent right owner.[262] A guarantee in form of a cash deposit or a letter of guarantee provided by a bank or other financial institution will also be accepted as security.[263] The security will be refunded to the patent owner or the guarantor's security liabilities will be lifted after the confiscated goods have been disposed of and the relevant expenses have been settled.[264] If the requirements for the request are met, the detention will be executed. Upon execution of detention, the requester as well as the sender or the recipient of the alleged goods will be notified (the latter, however, only if they are based in China).[265] **13.155**

For registered patent rights, the customs authorities will take note of supposedly infringing goods and immediately notify the patent right owner *ex officio*. The right owner is then expected to request detention and to provide the mentioned security within three working days.[266] If he fails to do so, the detained goods will be released.[267] The customs authorities may consent to an inspection of the supposedly infringing goods by the patent right owner and by the sender or recipient.[268] **13.156**

If the sender or the recipient of the allegedly infringing goods believes that the right owner's allegation is unfounded, they may lift the detention by providing a countersecurity which must correspond to the value of the detained goods. If no lawsuit is filed within a set deadline, this countersecurity will be refunded.[269] **13.157**

The customs authorities have 30 working days from the detention of goods to verify whether the patent at issue has been infringed upon. If infringement **13.158**

260 According to R. 28 Customs Protection Rules, the requester is liable for damages if neither customs authorities nor civil court establish patent infringement.
261 R. 14 Customs Protection Rules.
262 R. 25 Customs Protection Rules in connection with Art. 65 Chinese Patent Act.
263 R. 38 Customs Implementation Method.
264 R. 35 Customs Implementation Method.
265 R. 15 Customs Protection Rules.
266 For *ex officio* action, the security has a cap at 100,000 RMB, see R.23 Customs Implementation Method.
267 R. 16 Customs Protection Rules.
268 R. 17 Customs Protection Rules.
269 R. 19 Customs Protection Rules.

cannot be established, the patent owner shall be informed accordingly.[270] For the assessment of whether a patent is infringed, the customs authority may also hear the arguments and evidence provided by the sender or recipient.[271]

**13.159** The detention shall be ended and the goods released if:[272]

- the customs authorities do not receive a civil court order for assistance in execution within 20 working days for detention if the right at issue has not been registered;
- the customs authorities do not receive a civil court order for assistance in execution within 50 working days for detention if the right at issue is registered;
- the sender or recipient of the allegedly infringing goods has provided a security;
- the customs authorities, upon evidence provided by the sender or recipient, arrive at the conclusion that there is no infringement;
- the request for detention is withdrawn.

**13.160** Hence, customs protection procedure will only succeed if civil action is taken and a civil court order is issued. The further handling of the detained goods will be subject to the court's decision. Infringing goods will be confiscated and may be used for charity purposes, sold to the patent owner or auctioned off. The goods have to be destroyed if other ways to dispose of them would unduly prejudice the patent owner's interests, which may be the case if, for example, an infringing label cannot be removed without destroying the product.[273]

**13.161** It should be noted that foreign parties are required to appoint a representative and to provide an authorization for both the registration of a patent right and the request for detention.[274]

**13.162** A good practical account of customs enforcement in China is provided by the 2008 roadmap 'Customs Enforcement in China' which can be downloaded from http://www.ipr2.org/roadmap.

**13.163** Finally, it should be noted that whereas customs protection is a valuable instrument of patent enforcement, it is even more effective when it comes to the

270 R. 20 Customs Protection Rules.
271 R. 18 Customs Protection Rules.
272 R. 24 Customs Protection Rules.
273 R. 27 Customs Protection Rules.
274 R. 2 Customs Implementation Method.

protection of trademarks, as in the case of trademarks, customs authorities find it much easier to assess infringement than in the case of technically complicated patents.

### 2. Measures for the protection of patent rights during exhibitions

Another supplement to court litigation is a set of regulations aimed at protecting intellectual property during exhibitions. The 'Measures for the Protection of Intellectual Property Rights During Exhibitions' (展会知识产权保护办法), effective 1 March 2006 ('Exhibition Measures') are applied to the protection of patents, trademarks and copyrights during all kinds of commercial exhibitions, trade fairs, expositions, commodity fairs and shows within the territory of China.[275] **13.164**

For exhibitions which last for more than three days, the Administrative Department for Exhibitions[276] can require the organizer to set up an office in charge of intellectual property related complaints.[277] A patent owner can raise a complaint with this office or, alternatively, with the administrative department in charge of intellectual property (that is, in patent cases the patent administration authorities according to Article 60 Patent Act, see Rule 34 Exhibition Measures).[278] Within 24 hours, the mentioned office transfers complaints that comply with the formal requirements to the local patent administration authority.[279] A complete complaint contains the following information:[280] **13.165**

(1) patent certificate, text of patent announcement, identity certification of the patent owner, certification of the legal status of the patent;
(2) basic information about the parties which are suspected to have committed patent infringement;
(3) explanations and evidence supporting such suspect;
(4) a power of attorney in cases in which an agent has been entrusted to file the complaint.

Interested parties such as exclusive licensees do not possess the capacity to complain. Therefore, exclusive licensees are advised to strive for a clause in the license contract which obliges the patent owner to file the complaint. **13.166**

275 R. 2 Exhibition Measures.
276 'Administrative Department of Exhibitions' refers to the department in charge of examination and approval or registration of exhibitions, see R. 34 Exhibition Measures.
277 R. 6 Exhibition Measures.
278 R. 8 Exhibition Measures.
279 R. 11 Exhibition Measures.
280 R. 8 Exhibition Measures.

**13.167** If the required documents are found to be defective the complainant is given the opportunity to eliminate the defects.[281]

**13.168** Upon receipt of a complaint, the office will inform the exhibition organizer and the accused party.[282] If there is enough time, the accused party can be allowed to respond within a given deadline.[283] Failure to meet the deadline or no response at all has no effect on the decision of the patent administration authority.[284] If infringement has already been established by a court and the court decision has taken legal effect, the patent administration department can directly proceed with the implementation of the sanctions mentioned below.[285]

**13.169** Complaints which are based on fake documents or fabrications are held liable for the damages suffered by the accused party due to the false allegations.[286]

**13.170** The Patent Administration Department will prosecute the alleged infringement according to Articles 60, 63 and 64 Chinese Patent Act.[287] It may also collect evidence on the spot.[288]

**13.171** If the complaint is justified and patent infringement is established, the patent administration authority will order the infringer to stop the infringing act.[289] In particular, it will order the infringer to:[290]

- withdraw all items of infringement;
- destroy all publications introducing infringing articles;
- change exhibition boards introducing infringing articles.

**13.172** Under the following conditions, the IPR administrative department shall refrain from accepting a complaint:[291]

(1) an infringement lawsuit in this matter is already pending;
(2) an invalidation procedure against the asserted patent is pending;
(3) the asserted patent is subject to a dispute regarding ownership;

---

281 R. 9 Exhibition Measures.
282 R. 12 Exhibition Measures.
283 R. 13 Exhibition Measures.
284 R. 14 Exhibition Measures.
285 R. 29 Exhibition Measures.
286 R. 10 Exhibition Measures.
287 R. 16 Exhibition Measures.
288 R. 18 Exhibition Measures.
289 Since the 2008 amendment, 'offering for sale' is also regarded as infringing if design patents are at issue, so that the lighter sanctions provided by the regulation in case of design patents are now obsolete.
290 R. 25 Exhibition Measures.
291 R. 17 Exhibition Measures.

(4) the asserted patent has lost effect and the owner tries to restore it.

In particular, point (2) offers strategic options for putative infringers. If the likelihood of a complaint at an exhibition is high an invalidation request can be filed prior to the exhibition. In view of the moderate fee for invalidation,[292] this strategy may be a reasonable option in the case of important exhibitions in the course of which possible administrative actions could cause substantial harm to the alleged infringer. After the exhibition, the infringer can decide whether he wants to continue with invalidation. Good timing can keep the costs of such protective invalidation request at a moderate level. 13.173

Cases which remain unresolved until the end of the exhibition are to be transferred to the competent patent administration authority within 15 working days.[293] 13.174

## L. FUTURE PROSPECTS

Intellectual property laws remain with little practical meaning if intellectual property rights can be obtained but not enforced. Major strides have been taken in China but the system architects are keenly aware of the fact that enforcement is still lagging behind the majority of developed countries. 13.175

A fourth amendment to the Chinese Patent Act is under preparation. It is largely dedicated to enforcement issues. In particular, it aims at strengthening administrative enforcement.[294] The following short explanations will focus on those proposed changes which will impact on civil court enforcement.[295] 13.176

For instance, the proposed amendment to Article 46 Chinese Patent Act provides for the immediate effectiveness of Patent Re-examination Board (PRB) decisions in invalidation cases after their announcement. This amendment plan must be interpreted in light of another proposed amendment of 13.177

292 3,000 RMB for invention patents and 1,500 for utility models and designs.

293 R.33 Exhibition Measures.

294 New regulations relevant to administrative enforcement are that the administrative authority may:

- levy damages (Art. 60, Art. 65)
- confiscate illegal income and confiscate/destroy infringing products/equipment for manufacturing these products (Art. 60)
- impose a fine (Art. 60)
- use compulsory measures in the event of non-compliance (Art. 64).

295 The basis for the discussion of the fourth amendment is the second discussion draft. Explanations and text of this proposed amendment were published in 国家知识产权局文件, 国知发法字 [2013] 11 号.

Article 60 Chinese Patent Act and the corresponding official explanations. The amended Article 60 will call for prompt hearing or handling of a litigation lawsuit once the PRB has issued a decision.

**13.178** The rationale behind these amendment plans is to shorten the duration of infringement lawsuits which are stayed due to a concurrent invalidation procedure before the PRB.[296] According to current general practice, courts will render a decision on infringement only after validity has been decided.[297] This leads to major delay, especially when PRB decisions are appealed. However, only a small fraction of PRB invalidation decisions are reversed by the Beijing Intermediate People's Court No.1 which is in charge of dealing with appeals of PRB decisions at first instance, and the Bejing Higher People's Court at second instance. The amendment aims at enhancing the expediency of infringement cases. On the downside, the amendment is likely to entail major problems and legal uncertainty in cases in which PRB decisions are reversed upon appeal.

**13.179** One of these major problems is that due to the expedited infringement trial, it will become more likely that one of the above Beijing courts dealing with appeals of PRB decisions reverses a decision by the PRB to invalidate a patent only after the infringement court has established non-infringement due to the previous PRB decision, that is due to the patent's invalidation by the PRB.

(1) It is not clear whether damages have to be paid for the use of the patented solution during the period between the entry into effect of the PRB's invalidation decision and its reversal by the court. Moreover, even if no damages have to be paid, it remains unclear whether the above period will count towards the limitation for the collection of damages of two years preceding the infringement suit.[298]

(2) It is not clear what consequences such revival will have for third parties which have starting manufacturing the infringing product because they relied on the PRB decision. Would an 'intervening right' come into existence?[299] And would such an intervening right be limited to the scope of manufacturing at the date at which the patent has been revived?

---

296 Typically, it is infringement suits based on utility models and design patents that are stayed to have the stableness of the patent in suit checked in invalidation procedures first.

297 Clark, *Patent Litigation*, 102.

298 According to the statute of limitations in It. 23 of the 2001 Judicial Interpretation, damages can be collected for the two years preceding the file of the lawsuit.

299 Intervening rights are meant to protect good faith reliance on a given legal situation. For instance, restitution of a lapsed or rejected patent right will give rise to an intervening right according to Art. 123(5) of the German Patent Act if use of the patented technology has been prepared or has commenced during the period in which the patent was not effective.

Similarly, the fact that only the Beijing Intermediate People's Court No. 1 and, in second instance, the Beijing Higher People's Court, are competent to deal with invalidation cases has far-reaching implications. If the PRB upholds the patent, the infringement court may issue an injunction which can be executed right away after taking legal effect. If, however, the Beijing Intermediate People's Court No. 1 reverses the PRB decision, the execution of the injunction may already have caused substantial damage to the defendant in the infringement suit. For instance, factories may have been closed, employees dismissed, apparatus destroyed and so on. The reversal of the PRB decision now provides such a defendant with the opportunity to request a retrial (see section H.2) which would reverse the previous infringement decision and allow the defendant to recoup only the monetary damages paid to the patent owner. There is no legal basis, however, to recover the damage caused by the execution of the injunction.[300] **13.180**

In view of such a potential outcome, the Beijing court may hesitate to rule against PRB decisions. It goes without saying that such a bias would contravene the gist of what a fair appeal system is meant to guarantee. **13.181**

Low damages awards are another debated issue of the Chinese intellectual property system. The explanations of the proposed amendment identify the difficulty to raise evidence (举证难) as a key problem. The planned amendment to Article 61 Chinese Patent Act aims at remedying this situation, by supporting the plaintiff's endeavors to gain access to the evidence which is necessary for damage calculation. According to the planned amendments, the court shall, at the request of the plaintiff or his attorney, collect the evidence under the control of the alleged infringer. Uncooperative defendants would face compulsory measures. Infringers who overstep the bounds and commit criminal acts in preventing evidence collection may even face criminal sanctions. Such amendments are laudable and introduce elements which also exist in similar form in other jurisdictions.[301] **13.182**

Finally, Article 65 Chinese Patent Act may be amended to include damages for willful infringement. In such cases, the imposition of triple damages will become possible, irrespective of the applied damage calculation method.[302] Current law already provides for such a punitive element for damage calculation **13.183**

300 The situation is similar to the preliminary execution ('vorläufige Vollstreckung') in German law. Art. 717(2) of the German Civil Procedures Act provides for redress of the damage caused by preliminary execution. Presently, there is no such preliminary execution in Chinese patent litigation practice (see section H.1).

301 For example, 'Rechnungslegungsanspruch' and 'Auskunftsanspruch' according to the German Patent Act.

302 The present calculation scheme already permits the award of damages corresponding to a multiple of a reasonable license fee (see section G.2).

in license analogy, but it is rarely applied. The explanations leave no doubt that repeat infringement is to be sanctioned by strict application of punitive damages. The proposed amendments are more ambiguous, however, with regard to less reprehensive conduct. The term 'willful infringement' leaves much room for interpretation. It remains to be seen what level of care needs to be applied to rule out multiple damage sanctions. In view of breathtaking annual increases in patent applications and grants,[303] it will be increasingly burdensome for many companies to carry out in-depth patent clearings. Therefore, the proposed amendments will have to be accompanied by further clarifications, for example, as to whether negligent patent clearing already translates into exposure to triple damages.

**13.184** It remains to be seen whether the above amendment will be implemented in its present form. The amendment plans, nevertheless, demonstrate a certain commitment and political will to improve the enforcement of patents. Hereby, they integrate into the Chinese IP strategy which envisages that 'by 2020, China will become a country with a comparatively high level in terms of the creation, utilization, protection and administration of IPRs'.[304]

303 More than 2 million patent applications in 2012.

304 National Intellectual Property Strategy (published 2008).

# 14

# THE INTERPLAY BETWEEN INFRINGEMENT AND INVALIDITY PROCEEDINGS

**Nils Heide**[1]



1 The author would like to thank Dr. Quighong Xu, Lung Tin International and Mr. Dong Wei, P.C. & Associates for their helpful comments concerning their own case practice.

## A. SEPARATION AND INTERPLAY

### 1. Infringement procedure and revocation procedure as parallel systems

**14.01** The dualism of the revocation procedures and the infringement procedures is one of the characterising features of the Chinese patent system. There is not only a division of duties and competences, but there are also different procedural rules which govern the proceedings: Infringement proceedings are handled by the civil courts according to Civil Procedural Law and revocation proceedings are conducted by the Patent Reexamination Board according to Administrative Procedural Law.[2]

**14.02** Although both procedures follow parallel tracks there is an interplay between the proceedings which leads to complex issues concerning the procedural interdependence and the determination of the scope of protection of the patent which is subject to both procedures. The interplay also results in a playground for tactical considerations.

**14.03** In the normal course of an infringement dispute, the plaintiff initiates the infringement proceeding by filing a complaint with the infringement court having jurisdiction. After the court accepts the complaint, it is served to the defendant together with the court notification in which the court sets a deadline – 15 days for a Chinese party or 30 days for a foreign party without a residence or registered branch in China – for presenting the defence. During the defence period, the defendant can file a rebuttal brief with counter-arguments or contest the jurisdiction of the court or just remain silent, which does not preclude the defendant from presenting counter-arguments during the oral hearing. The defendant who takes the position that the patent is invalid has to file a request for invalidation at the Patent Reexamination Board and may file a request to suspend the infringement proceeding at the infringement court. The defendant cannot request revocation of the patent as a counterclaim in the infringement proceeding, because the infringement court has no power to invalidate the patent.

2 The different competences reflect that the granting of the patent is an administrative act which binds the civil judge so long as it is not invalidated. For the legal nature of the invalidation decision and the categorisation of the procedure, see He Huaiwen, 'Patent Invalidation Procedure: Limits of Judicial Power and Judicial Certainty', [2009] **3** *China Patents & Trademarks* 10, 11.

14.04 The infringement court decides at its own discretion whether to stay the infringement proceeding until a decision in the revocation proceeding is made. If the infringement procedure is not suspended, both proceedings will proceed within their own timeframe: Concerning the infringement proceedings there is a six months statutory time limit for the first instance, however, the six months period is not applicable if foreign parties are involved and, furthermore, does not include jurisdiction disputes or technical appraisals.[3] In the parallel invalidation procedure, the parties also enter into an evidence exchange after the Patent Reexamination Board has accepted the request for invalidation. The Patent Reexamination Board then schedules an oral hearing and issues a decision concerning the validity which can be appealed at the Beijing First Intermediate People's Court. The Patent Reexamination Board delivers its decision concerning the validity not only to the parties of the procedure, but also directly to the infringement court handling the parallel infringement case according to Part IV, Chapter 3, No. 3.7 (5) of the SIPO Guidelines for Patent Examination 2010.[4]

14.05 Decisions in the invalidation proceedings have no retroactive effect on decisions in infringement proceedings which have been delivered and enforced, with the exception that losses incurred by a party through malicious behaviour by or on behalf of the patentee shall be compensated according to Article 47 Chinese Patent Act. Consequently, generally it is not possible to request repayment of damages and compensation which have already been paid.

14.06 The principle of separation of infringement and validity also governs the other instruments available for enforcement of patents in China: The Patent Administration Authorities handling the administrative route of enforcement are not competent to issue decisions concerning the validity of a patent and therefore the defendant confronted with an investigation of the Patent Administration Authority has to start revocation proceedings at the Patent Reexamination Board. The Patent Administration Authorities then decide whether they will proceed with the administrative measures and sanctions during the parallel revocation proceedings.[5] Criminal investigations and public prosecutions in patent infringement cases also proceed parallel to the independent revocation proceedings.[6]

3 Cui Zhou, 'Recent Developments in Litigation Involving Intellectual Property in China', [2012] **43** *IIC* 21, 22.

4 The SIPO Guidelines for Patent Examination 2010 are available at http://www.sipo.gov.cn/zlsqzn/sczn2010eng.pdf.

5 With respect to the dual track system of patent enforcement in China see Liu Xiaohai, 'Enforcement of Intellectual Property Rights in the People's Republic of China', [2001] **32** *IIC* 141, 142.

6 Lin Ma and Junjie Zheng, 'Patent Criminal Enforcement in the People's Republic of China', [2010] **41** *IIC* 20.

## 2. Separated systems and combined systems – categorisation in the international patent system

**14.07** The separation of infringement and validity proceedings is an important, but not a unique feature of the Chinese patent system. An international comparison shows that a categorisation can be made between separated systems (usually called 'bifurcation') and combined systems. In most countries, the validity and infringement of the patent are handled simultaneously by one court.[7] A main advantage of such combined systems is that the validity of the patent is reviewed by the same judges who determine the scope of protection which is crucial for the question of an infringement, so that discrepancies concerning the interpretation of the claims can be avoided.[8]

**14.08** The separation of validity and infringement procedures is not only used in China, but also in several other countries throughout the world.[9] Under German Patent Law the infringement court is bound by a granted patent as long as the patent is formally effective and the infringement court is not authorized to question the legal validity of the patent which is the subject of a nullity procedure.[10] Separated systems are often preferred by patentees, because the defendant is forced to start separate revocation proceedings and can only stop the enforcement if the revocation proceedings lead to a suspension of the infringement proceedings. The separation can therefore accelerate the enforcement of patents and the division of competences between judges focused on validity or infringement issues can ensure a high quality of decisions in both procedures. The separation is one of the factors which can be used to explain

---

7 In Europe the litigation procedures in UK, France, Netherlands, Belgium, Luxembourg, and Italy are based on a combined system. For an overview, see Bruno Vandermeulen, 'Validity and Infringement: A Surrealist Distinction for the Belgium Patent Courts', in Christian Harmsen, Oliver Jan Jüngst and Felix Rödiger (eds.), *Festschrift für Wolfgang von Meibom zum 65. Geburtstag*, Cologne: Carl Heymanns Verlag 2010, 469, 470; Vito Mangini, 'The Legal Framework for Infringement and Revocation Proceedings in Patent Infringement Matters in Contracting States of the European Patent Convention', [1983] **14** *IIC* 776, 778; with respect to the new EU Unitary Patent System, Klaus Grabinski, 'Der Entwurf der Verfahrensordnung für das Einheitliche Patentgericht im Überblick', **2013** *GRUR Int.* 310, 314; concerning the comparison to the US system, see Wayne C. Jaeschke, Zhun Lu and Paul Crawford, 'Comparison of Chinese and US Patent Reform Legislation: Which, if Either, Got it Right?', [2012] **11** *J. Marshall. Rev. Intell. Prop. L.* 567, 567, 582.

8 *European Central Bank v Document Security System Inc.* [2008] EWCA Civ. 192.

9 In Europe, the separated system is used in Germany, Poland, Austria, Slovakia, and the Czech Republic. Concerning the German systems, see Thomas Kühnen, *Patent Litigation Proceedings in Germany*, Cologne: Carl Heymanns Verlag, 6th edn., 2013, No. 1574; Peter Meier-Beck, 'The Federal Patent Court and the Federal Court of Justice as European Patent Courts', in *Conference Volume Symposium 2011 – The National Patent Jurisdiction in Europe*, Munich, 2011, 17, 20; Hans Marshall, 'The Enforcement of Patent Rights in Germany', [2000] **31** *IIC* 646, 665.

10 German Federal Supreme Court, **2004** *GRUR* 710, 711 – Printing press tempering system.

why jurisdictions based on a separated system are often used as battlegrounds in international patent disputes.[11]

## B. PROCEDURAL ASPECTS OF THE INTERPLAY BETWEEN THE INFRINGEMENT AND THE REVOCATION PROCEDURES

### 1. Suspension of the infringement procedure

For a defendant confronted with an infringement lawsuit on the basis of a Chinese patent, a key question is how he can stay the ongoing infringement proceedings during parallel revocation proceedings. **14.09**

Infringement proceedings in China are not automatically suspended when revocation proceedings are initiated at the Patent Reexamination Board. An infringement judge who stays the infringement proceedings and awaits the outcome of the revocation proceedings has to consider that he hinders the enforcement of a granted patent. On the other hand, he has to weigh the risk that an infringement judgment is issued on the basis of a patent which later could be revoked. The principles governing the decision to stay the infringement proceedings are therefore crucial for the interplay between the infringement and the revocation proceedings. **14.10**

#### *(a) Chinese Civil Procedural Law*

According to Chinese Civil Procedural Law, a lawsuit shall be suspended if the ongoing proceedings depend on the results of other proceedings that have not yet been concluded. The infringement judge therefore has to consider the relevancy and the possible outcome of the revocation proceedings for his proceedings. A relevant connection has to be denied if the attacked product is not covered by the scope of protection of the patent or if the defendant can – besides the validity attack – rely on other relevant counter-arguments which would lead to a dismissal of the infringement claim. In these cases the infringement procedure does not 'depend' on the revocation procedure and therefore the judge is hindered by Chinese Civil Procedure Law from suspending the infringement procedure even if the defendant can also put forward relevant prior art. **14.11**

11 Peter Mes, 'Reflections on the German Patent Litigation System', in Wolrad Prinz zu Waldeck und Pyrmont, Martin J. Adelmann, Robert Brauneis, Josef Drexl and Ralph Nack (eds.), *Patents and Technological Progress in a Globalized World*, Berlin: Springer Verlag 2009, 401, 405.

*(b) Guidelines of the Supreme People's Court*

**14.12** The *Several Provisions of the Supreme People's Court on Issues Concerning the Law Applicable in the Trial of Patent Disputes*[12] ('SPC Provisions') further elaborate the main principles concerning the suspension of infringement proceedings in Items 8 to 11. The SPC Provisions consider in particular (1) the type of the intellectual property right which forms the basis of the infringement lawsuit, (2) whether the rights have been the subject of prior substantive examination, and (3) whether the defendant raised the validity argument in an early stage of the proceedings during the defence period.

*(i) Infringement proceedings based on invention patents or utility models or design patents which survived revocation proceedings*

**14.13** Item 11 Alternative 1 SPC Provisions establishes the general rule that the infringement court shall proceed with patent infringement proceedings even if revocation proceedings have been initiated by the defendant.

**14.14** In case the infringement concerns a utility model or design, the infringement judge shall also continue with the infringement proceedings if the utility model or design at stake has been maintained by the Patent Reexamination Board in revocation proceedings (Item 11 Alternative 2 of the SPC Provisions).

*(ii) Infringement lawsuits based on other utility models or design patents*

**14.15** Regarding utility models or designs which have not been the subject of a prior examination in revocation proceedings, Items 8 to 10 of the SPC Provisions provide further guidelines concerning the aspects to be considered by the infringement judge.

*(1) Evaluation report of SIPO*

**14.16** According to Item 8 SPC Provisions, the plaintiff instituting infringement proceedings concerning a utility model or design should present an evaluation report issued by the State Intellectual Property Office (SIPO) in order to substantiate the validity of the utility model or design. If the plaintiff fails to substantiate the validity by an evaluation report or other sufficient evidence, the infringement court will suspend the infringement proceedings after the defendant initiates a revocation proceeding. According to Article 61(2) Chinese Patent Act, the owner can obtain said patent evaluation report from SIPO. The patent evaluation report does not only include a search, but also a full legal opinion concerning the protectability requirements and therefore the report is used as *prima facie* evidence concerning the question of a suspension of

12 Fa Shi (2001) No. 21, June 19, 2006 available at http://www.chinaipr.gov.cn/lawsarticle/laws/lawsar/patent/200608/233034_1.html.

infringement proceedings.[13] The evaluation report issued by SIPO provides preliminary proof of the validity concerning the utility model or design. However, the evaluation report cannot be regarded as an equivalent to an invalidation decision.[14]

*(2) Initiating the revocation proceedings within the defence period*

The defendant who wants to stay the infringement proceedings has to start invalidation proceedings before the Patent Reexamination Board within the deadline for presenting the defence arguments in the infringement proceedings (Item 8 sentence 2 of the SPC Provisions). If the request for invalidation is filed belatedly, the infringement court has to reject the request for suspension in accordance with Item 10 SPC Provisions, if there are no specific circumstances which make it necessary to stay the infringement proceedings. **14.17**

*(3) General considerations according to Item 9 of the SPC Provisions*

Item 9 SPC Provisions provides, as a general principle, that infringement proceedings relating to utility models or designs should be suspended by the court if the defendant initiates revocation proceedings at the Patent Reexamination Board during the defence period unless one of the following exceptions is applicable: **14.18**

(a) no prior art document questioning the novelty or inventiveness of the utility model or design has been found in the evaluation report; or
(b) the evidence presented by the defendant is sufficient to prove that the technology used was already in the public domain; or
(c) the evidence and reasons presented by the defendant in the revocation proceedings are obviously groundless; or
(d) other exceptional circumstances.

In summary, the defendant confronted with an infringement lawsuit concerning a utility model or design has the chance to stay the infringement proceedings if he acts quickly and starts revocation proceedings within the time limits for submitting the defence arguments. A suspension is granted according to Item 9 SPC Provisions, unless one of the exceptional circumstances outlined in Item 9 apply.[15] If the intellectual property right forming the basis of the infringement lawsuit is a patent, a utility model or design which has been the **14.19**

13 Stefan Luginbuehl and Thomas Pattloch, 'The Awakening of the Chinese Patent Dragon – The Revised Chinese Patent Law' [2011] **42** *IIC* 130, 137.

14 Zhang Guangliang, 'Reflecting on Patent Evaluation Report System in China', [2010] **3** *China Patents & Trademarks* 84, 86.

15 Peter Ganea and Thomas Pattloch, *Intellectual Property Law in China*, The Hague: Kluwer Law International 2005, 306.

subject of a prior examination in invalidity proceedings before the Patent Reexamination Board (PRB), no suspension shall be granted.[16]

### *(c) Chinese court practice*

#### *(i) Efforts of the parties in the race between infringement and revocation procedures*

**14.20** The infringement court can exercise its discretion regarding the suspension of infringement proceedings in the case of parallel invalidity proceedings within the framework of the aforementioned rules.[17] The chances of a defendant convincing infringement judges to suspend the infringement litigation concerning invention patents are usually very low.[18] However, this cannot lead to the conclusion that all infringement proceedings concerning patents will continue despite parallel revocation proceedings. Very often tactical instruments are used by the defendant to delay infringement proceedings until a decision in the revocation procedure is made. The separated system leads to a 'race between the infringement case and the invalidation case'.[19] Requests to contest the jurisdiction of the infringement court or the evidence submitted by the parties are often filed to delay the infringement procedure in the light of parallel revocation proceedings.[20] In exceptional cases, in order to have a strong and reliable basis for the enforcement of the infringement judgment the plaintiff deliberately agrees to a time schedule of infringement proceedings which ensures that a decision, at least in the first instance, concerning the validity of the patent is issued before the infringement judgment. However, there is no formal suspension of infringement proceedings by consensus according to Chinese Procedural Law. The willingness of the defendant to delay infringement proceedings can only be reflected by the judges in the decision of the court concerning the time schedule of the procedure.

**14.21** In consideration of the aforementioned tactical aspects, both parties have to be prepared to act quickly and to deal with the procedural requirements of both

16 SIPO issued in February 2013 a draft of the new Patent Examination Guidelines which are now subject to public consultation. These guidelines encourage the examiners of SIPO to conduct searches on prior art concerning utility models and design patents. It has to be seen whether these revisions will have an impact on the future practice concerning the suspension of infringement courts based on utility models and design patents.

17 Dong Wei, 'A Refined Civil Procedural Law and Patent Litigation', *Managing IP*, March 1/2013.

18 Less than 5–10% of the invention patent infringement cases are stayed in the light of an invalidation proceeding, see Benjamin Bai, Peter J. Wang and Helen Cheng, 'How to Litigate Patents in China', *Managing IP*, China IP Focus 2007, 45, 45.

19 Xiaolin Dang, 'Patent Litigation: A Complex Procedure', *Managing IP*, March 2012.

20 If the defendant challenges the jurisdiction, the court issues a ruling which is independently appealable and which can result in a further delay. The verification of the evidence is also often used to delay the proceedings because, in complex cases, the court will arrange a pre-trial hearing to allow both parties to cross-examine the evidence.

parallel proceedings. The petitioner for a patent revocation has to submit within one month after the request for invalidity is filed the grounds and evidence concerning the revocation. The patentee has to respond within one month after a copy of the request is served to him. The fact that new prior art documents and evidence filed after the one month period will not be considered in revocation proceedings puts much pressure on the defendant in infringement proceedings, because there is a need to act within the defence period of the infringement proceedings while complying with the strict deadlines in revocation proceedings.[21]

#### *(ii) Adapting the time schedule of the infringement procedure*

The infringement judges sometimes also tend to adapt the timing of the infringement proceedings to the parallel invalidity proceedings. The willingness of the infringement judges to 'delay' the infringement procedure depends on the timeframe and the expected outcome of the revocation proceedings. The Chinese revocation procedure is governed by strict deadlines concerning the submission of evidence and the exchange of arguments.[22] Furthermore, there is a strict internal timeframe for the Patent Reexamination Board. However, the Patent Reexamination Board is suffering from a heavy workload resulting from the increasing number of disputes and increasing complexity of the cases.[23] **14.22**

Concerning the duration of the appeal filed in revocation proceedings with the Beijing First Intermediate People's Court and the Beijing Higher People's Court, statutory timeframes according to Chinese Administrative Law are applicable which stipulate that the appeal proceedings at Beijing First Intermediate People's Court shall be completed after three months and the proceedings at the Beijing Higher People's Court after two months. The short timeframe reflects that the appeal proceedings are usually focused on the question of whether there are violations of procedural law.[24] In practice, the duration of the appeal proceedings often exceeds the statutory timeline. The complete revocation proceedings for the first and second instance usually take one or two years. **14.23**

The average duration of the procedure in China is still fast in comparison to other countries. However, in individual cases when parallel infringement **14.24**

---

21 Within the timeframe it is necessary to collect documentary evidence, physical evidence, oral testimonies of witnesses, expert opinions and so on; Benjamin Bai, Peter J. Wang and Helen Cheng, 'What Multinational Companies Need to Know about Patent Enforcement and Patent Litigation in China', [2007] **5** *Nw. J. Tech & Intell. Prop.* 449, 454.

22 According to Part IV Chapter 3, No. 4.3.1 of the SIPO Guidelines for Patent Examination 2010, the requesting party has to submit the relevant prior art documents within 1 month of the start of revocation proceedings.

23 He Huaiwen, above note 2, 14.

24 Yonghong Li, 'From Patent Hearings based on Experts' Reports to a Rearrangement of the Reexamination and Appeal System in China', [2003] **34** *IIC* 242, 245.

proceedings take place and are stayed, the patentee often applies blocking tactics to delay the revocation proceedings and the enforcement of the final revocation judgment. On the other hand, the timeframe of the revocation proceedings can be painful for the patentee who failed with his request to stay the infringement proceedings and who is confronted with a quick decision in these proceedings on the basis of a patent which is under attack by the defendant.[25]

**14.25** The judges in the infringement proceedings try to balance the interests of both parties in light of the quality of the prior art documents and the progress of the proceedings. If the defendant can rely on substantive arguments in the revocation proceedings and makes reasonable efforts to pursue the proceedings, the infringement judges are often willing to delay the infringement proceedings until a decision in the first instance of the revocation proceedings is made. The defendant who has to rely on non-validity arguments therefore has to make every effort to accelerate the revocation proceedings and to inform the infringement court about the progress in the revocation proceedings.

#### *(iii) Judgments concerning corresponding patents in other countries*

**14.26** The defendant has to convince the infringement judge that there is a high likelihood of an invalidation of the patent. In international patent litigations there are often parallel proceedings in different countries involving infringement and validity issues. A revocation of foreign patents belonging to the same patent family in parallel jurisdictions will not justify a suspension of infringement proceedings in China, but they can support the arguments of the defendant that the revocation procedure started at the Patent Reexamination Board will come to the same result. The qualification of the foreign revocation judgments by the infringement court will depend on the individual circumstances of the case, in particular the wording of the claims and the procedural and legal principles applied in the parallel case.

#### *(iv) Consequences of the decision in the revocation procedure*

**14.27** A decision of the Patent Reexamination Board usually has a relevant impact on the course of infringement proceedings:

25 A defendant who has to rely on a complex obvious prior use in revocation proceedings will have problems in convincing an infringement judge to delay or to stay the infringement procedure.

- If the validity of the patent in dispute is confirmed, a quick infringement judgment can be expected even if an appeal is filed against the revocation decision with the Beijing First Intermediate People's Court.
- An appeal against the decision of the Patent Reexamination Board very often only has a minor effect on the timing of parallel infringement proceedings, because only a small number of decisions of the Patent Reexamination Board are amended in appeal proceedings.
- However, if the patent is declared invalid by the Patent Reexamination Board and an appeal is filed against the decision to revoke the patent it can be expected that the infringement judge will stay the infringement proceedings.
- A patentee who has withdrawn the infringement lawsuit in the light of a first instance decision resulting in a revocation of the patent in dispute can start new infringement proceedings if the validity of the patent is confirmed later in the appeal proceedings.

As mentioned above, according to Article 47 Chinese Patent Act, a revocation of the patent in suit has no retroactive effect on decisions in infringement proceedings which have been delivered and enforced. However, a defendant can claim compensation against the patentee if he can prove malicious behaviour. Article 47 Chinese Patent Act furthermore provides that the patent infringement compensation shall be wholly or partly refunded if a non-refund would be obviously contrary to the principle of fairness. The judges therefore have the option to order reimbursement of damage payments paid by the defendant on the basis of a judgment if the patent forming the grounds of the judgments is revoked. If the final infringement judgment has not yet been enforced by the patentee and the patent in suit is revoked, the defendant can request a court to stop further enforcement. **14.28**

A defendant who fails in revocation proceedings cannot file for new revocation proceedings concerning the same patent on the basis of the same grounds and evidence (*res iudicata*). However, a new request can be accepted by the Patent Reexamination Board on the basis of new grounds and new evidence.[26] **14.29**

#### (v) *The interplay of infringement and revocation procedures in settlement negotiations*

Pending revocation proceedings are often used by the defendant in infringement proceedings as an instrument to improve the position in settlement negotiations. Relevant prior art documents can be presented to put pressure on the patentee. Under Chinese patent law the request to revoke a patent can be **14.30**

26 Benjamin Bai, Peter J. Wang, and Helen Cheng, above note 21, 450.

withdrawn until a final decision is issued. This makes it possible that the potential infringer can use the offer to stop revocation proceedings as an element for a friendly settlement without risking that the Patent Reexamination Board continues with re-examination of the patent after the request has been withdrawn, because it will not continue with an *ex officio* examination of the validity of the patent.

### 2. Amendment of the claims in the infringement proceedings

**14.31** A plaintiff who intends to enforce a patent, utility model or design patent in China has to – as in all countries – carefully analyse the relevant prior art to ensure efficient enforcement of his rights and to avoid possible counterclaims by the defendant. If the patentee is aware of relevant prior art causing a problem concerning the validity of the granted claims, he might consider starting the lawsuit on the basis of a narrow claim.

**14.32** In China the plaintiff has to rely on the claims which are granted and cannot file a lawsuit on the basis of a new set of claims specifically adapted by him in the light of the prior art documents.[27] However, a plaintiff who anticipates conflicts concerning the validity of broad claims can focus on the granted dependent claims which cover the infringing products.[28] The patentee is furthermore allowed to voluntarily amend the granted claims in prosecution proceedings or during revocation proceedings if the amendments comply with the requirements under Chinese patent law, in particular the SIPO Patent Examination Guidelines and the Implementing Regulations to the Chinese Patent Act.[29] The new claims have to be reviewed for admissibility before they can form a basis for infringement proceedings.

### 3. Preliminary injunctions

**14.33** There are strict requirements under Chinese law to obtain a preliminary injunction.[30] Item 16 *Opinions of the Supreme People's Court on Giving Full Play to the Functional Role of Intellectual Property Rights in Advancing the Great*

27 Concerning the discussion under German Law whether it is possible to file an infringement lawsuit on the basis of alternative combinations of claims in case there are doubts concerning the validity of the patent in suit, see Thomas Kühnen, above note 9, No. 1611.

28 It. 1 of the *Interpretations of the Supreme People's Court Concerning Certain Issues on the Application of Law for the Trial on Disputes over Infringement of Patent Rights* issued on December 28, 2009 (Fa Shi (2009) No. 21) expressly states, that the plaintiff can proceed on the basis of dependent claims with additional technical features.

29 See Supreme People's Court in the cases *Shanghai Jahwa Pharm. Tech., Co., Ltd. v PRP*, case No. Zhixingzi 17/2011; see also He Huaiwen, 'Amendments to Claims in Patent Invalidation Proceedings: PRB's Scope of Examination ex officio', [2012] **2** *China Patents & Trademarks*, 47, 50.

30 Tilman Müller-Stoy, 'Patent Litigation in the People's Republic of China', [2007] **38** *IIC* 520, 543.

*Development and Prosperity of Socialist Culture and Promoting Independent and Coordinated Economic Development* released by the Supreme People's Court of China on 16 December 2011 (hereinafter '2011 SPC Opinion') expressly states that a preliminary injunction is not appropriate when the determination of an infringement is complicated or revocation proceedings are pending. The infringement court will therefore usually refuse to grant a preliminary injunction if the patent is under attack.[31] However, there are cases in which a preliminary injunction is not hindered by pending revocation proceedings, in particular if the patent in suit has been reviewed in prior revocation proceedings. The fact that the patent survived previous revocation proceedings will be qualified as an indication that the patentee can rely on a valid patent if the defendant cannot prove that he can present new relevant prior art documents that were not considered in prior procedures.

According to Rule 12 SPC Provisions, the court which decides to suspend the infringement proceedings can concurrently decide to issue a provisional injunction to cease the use if the plaintiff makes such a request. The positive decision on a preliminary injunction can also be combined with the order to provide a security deposit.[32] **14.34**

## C. CONSEQUENCES OF THE INTERPLAY CONCERNING THE CLAIM INTERPRETATION

One of the problems in all jurisdictions with a bifurcated system is that discrepancies concerning the interpretation of the patent in suit in parallel proceedings can occur. The features of the claim will be interpreted by the infringement court and according to the principles applied by the Patent Reexamination Board concerning the validity.[33] **14.35**

### 1. Different claim interpretations applied by the parties

The separation of infringement and validity can be used by the parties to apply different claim interpretations. The patentee can attempt to extend the scope of protection during infringement proceedings to cover the infringing product and then applies a narrow interpretation to defend the patent against prior art **14.36**

31 In other countries with a separated system, there are exceptional cases in which a preliminary injunction is granted if it is obvious that the decision of the first instance to revoke the patent is incorrect, see Higher Court of Düsseldorf, **2008** *GRUR-RR* 329, 331 – Olanzapin.

32 Peter Ganea and Thomas Pattloch, see above note 15, 306.

33 Rachel Wu, 'Awaking the Sleeping Dragon: The Evolving Chinese Patent Law and its Implications for Pharmaceutical Patents', [2011] **34** *Fordham Int'l L.J.* 549, 571.

documents cited in the revocation proceedings.[34] The infringer attacking a patent in an invalidation procedure will use a similar strategy, that is, present a narrow interpretation in infringement proceedings which excludes his products and present a broad scope of protection during revocation proceedings. The different lines of argumentation of the patentee and the infringer are presented in different proceedings to different judges and the strategy can therefore be successful if the other party does not reveal the discrepancies.

**14.37** However, parallel proceedings can sometimes also be used as an opportunity for parties to convince a judge to reconsider the claim interpretation: The infringement court and the Patent Reexamination Board can be reminded that the interpretation of the claim language should result in the same meaning. Differences can form a valid basis for appeal proceedings. Therefore, the defendant in infringement proceedings has to consider that the revocation proceedings can provide not only an instrument for invalidation of the patent, but can also motivate the infringement judge to review his own claim interpretation. This interplay between infringement and revocation proceedings becomes particularly obvious if the claim interpretation of the infringement judge would lead to a revocation of the patent in dispute in respective proceedings, because a feature with the applied meaning is disclosed in the prior art.

**14.38** The aforementioned risks and opportunities of different interpretations in parallel proceedings underline again that the timing in both proceedings is crucial, because a defendant in infringement proceedings is hindered from introducing a narrow interpretation of the claims once the judgment has become final. Judges in infringement proceedings also have to consider the risk of a divergence in the interpretation of the claims when they weigh the pros and cons of a suspension of the proceedings or when they fix the time schedule for the infringement proceeding during parallel revocation proceedings.

### 2. Estoppel Doctrine

**14.39** The Supreme People's Court applies the estoppel doctrine to avoid discrepancies between patent examination and revocation proceedings, on one hand, and

34 In the case *European Central Bank v Document Security Systems Inc.*[2008] EWCA Civ 192 this strategy has been described using the Angora cat as a metaphor: 'When validity is challenged, the patentee says his patent is very small: the cat with its fur smoothed down, cuddly and sleepy. But when the patentee goes on the attack, the fur bristles, the cat is twice the size with teeth bared and eyes ablaze.'

infringement proceedings, on the other hand.[35] The estoppel doctrine is used concerning infringement cases under the doctrine of equivalence.[36]

According to Item 6 *Interpretations of the Supreme People's Court Concerning Certain Issues on the Application of Law for Trial of Cases on Disputes over Infringements on Patent Rights*,[37] the infringement court 'must not recognise protection for the limitations of the claim so surrendered'. It is therefore necessary to identify the statements of the patentee which can be regarded as a 'surrender' of the scope of protection.[38] **14.40**

The quality of narrowing statements of the patentee made during revocation proceedings has to be carefully reviewed by the infringement court, because statements of the patentee often do not have an impact on the decision of the Patent Reexamination Board. It would lead to different interpretations of the claims if the infringement court used the interpretation of a feature used by the Patent Reexamination Board and the (narrowing) interpretation of the patentee during the invalidation proceedings. Therefore, it has to be determined by the court whether the narrow interpretation of the claims formed the basis of the decision in invalidation proceedings. **14.41**

### 3. Harmonisation of claim interpretation

Differences concerning the claim interpretation are often not only a result of the different lines of argumentation of the plaintiff and the defendant as described above, but also a result of the lack of harmonisation of the applicable interpretation guidelines applied by infringement courts and the Patent Reexamination Board. **14.42**

According to Item 13 2011 SPC Opinions, the claim language has to be interpreted in the light of the object of the invention. The object of the invention can limit the scope of the patent. In the interplay between infringement proceedings and revocation proceedings, it therefore has to be ensured that the infringement court and the Patent Reexamination Board come to the **14.43**

35 *Cyouta Corp. v Wangao Corp.*, Supreme People's Court Civil Judgment No. Mintizi 158/2010; Wushi Pharmaceutical, Supreme People's Court Civil Judgment No. Mintizi 20/2009; He Huaiwen, 'Claim Construction, Doctrine of Equivalence and Estoppel', [2011] **3** *China Patents & Trademarks* 10, 13.

36 Sun Hailong and Yao Jianjun, 'Application of Doctrine of Equivalence and Estoppel Doctrine in Patent Infringement Lawsuits', [2010] **2** *China Patents & Trademarks*; He Huaiwen, 'Doctrines of Estoppel in Patent System in China', [2010] **1** *China Patent & Trademarks* 10, 11.

37 Approved by Adjudicatory Committee of the Supreme People's Court of PRC at 1480th Session on December 21, 2009, Fa Shi (2009) No. 21.

38 It is difficult to prove the intent of the patentee and therefore an objective standard is used to determine whether the patentee surrendered a subject matter, see He Huaiwen, above note 36, 12.

same conclusion concerning the definition of the technical problem to be solved by the invention. The determination of the object of the invention requires the same understanding of the prior art. The application of the same standards is crucial in order to avoid that the interpretation results in a different scope of protection.

**14.44** There are claim categories, like product-by-process claims, which often result in substantive problems if they are treated differently in the examination/revocation proceedings, on one hand, and the infringement proceedings, on the other hand.[39] Due to the fact that there is no binding case law in China, there are several issues concerning the claim interpretation where no uniform standards exist. The guidelines for the Patent Reexamination Board and the Supreme People's Court judicial guidelines do not cover all issues in detail and, furthermore, do not lead to the same results concerning the interpretation of the claims in revocation and infringement proceedings.[40] However, as a general guiding principle in both proceedings, terms clearly defined in the claims cannot be interpreted in a different way.[41]

### 4. Binding effect of the claim interpretation in the revocation procedure

**14.45** In other jurisdictions having a bifurcated system, the reasons for the decision in opposition or nullity proceedings replace the original description as far as it is concerned by the decision if the patent is maintained in amended form or is partly nullified. In all other cases, statements made in opposition or nullity proceedings are not binding, but can provide the grounds for the infringement court to examine the statements possibly by an expert opinion if the court wishes to depart from the interpretation in the opposition or nullity decision.[42]

39 He Huaiwen, 'Product-by-Process Claim: Extent of Protection and Infringement Determination', [2011] **4** *China Patents & Trademarks* 10, 12.

40 The interpretation of means-plus-function claims provides examples for the different approaches, see *Beijing Yingtelai Muogen Co., Ltd. v Beijing Deyuan Kuaijie Doors and Windows Plant*, Beijing No. 2 Intermediate People's Court Civil Judgment No. Erzhongminchuzi 08543/2009; *Qu Shengbo v New World (China) Technology and Media Co., Ltd.*, Shanghai Higher People's Court Civil Judgment No. Hugaominsan (zhi) zhongzi 89/2010; Xiong Yanfeng, Wu Yuhe, Wang Jinjing, Johnston Li, Scott G. Wang, Daniel N. Cheng, Li Rongxin, Michelle Yang, Zhang Dongli and Chen Ran, 'A Comparative Study of Means-plus-Function Claims in China and United States', [2012] **2** *China Patents & Trademarks* 14, 18.

41 *Cui Jun v PRB and Zhao Donghong*, Beijing Higher People's Court Administrative Judgment No. Gaoxingzhongzi 751/2011, see the report by Liu Xiaojun and Chin Jinchuan, 'Latest Developments in Trial of IP cases by Beijing Higher People's Court in 2011', [2012] **2** *China Patents & Trademarks* 34, 35.

42 Linsenschleifmaschine, Federal Supreme Court, 12 May 1995, **1992** *GRUR* 839, 840; Regenbecken (Rainwater reservation), Federal Supreme Court, 5 May 1998, **1998** *GRUR* 895; however, in the case of a voluntary limitation by the patentee during opposition or nullity proceedings, the judgment does not include the reasoning for the limitation and therefore forms no basis for the interpretation of the patent, Ziehmaschinenzugeinheit I (Drawing machine I), Federal Supreme Court, 17 April 2007, **2007** *GRUR* 778; Thomas Kühnen, above note 9, No. 57.

In China there are no particular legal provisions dealing with the question as to what extent the infringement judge is bound by grounds provided in decisions of the Patent Reexamination Board concerning the interpretation of a patent. Although there is obviously no binding effect, the infringement court will not ignore the grounds of the revocation judgment. If the wording of the patent claims in dispute is amended during revocation proceedings, the description is not adapted to the new wording of the claims. The grounds of the revocation judgment therefore provide an additional basis for the interpretation of the amended claims. **14.46**

## D. ALTERNATIVE INSTRUMENTS IN THE INTERPLAY BETWEEN INFRINGEMENT AND VALIDITY ISSUES

A defendant in infringement proceedings who initiates revocation proceedings is confronted with the aforementioned procedural issues and problems related to the timing and will therefore consider alternative options to use the available prior art against the patent in the infringement proceedings. **14.47**

### 1. Prior art defence

One instrument of presenting prior art documents in infringement proceedings is the prior art defence (see in this regard also the contribution of *Bailey and Wang*, Chapter 8). The prior art defence was introduced in Article 62 Chinese Patent Act through the third amendment in 2009. It has been up-graded through the third amendment from judicial doctrine to codified law.[43] One of the reasons for the introduction of the prior art defence into Chinese law was to simplify the court proceedings in cases in which the accused infringer can provide evidence that the patented product or process is disclosed in the prior art.[44] The codification of the prior art defence is qualified as an indication that the split between infringement and revocation proceedings is diminishing in China.[45] **14.48**

43 Zhang Guangliang, 'Rules Applicable to Prior Art Defence: Difference in Law Provisions and Analysis thereof', [2010] **2** *China Patents & Trademarks* 55, 55.

44 Shoukang Guo, 'Some Remarks on the Third Revision Draft of the Chinese Patent Law', in Wolrad Prinz zu Waldeck und Pyrmont, Martin J. Adelmann, Robert Brauneis, Josef Drexl and Ralph Nack (eds.), above note 11, 713, 723; Rachel Wu, above note 33, 580.

45 Peter Ganea, 'Volkrepublik China – Neue höchstrichterliche Auslegungen und geänderte Durchführungsbestimmungen zum Patentgesetz', **2010** *GRUR Int.* 270, 272; Stefan Luginbuehl and Thomas Pattloch, above note 13, 149.

**14.49** According to the prior art defence, the infringer can argue that the patented product or process was part of the public domain prior to the filing of the patent application. In several countries, the defence of the free state of art is recognised in disputes in which the plaintiff relies on the doctrine of equivalence.[46] In China, the defence can also be raised in case of a literal infringement.[47] In other bifurcated systems, the application of the prior art defence in cases of literal infringement is denied, because of the division of duties in the different proceedings.[48]

**14.50** Under Chinese law the prior art defence also does not extend the power of the infringement court, but the application of the prior art defence in cases of literal infringement allows the judge to review prior art documents in all cases. As a consequence it has become a widely used instrument which is often considered to be more efficient than initiating revocation proceedings. However, the prior art defence raised in infringement proceedings only has an *inter partes* effect. Therefore, a defendant who wants to ensure freedom to operate for its customers, suppliers and so on has to obtain a revocation judgment with an *erga omnes* effect. In contrast to infringement proceedings the defendant in revocation proceedings is also allowed to raise patent invalidity grounds, such as insufficient disclosure or inadmissible broadening.

**14.51** In court practice, the prior art defence is extended to what is obvious to a person skilled in the art. Consequently, the scope of protection is not only limited to the exact prior art. The prior art defence can be used if the embodiment is identical to the prior art or forms an obvious variation of the prior art. This makes the prior art defence an important alternative tool in the interplay between the infringement and revocation procedure.

### 2. Counterclaims concerning malicious assertion of invalid patents

**14.52** Moreover, the defendant can attempt to file a counterclaim concerning the malicious assertion of an invalid patent. The first draft of the third amendment of the Chinese Patent Act expressly allowed a counterclaim if the patentee enforces a patent despite the fact that the patent would be invalid in the light of

46 German Federal Supreme Court, [1987] **18** *IIC* 795 – Formstein (Moulded Curbstone); [1999] **30** *IIC* 558 – Kabeldurchführung (Cable Duct I); [2001] **32** *IIC* 93 – Kontaktfederblock (Contact Spring Block). The so-called 'Formstein' objection which can be raised in cases based on the doctrine of equivalence does not imply any examination of the patentability, see Peter Meier-Beck, 'The Latest Issues in German Patent Infringement Proceedings', [2001] **32** *IIC* 505, 515.

47 Peter Ganea, above note 45, 272.

48 Alfred Keukenschrijver, in Jochen Pagenberg and William Cornish (eds.), *Interpretation of Patents in Europe*, Cologne: Carl Heymanns Verlag 2006, DE 71.

the existing prior art.[49] The counterclaim has not been codified in the final 2009 Chinese Patent Act, but the 2011 SPC Opinions confirmed in Item 16 the court practice that the enforcement of an invalid patent can lead to damage payments if the patentee sends a warning letter despite being aware of the prior art which could lead to a revocation of the patent.

An infringement court which is confronted with such a counterclaim therefore has to analyse the novelty-destroying quality of the prior art known to the plaintiff before sending a warning letter or starting further actions. There are different forms of wrongful patent enforcement, that is, unjustified enforcement due to the lack of infringement,[50] but the Supreme People's Court justifies only the enforcement of an invalid patent as a form of 'patent abuse' in its 2011 SPC Opinions. **14.53**

The 2011 SPC Opinions do not specify any detailed requirements, in particular which evidence has to be presented by the plaintiff concerning the prior art invalidating the patent and the knowledge of the patentee at the time when the claim is raised. The 2011 SPC Opinions also do not specify whether the judge handling the counterclaim can assess the validity or has to await a final decision concerning the invalidation issued in revocation proceedings. Therefore, it still has to be seen whether the counterclaim will develop into a relevant instrument in the interplay between infringement and revocation proceedings. **14.54**

## E. OUTLOOK

### 1. Timeframe of parallel proceedings – fourth amendment of the Chinese Patent Act

China is one of the most litigious countries in the world as far as patent litigation is concerned and the courts are confronted with a growing number of complex patent cases.[51] There also is a dramatic increase in revocation proceedings which already has and will have a future impact on the timeframe of the proceedings. Therefore, the aforementioned 'race' between the plaintiff and the defendant concerning the infringement and revocation proceedings will become even more important. In other countries with separate systems – like **14.55**

49 Jay Sha, 'Third Time Lucky', *Managing IP*, China IP Focus 2007, 29, 32.

50 Christopher Heath, 'Wrongful Patent Enforcement – Threats and Post Infringement Invalidity in Comparative Perspective', [2008] **39** *IIC* 307, 308.

51 According to a report published by the Supreme People' s Court of China, there was a 37.7% increase in IP lawsuits closed by Chinese courts in 2012 compared to the previous year, see http://en.chinacourt.org/public/detail.php?id=4675.

Germany – the delay caused by the duration of nullity proceedings in the past had been regarded as a problem which resulted in the modification of the procedural rules applicable to the first and second instance to accelerate the nullity proceedings.[52]

**14.56** China has made substantial efforts in recent years to improve the enforcement of patent rights[53] and has identified the timing of the parallel infringement and revocation proceedings as a problem which needs to be resolved in order to handle the increasing number of disputes.

**14.57** SIPO released in 2012 a draft of the fourth amendment to the Chinese Patent Act.[54] The draft version is subject to further revisions, but can be regarded as an indication of the expected changes. According to the proposed amendment, the decision of the Patent Reexamination Board in revocation proceedings would take effect immediately after announcement and publication of the decision irrespective of whether or not an appeal would have been filed by the other party. It could therefore be expected that the infringement court would not await the outcome of the appeal, but rather issue a judgment on the basis of the decision of the Patent Reexamination Board in the first instance.

**14.58** The proposed change in the fourth amendment of the Chinese Patent Act would have a relevant impact on the interplay between the infringement and revocation proceedings. It also provides an indication that there are no different concepts that apply in infringement and revocation proceedings,[55] but rather a pragmatic and efficient approach to respond to problems identified after the third amendment. However, it has to be seen whether the proposed change will find its way in the final version of the new law because it affects the position of the party using the legitimate right to appeal the decision of the Patent Reexamination Board.

---

52 See the German Patent Modernisation Act dated 1 August 2009, *Federal Law Gazette* 2009, 2521; Concerning the individual procedural elements to accelerate the proceedings, see Jochem Gröning, 'Angriff und Verteidigung im reformierten Patentnichtigkeitsberufungsverfahren', **2012** *GRUR* 996 et seq.

53 Concerning the development of the enforcement activities, see Peter Ganea, 'Can China be forced to enforce IP Rights', in Wolrad Prinz zu Waldeck und Pyrmont, Martin J. Adelmann, Robert Brauneis, Josef Drexl, Ralph Nack (eds.), above note 11, 379 et seq., Andrea Wechsler, 'Sino-German IP Conference – IP Enforcement: A Comparison of Chinese and German Experiences', Conference Report (Munich, 15–17 October 2008), [2009] **40** *IIC* 839, 840.

54 An English translation of the modified Articles is available at http://chineseip.jmls.edu/sites/en/4th-amendments-chinese-pa.

55 Deming Liu, 'The Transplant Effect of Chinese Patent Law', in [2006] **5** *Chinese Journal of International Law*, No. 3, 733, 749.

## 2. High quality standards in the examination proceedings

The separation of infringement and invalidity proceedings is founded on the presumption that the patent which forms the grounds of the infringement proceedings is valid and has been the subject of detailed substantive examination in examination proceedings. The infringement judge has to rely on the correctness of the granted patent and cannot review the legitimacy of the patent if he examines the infringement claims. The quality of the examination process therefore is the key feature in those systems which are based on a separation between the infringement and validity procedures. **14.59**

The SIPO examination procedure gained a sufficiently good reputation so that a patent granted by SIPO is regarded as *prima facie* valid. However, the enormous growth of the number of patent applications during recent years raises concerns related to the quality standards of the examination procedure.[56] There is substantial technological progress in China, but the dramatic increase of utility model, design patent and invention patent applications[57] cannot only be explained by a historical boost in innovation. The re-examination in the invalidation procedure will therefore become an even more important element in the Chinese litigation system. **14.60**

The constantly increasing number of applications and the remarkably short periods available to SIPO to examine patent applications lead to a high pressure on the examiners. It has to be seen whether the quality standard in the examination procedure can be maintained if the examination period is not extended and the number of examiners is not increased.[58] **14.61**

The judges in infringement proceedings have to consider the aforementioned developments in the examination procedure if they decide to proceed with the infringement litigation after revocation proceedings have been started. They have to analyse in the decision making process concerning the suspension of the infringement proceeding whether the prior art documents cited in revocation proceedings have been considered in the prosecution process and have been properly reviewed. The judges in the infringement proceedings have the knowledge and experience to assess not only the infringement situation, but **14.62**

56 Stefan Luginbühl and Thomas Pattloch, above note 13, 135.

57 Concerning the statistics, see the detailed analysis of Mark Liang, 'Chinese Patent Quality: Running the Numbers and Possible Remedies', [2012] **11** *J. Marshall Rev. Intell. Prop. L.* 478, 478, 492.

58 With respect to the risk of an understaffing at SIPO and the impact on the quality of the prosecution process, see Mark Liang, above note 57, 492.

also validity issues,[59] and therefore should review the prior art submitted by the defendant to decide whether there is a strong basis for invalidation or whether revocation proceedings have been launched for tactical purposes only.

**14.63** The patent evaluation report – which was newly introduced through the third amendment of the Chinese Patent Act in 2009 – provides a flexible instrument for review of the protectability of designs and utility models. Due to the fact that the statistics show an immense increase in applications for utility models and designs, these intellectual property rights will often form the basis of infringement litigations. The evaluation therefore plays an important role in the decision of the infringement judge to proceed or to stay infringement proceedings. However, it has to be considered that the evaluation report cannot be challenged in separate proceedings and therefore has to be reviewed by the infringement judge in the light of the further arguments presented by the parties before a decision is made concerning the suspension of infringement proceedings.

### 3. Harmonisation of the patent interpretation in infringement and revocation procedures

**14.64** Possible discrepancies between the claim interpretation in infringement proceedings and parallel revocation proceedings are identified as a main problem of separated systems. The statements issued by the Supreme People's Court and SIPO provide only general guidelines, but no definitive answers to all detailed questions of claim interpretation. This increases the risk of differences arising in the claim interpretation in infringement and revocation proceedings. It also enables the patentee and the potential infringer to use different interpretations in the two proceedings. Further harmonisation of the interpretation of claims by a binding case law would improve the interplay between infringement and revocation procedures.

**14.65** It also can be expected that the increasing number of parallel infringement and revocation proceedings in China will require detailed guidelines concerning the question as to what extent the grounds of the revocation judgment are binding

59 Regarding the legal and technical background of infringement judges, see Rongjie Lan, 'Are Intellectual Property Litigants Treated Fairer in China's Courts? An Empirical Study of Two Courts', [2012] **43** *IIC* 751, 770; Zhang Guangliang, 'Discussion on IP Judicial Institution, Judges and Ways to Hear IP Cases', [2011] **2** *China Patents & Trademarks* 80, 81.

in infringement proceedings. In other bifurcated systems the decisions amending the patent claims replace the original description.[60] However, Chinese courts have to carefully review such an approach because third parties would need full access to the revocation decisions and it also needs to clarify the categories of statements in revocation decisions which would replace the description of the patent. The future development of the interplay between infringement and revocation procedures in China will therefore also be interesting for other jurisdictions which apply a bifurcated system.

60 In Germany the opposition or nullity decision replaces the patent specification if the patent is partially nullified, see above note 42; Linsenschleifmaschine, Federal Supreme Court, 12 May 1995, **1992** *GRUR* 839, 840; Thomas Kühnen, above note 9, No. 56.

# 15

# CHINESE CHARACTERISTICS OF CLAIM INTERPRETATION BY COURTS

**Li Jian**



## A. BRIEF REVIEW OF CHINA'S PATENT LITIGATION PRACTICE

**15.01** China's patent law has been in effect since 1984. Until 2008, it has undergone three amendments, inter alia, to adapt it to the requirements of the TRIPS Agreement and to encourage innovation. The Supreme People's Court (SPC) has issued two judicial interpretations[1] on patent infringement cases, the Interpretation of Several Issues Relating to Application of Law to Trial of Patent Cases[2] ('2001 Judicial Interpretation') and the Interpretation of Several Issues Relating to Application of Law to Trial of Cases of Disputes Arising from Patent Infringement[3] ('2009 Judicial Interpretation'). Both Interpretations are binding and can be cited by lower courts as a legal resource.

**15.02** As far as patent jurisdiction is concerned, the SPC has designated 64 Intermediate People's Courts which are competent to deal with patent cases in the first instance. The second instance is the Higher People's Courts at the provincial or autonomous region level, and the third and last instance is the SPC. Due to the

1 Judicial interpretations are a specialty of the Chinese judicial system. The SPC is entitled to issue such interpretations of the laws enacted by the People's Congress, so as to provide guidance for the People's Courts throughout the country with regard to the understanding of complicated legal terms.

2 *Fashi* [2001] No. 21.

3 *Fashi* [2009] No. 21.

vast volume of IP litigation coming through the courts, many judges have gained profound experience in the patent field. Moreover, an increasing number of judges look back on studies abroad or on specialized IP training in law schools.

As a consequence of the ongoing improvement of judicial intellectual property protection and enforcement (*Luginbuehl*, Chapter 1) as well as of the revision of the Civil Procedures Law in 2009, the courts' workload from patent infringement litigation has increased over the past years and reached 7,130 suits filed throughout the country in 2012. It is generally understood within China's judiciary that both domestic and foreign companies have a legitimate interest in effective IP protection. In a qualitative respect, 2012 has seen a relatively high amount of unprecedented, novel cases of high complexity and remarkable social impact. These cases were quite challenging and demanding in terms of professional and technical expertise. **15.03**

In the course of patent litigation, the interpretation of the claims is pivotal when deciding whether the patent is valid and whether the defendant's technical solution is infringing. **15.04**

## B. PRINCIPLES OF CLAIM INTERPRETATION

As an important feature of patent law in general, the scope of the claims forms the boundary of the exclusive patent right. Article 59(1) of the Chinese Patent Act stipulates that the scope of protection of the patent right for inventions or utility models shall be determined by the terms of the claims. Therefore, through the process of claim interpretation, the scope of protection will be determined. Consequently, the generousness or strictness of claim interpretation is decisive for the determination of the scope of protection and also has, from a broader perspective, a great impact on the balance of interests between the patentee and the public. **15.05**

There are two extreme theories on claim interpretation. The rather generous one is the 'theory of central definition'. According to this theory, the patent protects the inventive concept, with the claim as just an example of such inventive concept. Claim interpretation should not stick to the literal meaning of the claim but, by focusing on the technical solution described by the claim, cover the overall concept of the invention with the help of the description and the drawings so as to expand protection to the scope desired by the patentee. The other, rather strict theory is the 'theory of peripheral definition'. According to this theory, the patentee has limited the scope of the protected subject-matter **15.06** by the claim, so that the wording of the claim should be interpreted strictly according to its literal meaning. To harmonize these two extreme interpretation principles, the Protocol on the Interpretation of Article 69 European Patent Convention, for instance, has determined another principle, namely that of 'eclectic interpretation', which is largely followed by Item 2 of the 2009 Judicial Interpretation. That is, the interpretation of the claim should, on the one hand, properly protect the patentee's interests, but on the other hand, it should also send a clear signal to the public with regard to the boundary of the patent. As a matter of fact, the application of the doctrine of equivalents as well as its limitations, originates from this interpretation principle.

**15.07** Item 2 of the 2009 Judicial Interpretation stipulates that the courts shall determine the content of the claim as prescribed in Article 59(1) Chinese Patent Act[4] in combination with the understanding of an ordinarily skilled person in the art who has considered the description and the appended drawings.

**15.08** The 'person skilled in the art' is the key concept behind the eclectic interpretation theory. Such person is a legal fiction and an abstract concept. It refers to a technician who, at the time of infringement, possesses an average level of knowledge in the relevant technical field, neither to a technical expert nor to an ordinary person without any skills in the art. The 'person skilled in the art' is explicitly mentioned in Article 26(3)[5] Chinese Patent Act, pursuant to which the description shall set forth the invention or utility model in a manner sufficiently clear and complete so as to enable a person skilled in the relevant field of technology to carry it out. In other words, the technical solution for which the claims seek protection is to be obtained, directly or by generalization, from the description and drawings by a person skilled in the art. Therefore, the scope of protection should be defined in a way that it encompasses the scope of comprehension of the claims by a person skilled in the relevant field of technology upon reading the description and the drawings. That is, when determining the scope of protection, the judge shall understand and interpret the claim from the angle of a person skilled in the relevant field of technology.

4 'For the patent right of an invention or a utility model, the scope of protection shall be subject to the content of claims, and the written description and the pictures attached may be used to explain the content of claims.'

5 'A description shall describe the invention or utility model in a clear and comprehensive way to enable a technician in the relevant technology field to carry it out; when necessary, pictures shall be attached. An abstract shall briefly introduce the main technical points of an invention or utility model.'

## C. THE BASIS OF CLAIM INTERPRETATION

Item 1 of the 2009 Judicial Interpretation stipulates that the right holder may choose one or more claims before the end of the court hearing in the first instance so as to determine the scope of protection sought against the allegedly infringing technical solution. The reason for such provision is that each claim forms a complete technical solution, and that it should be up to the right holder to choose those claims which will henceforth outline the scope of protection he seeks. Specifically, Rule 21(1) Implementing Rules to the Chinese Patent Act stipulates that the claims shall comprise one independent claim and may also contain subordinate claims. As the 'claim', as specified by Article 59 Chinese Patent Act, is not confined to 'independent claim', 'subordinate claims' may also be included. Therefore, the right holder is allowed to choose subordinate claims so as to further determine the protection scope. In addition, as the scope of protection of the patent as defined by the subordinate claims is necessarily narrower than the scope of the independent claim, such option to choose the appropriate subordinate claims cannot result in overprotection and therefore does not bear the danger of harming the general public interest. **15.09**

If a patent claim involves multiple claims, the right holder shall identify during the pleadings those claims for which he seeks protection. If he merely complains in general terms that the alleged infringing technical solution falls into the scope of protection of the patent, but does not clarify the claim or claims which define such scope of protection, the judge shall instruct him to determine those claim(s) on grounds on which he intends to prosecute infringement. If the right holder has already clarified such claims during the first-instance hearings, the court shall determine whether the alleged infringing technical solution falls into the independent claim or the subordinate claims. If the court, upon examination, finds that the alleged infringing technical solution does not fall into the scope of protection as defined by the independent claim, he or she must arrive at the conclusion that the defendant's solution does not fall into the subordinate claim, as the scope of the independent claim is necessarily broader than the scope of the subordinate claim. In such case, the court no longer has to carry out a one-by-one comparison of the technical features of the subordinate claim and of the alleged technical solution, but may determine directly whether the allegedly infringing solution falls into the scope of protection. However, if the court finds, upon examination, that the allegedly infringing technical solution falls into the scope of the independent claim, it still has to determine whether such solution also falls within the scope of the subordinate claim. That is, the fact that the defendant's solution falls into the scope of the independent claim does not automatically mean that the scope defined by the subordinate claim is also infringed upon. **15.10**

**15.11** In practice, it may occur that the claim asserted by the right holder is declared invalid. There are views that if such invalidity is established prior to the first-instance judgment, the patent right shall remain valid on the basis of the other claims. If, according to such view, the right holder requests determination of the protection scope with reference to other claims, the People's Court shall consider such request if the above declaration of invalidity is made after the first-instance judgment and before the second-instance judgment. That is, if the right holder requests determination of the protection scope with the help of claims that have not been asserted in the first instance, the second-instance court may make an attempt to conciliate between the parties with regard to the new choice of claims. If conciliation fails, the court shall instruct the right holder to file another lawsuit. As for the claim that the right holder has asserted, if the People's Court of the first instance does not make a judgment, the People's Court of the second instance may conciliate relevant claims between the parties on a voluntary basis. If the conciliation fails, the case shall be remanded to the original court for retrial.

**15.12** However, to avoid a back and forth between first and second instance caused by such a random change of asserted claims, the Interpretation has not adopted the above views but refers to the general provisions on the change of litigious claims as specified by Item 156 *Opinions of the Supreme People's Court on Some Issues concerning the Application of the Civil Procedure Law of the PRC*, according to which the right holder can change the asserted claim until the end of the first-instance hearing. That is, changes afterwards will not be considered but the right holder is free to assert other claims in a separate court trial.

**15.13** Even if the claim asserted by the right holder is declared invalid, the patent remains valid on the basis of other claims. However, as the plaintiff has not asserted these other claims, the judge will not consider them but dismiss the plaintiff's claim, as the legal ground for his accusations against the defendant has fallen away.

## D. SPECIFIC RULES ON CLAIM INTERPRETATION

**15.14** The 2001 Judicial Interpretation has established the doctrine of equivalents. It provides that the scope of protection of a patent does not only include the scope as determined by the technical features described in the claims, but also the scope as determined by equivalent features. The doctrine of equivalents is an important instrument to avoid an overly restrictive interpretation which would remain limited to the wording of the claim, so as to achieve a fair protection of the patent right. Therefore, on the one hand, the doctrine of equivalents compensates for the inadequacy of literal claim interpretation. On the other hand, however, it bears the danger of being applied in an excessively broad and arbitrary manner. The latter should be avoided, so as to prevent an inadequate expansion of the protection scope which would narrow the leeway for innovative competition and harm the public interest.

## 1. Intrinsic evidence preferred over extrinsic evidence

According to Item 3 of the 2009 Judicial Interpretation, the courts may interpret a claim by referring to the description and the appended drawings, relevant claim(s) in the claims portion and the patent prosecution history. Where the description has specifically defined an expression in the claim, such specific definition shall be adhered to. **15.15**

Furthermore, the description and the drawings, as well as further relevant claims, are all components of the same set of patent grant documents and therefore, due to their close relation to the claim at issue, the best available guidance to clarify controversial terms. The patent examination file may also serve as guidance. Even though it is not part of the patent authorization document, it is open to the public and the terms used therein shall be understood by the infringement judge in the same way as the patent examiner has understood them. Therefore, the patent examination file plays an important role in the course of claim interpretation. **15.16**

In contrast to the above patent grant documents and the examination file which pertain to so-called 'intrinsic evidence', 'extrinsic evidence' encompasses reference books, textbooks which are not kept in relevant patent documents and files of the patent office. In general, such external evidence remains unconsidered unless the internal evidence is not sufficient to enable a clear interpretation. Of course, all these interpretation instruments do not have to be considered if the description alone suffices to clarify the meaning of the claims. **15.17**

In practice, there are only a few cases in which the scope of protection remained unclear, so that courts found it difficult to determine infringement. Nevertheless, these cases stirred many discussions. In *Bai Wanqing v Tianxiang Co.*[6] for instance, the claim of patent read as follows: **15.18**

> Electro-magnetic pollution-proof clothes, including top and bottom, radiation-proof metal web or membrane embedded in the shell fabric, radiation-proof metal web or membrane composed of metal threadlets or powder with high magnetic inductivity and, consequently, no residual magnetism.

---

6 [2012] *Min Shen* No. 1544.

**15.19** In contrast, the accused product had been described as follows:

> An electro-magnetic pollution proof top, radiation-proof metal protection web in the shell fabric, the metal protection web is composed of stainless steel fib.

In its final decision, the SPC held that the claim used the ill-defined technical term 'high magnetic inductivity' to describe the metallic material used in the 'electro-magnetic pollution proof clothes', and failed to define the specific numerical range of this high magnetic inductivity as well as other parameters affecting magnetic inductivity in its patent claim or manual. Furthermore, during the court hearing, the plaintiff has not provided a commonly recognized definition of 'high inductivity' of radiation-proof clothes. Therefore, the SPC decided that the defendant's accused product would not fall into the scope of patent protection.

**15.20** In addition, a decision which involved the invalidation of a patent for a Precision Rotating Compensator[7] held as follows: if an error in a drafted claim is one a person skilled in the art, due to his or her general knowledge, can detect simply upon reading the claim, and if such general knowledge guides the skilled artisan to the only correct answer just upon reading the description and the appended drawing, such person skilled in the art will naturally construe the technical solution based on his sole correct interpretation, and will naturally understand the technical solution on the basis of self-correction of the obvious error when he or she runs into the technical solution of the invention or utility model again. That is, he or she will not mechanically 'understand it wrongly'. For a person skilled in the art, the technical feature and the meaning of a technical term used in the claims are definite, and his or her corrective understanding of an obvious error would neither entail a change in the scope of protection nor render the boundary of the claims unclear or cause prejudice to the public interest.

**15.21** It should be noted that in general, the terms used in the claims should be construed in a way that their usual meaning within the relevant technical field remains unchanged. In special cases, if the description indicates that a certain term has a patent-specific meaning, and the scope of protection of the claim is defined clearly enough in the description, such special definition from the description should be used to interpret the meaning of the same term in the claim. Such practice does not contradict the view that restrictively interpretable terms from the description shall not be read into the claims; the latter only

---

7 *Hong Liang v. Patent Reexamination Board and Song Zhanggen* [2011] *Xing Ti* No. 13.

means that embodiments from the description shall not be used to reduce the scope of protection.

## 2. All elements rule

According to the 'all elements rule', patent infringement can only be determined if the alleged infringing technical solution comprises all technical features of the patented technical solution. Additional technical features of the alleged solution will not be considered. Only in the case of composition patents characterized by so-called closed claims, will the alleged solution also be regarded as non-infringing if it contains elements which are not contained in the patent claim. Such practice does not contradict the all elements rule, as 'closed claim' means that the claimed composition does not contain any other components apart from the components explicitly mentioned in the claim, so that the exclusion of other components must be regarded as another feature of the claim. Exactly this particular feature, however, is absent from the alleged technical solution if it contains additional components which are not mentioned in the claim. **15.22**

As far as the controversially debated 'superfluous definition' is concerned, Item 7(1) of the 2009 Judicial Interpretation expressly stipulates that all technical features described in the claims shall be examined, irrespective of whether they are necessary to achieve the inventive aim. That is, the SPC explicitly prohibits the application of the 'superfluous definition' doctrine, thereby putting an end to previous, rather generous lower court decisions in this matter.[8] Hereby, the SPC considered the role of the claim which is to determine the scope of protection of the patent, or, in other words, to clearly indicate the boundaries of the subject-matter for which protection is sought, so as to signal to the public what acts can be performed without intruding into such boundaries and to avoid unpredictable changes to the claimed subject-matter. Such clarity and legal certainty can only be achieved if all the features included in the claim by the right owner himself are comprehensively and fully respected by the courts, irrespective of whether they later turn out to be unnecessary to achieve the inventive aim. It should be noted that the German Federal Supreme Court is similarly reserved towards the 'superfluous definition' doctrine.[9] **15.23**

8 The non-binding 'Opinions on Several issues Relating to the Establishment of Patent Infringement' of 2002, of the Beijing Higher People's Court, for instance, explicitly acknowledged the superfluous definition rule in its items 47–55; see also decision of the Intermediate People's Court of the City of Beijing of 15 May 1995 (Higher People's Court of the City of Beijing (ed.), *Zhishi chanquan jingdian panli* (Classical IP Cases), vol. 3 (2003), 38).

9 See for example *Behheizbarer Atemluftschlauch* (Heatable breathing air hose), Federal Supreme Court, 24 September 1991, **1992** *GRUR* 40, 41.

### 3. Dedication rule

15.24 'Dedication rule' means that a potentially patentable technical solution described in the description but not mentioned by the claims will be considered as dedication to the public by the patentee, and that the patentee cannot claim that such dedicated content shall be included in the scope of protection under the doctrine of equivalents. In essence, the dedication rule restricts the application of the doctrine of equivalents. It is based on the frequently observed phenomenon that applicants, in order to facilitate the grant, adopt a subordinate concept in the claim while expanding its interpretation to the description and the drawings. Then, in an infringement suit, the patentee asserts such expanded part as equivalent features, which forms an undue expansion of the protection scope.

15.25 For example, a claim explicitly mentions 'one part held together by three screws' as a technical feature, whereas the description states that these screws may also be five, eight or ten. If the corresponding feature of the allegedly infringing product involves eight screws, the right holder will not be able to convince the court that such feature shall be regarded as equivalent to the claimed technical solution, as it is only outlined in the description but not in the claims portion.

15.26 As a matter of fact, this is just another example of 'buttering both sides of the bread'. The patent system is not only there to protect patentees but has the simultaneous function of safeguarding the public interest. The establishment of the dedication rule is conducive to safeguarding that patent claims are interpreted in the light of the public interest.

### 4. Estoppel rule

15.27 'Estoppel rule' refers to the principle that third parties should be able to rely on acts performed by a party in the past, in a way that such party is banned from undoing its past acts. In the area of patent law, the estoppel rule forms a limitation to the application of the doctrine of equivalents. That is, whatever the patentee has abandoned during the grant or invalidation procedure cannot be reincorporated into the scope of protection through the application of the doctrine of equivalents in an infringement trial. To enhance the operability of the estoppel rule, Item 6 of the 2009 Judicial Interpretation emphasizes that subject-matter abandoned by the applicant or patentee in the course of patent grant and patent invalidation procedures through amendments to the claims or description or through a statement shall not be reincorporated into the protection scope. Hereby, it is irrelevant whether such amendment or statement has been made at the right owner's initiative or at the patent examiner's request, as long as there exists a legal causality between such amendment or right owner's statement and the final scope of protection as granted.

In the case *Zhongyu Co. v Jiuying Co.*,[10] for instance, the claims of patent read as follows: **15.28**

> 1. A steering gear model composed of rack, electric motor, feed and slider. The electric motor is located in the seat, one active gear is attached to one side of the motor, the feed runs through the slider, a passive gear attached to one end of the feed is engaged with the passive gear. At the bottom of the slider is an electric brush. 2. The steering gear in claim one is characterized by a fixed hole on the rack fixed in a motor drive circuit board. 3. The steering motor in claim 2 is characterized by a motor drive circuit board printed with a bar-type carbon film and silver skin, the rack fixed in the motor drive circuit board through the fixed hole, and the electric brush at the slider seat engaged with the carbon film and silver skin.

However, the Patent Reexamination Board had declared claim 1 and 2 invalid and upheld validity only on the basis of claim 3. The accused product's features were as follows: **15.29**

> The steering gear's drive circuit board is printed with a bar-type carbon film and gold-plating copper bar, and the electric brush at the slider seat is engaged with the carbon film and gold-plating copper bar.

In its final judgment, the SPC held that the prosecution history estoppel shall be applied to narrowing amendments, statements or opinions made voluntarily by the applicant or patent owner. If, however, the Patent Reexamination Board has invalidated an independent claim but upheld the validity of the subordinate claim, such amendment can no longer be regarded as made voluntarily by the patent owner. The SPC therefore held that full attention shall be paid to this circumstance, so as to strictly assess whether the prerequisites for an estoppel are met. **15.30**

In contrast, in *Honeywell International Inc. v Hamilton Sundstrand Co.*,[11] the United States Court of Appeals Federal Circuit opined as follows: **15.31**

> It is therefore clear that the addition of a new claim limitation can give rise to a presumption of prosecution history estoppel, just like an amendment that narrows a preexisting claim limitation. In either case, the narrowing amendment, if made for a reason related to patentability, will give rise to a presumption of surrender. If only

10 [2012] *Min Ti* No. 306.
11 *370 F.3d 1131 (Fed. Cir. 2004).*

> narrowing amendments to preexisting claim limitations could give rise to the presumption, the purpose of preventing patentees from recapturing subject matter conceded during prosecution would be undermined. Astute practitioners could, through clever claim drafting, elect to treat most, if not all, amendments as merely adding new claim limitations rather than narrowing preexisting ones. For these reasons, we hold that an amendment adding a new claim limitation constitutes a narrowing amendment that may give rise to an estoppel.

Circuit Judge Newman, however, dissented in part.[12]

15.32 Hence, the application of the estoppel depends to a certain degree on the circumstances under which the practice of patent prosecution has developed or is still developing. That is, theory does not provide for any standards on grounds of which the application of such estoppel could be regarded as 'correct' or 'wrong'. If the applicant is expected to pay more attention to the expressions used in the claims, the stricter standard, as applied by the majority in the *Honeywell* case, appears to be justified. Otherwise, the view of the SPC as expressed in the *Zhongyu* case is also appropriate.

## E. INTERPRETATION OF SPECIAL CLAIMS

### 1. Product-by-process claim

15.33 Method patents are technical solutions which comprise a series of processes or operation steps used in order to resolve a specific technical problem. There are differing opinions as to whether the sequences of the actual steps of a patented process limit the scope of protection when the patent claim fails to specify such order.

---

12 Ibid.

> A claim is not narrowed by canceling its antecedent claim. By statute it is irrelevant whether a claim is in dependent or independent form; it is not a narrowing amendment to go from dependent form to independent form. The majority opinion searches for and finds a narrowing amendment in the cancellation of the broader antecedent claim. However, for the claims here at issue, there was no narrowing amendment of any of the elements or limitations at issue, in any claim. The majority opinion changes the basic premise of presentation of claims of varying scope and divergent content, in holding that by dropping a broader claim, the claims subordinate to that claim became subject to presumptive estoppel, whether or not the subject matter at issue was included in the broader claim. That is far removed from the Court's holding in *Festo*. Although the majority quotes the Court's statement that 'a narrowing amendment made to satisfy any requirement of the Patent Act may give rise to an estoppel,' restating a dependent claim into an independent claim of identical scope is not a narrowing amendment; and canceling a broader claim (especially one that does not mention the element at issue for equivalency) is not a narrowing amendment.

In *OBE-Werk Ohnmacht & Baumgärtner GmbH & Co. KG v Zhejiang Kanghua Glasses Co., Ltd*,[13] the SPC held that when applying the doctrine of equivalents to method patent cases, patent specification and drawings, patent examination files, technical solutions written in the claim and the logical connections between the different steps should be considered in totality to determine if the various steps of the patented process shall be followed in a specific sequence if the claim itself remains silent on such sequence. The steps themselves and their sequence would then both limit the scope of protection of the method patent. The facts of the case were as follows. **15.34**

On 24 April 1996, OBE-Werk Ohnmacht & Baumgärtner GmbH & Co. KG (OBE) filed with the State Intellectual Property Office (SIPO) an invention patent application for the manufacturing method of its 'spring-loaded hinge'. The company was granted a patent on 24 October 2001. Claim 1 of the patent states: **15.35**

> 1. A method for manufacturing spring hinges that comprise at least a housing, a hinge pin and a spring; the distinguishing features of the method are its steps described as follows: provide a metal strip for producing the hinge pin; cut out a section similar in shape as the hinge pin; press the section to form a round area in order to shape the shoulder on the hinge pin; punch holes on the hinge pin.

On 24 June 2002, OBE filed a lawsuit against Zhejiang Kanghua Glasses Co., Ltd (Kanghua) which, in OBE's opinion, manufactured, used, offered for sale and sold for business purposes its spring-loaded hinge by making infringing use of OBE's patented process. The Beijing Intermediate People's Court No.1 found in the first instance that Kanghua's hinge pin production process functioned as follows: **15.36**

> 1. Die cut a hinge pin by manually feeding the metal strip into the punch;
> 2. Use a clamp to manually hold the hinge pin's front portion, and use a forging press to hammer the hinge pin's rear portion into a rounded shape;
> 3. Use a clamp to manually hold the hinge pin's front portion, and insert the hinge pin into a punching machine to punch holes;
> 4. Use a lead wire to manually thread through the round hole in the front part of the hinge pin; after threading several hinge pins, polish the hinge pins together using a polisher.

The court found that claim 1 of the patent at issue consisted of four steps, and Kanghua's process also consisted of four steps. When the hinge pin is cut from the metal strip, a reversal of the sequence of forging and hole-punching would **15.37**

13 [2008] *Min Shen* No. 980.

not produce a different result. Therefore, Kanghua's method would be equivalent to the method under claim 1, hence it is within the scope of protection. According to Beijing Higher People's Court's second-instance judgment, however, which focused on the specifications of the patent at issue, the technical aim of the patent would only be achieved by observing the sequence of the steps. Any change to such sequence would prevent the achievement of the desired technical effect. Kanghua's manufacturing method consisted of four steps, of which 'rounding' and 'hole-punching' may be interchanged. This would be different from the patented solution's sequence of steps. Hence, the allegedly infringing product's manufacturing method would be neither identical with nor equivalent to the patented method, and therefore not fall within the scope of protection. The court reversed the decision of the trial court and dismissed OBE's claims. OBE petitioned to the SPC to reopen the case. On 29 August 2009, the SPC dismissed the petition.

**15.38** The SPC held that in method patent infringement cases, the limiting effect of a specific sequence of steps should not be ignored just because the patent claim has not specified such sequence as a limitation to the protection scope. Instead, patent specifications and drawings, patent examination files, technical solutions contained in the claim and the logical connection between the different steps should be considered in totality from the perspective of a person with ordinary skills in the art, so as to determine whether the various steps should indeed be followed in a specific sequence.

**15.39** For method inventions involving sequences of steps, both the step itself and the sequence of the steps to be followed limit the scope of protection. In the above-mentioned case, claim 1 included four steps. First, the purpose of the 'material feeding step' is to provide processing material for other steps; hence, material feeding must take place before other steps. Second, the purpose of the 'cutting step' is to cut out a section similar in shape to the hinge pin. Based on the specifications and drawings of the patent, the 'section' described includes the 'basic shape used to form the shoulder (9)' and 'at least a part that comprises the hinge hole area (497)'. As the 'pressing step' involves pressing the 'basic shape created from the "cutting step" to be used to form shoulder (9)' and the 'hole-punching step' involves making hinge holes on 'Area 497' created from the 'cutting step', on top of which, the patent specifications contain no technical information indicating that 'hole-punching' or 'pressing' may be made before cutting or provide the relevant technical indication, a person of ordinary skill in the field may not know that the purpose of the disputed patent invention or the same technical effect may be achieved by performing 'hole-punching' or 'pressing' before 'cutting'. Hence, 'cutting' in claim 1 should be made before 'pressing' and 'hole-punching'. Based on the patent specifications, although 'pressing' and 'hole-punching' may be interchanged, in practice, the sequence of the two steps, once determined, has to be followed. Therefore, a fixed sequence of the four steps of claim 1 exists.

### 2. Means-plus-function claim

With regard to certain claims, technical characteristics cannot be expressed with the help of structural features, so that it appears more appropriate to define such characteristics with the help of functional features, that is, features defined by a certain function or by the effect that they achieve. As the literal meaning of such functional features is, by nature, rather general, the 2009 Interpretation Rules prescribe that they shall be interpreted in combination with the specific method of implementation laid down in the description and in the drawings, as well as with equivalent implementation methods. Such interpretation aims at achieving a fair balance between the interests of the patent holders and the public. The reason for the use of the expression 'in combination with' is that in rare cases, according to current examination practice, description and drawings do not describe a specific implementation method. **15.40**

There are views that such interpretation method is not consistent with Part II, Chapter 2, 3.2.1 Examination Guidelines pursuant to which the 'technical features of a claim which are defined by their function shall be construed as embracing all the means which are capable of performing the function'. This provision, however, applies to the subject-matter of patent protection, namely the technical solution, not just the function or effect of a technical feature. **15.41**

Moreover, according to the current patent examination practice, it is hard to completely search and examine all possible methods of implementing the stated functions. Therefore, 'equivalent implementation methods' shall be determined in accordance with the facts of the individual case. **15.42**

## F. CLOSING REMARKS

The growing number of novel and highly complex cases has brought to light several deficiencies of the legal system. Through patent adjudication, the SPC has nevertheless promptly explored and appropriately addressed new areas and provided the courts throughout China with guidance and new rules. The judicial interpretations enacted and precedents set by SPC reflect its innovative approach towards balancing legal stability and change, private rights and public interests so as to satisfy both legal requirements and social expectations. As China's highest judicial authority, the SPC does not stop at settling disputes but **15.43** it also establishes codes of conduct for the general public and guidelines for competition between business enterprises. Interpretation rules and case law also serve as guideposts for industrial development and sector development. To some extent, the current rules on claim interpretation such as the estoppel rule or the dedication rule, have been influenced by corresponding US practice, in spite of the fact that the Chinese patent system has its historical roots in German patent law. The vital goal of SPC adjudication and rulemaking is to clarify the boundaries of protection, so as to enhance the predictability and uniformity of court decisions. Without doubt, the SPC's unique competence to enact binding interpretations as well as the leading cases will contribute to further enhancing the rule of law in the area of intellectual property.

# 16

# PREDOMINANTLY PROCESS PATENT-RELATED ASPECTS OF INFRINGEMENT

**Peter Ganea**



## A. INTRODUCTORY REMARKS

As an economy which supplies the world with a great variety of products, China has a huge interest in the inflow of sophisticated manufacturing processes, not least because the country endeavours to climb up the value chain and to become an 'indigenous innovation'-based economy (*Luginbuehl*, Chapter 1). Hereby, China is still dependent on advanced knowledge generated abroad.[1] **16.01**

Unlike the majority of tangible products which, once put into market circulation, can be quite easily re-engineered so that patents are the only option to protect them against imitation, processes are normally carried out behind factory walls and have better chances of being kept secret. That is, process patent holders often have the choice between patent or know-how protection. **16.02**

China, on the other hand, can be assumed to have a greater interest in motivating foreign investors, joint venture partners, and so on to disclose their **16.03**

1 Recently emphasized by China's President Xi Jingping during his visit to Germany in March 2014, see Christian Geinitz, 'Was China von uns will' (what China wants from us), http://www.faz.net/aktuell/wirtschaft/fruehaufsteher/xi-jinping-in-deutschland-was-china-von-uns-will-12868185.html.

process-related knowledge through patent applications, rather than to keep it secret. Even the implementation of patented manufacturing processes is hardly possible merely on grounds of the information revealed by the patent application but requires additional know-how. The desired knowledge spill-over on national joint venture partners, suppliers, and so on, can only be fully generated if the foreign company provides locals with insights into their implicit knowledge and other know-how that accompanies the patented technology.

**16.04** Far-reaching secrecy out of distrust in the local IP protection framework, accompanied by measures such as splitting up manufacturing processes and entrusting each step to different joint venture partners so as to prevent a single local company from acquiring all necessary knowledge,[2] would be detrimental to China's ambitious plans towards 'indigenous innovation'. On the other hand, the country's sheer size enables the government to impose unfavourable conditions on foreign and multinational companies who want to be present in China's market. Foreign investors bemoan, inter alia, pressure to transfer or to license their IP to domestic companies or to enter joint ventures with domestic partners.[3]

**16.05** This chapter deals with predominantly process patent-specific aspects of litigation, in particular with patent exhaustion, new rules which interpret some flexibly interpretable TRIPS provisions on process patent protection, acts which would be regarded as 'indirect infringement' in other jurisdictions and, briefly, with process patent-specific aspects of claim interpretation.

## B. PRODUCT AND PROCESS PATENT-RELATED ASPECTS OF EXHAUSTION

**16.06** The amendments to the Patent Act of 2008 introduced a new provision in Article 69 No.1 which clarifies that using, offering for sale, sale or import of patented products or products directly obtained from a patented process, which have been made by the patentee or with the patentee's consent, shall not be regarded as infringement. That is, the patent exhausts upon first sale, within

2 In 2005, and therefore at a time when European businesses perceived China's IP enforcement as more problematic than today, the *Guidelines for Entrepreneurs: Technology Transfer to China* issued by the German Asia Pacific Committee, an organization jointly established by the German Federation of Industries, the Association of German Chambers of Industry and Commerce, and other business federations, openly advised German investors in China to take these and other measures in order to protect their manufacturing know-how.

3 Testimonials of Robert D. Atkinson and Dennis C. Shea before the US House of Representatives at http://science.house.gov/hearing/subcommittee-investigations-and-oversight-%E2%80%93-impact-international-technology-transfer; see also the USTR's 'Priority Watch List' 2012 of countries which have shown disobedience to US demands related to IP protection; Thomas M. Hout and Pankaj Ghemawat, 'China vs the World: Whose Technology is it?' [2010] **88** *Harvard Business Review* 94.

China and abroad ('international exhaustion'). Holders of Chinese patents cannot proceed against the parallel import of products protected under a parallel patent abroad and made and sold there by themselves or with their consent. The exhaustion rule complies with the flexibility set forth in Article 6 of the TRIPS Agreement which stipulates that 'nothing in this Agreement shall be used to address the issue of the exhaustion of intellectual property rights'.

The new provision has eliminated some of the uncertainties associated with the previous version of the Patent Act which remained silent on exhaustion and tacitly delegated the interpretation of this issue to the courts. Chinese courts, however, have not yet had many opportunities to decide on exhaustion cases.[4] Item 94 of an early draft interpretation on patent litigation issues published by the Supreme People's Court (SPC) in 2003 proposed the adoption of the English implied licence.[5] Chinese scholars instead favoured a – finally adopted – statutory rule on international exhaustion which would be in China's national interest as an emerging market.[6] During the drafting process, SIPO justified the plan to introduce such rule with China's 'dependence on the import of foreign technologies'[7] – a justification which appears a bit odd at first, as exhaustion is normally related to the products which incorporate a technical idea, not to the technical idea *per se*. However, in the following we will see that exhaustion rules actually do have the potential to facilitate or to hamper the inflow of technical knowledge, in particular in context with process patents. 16.07

Before dealing with process patent-related exhaustion issues, however, let us have a look at another, product patent-related aspect. To date, neither the law nor the accompanying State Council's implementing rules or the relevant SPC interpretations contain provisions, for example, on the recycling of disposable patented cameras or empty ink cartridges under patent protection. Does the 16.08

---

4 AIPPI Yearbook 2008 / III (Q205: Exhaustion of IPRs in cases of recycling and repair of goods), 87 et seq.; https://www.aippi.org/download/yearbooks/2008/book-III.pdf.

5 Implied patent licence means that the patented product can be unrestrictedly recirculated and used by the lawful purchaser unless the patent owner has made a declaration of will, for example, by marking the product correspondingly, that only certain uses, sale within a certain territory, and so on are permitted. The solution found by the Japanese Supreme Court in the landmark BBS decision of 1 July 1997, [1998] **29** *IIC* 331, with regard to parallel trade in design protected goods, for instance, comes close to the implied licence doctrine; note that the SPC proposal is no longer available on the internet and should have lost all relevance after the amendments of 2008; it has been mentioned in Peter Ganea and Thomas Pattloch, *Intellectual Property Law in China*, The Hague: Kluwer Law International 2005, 13 (72 with regard to exhaustion and parallel imports); see also Katrin Blasek, 'Erschöpfung und Paralleleinfuhr in der VR China – Rechtslage und Ausblick' ('Exhaustion and Parallel Imports in China – legal situation and prospects'), **2006** *GRUR Int.*, 568, 570.

6 See, for example, Xiang Yu, 'Exhaustion and Parallel Imports in China', in Christopher Heath (ed.), *Parallel Imports in Asia*, The Hague: Kluwer Law International 2004, 25 et seq., who, however, would have favoured a regulation within an SPC interpretation which would have been more flexibly adaptable than a legal provision.

7 EU China IPR2 Project: *Third Revision of China's Patent Law – legal texts and documents on the drafting process 2006 – 2008*, at http://www.ipr2.org/images/eu_patent_law-final.pdf, 65.

resale of such once legally sold, collected and recycled products in direct price competition with the sale of original parts by the patent owner fall under the exhaustion doctrine, or does it form patent infringement? Relevant case law from the US, Japan and Germany is abundant, and courts there have developed sophisticated doctrines.[8] Chinese case law is almost non-existent, apart from one decision of the Shandong High Court of 2000 (exact date not available). In *Ju Aijun v Gubeichun Co.*, the court decided that collecting and refilling design protected wine bottles would not constitute design patent infringement, due to the exhaustion of the design right.[9]

**16.09** In spite of the lack of case law, the Beijing Higher People's Court seems to have considered the possibility that related disputes may arise at a relatively early stage. Item 95 of a former, non-binding set of published court interpretations, the Beijing Higher People's Court's 'Opinions on Patent Infringement Litigation (tentative)' of 29 September 2001,[10] contained the following provision:

> Patent exhaustion. Use or resale of a patented product which has been made and sold by the patent owner or with the patent owner's consent does not form patent infringement. This includes the following:
>
> (1) upon its sale, the use or resale of a part of a patented product, whereby such part has been made by patent owner or with the patent owner's consent, shall be regarded as being carried out with the patent owner's implicit permission
> (2) … .

Paragraph (1) is quite broadly interpretable but if, for example, refilling empty ink cartridges as part of a patent for a printer can be subsumed under the mentioned acts, the provision could mean that the patent right exhausts upon first sale in such a manner that it cannot work against the recycling and subsequent resale of product parts intended for disposal.

**16.10** Meanwhile, these 'Opinions' have been replaced by the Beijing Higher People's Courts 'Guidelines on Patent Infringement Litigation' of 4 September 2013[11] (hereinafter 'Guidelines'). Item 119(3) of the Guidelines reads as follows:

> 119. Upon sale of a patented product or a product directly obtained from a patented process by the patent owner or an authorized entity or individual, the use, offer for sale,

8 A comprehensive overview is given by Mineko Mohri, 'Patents, Recycling and Repair from a Comparative Perspective' [2010] **41** *IIC* 779.

9 Case reported in AIPPI Yearbook 2008/III, above note 4, and on the website of the Beijing Intellectual Property Institute http://www.bipi.org/html/zhurenzhuanlan/anlifenxi/200812/22–230.html (Chinese).

10 Translated into German by Yuanshi Bu, *Patentrecht und Technologietransfer*, Munich: C.H. Beck 2010, 279 et seq.

11 http://bjgy.chinacourt.org/article/detail/2013/10/id/1104565.shtml (Chinese).

sale or import of such product is not regarded as patent infringement. The aforementioned includes:

…

(1) Upon the sale of a specific part of a patented product by the patent owner or an authorized person, the use, offer for sale or sale of such part or its assembly with the patented product.

This new provision appears to point even clearer towards the exhaustion of the patent right in spare parts upon first sale, in a manner that also recycling and reusing parts of patented products, inter alia, by reassembling them with the patented product seems to be permissible. It should be noted, however, that these provisions are not binding for all other Chinese courts. Only one court, the SPC, has the authority to enact binding court interpretation rules which clarify difficult legal questions or detail the meaning of broadly interpretable legal provisions, so as to provide guidance to all People's Courts throughout the country. The practical importance of the Beijing Higher People's Court's interpretation guidelines for other, less experienced courts should not be underestimated, however. The former 'opinions', for instance, have been frequently quoted in literature until recently, and it is well imaginable that also local judges tacitly resort to them.

In sum, Chinese legislature and judiciary have not yet had too many opportunities to deal with the question of exhaustion in recycling and repair cases. It is hardly conceivable, however, that courts will not sooner or later be confronted with this issue, given the fact that the country is one of the world's largest consumer markets, with plenty of business opportunities for collectors and recyclers of thrown-away disposables. **16.11**

Now, let us turn back to process patent-related aspects of exhaustion. Whereas, in spite of rapidly increasing prices, owners of Chinese patents do not yet seem to suffer under rampant parallel importing, the question of sale/import of machinery and equipment used for the implementation and operation of patented manufacturing processes is highly topical. **16.12**

In this context, the question of whether the owner of the process patent who has sold patented or non-patented equipment which enables the operation of said process, is still in the position to control the use of such apparatus to carry out the patented process, or whether the process patent has been exhausted upon sale of the apparatus is debated worldwide. German courts are comparably reluctant to utilize a generous application of the exhaustion doctrine. In its **16.13** landmark decision *Fullplastverfahren*,[12] for instance, the Federal Supreme Court regarded the process patent as not yet exhausted upon sale of the (non-patented) apparatus. It should be noted, however, that the main point of departure for the Federal Supreme Court had been the sales contract between the parties respectively the implied licence to use the apparatus in the intended manner that went along with it, namely to realize the patented process.[13] The US Supreme Court's *Quanta Computers v LG* decision of 9 June 2008[14] also had to deal with the question of process patent exhaustion. It arrived at the conclusion that the method claim in the operation of a computer component shall exhaust if it is largely embodied in the sold product in a way that apart from implementing the process, no other non-infringing uses were possible.

**16.14** As said, China's courts have not yet had many opportunities to decide in patent exhaustion cases. However, especially the above raised process-related questions are of significant relevance for China as a net technology importer. China's manufacturing industries are still highly dependent on the supply with manufacturing knowledge and the associated production lines from abroad. Implementing and using such tangible apparatus also generates implicit and explicit knowledge, and therefore almost necessarily entails technology transfer. A right in the hands of process patent holders to prohibit uses for which such apparatus had originally been designed would hardly be in the interest of China's industries, as it would render the inflow of advanced manufacturing knowledge more expensive.

**16.15** A hint that the Chinese judiciary is indeed reluctant to give too generous treatment to patent holders had already been contained in Item 95 of the above-mentioned, now obsolete, Beijing Higher People's Court's 'Opinions':

> Item 95: Patent exhaustion. Use or resale of a patented product which has been made and sold by the patent owner or with the patent owner's consent does not form patent infringement. This includes the following:
>
> (1) …
> (2) the use of apparatus which is specifically designed to implement a patented process and which has been made by the patent owner or with the patent owner's consent, for the purpose of implementing said process

As mentioned, these 'Opinions' are now obsolete but the provision in Item 95 has been transplanted into Item 119(4) of the mentioned 'Guidelines':

---

12 Decision of 24 September 1980, **1980** *GRUR* 28 (in German).

13 See also the Federal Supreme Court decisions of 16 September 1997, **1998** *GRUR* 130, 132 ('Handhabungsgerät') and of 27 February 2007, **2007** *GRUR* 773, 776 ('Rohrschweißverfahren').

14 553 U.S. 617.

> Upon sale of apparatus specifically designed for the implementation of a patented process by the patent owner or by an authorized person, the use of such apparatus for the implementation of the patented process

That is, the Beijing Higher People's Court is of the opinion that the process patent owner cannot prevent the legal purchaser of apparatus designed for the implementation of the process from using it in the designated manner, obviously irrespective of whether the apparatus itself is patented or not. As these guidelines are only non-binding recommendations, it may well be that other courts will arrive at a contrary interpretation. In the light of the rather restrictive stance the legislature and judiciary have taken towards the scope of substantive patent protection (*Li*, Chapter 15, *Bailey and Wang*, Chapter 8 and *Pattloch*, Chapter 17), however, patent holders are well advised to expect a rather generous application of the exhaustion doctrine in future decisions.

## C. PROCESS PATENT-SPECIFIC LITIGATION PROVISIONS

### 1. Reversal of burden of proof

Process patent infringement is often hard to prove, as the plaintiff cannot rely on evidence obtained from, for example, examining products which are openly available on the market, as in case of product patent infringements, but would need access to the premises of the alleged infringer. The defendant, on the other hand, has a legitimate interest in denying the plaintiff, who is almost necessarily a competitor, such access. **16.16**

Article 34.1 of the TRIPS Agreement aims at balancing the interests of the disputing parties, by stipulating that courts shall be authorized to order the defendant to prove that the process to obtain an identical product is different from the patented process, if (a) either the product obtained by the patented process is 'new' or (b) there is a substantial likelihood that the identical product was made by the process and the owner of the patent has been unable through reasonable efforts to determine the process actually used. That is, Article 34.1 regulates a reversal of burden of proof, as an exception to the general civil procedures principle that the plaintiff has to prove his case. **16.17**

The corresponding Chinese Patent Act provision in Article 61(1) has opted for the first alternative, that is, the defendant can be ordered to prove that his process is different from the patented process if the product obtained by the patented process is 'new'. The legal provision has remained unchanged during the amendment of 2008. Its text is as broadly interpretable as the corresponding **16.18**

TRIPS provision in Article 34.1(a), in that it merely requires such product to be 'new' to justify the reversal of burden of proof, but remains silent on *how* new the product shall be,[15] for example, new in the meaning of patent 'novelty' or 'new on the market'?

**16.19** It was up to the SPC to define 'new' in its Interpretation of Issues Concerning the Application of Law in the Trial of Disputes over Infringement of Patent Rights of 2009 (Interpretation 2009).[16] Note that the Interpretation 2009 is issued by the SPC and therefore binding for all courts in China. Item 17 of the Interpretation 2009 clarifies that 'new' under Article 61 Chinese Patent Act is to be understood as follows:

> If the new product or the technical means to manufacture such new product is already publicly known in China or abroad at the patent application date, the People's Court shall determine that such product does not pertain to 'new product' pursuant to Article 61(1) of the Patent Act

The reference date is therefore the same as for 'novelty' as a patent prerequisite, namely the application date. Also in qualitative respect, such 'newness' requirement for a reversal of burden of proof comes close to the novelty requirement for patentability.

**16.20** On the one hand, regulating 'new' as not yet known at the application date is more patent-owner friendly than reference to later dates which may also be subsumable under Article 34.1(a) TRIPS. This is because considerable time may have passed since the filing of the patent application, with a correspondingly high likelihood that the defendant uses an alternative process which has been developed since then in order to get the new product. In spite of such likelihood, the defendant can still be ordered to prove that his process is different from the patented one and thus not infringing. On the other hand, due to the clarification that 'new' has to be understood as 'not publicly known worldwide', the provision falls behind the previous judicial Chinese practice in terms of patent-holder friendliness. Previous court practice tended towards interpreting 'new' in relative terms, that is, as not yet publicly known *within* China at the application date, so that the court could still order the defendant to prove that his process is different even if the product was already publicly

15 Nils Heide, 'Harmonisierungsaufgaben im internationalen Technologietransfer – Zum Schutz von Herstellungstechnologien in der Volksrepublik China' ('Harmonization tasks regarding international technology transfer – about the protection of manufacturing technologies in the People's Republic of China'), **2008** *GRUR Int.* 12.

16 English translation available on the website of China Patent Agents http://www.cpahkltd.com/UploadFiles/20100317113813391.pdf.

known outside China. Also according to the now obsolete Item 122 of the non-binding 'Opinions' of the Beijing Higher People's Court of 2001, a 'new product' pursuant to the corresponding Patent Act provision meant 'a product which had been manufactured in China for the first time and which is clearly distinct in terms of composition, design or in terms of quality, performance and function from equivalent products that existed prior to the application date'.[17] The new SPC Interpretation has put an end to such patentee-friendly interpretation.

The effect of the new legal regime on process patent holders is somewhat mitigated by a more recent set of rules issued by the Supreme People's Court, the 'Opinion on Several Issues Relating to Sufficient Utilization of IP Adjudication to Foster Development and Prosperity of Socialist Culture and to Promote Autonomous and Coordinated Economic Development' of 16 December 2011,[18] which allows courts to shift the burden of proof even if the product at issue is not 'new'. Item 15 regulates three alternatively applicable circumstances under which the court may require the defendant to prove that he or she does not infringe, namely: **16.21**

- the patent owner can prove that both products are identical;
- the patent owner is unable to prove infringement in spite of reasonable efforts;
- the court arrives at the conclusion that it is very likely that the infringer uses the patented process.

## 2. Product directly obtained from a patented process

Another process patent-related issue is the extension of process patent protection to the products directly obtained from the patented process. The EPC, for instance, has regulated such product-by-process protection since 1973 (Article 64). The corresponding TRIPS provision in Article 28.1(b) pursuant to which the process patent owner shall have the rights to sell, offer for sale, and so on, at least in products obtained directly from the patented process, does not contain a definition of the products encompassed by the expression 'directly obtained by the process', that is, whether it is limited to products which are the immediate result of the last process step, or whether it extends to products which have undergone further processing? The TRIPS requirement has been implemented in Article 11(1) Chinese Patent Act but without a clarification as to the **16.22**

17 An older SPC decision of 17 June 2003 (*Eli Lilly v Jiangsu Haoshen Pharmaceutical Industries*) is also frequently referred to as interpreting 'new' as 'new within China'; see also Yuanshi Bu, above note 10, 134 et seq.

18 Available at http://www.law-lib.com/law//law_view.asp?id=370632 (in Chinese).

meaning of 'directly obtained'.[19] It was, again, up to the SPC to formulate a definition in Item 13(2) Interpretation 2009 which reads as follows:

> Where a follow-up product is obtained by further processing or disposing of the original product, the courts shall determine the act as 'use the product directly obtained by the patented process' as prescribed in Article 11 of the Patent Law.

**16.23** That is, the act of further processing the directly obtained product forms infringing 'use'. Pursuant to the SIPO, however, such protection does not extend to follow-up products manufactured with help of these further processed materials or products.[20]

## D. INDIRECT INFRINGEMENT

**16.24** Indirect infringement forms a patent-specific category of infringement which does not require collaboration between the assisting and the immediately infringing act. That is, the assisting act can be prosecuted, even if there is no collaboration between the indirect and the direct infringer with the aim of infringing. Indirect infringement basically means to provide the infringer with the necessary means of infringement. Such apparatus, material or preliminary products themselves do not have to be infringing but they have to be indispensable for carrying out the infringing act. Moreover, important jurisdictions which have adopted patent-specific indirect infringement provisions require that the indirect infringer – insofar as there is also a subjective requirement – must have had a certain degree of knowledge or at least sufficient reason to know that the means he delivers can or will be used for infringement.[21]

**16.25** Rules on indirect infringement have been introduced by important jurisdictions, in particular because general civil law provisions on joint infringement have turned out to be insufficient, for example, to cover the delivery of equipment, so that their meaning had to be unduly overstretched to achieve a patent-owner friendly result.

**16.26** Process patents are especially prone to indirect infringement, for example, by the delivery of non-patented apparatus which enables the use of the patented process. Moreover, due to the reasons outlined above at 16.16 et seq., process patent owners find it especially difficult to prove the direct infringement.

---

19 Nils Heide, above note 15.

20 Reported by Yuanshi Bu, above note 10, 29.

21 Comparative overview provided by Georg Andreas Rauh, 'Mittelbare Patentverletzung in Deutschland, Japan und den USA' ('Indirect infringement in Germany, Japan and the US'), 2010 *GRUR Int.* 459.

Patent-specific rules on indirect infringement instead enable them to hold the suppliers of equipment and other means liable, without having to evidence the liability of the actual infringer.[22] Hereby, the German provision in Article 10 of the Patent Act seems to be comparably far-reaching in terms of patent-owner friendliness, in that it, for instance, does not even require the indirect infringer to have known about the patent at issue; mere 'obviousness' of the fact that the supplied equipment or material can be used for infringement or is intended for infringement is sufficient.[23] With some justification, critics of this provision refer to the enhanced legal uncertainty among suppliers of machinery, preliminary products, and so on, who are burdened with an enhanced duty of care to ascertain that purchasers will use their products for non-infringing uses only.[24]

Out of similar concerns, the Chinese legislature has abandoned the idea of introducing a provision on indirect patent infringement. In the course of the debates that preceded the amendment, SIPO justified the legislature's reluctance to introduce a corresponding rule as follows: 16.27

> The essence of adding provisions on stopping of an act of indirect patent infringement to the Patent Law is to expand the protection for patent right to the product which is associated with the patented technology and itself is not granted the patent right. Therefore, the problem of indirect patent infringement has fallen into the highly sensitive grey area of the interests between the patentee and the public, and relevant rules, if established and applied in an improper manner, will harm the right of the public to freely use the prior art. In consideration of the above factors, the SIPO is of the view that the time is not yet ripe to provide indirect patent infringement in the Patent Law, since the patentee may claim right over the direct infringer and look into joint liabilities of the relevant person based on the provisions on contributory infringement under the General Principles of Civil Law.[25]

Also, the SPC had regulated a provision on indirect infringement in a previous draft version of its Interpretation 2009, but finally decided to abandon it.[26] 16.28

What remains are the general civil provisions on joint liability as mentioned by SIPO. The corresponding provisions are contained in Articles 8 and 9 of the new Chinese Act on Torts of 26 December 2009.[27] Both provisions have been transferred from Article 130 of the General Principles of Civil Law of 12 April 16.29

22 Rudolf Kraßer, *Patentrecht* ('Patent Law'), 6th edn., 2009, § 33 VI a.

23 Rudolf Kraßer, ibid., § 33 VIb; Georg Andreas Rauh, above note 21.

24 See, for example, Bernd Fabry and Michael Trimborn, 'Die mittelbare Patentverletzung – das unterschätzte Geschäftsrisiko' ('Indirect patent infringement – the underestimated business risk'), **2008** *GRUR* 861 et seq.

25 IPR2 Programme, p. 73, at http://www.ipr2.org/images/eu_patent_law-final.pdf.

26 As envisioned by Patent Law Amendment Research Group China Patent Agent (H.K. Ltd), http://www.cpahkltd.com/EN/static/20100416101302417114.html.

27 In English at http://www.wipo.int/wipolex/en/text.jsp?file_id=182630.

1986, China's first Civil Code after the start of the opening and reform policy in the late 1970s which is now subsequently replaced by new separate codes on specific aspects of Civil Law, and from Article 48 of the SPC's 'Tentative Opinions on Several Questions Regarding the Application of the General Principles of Civil Law' of 1988. In the following, reference will be made to the new Torts Act provisions but it should be noted that the older court decisions still refer to the previous provisions contained in the General Principles and the Court's 'Tentative Opinions'. The Tort Act provisions read as follows:

> Article 8
> Where two or more persons jointly commit a tort, causing harm to another person, they shall be liable jointly and severally.
>
> Article 9
> One who abets or assists another person in committing a tort shall be liable jointly and severally with the tortfeasor.

**16.30** According to the Chinese legislature and, obviously, also the SPC Opinion, only these provisions should be applied to acts of contributory/indirect infringement. Even though their wording leaves some room for interpretation, it seems that only intentional acts of abetting or assisting entail liability for joint infringements. More or less innocent suppliers of apparatus who had no clear intent to infringe, even though they had reason to know that their products may be used for infringing purposes, should therefore be exempted from liability.

**16.31** Interestingly, a number of older court decisions have demonstrated a quite generous stance towards patent holders, by extending the liability of joint tortfeasors to parties who hardly met the degree of intent and knowledge normally required under the general civil rules on joint liability (which, in turn, may have prompted the legislature to expressly dismiss the idea of adopting provisions on indirect infringement). For instance, a much-criticized decision of the Intermediate People's Court No.1 of the City of Shanghai of 2003 (exact date not available) held that delivering non-patented parts which nevertheless enabled the infringer to assemble a product that infringed upon the plaintiff's patent, formed joint infringement. At least, the court found it worth mentioning that certain subjective preconditions to establish joint liability were met, namely intention on the part of the defendants, as well as the fact that the components delivered by the joint infringer could not be used for anything other than infringing purposes.[28]

---

28 Criticized as violating the rules of patent scope determination by Wei Zheng, 'Doctrine of Indirect Infringement of Patent Should not be Given Room for Application in China', [2008] **1** *China Patents & Trademarks* 39; also reported by Wu Yuhe and Cao Wen, 'Establishment of Indirect/Contributory Infringement in China', [2007] **4** *China Patents & Trademarks* 13; unfortunately, the original text of the decision could not be traced.

Seemingly, the Higher People's Court of Jiangsu in its decision *Song Zhi'an v Wuxi Furnace Factory*[29] went even further in lowering the bars for establishing joint liability. In this dispute, the plaintiff Song Zhi'an accused the defendant Wuxi Furnace Factory (Wuxi) of having infringed upon his utility model in a coal feeding machine. Wuxi had manufactured the coal feeding machine on grounds of a utility model assignment contract with the firm Beijing General Energy Power Corporation (BGC), that is, it had been assigned a worthless, infringing utility model. In addition, BGC had also provided Wuxi with plans, technical documentation, and so on. In its final second-instance decision of 2003, the Higher People's Court of Jiangsu province held that both Wuxi and BGC were jointly liable for utility model infringement. With regard to BGC's joint liability, the court made the following statement: **16.32**

> As the Wuxi Furnace Factory has carried out the infringement upon a patent assignment contract with the respondent BGC, BGC is civilly liable pursuant to Article 148 (1) of the Supreme People's Court's 'Tentative Opinions on Several Questions Regarding the Application of the General Principles of Civil Law' (One who abets or assists another person in committing a tort shall be liable jointly and severally with the tortfeasor).

Even at the risk of over-interpreting the court's findings, it seems that the question whether BGC had knowledge about the infringing character of its utility model and therefore acted intentionally, did not play a major role in the decision. For the court, it seemed to be sufficient that BGC had contributed to the infringement by merely assigning a utility model that should not have been granted in the first place (more about bogus utility model applications in *Luginbuehl*, Chapter 1), to the immediate infringer. It also seems that the mere assignment of the utility model sufficed to establish joint liability. BGC's technical guidance in the form of providing Wuxi with plans and documentation, which can at least be regarded as 'means' under the various indirect infringement doctrines, was not particularly emphasized by the court to further support its view that BGC's acts met the prerequisites for joint liability. It should be noted, however, that the decision clearly contravenes the above-mentioned legislature's express decision to abstain from adopting the indirect infringement doctrine, in that it overstrained the interpretation of the general provisions on joint liability to an extent that even exceeds the scope of the indirect infringement provisions introduced by many other legislatures. That is, patent holders should not feel too confident that they can continue to succeed that easily against third-party infringers. **16.33**

---

29 An unofficial text without exact decision date can be found on the internet at http://www.chinalawedu.com/news/21604/6500/69/2003/10/he07871227341701300211060_89460.htm.

**16.34** Finally, for the sake of completeness, it should be noted also that the above-mentioned, now obsolete 'Opinions' of the Beijing Higher People's Court contained provisions on 'Indirect Infringement'. Pursuant to Item 73 of the 'Opinions', those who tempt, induce or abet another party to infringe upon a patent, shall be liable for indirect infringement. Item 75 provides that with respect to product patents, indirect infringement means to offer, sell or import the raw materials or parts which are necessary to manufacture the patented product, whereas with respect to process patents, indirect infringement shall mean the offer, sale or import of the materials, apparatus or specific machinery which are necessary to carry out the patented process. The 'Opinions' are a little unclear about the connection between direct and indirect infringement, in that Item 78 regulates that 'indirect infringement, in general, presupposes the emergence of direct infringement, without which there exists no indirect infringement', a wording which, according to this author's experience, has misled some practitioners to believe that indirect infringement can only be established if direct infringement has already started. Such strong connection, however, would render any special regulation of indirect infringement obsolete. Therefore, interpreting the above provision in a manner that indirect infringement can be established if it inevitably amounts to direct infringement if not stopped, appears to be more plausible. It would also comply with the preceding Item 77 of the 'Opinions' ('If a party knows that another party is in the course of preparing a patent infringement but nevertheless provides it with the means which are necessary for carrying out the infringement, indirect infringement is to be established'), which is clearly aimed at acts supporting imminent direct infringement.

**16.35** The above exegetic exercises with regard to a possible judge-made indirect infringement doctrine seem to be of largely historic relevance, however. As mentioned, the legislature has explicitly abandoned the 'indirect infringement' doctrine. Consequently, also the new 'Guidelines' of the Beijing Higher People's Court no longer contain the notion of 'indirect infringement' but confine themselves to 'joint infringement' within the scope of the general civil law provisions.

## E. PROCESS PATENT-SPECIFIC CLAIM INTERPRETATION

**16.36** Chapter 15 has already treated this topic exhaustively, so that the following explanations will only briefly refer to the SPC's landmark decision *OBE v Kanghua*. It implies that patent applicants are well advised to take great care already at the stage of drafting the claims and specification, as Chinese courts are held to reduce the claim's literal scope, inter alia, to specific technical features mentioned on the specification and the embodiment. If the specification, for instance, reveals a specific sequence of process steps, the court is likely to regard the defendant's processes as non-infringing if it does not provide for exactly the same sequence, irrespective of whether the claim is silent on such sequence. It also seems that, in particular, the strong adherence to the content of the specification has found its way into Item 3 Interpretation 2009 which states as follows:

> The courts may interpret a claim using the description and the appended drawings, relevant claim(s) in the claims set, and patent prosecution history. *Where the description has specifically defined an expression in the claim, such specific definition shall be adhered to.*[30]

Also Item 4 Interpretation 2009, according to which in a case of so-called means-plus-function claims, the scope of protection shall be limited to what has been outlined by the concrete embodiments in the description (as well as to equivalent embodiments) points towards a comparably restrictive claim interpretation. **16.37**

## F. CONCLUDING REMARKS

The Chinese reforms between 2008 and 2010 have clarified a number of important questions and therefore contributed to enhancing the general legal certainty for litigants in the area of process patent protection. On the other hand, a number of clarifications have narrowed the scope of substantive protection, as compared to the scope Chinese courts had been willing to grant when their interpretation freedom was less limited. That is, some courts will have to rethink their previously quite patent-owner friendly decision practice. As far as incentives for foreign manufacturers to invest in China are concerned, however, it may well be that the positive effect of enhanced legal certainty and predictability of future court decisions will prevail over concerns that the scope of substantive protection has become narrower in a number of areas. **16.38**

30 Emphasis added by author.

16.37

## CONCLUDING REMARKS

16.38

# Part E

# MARKET POWER – RELATED ASPECTS

# 17

# CHINESE ANTI-MONOPOLY LAW

**Thomas Pattloch**



## A. INTRODUCTION

Only a decade ago, an observer of the Chinese economy would have laughed at the prediction that a Chinese anti-monopoly law would be actively applied. Today, in 2013, news about the National Development and Reform Commission (NDRC) investigating price-fixing behaviours by baby powder producers (including their relationship between manufacturers, distributors and retailers),[1] **17.01**

1 Julie Zhu, 'Danone cuts prices in China as confidence in local baby formula stays low', *Financial Times* 8 July 2013; Kathrin Hille, Leslie Hook and Patti Waldmeir, 'China's watchdogs show they have teeth', *Financial Times* 5 July 2013; Zhou Wenting and Zhao Yinan, *China Daily* 2 August 2013 p. 1: Investigation targeted also foreign producers such as Wyeth, BiosTime and Dumex.

fining LCD panel manufacturers for price-fixing cartels[2] and probing drug pricing[3] govern the headlines of the *China Daily* and *Financial Times*. No doubt, anti-monopoly law is about to become an actively applied part of the Chinese legal system.

## 1. History

**17.02** Work on relevant legislation started as early as 1987. In 1994, the drafting of a cartel law was finally included in the Legislative Plan of the National People's Congress.[4] The Anti-Monopoly Law AML was passed on 30 August 2007 and became effective on 1 August 2008. The drafting process had been a difficult issue which also involved turf battles between different Chinese authorities.[5] Very quickly within the first year of enacting the new law, all involved enforcement agencies demonstrated a proactive approach on gathering expertise and improving the enforcement transparency and certainty.[6] A plethora of related administrative regulations has been passed since. The legislator's foundation of an actively applied anti-monopoly law is still under construction and currently still appears somewhat influenced by case law and experiences from US and European counterparts.

## 2. Legislation

**17.03** The following overview only lists the most important laws and regulations which can be applied to anti-monopoly cases. Some general laws such as the Contract Act in its Article 329 also contain provisions which may be applicable in individual cases:

**17.04** General legislation:

- Anti-Unfair Competition Law, promulgated on 2 September 1993
- Price Law, promulgated on 19 December 1997

---

2 Zhuowei (Joyce) Li, Ying (Tracy) Zhou and Haoze Li, Han Kun Law Office 'NDRC Punished Enterprises outside Mainland China for Price-related Anti-competitive Activities for the First Time', Newsletter 8 January 2013. 'On January 4, 2013, the National Development and Reform Commission of the People's Republic of China announced a crackdown against six leading international LCD panel manufacturers including Samsung, LG, Chimei, AU Optronics, Chunghwa Picture Tubes and HannStar for price-fixing cartel among them from 2001 to 2006. The total penalty imposed against the Group was RMB 353 million.' It should be noted, however, that punishment in this case was issued under the Price Law.

3 Patti Waldmeir and Andrew Jack, China launches drug pricing probe, *Financial Times* 5 July 2013; according to the *China Daily* 2 August 2013 the Shanghai High People's Court has further announced investigation probes into the Belgian pharmaceutical company UCB and Swedish company Tetra Pak International.

4 Ding Guofeng, *Fanlongduan Falü Zeren Zhidu Yanjiu*, Beijing: Falü Chubanshe July 2012, 342.

5 Wang Xiaoye, 'Erlass und Ausführung des chinesischen Kartellgesetzes', **2008** *RIW* 417.

6 Yuanshi Bu, *Chinese Business Law*, 159.

- Provisions of the State Council on Prohibiting Regional Barriers in Market Economic Activities, issued on 21 April 2001
- Anti-Monopoly Law, promulgated on 30 August 2007 and in force since 1 August 2008
- Ministry of Commerce ('MOFCOM') Anti-Monopoly Guidelines on Defining the Relevant Market, issued on 24 May 2009

Price-fixing related legislation: 17.05

- NDRC Anti-Price Monopoly Regulations, issued on 29 December 2010, in force since 1 February 2011
- NDRC Regulations on Anti-Price Monopoly Administrative Enforcement Procedures, issued on 29 December 2010, in force since 1 February 2011
- NDRC Procedural Provisions for Administrative Penalties on Price-related Illegal Activities, issued 6 March 2013, in force since 1 July 2013

General monopoly agreements/abuse of dominant position: 17.06

- State Administration for Industry and Commerce (SAIC) Procedural Rules of Administration of Industry and Commerce on Investigation of Cases regarding Monopoly Agreements and Abuse of Dominance, promulgated on 5 June 2009, effective since 1 July 2009
- SAIC Procedural Rules of Administration of Industry and Commerce on Prohibition of Abuse of Administrative Power to Eliminate or Restrict Competition, issued on 26 May 2009, effective since 1 July 2009
- SAIC Provisions on Prohibiting Monopoly Agreements, issued on 31 December 2010, effective since 1 February 2011
- SAIC Provisions on Prohibiting Abuse of Dominance, issued on 31 December 2010, effective since 1 February 2011
- SAIC Provisions on Preventing Abuse of Administrative Power to Eliminate or Restrict Competition, issued on 31 December 2010, effective since 1 February 2011

Merger control: 17.07

- State Council Provisions on Thresholds for Reporting of Concentrations of Undertakings, promulgated and entered into force on 3 August 2008
- MOFCOM Guiding Opinions on Reporting of Concentrations and Undertakings, promulgated and entered into force on 5 January 2009, revised and substantially revamped by a new form issued in July 2012

- Guiding Opinions on Documents and Materials Required for Reporting of Concentrations of Undertakings, promulgated and entered into force on 5 January 2009
- MOFCOM Measures on Calculating the Turnover of Financial Institutions for Merger Control Purposes, issued on 15 July 2009 and entered into force on 15 August 2009
- MOFCOM Measures on the Notification of Proposed Concentrations, issued on 21 November 2009
- MOFCOM Measures on the Review of Notified Concentrations, issued on 24 November 2009
- MOFCOM's Interpretation of the Measures on the Notification of Proposed Concentrations and of the Measures on the Review of Notified Concentrations, issued on 12 January 2010
- MOFCOM Guidelines on Procedures for Merger Review, issued on 3 March 2010
- MOFCOM Interim Measures concerning the Divestiture of Assets or Businesses when Implementing Concentrations of Undertakings, issued on 5 July 2010
- State Council Notice on the Establishment of a Security Review System for Foreign Acquisitions of Domestic Enterprises, issued on 3 February 2011
- MOFCOM Implementing Regulations of the Security Review System for Foreign Acquisitions of Domestic Enterprises, issued on 25 August 2011
- MOFCOM Interim Regulations on the Assessment of the Competitive Effect of Concentrations of Undertakings, issued on 29 August 2011
- MOFCOM Interim Measures on the Investigation of Concentrations Not Notified, promulgated on 30 December 2011, in effect since 1 February 2012

**17.08** Enforcement:

- Supreme People's Court Notice on Carefully Studying and Implementing the Anti-Monopoly Law, issued on 28 July 2008
- Supreme People's Court of China Provisions on Several Issues Concerning the Trial of Civil Cases Caused by Monopolistic Conducts, issued on 8 May 2012, in force as of 1 June 2012

**17.09** Important draft regulations:

- State Council Draft Provisions on Restrictive Conditions Attached to Concentration of Undertakings, issued on 28 March 2013

- SAIC Guide on Anti-Monopoly Law Enforcement in the Field of Intellectual Property Rights (fifth draft; note that supposedly there is already a sixth draft in the making)
- MOFCOM Provisions on Applying Fast-Track Procedure in Concentration Cases

### 3. Structure of authorities

The AML stipulates in its Article 9 the set-up of an Anti-Monopoly Commission reporting directly to the level of the State Council. According to the relevant official notice from the State Council, the Anti-Monopoly Commission is composed of the principals of relevant departments and organs of the State Council. The Anti-Monopoly Commission is in charge of organizing, coordinating and supervising AML-related activities. However, no real formal supervisory mechanism has been established so far, which was early on predicted due to the difficulty of establishing this body at all between feuding ministries.[7] **17.10**

With a very limited functioning and vague responsibilities[8] of the Anti-Monopoly Commission, the second level under the Commission, the Anti-Monopoly Law Enforcement Authorities (AMEAs) designated by the Anti-Monopoly Commission in accordance with Article 10 AML are primarily tasked to enforce the AML. Responsibilities may be delegated from central to provincial level, which has been done in some instances. The responsible AMEAs are MOFCOM, the National Development and Reform Commission (NDRC) and the State Administration for Industry and Commerce (SAIC). **17.11**

MOFCOM is responsible for merger review, the NDRC has the authority to inspect price monopolies and the SAIC is responsible for the inspection of monopoly agreements, conduct of exclusive or restrictive behaviours and abuse of dominant position other than business concentration and monopoly pricing. **17.12**

The Chinese courts are responsible for private lawsuits brought in accordance with Article 50 AML which provides that business operators found liable for monopolistic conduct and causing loss to others shall bear civil liability according to the law. Within the courts, an SPC circular issued in 2008 and a later Judicial Interpretation endowed the IP tribunals of the Chinese courts **17.13**

7 Wang Xiaoye, above note 5, 419.

8 Lutz-Christian Wolff, *Mergers & Acquisitions in China, Law and Practice*, CCH Hong Kong Limited, 2nd edn. 2008, 17–330.

with the competence to deal with such private lawsuits. Lawsuits usually start at Intermediate People's Court level. Judges in these divisions are well trained and deemed to be more capable of dealing with complex anti-monopoly cases.

**17.14** Administrative lawsuits brought against decisions concerning, for example, merger control, or SAIC or NDRC decisions can be challenged through the administrative review procedure and/or a direct administrative action. Review of merger control decisions will first require administrative review (Article 53 AML).

## B. SCOPE OF APPLICATION AND MAIN CONTENT

### 1. Applicability of the law, key definitions

**17.15** Article 2 AML stipulates that the law applies to monopolistic conduct in economic activities within the territory of the People's Republic of China (PRC), including monopolistic conduct outside the territory of the PRC that has the effect of eliminating or restricting competition on the domestic market of China.

**17.16** Article 3 AML defines monopolistic conduct as (1) monopoly agreements reached between business operators; (2) abuse of dominant market position by business operators; and (3) concentration of business operators that may have the effect of eliminating or restricting competition.

**17.17** The term business operators is broadly defined and includes any legal person, private person, economic organization, trade association, hospitals, law firms, auditors and so on who conduct commercial production or engage in commercial trade or commercial provision of services, without the need to be part of a specific relevant market in order to apply the AML.[9]

**17.18** The new AML also attempts to cover trade associations which very often possess semi-governmental functions within the Chinese economy, taking an active role in organizing and coordinating competition.[10] Concerns were raised following a scandal concerning price-fixing and anti-competitive behaviours by noodle manufacturers who had organized an attempt to agree on a minimum

9 Ding Guofeng, above note 4, 43; more detailed explanations in Lorenz and Liu, 'Der Unternehmensbegriff des chinesischen Kartellrechts', **2009** *RIW* 33 et seq.

10 Michael Zhang and William Zhen, 'Suggestions on Regulatory Compliance with the New Anti-Monopoly Law for Multinational Companies in China', *CLP* October 2007, 26.

price.[11] Article 16 AML addresses this concern. If a trade association engages in illegal cartels, both the association and its members may be sanctioned separately. The trade association itself may be subject to a fine up to RMB 500,000, and in serious cases it may even be dissolved.[12]

Article 56 AML provides a limited exemption for agricultural producers and rural economic organizations in economic activities such as production, processing, sales, transportation and storage of agricultural products. **17.19**

Article 7 AML stipulates that the state shall protect legitimate business activities of state-owned enterprises which control industries concerning state economic vitality and national security and those activities of state-owned enterprises in industries with state monopoly, to supervise and regulate their business conduct and prices, safeguard the interests of consumers and foster technological progress. Some have interpreted this provision to provide a more lenient treatment of state-owned enterprises and restricted ability to apply the Anti-Monopoly Law by the relevant enforcement authorities due to conflicts of interest with specific sectorial regulators.[13] **17.20**

These fears seem to have been addressed by the recent practice: shortly after passing the AML, NDRC investigated China Telecom and China Unicom for abuse of a dominant position in the 3G broadband market. The inquiry began in April 2011 and resulted (based on Article 45 AML) in a promise issued on 2 December 2011 by both companies to lower their prices by up to 35 per cent within the next five years. The agreement was subsequently monitored through follow-up reports submitted in February 2012 and further statements made in December 2012.[14] **17.21**

*(a) 'Monopolistic agreement'*

Article 13 (2) AML defines monopolistic agreements as 'agreements, (written or oral) decisions or other concerted behaviors that may eliminate or restrict competition', which is further expanded by Rule 2 of the SAIC's 'Prohibiting Conclusion of Monopoly Agreements Provisions' addressing agreements, decisions or concerted behaviours 'which are reached among business operators or are reached by them through organization by industrial associations in violation of Articles 13, 14 and 16 of the Anti-Monopoly Law'. **17.22**

---

11 Wang Xiaoye, above note 5, 422.

12 See the paper manufacturing cartel decision of the NDRC promulgated on 4 January 2011 with the maximum fine of RMB 500,000 levied on the trade association, but based on the Price Law.

13 Wang Xiaoye, above note 5, 420; Yuanshi Bu, above note 6, 160, with further references.

14 See reports on http://industry.caijing.com.cn/2012-03-15/111746005.html.

**17.23** Difficulties are sometimes encountered when determining 'concerted behaviors', in spite of Guidelines issued by NDRC and SAIC which list specific behaviours regarded as concerted behaviours.[15]

*(b) 'Relevant market'*

**17.24** The concept of relevant market is defined in the Guidelines of the Anti-Monopoly Commission of the State Council. As in other jurisdictions, the definition of the relevant market is crucial for the scope of application of the law.[16] The Guidelines employ criteria which pertain to common international practice, that is, commodity/services, locality and time, and have therefore not developed an independent theory.[17] In particular, the Guidelines make reference to product markets, geographical markets and technology markets. The basis for definition of the relevant market is objective existing data and economic analysis. Case law indicates that interaction between the markets may be interpreted more narrowly than in Western jurisdictions.[18]

**17.25** According to Rule 3 of the Guidelines on the Definition of the Relevant Market such market is the scope of products and the geographic area within which the business operator competes with others with respect to a specific product or service for a certain period of time. The product market comprises products which are substitutable from the demand perspective. The geographic market is the regional boundary within which consumers can acquire substitutable products, even in case of extra transport costs. Temporal factors such as production cycle, product life, fashion style or protection periods of intellectual property rights have to be taken into account when determining the market.

**17.26** With respect to technology transfer and licensing agreements, the Guidelines merely indicate the possibility of defining the relevant technology market,

15 Herbert Smith, *A Guide to China's Anti-Monopoly Law*, 10 available at http://uk.practicallaw.com/resource/4–514–6509?q=&qp=&qo=&qe=; R. 3 of the SAIC Prohibiting Conclusion of Monopoly Agreements Provisions stipulates the criteria of uniformity in the market acts committed by business operators; communication of intention or exchange of information between business operators; and whether business operators are able to give reasonable explanation for their concerted practices. R. 6 of the NDRC Anti-Price Monopoly Regulations makes for example reference to 'consideration of market structure and market changes' and requires communication of intention between the parties and consistency of price adjustment activities of the business operators.

16 External experts therefore are allowed and heard in cases accepted by the court, see the famous *Qihoo v Tencent* cases decided by the Guangdong High People's Court, cited by Susan Ning, 'Judicial Practice under Code of Conducts in China's Anti-Monopoly Law', [2012] *Competition Policy International* 2.

17 Susan Ning, 'Overview of the Anti-monopoly Law', *CLP* October 2007, 23.

18 See MOFCOM Merger Control decision 18 March 2009 Coca Cola and Huiyuan, see Zhan Hao, 'Anti-Monopoly law: one year on', *CLP* September 2009, 37.

without, however, having provided explicit and more detailed provisions on this issue so far.[19]

Substitutability is further divided into manufacturing and supply substitutability. Manufacturing substitutability is the primary criterion for the delineation of relevant markets. Supply factors only serve as a supplement if so required by the specific case (Rule 7 Guidelines). Factors to be included concern product characteristics, quality, purpose, price and availability. The supply stability analysis focuses more on market entry barriers, such as investment incurred for changing equipment and risk of failure with regard to a new product, time needed by a product to enter the market, and so on. It should further be noted that the SSNIP test (small but significant non-transitory increase in price) is also allowed under the new law. **17.27**

## 2. Horizontal monopoly agreement

Article 13 AML lists prohibited horizontal monopoly agreements,[20] such as price fixing, restricting the output or sales volume, dividing sales markets or raw materials purchasing markets, restrictions on purchasing new technology or new facilities, restrictions to the development of new technologies or products, and joint boycotts. The SAIC Prohibiting Conclusion of Monopoly Agreements Provisions ('SAIC Monopoly Provisions') defines the scope of application further, inter alia, by clarifying that such AML-relevant agreements must have been concluded between 'competitors'. **17.28**

According to Rule 4 SAIC Monopoly Provisions, competing operators are prohibited from concluding monopoly agreements on *limiting the production quantity or sales quantity* of commodities by (1) limiting the production quantity of commodities or the production quantity of a specific variety or model of commodities by way of limiting production output, setting a fixed production output, suspending production, and so on; and (2) limiting the sales quantity of commodities or the sales quantity of a specific variety or model of commodities by way of refusing to supply commodities or limiting the distribution quantity of commodities, and so on. **17.29**

19 R. 8 of the 5th SAIC Draft Guide on Anti-Monopoly Law Enforcement in the Field of IP makes reference to 'technology markets' and in its paragraph 3 provides the following definition: 'As IPRs inherently possess product attributes, with reference to factors such as characteristics, use and price of the IPR, a group of IPRs which demanders believe to be possessing a more closely substitutable relationship or a class of IPRs can be defined as the relevant technology market.'

20 Wang Xiaoye, above note 5, 422.

**17.30** Rule 5 SAIC Monopoly Provisions prohibits *dividing sales markets or raw material procurement markets* by (1) dividing sales regions, sales targets, or the varieties or quantity of the commodities; (2) dividing the procurement regions, varieties, or quantity of materials, semi-finished products, components and parts, relevant equipment, and other raw materials; and (3) dividing the suppliers of materials, semi-finished products, components and parts, relevant equipment, and other raw materials.

**17.31** Rule 6 SAIC Monopoly Provisions addresses *limiting the purchase of new technologies* or new equipment or *limiting the development of new technologies or new products*, prohibiting (1) limiting the purchase or use of new technologies or new processes; (2) limiting the purchase, lease, or use of new equipment; (3) limiting the investment in or research and development of new technologies, new processes, or new products; (4) refusing to use new technologies, new processes, or new products; and (5) refusing to adopt new technological standards.

**17.32** Rule 7 SAIC Monopoly Provisions prohibits *horizontal boycott* in the form of (1) jointly refusing to supply or sell commodities to specific business operators; (2) jointly refusing to purchase or sell the commodities of specific business operators; and (3) jointly restricting specific business operators from transacting with their competitors.

*(a) Exemptions*

**17.33** Article 15 AML, in turn, provides a non-exhaustive list of exemptions to prohibited horizontal and vertical monopoly agreements. To the extent that an agreement serves the purpose of improving technologies or researching and developing new products, restrictions may be deemed as being compliant with the AML.[21]

**17.34** If an agreement serves the purpose of improving product quality, reduces costs and promotes efficiency, unifies product specifications and standards, and contributes to a professional division of labour, it may, in spite of its restrictions, be regarded as compliant with the AML.

**17.35** Further exemptions relate to agreements with the purpose of enhancing the competitiveness of SMEs, of promoting of the public interest, for example, by aiming at saving energy, protecting the environment, providing disaster aid, alleviating severe decreases in turnover or overproduction caused by the economic downturn, safeguarding legitimate interests and promoting foreign trade

21 See also R. 14 SAIC Monopoly Provisions.

and cooperation with foreign countries. Last but not least, all cartels allowed by AML enforcement agencies are exempted from the application of the AML.

In order to be exempted, enterprises have to prove that market competition will not be severely restricted and that consumers can share the benefits derived from the agreement (Article 15 (2) AML). Business operators have to self-assess whether one of the exemptions is applicable to their specific case. Interestingly, the Shanghai Higher People's Court in the *Johnson & Johnson v Rainbow Medical* decision noted that, for example, resale price maintenance also 'can have positive effects, such as improving the quality of products in the market and allowing new brands to enter the market'.[22] This comment gives further rise to a still unanswered question, namely to what extent a rule of reason principle also applies under Chinese law.[23] **17.36**

### *(b) Case law: dividing up sales markets*

In a decision published by the SAIC on 26 January 2001 concerning a cement cartel, a trade association for construction material and machinery in Jiangsu was found liable for having colluded with concrete producers for dividing up sales markets and restricting competition: while some members of the association cooperated and were spared fines, the trade association was levied a fine of RMB 200,000 together with the confiscation of profits of five members: Moreover, these members had to pay a fine of more than RMB 530,000.[24] **17.37**

### *(c) Case law: restriction on cooperation with third parties*

In a case decided in 2009 by the Gansu Intermediate People's Court, *Lanzhou Xitaihua Industry and Trade Group and Lanzhou Hailande Pump Co. Ltd v Magnetic Advice Research Institute of Gansu Academy of Science* [Ganmin Sanzhongzi No. 36], the parties had jointly established Hailande Pump Co., Ltd. The Magnetic Advice Research Institute agreed that it would cooperate only with Hailande on the development of technology related to the magnetic pump and would not cooperate with a third party. The court decided that the restriction in the agreement was related to the scope of technology development, not to the technology *per se*, and that the agreement should not be considered as 'illegally monopolizing technology and impairing technological progress'. While this case refers to Article 329 Contract Act, it made an important distinction between restrictions on the development of new technology and restrictions in the course of cooperation on specific technology projects. **17.38**

22 Zhu Dan, President of IP Tribunal of IP High Court, quoted in *China Daily* 2 August 2013 p. 2.

23 See Wang Xiaoye, above note 5, 423, Susan Ning, above note 17, 23 pointing out the applicability of Art. 15 AML also to monopoly agreements in Art. 13 AML.

24 Cited by Herbert Smith, above note 15, 11.

### 3. Vertical agreements

**17.39** Vertical agreements are regulated in Article 14 AML, which prohibits resale price fixing and maintenance of minimum resale price. No regulations are contained in the law on restrictive trade practices such as selective distribution. However, the SAIC rules subsequently declared related types of vertical restraints illegal under the law. Some commentators have noted that further clarification will be required by the legislator and AMEAs in order to clarify the scope of application of the AML to vertical agreements.[25] This has been partially done by the NDRC: Rule 8 NDRC Anti-Price Monopoly Regulations stipulates that fixing the price for resale or setting a minimum price should be regarded as monopolistic agreement.

**17.40** In practice, vertical agreements have – somewhat unexpectedly – quickly become the focus of recent NDRC decisions on resale prices.

#### *(a) Case law: resale price fixing*

**17.41** *Maotai* and *Wuliangye*, two of the most famous '*baijiu*' (a strong liquor) producers in China, requested their distributors to sell their products at a minimum price. The provincial NDRC determined that this behaviour violated Article 14 AML, and in light of active cooperation by both companies issued a relatively light fine, taking only turnover of the sales subsidiaries into account.[26]

**17.42** Other case law in Chinese courts indicates that resale price maintenance may soon become a frequent reason for private parties initiating anti-trust litigation: the *Johnson & Johnson v Rainbow Medical* case decided in 2013 by the Shanghai court regarding resale price maintenance was a case in point, leading to determination of a monopolistic agreement and liability for damage compensation by the subsidiaries of *Johnson & Johnson* in China.[27]

### 4. Abuse of dominant market position

**17.43** Article 17 AML contains a non-exhaustive list of abusive market behaviour by holders of a dominant position. Whereas immediately after issuance of the law many commentators presumed that it would take time for this provision to be applied in practice, the opposite seems to be the case in the light of the relatively

25 Wang Xiaoye, above note 5, 424.

26 Michael Gu and Zhan Hao, Key Developments of 2012 in Merger Control Enforcement, *Anjie Legal Studies Antitrust* Mar-April 2013, 24.

27 Zhou Wenting and Zhao Yinan, *China Daily* 2 August 2013, 2.

high number of current investigations into possible abuses of market dominance.[28] Concerning private anti-monopoly law litigation, it is also reported that cases of abuse of a dominant position in Chinese courts outnumber cartel cases.[29]

### (a) Dominant position

A dominant market position is defined as a market position that enables a business operator to control product pricing, quantity and other transaction conditions (such as commodity price and quantity that have substantial effect on transactions in the market, including commodity quality, payment terms, delivery method and after-sale services), or to hinder or affect the entry of other business operators into the relevant market by exclusion, delay or rendering cost-efficient competition impossible (Article 17(2) AML, Rule 3 SAIC Provisions on Prohibiting Abuse of Dominance). **17.44**

Article 18 AML further describes factors to be considered when assessing dominance, such as the market share and competitive status in the relevant market, ability to control sales or raw material supply markets, financial and technological conditions, degree of reliance on the business operator by other business operators in the transactions, degree of difficulty for other business operators to enter the relevant market, and so on. **17.45**

According to Article 19 AML, market dominance is presumed for certain percentages of market share (at least 50 per cent in the case of one business operator, 66 per cent in the case of two operators and 75 per cent in the case of three operators). Such legal presumption of percentages giving reason for dominance can be rebutted by countervailing evidence. Enterprises with a market share of less than 10 per cent of the relevant market are excluded from the presumption of a dominant market position. **17.46**

### (b) Excluded behaviours

Article 17(1) AML prohibits imposition of unfairly high selling prices or unfairly low purchasing prices, sale of products at prices below cost without justification, refusal to deal, restrictions on the choice of trading partners, discriminatory treatment of trading partners with equal standing and other behaviours deemed to be abusive. **17.47**

---

28 Kathrin Hille, Leslie Hook and Patti Waldmeir, 'China's watchdogs show they have teeth', *Financial Times* 5 July 2013.

29 Susan Ning, above note 17, 2.

**17.48** The SAIC Provisions on Prohibiting Abuse of Dominance ('SAIC Abuse Provisions') provide more detailed stipulations with sometimes more wide-ranging obligations in its Rules 4 to 7, which address exploitative and discriminatory behaviour. Business operators which have attained a dominant market position can escape liability by providing 'justified reasons', a term defined in more detail in Rule 8 SAIC Abuse Provisions. Accordingly, an operator will not be held liable for abuse if it can prove that the relevant act pertains to its normal business activities or serves its normal benefit. In this respect also the impact of such act on economic operation efficiency, public interest and economic development will be taken into account.[30]

**17.49** Rule 4 SAIC Abuse Provisions provides that business operators with market dominant positions shall not, without justified reasons, *refuse to trade* by way of (1) reducing the existing quantity of trade with their trading counterparties; (2) putting off or suspending the existing trade with their trading counterparties; (3) refusing to enter into new trades; (4) setting restrictive conditions in order to aggravate the continuance of trade activities by the trading counterparties; or (5) rejecting trading counterparties' requests to use necessary facilities of said business operator on reasonable terms during production activities and business operations (taking into account the feasibility of investing in and constructing such facilities separately or of developing and constructing them separately, the dependence of trading counterparties on such facilities to effectively carry out production activities and business operations, the actual ability of business operators to provide such facilities, the impact of the use of such facilities by trade counterparties on the business operator's own production activities/business operations, and so on).

**17.50** Rule 5 SAIC Abuse Provisions prohibits *restriction of trade* without justified reasons by (1) forcing trading counterparties to trade exclusively with the dominant business operator; (2) forcing trading counterparties to trade exclusively with designated business operators; or (3) preventing trading counterparties from trading with competitors.

**17.51** Rule 6 SAIC Abuse Provision forbids *tie-in sales* without justified reasons or imposition of other unreasonable trading conditions in the course of trading, for example, (1) compulsory tie-up arrangement or bundling of different commodities in violation of established trading practices, purchase habits, and so on, or in disregard of the functions of the commodities at issue; (2) imposing other unreasonable restrictions on contractual terms, way of payment, mode of

30 According to R. 13 SAIC Provisions the justification has to be provided within the time limit stipulated by the SAIC.

transportation and delivery of commodities or method of providing services; (3) imposing further unreasonable restrictions on sales regions, sales targets, after-sales services and so on; or (4) imposing other trading conditions which are irrelevant to the items traded.

Rule 7 SAIC Abuse Provisions prohibits business operators with dominant market positions from applying the following *differentiating treatment to their trading counterparties* under the same conditions: (1) to apply different trading quantities, kinds, or quality grades; (2) to apply different preferential conditions such as quantity discounts; (3) to apply different payment conditions or delivery methods; and (4) to apply different after-sale services such as content and period of warranty, content and time of maintenance, supply with spare parts and technical support. **17.52**

### *(c) Case law*

Whereas the SAIC has been comparably slow in picking up cases related to abuse of a dominant position, private parties have quickly seized the opportunities provided by the new legal provisions. **17.53**

In the case filed by the individual Zhou Ze against China Mobile Group Beijing Co. Ltd. and China Unicom Group Beijing Co. Ltd. on 4 March 2009, the defendants were alleged to have abused their dominant position in the form of a mandatory monthly subscription fee for a specific global tariff. The case was finally settled, with Zhou Ze receiving an 'award' of RMB 1,000 and his monthly subscription fee cancelled.[31] **17.54**

On 18 December 2009, Beijing No. 1 Intermediate People's Court released a decision in the matter *Renren Information Service Co. Ltd. v Beijing Baidu Internet Information Technology Co. Ltd.* The plaintiff alleged that traffic on its website had suddenly dropped. It stated that while Google still listed its website after a search for its related services, Baidu only listed four pages without the plaintfiff's website, thus shutting out Renren and abusing its dominant position in the search engine market. Baidu countered that the site of the plaintiff contained too many spam-links which would justify its exclusion from the search results. The court upheld Baidu's argument and noted in addition that the plaintiff had not provided sufficient evidence to assume a dominant market position of Baidu. **17.55**

31 http://news.xinhuanet.com/tech/2009–10/27/content_12336944_1.htm.

**17.56** *Qihoo 360 v Tencent QQ*: The '3Q war'[32] concerning mainly claims of unfair competition had started with an exchange of false allegations and ended in a series of lawsuits which are still ongoing. Qihoo, the producer of an anti-virus program called *360 Safeguard*, faces competition from *QQ Doctor*, which, within a very short time, had gained a domestic market share of 40 per cent when it bundled with the extremely popular instant chatting software *Tencent QQ*. Qihoo retaliated by updating the privacy guard to block ads in *QQ*. Tencent, in turn, raised an unfair competition lawsuit and issued a software update that blocked itself from running *QQ* on machines with *360 Safeguard* installed. Henceforth, hundreds of millions of Chinese netizens[33] were forced to choose one side, to either uninstall *QQ* or to remove *360*'s privacy guard.

**17.57** On April 18, 2012, Qihoo accused Tencent of anti-trust violation and sued in the Guangdong Higher People's Court, alleging that Tencent stopped user services at their own discretion *during* the 3Q war, installed *QQ Doctor* under the name of updating the *QQ Software Manager*, misused market dominance by forcing users to uninstall *360* software that had been installed, and deprived the users of their right to choose, which would constitute an act of limiting transactions and conditional sale. Qihoo claimed RMB 150 million from Tencent on the basis of the AML.

**17.58** On 28 March 2013, against the expectations of observers, the Guangdong High Court ruled against the assumption of a dominant position, based on lack of sufficient evidence presented by the plaintiff and a broader definition of the relevant market which, due to the global nature of the internet, also included territory outside China.[34] The case is currently subject to a heated debate on how to determine relevant markets in the internet, on the standards to be applied[35] and on the extent of the plaintiff's burden of proof.[36] Qihoo has announced that it will appeal in the Supreme People's Court.

### 5. Abuse of intellectual property rights

**17.59** Article 55 AML states that in principle, exercise of intellectual property (IP) rights including their enforcement shall not be regarded as anti-monopolistic

32 http://www.lexology.com/library/detail.aspx?g=0f2d83f4-1d84-4490-9ef6-5e25c2ff72d9.

33 There are an estimated 600 million users using QQ software, see Electronic IP, April 2013, 23.

34 Zhan Hao, 'Ping 360 su Tengxun longduan xingwei qinquan jiufen yishen panjue: Zhongguo fanlongduan minshi susong zhidu goujian de shouci zhenshi changshi', *Electronics Intellectual Property* April 2013, 28, 29.

35 Meng Yanbei, 'Hulianwang hangye xiangguan shichang jieding de tiaozhan', *Electronics Intellectual Property*, April 2013, 42 et seq.

36 Zhan Hao, above note 34, 24 et seq.

behaviour; however, the AML shall be applicable to abuses of IP rights which eliminate or restrict competition.[37]

Article 48(2) Patent Act refers to the AML and allows the grant of a compulsory licence if the 'patentee's act of exercising the patent rights is determined as a monopolizing act and it is to eliminate or reduce the adverse consequences of the said act on competition'. Statements made by government officials of SIPO in the course of the EU-China IP Dialogue have confirmed the understanding that adjudication of determination of a 'monopolizing act' lies with the authorities responsible for applying and interpreting the AML, rather than SIPO.[38] **17.60**

The exercise and enforcement of IP can thus become subject to application of the AML under two conditions: (1) abusive behaviour and (2) elimination of or restrictions to competition. It should be noted that in many cases, a dominant position is not required to declare a contract void due to monopolistic conduct. Such declaration would then not be based on the AML but on Article 329 of the Contract Act which prohibits 'illegally monopolizing technology and impairing technological progress'. A judicial interpretation of the SPC which defines the Contract Act in more detail, excludes, for example, unilateral grant-back clauses.[39] **17.61**

Article 55 AML has raised substantial criticism from abroad, but also internally: Chinese scholars have made the criticism that 'abuse of IP' is not a *requirement* for application of the law, but should rather be seen as a *result* in those cases where the enforcement of IP or refusal to license it is judged as unjustified behaviour violating the *general regulations* of the AML.[40] **17.62**

The difficulties associated with the term 'abuse of IPRs' are highlighted by the absence of any specific definition in Chinese law so far.[41] It is generally recognized that legally obtaining a monopoly, for example, through exclusive intellectual property rights, should not be regarded as illegal monopolistic **17.63**

---

37 Art. 55 AML: 'This law shall not apply to the conduct of business operators to exercise their intellectual property rights according to the laws and relevant administrative regulations on intellectual property rights; however, this Law shall apply to the conduct of business operators to eliminate or restrict market competition by abusing their intellectual property rights.'

38 Clarified also in the 5th Draft by the SAIC Guide on Anti-Monopoly Law Enforcement in the Field of IPRs.

39 Peter Straub, 'Der Missbrauch geistiger Eigentumsrechte im chinesischen Kartellrecht', **2011** *RIW* December, 830 et seq.

40 Zhang Weijun, 'Lanyong zhishi chanquan: weifan "fanlongduanfa" de qianti haishi jieguo' in: Zhang Weijun and Zhang Taolüe, *Zhishi chanquan yu jingzhengfa yanjiu*, Falü Chubanshe October 2012, 94.

41 Zhang Weijun, above note 40, 97.

behaviour.[42] However, there may exist a tendency to establish anti-competitive behaviour associated with the enforcement and utilization of IPRs not solely on grounds of the competitive situation but also with reference to industrial policy and public interest. This becomes apparent from the following statement in the 5th draft of the SAIC for a Guide on Anti-Monopoly Law Enforcement in the Field of IPR ('Draft Guide') Rule 3: 'The abuse of IPRs refers to violations of the relevant intellectual property laws as well as the boundaries and purposes of administrative regulations. The unfair exercise of IPRs harms others' interests and public interests.'

**17.64** For the purpose of safeguarding the public interest, the Draft Guide proposes a future possibility to oblige the IP owner who is assumed to hold a dominant market position to license and to grant access in the area of patents and standards. Rule 9 states that 'if a patent of an undertaking is being included as a basic patent of international standards or national, mandatory industry standards, the State Council Anti-Monopoly Law enforcement agencies can infer the dominant market position of the undertaking in the relevant market according to the specific circumstances of the market structure and competitive situation; however, the presence of evidence to the contrary may rebut the interference'.

**17.65** Whereas this rule does not require abusive behaviour as a prerequisite for its application, Rule 17 Draft Guide defines further abusive circumstances which may lead to application of the AML: Rule 17(1) Draft Guide on dominant market positions does apply the AML in a case of 'unfair and discriminatory refusal to license' and Rule 17(2) shall apply to 'IPR which the undertaking with dominant market position refuses to license [which] is an essential element for the licensee to compete in the relevant market, and the refusal to license that IPR will prohibit the licensee from competing effectively in the relevant market, which adversely impacts on competition and innovation in the relevant market, and as a result cannot fulfill reasonable demands from consumers'. This interpretation targets a demand-orientated interpretation of abuse and adverse innovative effects in the relevant market and according to the Draft Guide appears even to exclude recourse to Article 15 AML, which permits exemptions if the alleged conduct has the potential to contribute to the improvement of technology and to the enhancement of R&D.

**17.66** Rule 22 Draft Guide includes further detailed but also partially vague obligations on patent holders who participate in standard setting, including the obligations to notify licence fee caps, to adhere to disclosure rules to prevent

42 Wang Xiaoye, above note 5, 426.

patent hold-ups and, most importantly, the rule that a 'patent holder or patent applicant knows or should have known that its patents or pending patent applications may be included in the relevant standard'. While this rule is intended to prevent patent ambushes and hold-ups, it may very well be applied in such a way as to force patent owners to commit their patents to a Chinese standard in order to avoid abusive behaviour.

Rule 19 of the Draft Guide further prohibits companies with a dominant market position from imposing unreasonable trading conditions which involve IP, such as requiring the counterparty to revert improvements it has made to the patented technology exclusively to the right holder, prohibiting the counter-party from challenging the validity of the IP at issue or preventing the counterparty after the expiry of a licence from manufacturing, using or selling competing goods or technology. It remains unclear how far commissioned research agreements and know-how licences are affected by such a rule. It should be noted, however, that some of these regulations can also be found in the SPC Interpretation on Technology Contracts in conjunction with Article 329 Contract Act.[43] **17.67**

Rule 20 Draft Guide expands the application of merger control rules on exclusive licence agreements. In such case, MOFCOM would initiate a review procedure as to whether the alleged undertaking exerts control or possesses the ability to exert a decisive influence on other undertakings. Such review could ultimately result in structural changes to licence contracts under Article 48 AML. **17.68**

The various proposals made by the Draft Guide demonstrate the challenge of legally defining abusive utilization and enforcement of intellectual property rights. Supposedly, the 5th Draft Guide has been revised again, due to numerous comments and criticism. It remains to be seen whether and how abuse of IPRs will have to adhere to more detailed obligations stipulated under the framework of the AML. In any case, such new regulations may have a significant impact on licence contracts, R&D including commissioned research, licensing fees and know-how protection. **17.69**

43 It. 10 'Interpretation of the Supreme People's Court concerning Some Issues on Application of Law for the Trial of Cases on Disputes over Technology Contracts', adopted at 1335th meeting of the Judicial Committee of the Supreme People's Court on 30 November 2004, in force since 1 January 2005.

## 6. Merger control

**17.70** The AML follows a conglomerate effects-based approach for mergers and is applicable to all concentrations, including foreign-to-foreign party transactions, which may eliminate or restrict competition in the Chinese market. Intended mergers have to be filed with MOFCOM in the financial year which precedes the transaction. The term 'concentration' covers a wide variety of transaction structures such as mergers, the acquisition of shares or assets, the creation of joint ventures and the acquisition of control or decisive influence through contractual arrangements.[44]

### *(a) Filing obligation*

**17.71** The Chinese merger control features pre-defined thresholds, that is, if the worldwide aggregate (revenues net of taxes, group-wide, across all products) turnover of all parties involved exceeds RMB 10 billion or if the Chinese aggregate turnover of all parties involved exceeds RMB 2 billion, the merger must be filed. The same applies if at least two of the parties involved have a turnover in China which exceeds RMB 400 million. It is important to note that even if none of these thresholds is met, MOFCOM remains competent to assume that a transaction may have eliminating or restricting effects on competition and to act *ex officio*.[45]

**17.72** If the proposed transaction meets the requirements for merger control, the parties are required to seek prior approval from MOFCOM. Failure to seek such mandatory approval in accordance with Article 48 AML may give rise to the termination or unwinding of the transaction or imposition of other measures to restore the premerger conditions. Moreover, fines of up to RMB 500,000 can be imposed. Additionally, the parties to the merger may be held liable by third parties for any losses attributable to the unapproved business concentration. Additional special rules address the penalization of companies which do not comply with their notification obligations. They entered into force on 1 February 2012. So far, no punishment decisions have been reported.

### *(b) Guiding principles*

**17.73** Pursuant to Article 27 AML, MOFCOM will consider the following factors: market share of each transaction party of the relevant market in the control power of the market, degree of concentration in the relevant market, impact of the business concentration on market entry and technology improvements, on

44 Michael Dietrich, Maria Hou and Johnny Zhao, 'MOFCOM's Review Processes Explained', *CLP* Sept/Oct 2012, 13.

45 Herbert Smith, above note 15, 4.

consumers and other related business operators and on the development of the national economy. According to some observers who have reviewed the decisions MOFCOM has published to date, the agency appears to have relied heavily on market definition and market shares in making its substantive assessments, and sometimes simply equated high market shares with market power.[46]

It has also been reported that in practice, MOFCOM has quickly emancipated itself from foreign authorities. In some cases, MOFCOM has been the only major authority to impose remedies on global transactions.[47] **17.74**

MOFCOM appears to prefer behavioural remedies over structural remedies when imposing conditions, however, also with a new tendency to demand, upon an independent assessment, remedies which are different from those imposed by European or US authorities.[48] **17.75**

MOFCOM has published four conditional approval decisions since January 2012; whereas 92 per cent of all 201 cases notified in 2012 were approved without any conditions.[49] **17.76**

### *(c) Procedure*

Merger control goes through three phases, with a clearance possible in each phase. The first review phase begins with the official acceptance of the notification by MOFCOM and lasts 30 days after official acceptance. During this phase, MOFCOM will conduct a preliminary review and decide whether the concentration merits an in-depth Phase II review. **17.77**

---

46 Herbert Smith, above note 15, 5, citing the *Mitsubishi/Lucite* case with a combined market share of 64%. This seems to be confirmed by MOFCOM decision on acquisition of Goodrich by United Technologies Corporation. Both companies were active in the production and sale of aviation equipment on a worldwide basis. MOFCOM's analysis focused on the global market for alternate current (AC) power generators, where the combined market share of the parties amounted to 84%.

47 See General Motor's acquisition of Delphi in 2009, Seagate's acquisition of Samsung in 2011 and Google's acquisition of Motorola Mobility in 2012, cited by Susan Ning and Hazel Yin, 'China's Anti-Monopoly Law: Retrospect and Prospect on the Fourth Anniversary', *King & Wood Malleson Newsletter* 2012. Michael Dietrich, Maria Hou and Johnny Zhao, above note 44, 14, report for the acquisition of Motorola Mobility by Google that MOFCOM's decision in this case was taken after a total review time of almost eight months at the end of Phase III. While other regulators, particularly the US and EU authorities, approved this transaction unconditionally, MOFCOM imposed behavioural remedies with regard to the licensing conditions of Google's mobile software Android and Motorola's patents.

48 Michael Gu and Zhan Hao, above note 26, 35, 36.

49 Michael Gu and Zhan Hao, above note 26, 32; since 2008, reportedly 450 cases have been reviewed by MOFCOM with an average of 95% being held valid without further conditions, Susan Ning and Hazel Yin, 'China's Anti-Monopoly Law: Retrospect and Prospect on the Fourth Anniversary', *King & Wood Malleson Newsletter* 2012.

17.78 In practice, even unproblematic reviews normally enter Phase II.[50] For mergers which have entered Phase II, the whole review period lasts 90 days. In cases which give rise to substantial competition concerns, Phase III will be initiated and the review process is extended by another 60 days.[51]

17.79 It should be noted that in practice the procedure before accepting a merger notification can be regarded as an additional phase. After the submission of the initial notification, MOFCOM will accept the filing only if it deems the accompanying documentation complete. The AML does not stipulate a time limit for this pre-acceptance review, thereby leaving it to the sole discretion of MOFCOM whether and when to accept a filing.[52]

#### (d) Fast-track procedure

17.80 Sources within MOFCOM have revealed that an internal draft for establishing a fast-track procedure has been circulated. Accordingly, transactions will be classified as simple, normal and major cases based on criteria such as market share and the Herfindahl-Hirschman Index, with different review timelines set for each type. Moreover, the draft seems to contain provisions which oblige MOFCOM to consider industrial or political factors when determining the type of a case. For example, a transaction will be deemed to form a major case if it involves the acquisition of well-known trademarks or time-honoured brands[53] or if it concerns industries with restrictions for foreign investment.[54]

### 7. Abuse of administrative power

17.81 Articles 32 to 37 AML contain numerous provisions aimed at prohibiting government restraint which eliminates or restricts competition. While this chapter had given rise to especially heated discussion in the draft process of the law,[55] it contains wide-ranging rules against governmental bodies imposing restrictions on purchasing products from other regions or hampering the inflow of products from other regions by way of price discrimination, discriminative technical standards and additional administrative permissions, as well as market access barriers, barring of non-local undertakings from participation in local tenders and bidding procedures or barring them from making investment or compelling business operators to engage in anti-competitive conduct.

---

50 Michael Dietrich, Maria Hou and Johnny Zhao, above note 44, 13.

51 Michael Dietrich, Maria Hou and Johnny Zhao, above note 44, 13.

52 Michael Dietrich, Maria Hou and Johnny Zhao, above note 44, 13.

53 A reason which was suspected to have played a role in the denial of acquisition of Chinese juice maker Huiyuan by Coca Cola.

54 See in detail Michael Dietrich, Maria Hou and Johnny Zhao, above note 44, 14, 15.

55 Wang Xiaoye, above note 5, 420.

The provisions on government misconduct have been especially warmly welcomed by many Chinese commentators, as abuse of administrative powers in local areas has quite frequently occurred as a form of local protectionism. Many discussions had arisen around the adoption of such provisions, and indeed, the first anti-monopoly lawsuit under the AML had been raised against the governmental body AQSIQ, for alleged abuse of administrative power.[56] **17.82**

The AML is strongly criticized for lacking an efficient enforcement mechanism against abuse of administrative monopolies.[57] According to Article 51 AML, in the case of government restraint by a government agency, the superior authority may order rectification and impose penalties on the directly responsible persons. SAIC, as well as its local branches at provincial level, cannot take more serious measures. They are only competent to issue recommendations. **17.83**

## C. ENFORCEMENT

Sanctions and remedies in the case of monopolistic agreements are contained in Article 46, remedies in case of abuse of a dominant position in Article 47 and sanctions in case of merger control violations in Article 48 AML. **17.84**

In general, AML enforcement can be carried out through two routes: through administrative authorities, that is, the AMEAs in charge of different aspects of anti-trust law, or through private lawsuits in Chinese courts (Article 50 AML). The jurisdictional relationship between the administrative agencies and the courts remains unclear, in particular as regards the question of recognition of a prior administrative decision in court.[58] **17.85**

56 http://www.bjreview.com.cn/business/txt/2008–09/01/content_148184.htm, 1 September 2008, reported by Tan Wei: 'On August 1, the day the Anti-Monopoly Law (AML) came into force, four Beijing-based companies filed the first lawsuit against the General Administration of Quality Supervision, Inspection and Quarantine (AQSIQ). The companies … all engaged in digital anti-counterfeiting technologies, believe the agency is an administrative monopoly. … Statements submitted by the companies say AQSIQ has been promoting the services of the China Product Identification, Authentication and Tracking System (PIATS) operated by a firm called China Credit Information Technology Co. Ltd. (CCIT) since April 2005. They say the agency has unfairly promoted PIATS in its circulars and at various conferences. The AQSIQ has required the companies to pay certain service charges to PIATS and print supervision codes on their product packages, and stipulated that products made by companies in nine industries, such as home appliances, food and cosmetics, cannot be sold without the supervision codes and access to PIATS. Meanwhile, the AQSIQ also has linked the promotion of PIATS with appraisals of famous Chinese brands and products that are exempt from product inspections.'

57 Wang Xiaoye, above note 5, 418–419 in relation to State-Owned Enterprises and 420, 421 in relation to Art. 51 AML speaks of cartel authorities as a 'tame tiger'.

58 Susan Ning, above note 17, 2.

### 1. Administrative enforcement

**17.86** The AML encourages whistleblowing (see Articles 38(2) and (3) AML). In fact, a number of cases were initiated following complaints by competitors.[59]

### 2. Leniency

**17.87** Article 46(2) AML allows for leniency at the discretion of the administrative authorities in case of monopoly agreements. Rule 11 SAIC Monopoly Provisions provides further guidance by stipulating that authorities shall make their decisions based on time and sequence of voluntary reports, importance of evidence provided, information pertaining to conclusion and implementation of monopoly agreements, and co-operation in the investigation.

**17.88** The AMEAs in accordance with Article 39 AML enjoy broad investigation power. They may enter business premises, obtain information from any relevant entity or individual, seize and detain evidence and inquire into bank accounts. Business operators or individuals subject to scrutiny can make statements, but in practice, they have limited means to fight an investigation. Lack of co-operation may be subject to fines up to RMB 200,000 for individuals and RMB 1 million for companies in serious cases (Article 52 AML). If a violation of the AML is found, the AMEAs are authorized to publish a punishment decision (Article 44 AML).

### 3. Sanctions

**17.89** Sanctions in the case of monopoly agreements comprise the order to stop violations, confiscation of illegal gains and a fine of 1 to 10 per cent of the sales revenue made in the previous year by the direct violator. In cases in which an illegal monopoly agreement has not been fulfilled, a fine of less than RMB 500,000 may be imposed (Article 46 AML).

**17.90** Trade associations can be subject to a fine of up to RMB 500,000 and even face deregistration in serious cases (Article 46(2) AML).

**17.91** Sanctions for abuse of dominance likewise include cease-and-desist orders, confiscation of illegal gains and fines. The levels of fines that can be imposed range from 1 per cent to a maximum of 10 per cent of the infringer's turnover in the previous year (Article 47 AML).

---

59 Michael Gu and Zhan Hao, above note 26, 37 et seq.

Article 49 AML stipulates that for the determination of a fine, the AMEA shall consider such factors as the nature, extent and duration of the violations. 17.92

Finally, in the case of merger control violations, sanctions include an order to stop the concentration, to dispose of shares or assets, to transfer the business or to adopt other necessary measures to restore the market situation before the concentration within a specified time limit, and a fine of less than RMB 500,000. 17.93

## 4. Level of activity by administrative authorities

According to a statement of Ren Airong, the director-general of the enforcement bureau of the Anti-monopoly and Anti-unfair Competition Department of SAIC made in July 2011, his office had authorized provincial AICs in the provinces Jiangsu, Jiangxi, Henan, Zhejiang, Sichuan, Liaoning, Hunan, Heilongjiang, and Yunnan to launch investigations in a total of 14 cases, of which three have been closed and one has been suspended. Relatively few cases are still reported, so that SAIC falls behind NDRC in terms of strength of enforcement. 17.94

NDRC established its reputation as a powerful AML enforcement agency in November 2011, when it announced a groundbreaking investigation of China Unicom and China Telecom for their abuse of dominance in the broadband access market. Shortly thereafter, the NDRC fined two Shandong pharmaceutical companies an amount of roughly RMB 7 million for their abuse of dominance by selling a key ingredient to a popular hypertension medicine at an excessively high price. 17.95

## 5. Private actions in Chinese courts

Reportedly, by the end of 2011, 61 private AML actions were filed and 53 cases were closed. Most cases were related to abuse of dominance and in almost all cases the plaintiffs lost, for failure to prove the defendants' dominance. 17.96

### *(a) Standing to sue*

According to Item 1 SPC Provisions of the Supreme People's Court on Certain Issues Relating to the Application of Law in Hearing Cases Involving Civil Disputes Arising out of Monopolistic Acts[60] ('Judicial Interpretation'), natural persons, legal persons, and other organizations can file civil lawsuits with the people's courts for disputes over losses caused by monopolistic conduct or 17.97

60 *Fashi* 2012 No.5.

violations of the AML by contractual provisions, bylaws of industry associations, and so on. Plaintiffs shall have a direct interest in the case, which also includes consumers as indirect victims. Popular actions are not possible.

*(b) Burden of proof*

**17.98** In practice, burden of proof is the most difficult challenge for a plaintiff to overcome in court. Rules on the shift of burden of proof, lower thresholds for admission of evidence or additional means of proof therefore have a high significance in Chinese court procedure.

**17.99** For horizontal monopoly agreements which are explicitly mentioned in Article 13 No. 1 to 5 AML, a plaintiff does not have to prove the anti-competitive effects of the agreement (Item 7 Judicial Interpretation). In contrast, if the abuse of a dominant position is disputed, the plaintiff has to demonstrate both that the defendant is dominant in the relevant market and that it has abused its market dominant position (Item 8 Judicial Interpretation). Plaintiffs may, however, rely on information made public by the defendant as evidence to prove the dominant position. The court may then, based on such public information, determine that the defendant is dominant in the relevant market, unless there is sufficient evidence to the contrary (Item 10 Judicial Interpretation).

**17.100** In the case of abuse of a dominant position by a public utility enterprise or other business operators with an exclusive status established by law, the court may also directly determine that the defendant is dominant in the relevant market according to the specific circumstances of the market structure and the competition situation, unless proven otherwise (Item 9 Judicial Interpretation). Most of China's public utilities for water, electricity, and so on, enjoy a natural monopoly position.

*(c) Economic experts and economic analysis report*

**17.101** According to Item 12 Judicial Interpretation, the parties may request the invitation of experts with professional knowledge in specific areas to explain difficult subject matter in court. The Judicial Interpretation does not provide for further specific requirements regarding the qualification of such professionals. The standards applied here may therefore deviate from the standards applied to expert witnesses in normal civil procedures who are usually required to be authoritative and independent. In the previously mentioned *Qihoo 360 v Tencent* monopoly dispute, both parties had invited several persons with professional knowledge in the internet market to assist the People's Court in its forensic investigation.

Item 13 Judicial Interpretation provides that the parties to a case may request the People's Court to entrust professional institutions or individual professionals with the preparation of a market survey or economic analysis report on specific issues. With the consent of the court, such professional institutions or professionals may be determined by both parties through consultation, and shall be designated by the People's Court if consultation fails. **17.102**

As professional institutions or professionals are determined by the parties or designated by the court, their identity or independence cannot be challenged. However, the contents of their reports can be examined. **17.103**

### *(d) Limitation of action*

According to Item 16 Judicial Interpretation a report or application to administrative authorities can suspend the limitation period for the duration of an investigation. Actions undertaken by authorities thus can considerably prolong the risk of additionally being held liable for damages of a private third party. **17.104**

### *(e) Remedies*

Remedies include cease-and-desist orders and damage compensation. In line with the General Principles of Civil Law, even broader remedies depending on the individual case may be granted to 'eliminate the negative effects'. Regarding damage compensation, Item 14 Judicial Interpretation explicitly stipulates that upon a plaintiff's claim, the court may include the plaintiff's reasonable expenses on investigation and prevention of the monopolistic conduct in the scope of compensation for losses. **17.105**

## D. SUMMARY

With the high degree of activity displayed by both administrative authorities as well as private litigators, business operators must be more alert than ever with regard to ascertaining the AML compliance of their activities and the possibility of being faced with litigation. Case law from US and European authorities may still provide Chinese authorities and courts with some guidance, but in a number of areas such as merger control or abuse of IP, Chinese authorities seem to be eager to develop China-specific approaches and to break new ground. Business operators which are active in China will have to closely observe further legislation and case law, so as to anticipate important developments in the application of Chinese Anti-Monopoly Law. **17.106**

# 18

# STANDARD-ESSENTIAL PATENTS AND INJUNCTIVE RELIEF

**Cui Guobin**[1]



## A. INTRODUCTION

**18.01** Technical standardization helps to improve the quality, security and interoperability of products or services, having affected every aspect of modern social life. However, the relationship between technical standards and patents has not become a worldwide concern until recent decades. In the past, a technology usually had already been in the public domain before it became a technical standard. Therefore, patent protection for technology had no substantial impact on technological standardization. However, in recent decades, things have drastically changed. Technologies in the fields of electronics, telecommunications, software and the internet progress very quickly, and standardization thereof accelerates accordingly. Many technologies become *de facto* or *de jure* standard and are still effectively protected by patents. These patents that cover the technical standard are referred to as 'standard-essential patents' (SEPs). Anyone who implements the standard will necessarily infringe these SEPs.

1 This author is deeply indebted to Prof. Dr. Heinz Goddar, Prof. Dr. Jan Bernd Nordemann and Prof. Dr. Christian Czychowski. Their insightful comments on this draft and other valuable help are highly appreciated. This author remains accountable for any remaining errors.

That is, *such infringement could not have been avoided by another technically feasible non-infringing implementation* of such standard.[2]

Once a patent becomes a 'standard-essential patent', the patentee's bargaining power in patent licensing negotiations will be greatly enhanced, except that the patented technology from the very beginning was the only choice in the market. After a technical standard has been widely implemented, if the market was forced to adopt alternative technical solutions, standard implementers would have to bear enormously high switching costs.[3] The owners of SEPs could take advantage of these to impose restrictive patent licensing terms on standard implementers.[4] Therefore, many patent owners wish their patents to be implicated in *de facto* or *de jure* technical standards, thus maximizing the market value of their patented technologies. **18.02**

In high-tech fields, many technical standards implicate patents. The society needs effective measures to prevent SEP holders from abusing their market power and holding up technical standards. For this purpose, many standard-setting organizations (SSOs) develop so-called intellectual property (patent) policies, requiring those involved in a standard-setting process to disclose their owned SEPs and promise to grant patent licenses to all standard implementers on 'fair, reasonable and non-discriminatory' (FRAND or RAND) terms.[5] A FRAND commitment prevents a patent holder from using its own market power to extract excessive licensing fees or set other discriminatory licensing terms, since this commitment actually deprives the patent holder of the final say in pricing its own patents and choosing licensees.[6] **18.03**

As a FRAND term is inherently vague, an SEP owner and a standard implementer in a patent licensing negotiation often dispute over whether a specific licensing offer is consistent with the FRAND commitment. If two parties failed to resolve the dispute, a common strategy for the SEP owner is to file a patent infringement suit, seeking injunctive relief against the standard implementer. So, today it is not surprising to see that leading IT companies **18.04**

2 AVS, Intellectual Property Rights Policy of the Audio Video Coding Standard Working Group of China, Art. 2; CESI, IT Standard Drafting Organization's IPR Policy Template, Ch.2, Section 4 Definitions; IEEE-SA Standards Board Bylaws Section 6.1 Definitions.

3 DOJ & USPTO Policy Statement on Remedies for Standard-Essential Patents Subject to Voluntary F/RAND Commitments (8 January 2013), 4, http://www.justice.gov/atr/public/guidelines/290994.pdf.

4 US Department of Justice & Federal Trade Commission, Antitrust Enforcement & Intellectual Property Rights: Promoting Innovation and Competition (17 April 2007)(hereinafter 'DOJ IP2 Report'), 38, http://www.usdoj.gov/atr/public/hearings/ip/222655.pdf.

5 See ANSI, ETSI, IEEE, AVS and other SSOs' Intellectual Property or Patent Polices.

6 Daniel G. Swanson and William J. Baumol, 'Reasonable and Nondiscriminatory (RAND) Royalties, Standards Selection, and Control of Market Power', [2005] **73** *Antitrust L.J.* 1, 54.

have filed so many SEP infringement lawsuits in the United States and Europe. Philips, Google, Microsoft, Motorola, Apple, Samsung and Huawei are all involved. Obviously, a judicial court's interpretation on the availability of injunctive relief in these cases, will directly affect the bargaining power of patentees and standard implementers in such a FRAND licensing negotiation. Such a judicial decision will also bring a significant impact on the legal order in high-tech industries.

**18.05** In this context, this chapter focuses on the enforcement of SEPs under Chinese law, especially the availability of injunctive relief in an SEP infringement case. In Section B, it analyzes the ambiguity in the legal nature of a FRAND commitment and the practical difficulties faced by SSOs in eliminating such ambiguity. In Section C, applying contract law theories, it explains Chinese courts' two possible options in interpreting FRAND commitments, that is, either an offer to grant a patent license to all standard implementers, or a contract with a third-party beneficiary. In both of these two options, the court might hold that a patent license has been established between an SEP holder and a standard implementer and therefore injunctive relief shall be excluded. In Section D and Section E, it discusses how a Chinese court would deal with injunctive relief under the Patent Act and the Anti-Monopoly Law (hereinafter 'AML').

## B. THE AMBIGUITY IN THE LEGAL NATURE OF A FRAND COMMITMENT

**18.06** For the purpose of reducing patent holdups over technical standards, SSOs usually set up patent policies requiring SEP owners to disclose their SEPs and promise to license their patents on fair, reasonable and non-discriminatory terms (FRAND) to all standard implementers. Different SSOs' patent policies on FRAND commitment might vary from each other, but their spirit is broadly consistent.

**18.07** According to general contract law theory, an SEP owner's FRAND commitment could be viewed as either an offer to license SEPs to all standard implementers, or as a contract between SEP owners and the SSO with a third-party beneficiary (standard implementers). If wished, an SSO could freely define the legal nature of a FRAND commitment in its patent policies, and further clarify whether an SEP owner has a right to seek injunctive relief against standard implementers who fail to conclude specific licenses with him. Once an SSO did so, a court, when interpreting the FRAND commitment, should rely on the specific content of the patent policy and respect the real intention of the relevant parties, as expressed by them. This is the essence of the principle of freedom of contract.

Unfortunately, so far, the vast majority of SSOs' intellectual property or patent policies are very simple, in which the FRAND commitment often only has a few lines. For example, the ANSI (American National Standards Institute), in its patent policies, requires SEP holders to make a FRAND or RF (royalty free) commitment. The FRAND commitment reads as follows: **18.08**

> A license to such essential patent claim(s) will be made available to applicants desiring to utilize the license for the purpose of implementing the standard … under reasonable terms and conditions that are demonstrably free of any unfair discrimination.[7]

Similarly, the patent licensing commitment in IEEE's patent policies is very concise, in which an SEP owner is required to make the following statement in a so-called 'Letter of Assurance':

> A license for a compliant implementation of the standard will be made available to an unrestricted number of applicants on a worldwide basis without compensation or under reasonable rates, with reasonable terms and conditions that are demonstrably free of any unfair discrimination.[8]

The famous SSO in Europe, ETSI, has the same problem. It only requires its members to fill in an IPR Licensing Declaration Form, promising to grant irrevocable licenses under Clause 6.1 of the ETSI IPR Policy. The Policy states that an SEP owner 'is prepared to grant irrevocable licenses on fair, reasonable and non-discriminatory ("FRAND") terms and conditions'.[9] Chinese SSOs, such as AVS or IGRS are no exception.[10]

The China National Standardization Committee and the State Intellectual Property Office should be in a position to clarify the legal nature of a RAND commitment but have failed to do so. On 19 December 2013, they jointly issued the 'Regulations on National Standards Involving Patents (Tentative)' which, however, remain silent on the availability of injunctive relief for patentees. According to the Regulations, when setting up or revising a national standard involving patents, its technical committee or other responsible entity shall obtain RF or RAND patent licensing declarations from the patentees or patent applicants in a timely manner.[11] If the patentee or applicant refuses to make **18.09**

7 ANSI Patent Policy, Section 3.1.1. http://publicaa.ansi.org/sites/apdl/Reference%20Documents%20Regarding%20ANSI%20Patent%20Policy/62–2007%20ANSI%20Patent%20Policy%20Revision.pdf.

8 IEEE-SA Standards Board Bylaws Section 6.2 Policies, available at https://standards.ieee.org/develop/policies/bylaws.

9 Clause 6.1 of the ETSI IPR Policy, available at www.etsi.org/images/etsi_ipr-policy.pdf.

10 AVS IPR Policy, Art. 11 and Art.12, available at http://www.avs.org.cn/english/Doc/AVS%20IPR%20Policy%20(Mar29%202008-Dual%20Languages).doc.

11 R. 9 Regulations on National Standards Involving Patents (Tentative).

such a declaration, the standard shall not implicate their patents unless the standard is a mandatory one.[12] The Regulations allow a mandatory standard, where necessary, to implicate patents. If the patentee refuses to make an RF or RAND commitment, the National Standardization Committee, SIPO or other relevant governmental departments, shall negotiate with the patentee so as to arrive at a solution.[13] It is unclear, however, what will happen upon failure of such negotiations. Most likely, the patentee will face a compulsory license under the Patent Act or a remedy under the Anti-Monopoly Law.

**18.10** SSOs prefer a simple and ambiguous FRAND statement for several possible reasons. First, an SEP owner's claim for injunctive relief against standard implementers historically has never become a serious threat to SSOs as we see today, so SSOs did not realize the importance of this issue and the necessity of responding to it in patent policies. Second, prior to the setting of a standard, a clarification of the legal nature of a FRAND commitment may cause too much controversy and unnecessarily slow down the standard-setting process. Thus, many SSOs deliberately keep silent on this issue, so that it is easier for all participants to compromise and reach a consensus. Third, some SSOs might believe that keeping this ambiguity in patent policies does not prevent SEP owners and standard implementers to eliminate it through *ex post* private negotiations. Finally, some SSOs have anti-trust concerns as to the possibility of forming an illegal horizontal cartel if they get too much involved, for example, into setting prices (royalties) for SEPs. That may be the reason why so many FRAND commitments lack specific royalties.

**18.11** Theoretically, an SSO could eliminate the existing ambiguity of a FRAND commitment by revising its patent policy. However, in practice, it would not be an easy task.

**18.12** First, an SSO's patent policies are a legally binding contract between the SSO and its members. Before revising the policy, all SSO members must first reach a consensus. Many influential SSOs administrate tens or hundreds of technical standards, which share the same patent policy.[14] Revising such a patent policy will affect hundreds or thousands of members' core interests. It would certainly be time-consuming for an SSO to reach a consensus on how to revise the patent policy. So, until left without choice, an SSO would not re-start such a re-negotiating process.

---

12 R. 10 Regulations on National Standards Involving Patents (Tentative).

13 R. 15 Regulations on National Standards Involving Patents (Tentative).

14 For example, ANSI has approved or accredited more than 1000 standards as American National Standard. http://www.ansi.org/about_ansi/introduction/introduction.aspx?menuid=1.

Second, revising the patent policy may trigger anti-trust or unfair competition law concerns, usually disturbing enough for an SSO. For SEP holders and standard implementers, market situations before and after a standard has been set up are quite different. Prior to an adoption of a standard, an SEP owner, if dissatisfied with the SSO's patent policy, might refuse to participate in the standard-setting process, and a non-SEP owner may take measures to block the standard-setting process in advance. After a standard has been widely implemented, the above strategies would no longer be available. In which direction an SSO might revise its patent policy then depends largely on the 'ecological environment' within the SSO. If SEP owners control the SSO's decision-making process, the SSO is likely to clarify that a FRAND commitment should not affect an SEP owner's claim for injunctive relief. Conversely, if non-patent holders are dominant within the SSO, the revision will move in the opposite direction. No matter which party controls the revision process, there would always be a losing party. After failing to affect an SSO's revision process, the losing party might resort to anti-trust law or unfair competition law to challenge the revision, alleging that either SEP owners are seeking an illegal monopoly or non-patent holders are jointly boycotting SEP owners. 18.13

Last, when revising patent policy in a country like China, an SSO has to face extra challenges because the government heavily regulates standard-setting activities. Once a standard together with relevant patent policies is approved by the government as a mandatory national standard or industrial standard, it functions as a technical regulation in China.[15] If an SSO's revision of the patent policy threatened the government's established policy goal in its previous approval of the standard, the government would probably not allow such a revision. Such a risk would force many SSOs to think twice before starting a revision of their patent policies. 18.14

Through the above analysis, we find that SSO's revising an established standard patent policy is theoretically possible, but in practice it would be quite difficult and legally risky. So it is safe to predict that the parties in the majority of FRAND disputes would choose to resolve the problem before a court or arbitration committee, rather than push an SSO for clarification or revision of its patent policy. In other words, in most cases, SSO's timely clarification would not be available, and a court has to face the ambiguity in a FRAND commitment. 18.15

15 See Art. 7 Standardization Law (1988).

## C. INTERPRETING A FRAND STATEMENT UNDER CHINESE CONTRACT LAW

**18.16** There is no dispute that a contract exists between an SSO and its members. The SSO's patent policies usually require an SEP owner to be committed to a FRAND license. Such a FRAND commitment is part of the contract. If an SEP owner later refuses to grant a FRAND license to standard implementers, it will violate the SSO's patent policies and should be liable for breaching the contract. The SSO can kick the SEP owner out from the SSO or require the owner to compensate the SSO for its losses. However, such contractual remedies are not available to standard implementers for they are not parties to the above contract. Without a binding contract, standard implementers would be unable to counter against an SEP owner's claim for injunctive relief.

**18.17** The above analysis is based on a presumption – the SEP's FRAND statement has no legal implications on the relationship between an SEP owner and standard implementers. Actually, this presumption is not always reliable. Under the Contract Act, a FRAND statement might be interpreted in two different ways, either as an offer to grant a license to all standard implementers made by an SEP owner, or as a contract term with third-party beneficiary (standard implementers). Both these two interpretations avail standard implementers of a counterargument against an SEP's accusation of patent infringement. The underlying rationality of the two interpretations is explored respectively in the following Sections C.1 and C.2. After that, the Chinese Supreme Court's possible attitude in interpreting a FRAND statement is further discussed.

### 1. An offer to standard implementers

**18.18** According to the Contract Act, an offer shall satisfy the following requirements: (1) it shall suggest an offeror's intent to contract; (2) it shall aim at an offeree whom the offeror wishes to contract with; (3) it shall be specific and definite.[16]

**18.19** When making a FRAND statement, an SEP owner usually discloses a list of SEPs implicated by a standard, its willingness to grant patent licenses to any standard implementer in the future, the basic conditions for the patent license, that is, FRAND commitment. The FRAND commitment is usually irrevocable.[17] According to most SSOs' patent policies, if such a disclosure of SEPs

16 Art. 14 Contract Act (1999); See also Wang Liming, *Hetongfa yanjiu (Contract Law Studies)*, 1st vol., Renmin University of China Press 2002, 206–11.

17 OASIS Intellectual Property Rights (IPR) Policy, Section 11; AVS IPR Policies, Art. 31.

were inadequate or incomplete, later-discovered SEPs would be automatically included in the scope of the FRAND statement.

Compared with a common patent license agreement, a FRAND statement is very general and abstract. So it is widely disputed whether such a statement constitutes an offer under the Contract Act. The trial judges in *Huawei v IDC* have opined such a doubt. They published a law review article, saying that a FRAND commitment is not an offer in the sense of the Contract Act: **18.20**

> Before an owner of SEPs and a standard implementer start their negotiation for a patent license, the owner has not made any offer. ... Only after the parties have entered into a negotiation, the owner's disclosure to the licensee of specific royalty rate and other licensing terms could be called an offer. And only after the standard implementer has accepted such an offer, a license agreement is formally concluded.[18]

The judges did not further explain in their article why such a FRAND commitment should not constitute an offer and why only an SEP owner's *ex post* detailed proposal in a license negotiation could be an acceptable offer.

This chapter argues that completely ruling out the possibility of a FRAND statement being an offer under Contract Act is not legally reliable. The reasons are specified as follows. **18.21**

First, through a FRAND statement, the SEP owner declares its willingness to license, which may be viewed as an obvious declaration of 'intent to contract'. Even if an SEP owner's statement is vague, it should not always be an insurmountable obstacle for a court to recognize the statement as an offer to standard implementers. In many cases, the following holds true: **18.22**

> Although one party does not clearly express in words that he is to be bound by his declaration of intent after the counterpart's acceptance, if the counterpart, after combining the party's declaration of intent and industrial practices, could reasonably infer that the party intends to be bound by his declaration of intent, what the party says should be viewed as an offer.[19]

In a FRAND license dispute, from the fact that an SEP owner participates in a standard-setting process, discloses its SEPs, and makes a FRAND statement, it

18 Ye Ruosi, Zhu Jianjun and Chen Wenquan, 'Biaozhun biyao zhuanli shiyongfei jiufenzhong FRAND guize de sifa shiyong (The Judicial Application of FRAND Rules in Cases concerning Licensing Fee for SEPs)', [2013] **4** *Dianzi zhishi chanquan (Electronic IP)* 60.

19 Wang Liming, above note 16, at 207.

might be reasonable for a court to infer that the patent owner has shown the intent to contract embodied in an offer.

**18.23** Second, an SSO's patent policy and an SEP's FRAND statement include the main components of a typical license agreement, such as a list of licensed patents, territorial scope of the license (usually worldwide), licensing conditions (FRAND) and so on. For both sides, more detailed licensing terms are absent. For example, a royalty rate is not fixed by a FRAND commitment. Nevertheless, when a dispute on a royalty rate arises, an SSO's patent policy usually requires the disputing parties to accept a reasonable royalty rate determined through a judicial or arbitration process. Under the Contract Act, as long as a contract price is fixed afterwards, the absence of contract price in an offer does not prevent it to be deemed 'sufficiently certain' if the parties have agreed upon a procedure to determine the price.[20]

**18.24** In the field of IP licensing, Chinese courts have already confirmed this rule. *Beijing Xichuan Advertisement Co., Ltd. v Beijing Haitian Training School* is an example. In this case, one party commissioned the other party to design a business logo and the parties failed to reach an agreement on a contract price. After the former finished his work, disputes on the contract price arose. The court held as follows:

> As to the contract price, in normal circumstances, the parties often expressly agree upon it at the time of concluding the contract. But we shall not exclude the possibility that the parties do not negotiate for a price until they begin to perform the contract. Put it differently, as long as the parties have reached a consensus for signing a contract, leaving the problem of ascertaining contract price for future consideration would not prejudice the establishment of the contract. Under China's Contract Act, if two parties are unable to reach a supplementary agreement on price after a contract comes into effect, the contract price could be determined according to relevant provisions of the contract or trade practices.[21]

Thus, following the same principle, even if a FRAND statement does not indicate a detailed royalty rate, it still could be an offer to grant a license under the Contract Act.

**18.25** Third, the fact that the FRAND statement is declared to the general public, not to a specific standard implementer, does not prevent it from being viewed as an

---

20 Art. 14 United Nations Convention on Contracts of International Sales of Goods; § 2–204 Uniform Commercial Code.

21 *Beijing Xichuan Advertisement Co., Ltd, v Beijing Haitian Training School*, No. 7082 Decision of the Civil Tribunal, the Haidian District Court, 2004.

offer. Contract Act does not strictly prohibit an offer to the general public. For example, a reward advertisement to the general public has long been treated as an offer under China's Contract Act.[22]

When a FRAND statement is an acceptable offer, a standard implementer may enter into a patent license agreement by accepting the offer. According to Article 22 of the Contract Act, a notice of acceptance should be sent to the offeror. But the law does not restrict the form or format of the notice. Generally speaking, once a standard implementer has informed an SEP owner of his plan to implement a standard and accept all FRAND licensing terms, he may satisfy the requirement for an acceptance under the Contract Act. After concluding a license contract, if the parties could not reach consensus on some licensing terms, they could resolve their difference through judicial procedure or another alternative dispute resolution process. The dispute on how to interpret the FRAND requirement itself would not endanger the validity of a license contract. **18.26**

If a patent licensee refuses to pay a royalty determined by a court or an ADR institution, he would breach a license contract in a substantial way. The SEP owner could terminate the license contract and sue the standard implementer for patent infringement. Once patent infringement is established, the SEP owner could seek injunctive relief. **18.27**

### 2. A contract with a third-party beneficiary

An alternative interpretation under the Contract Act is to treat a FRAND statement as part of the contract between an SSO and its members involving a third-party beneficiary. According to Articles 64 and 65 of the Contract Act, contractual parties could agree in a contract that one party shall perform contractual obligations to a third party, or a third party shall perform contractual obligation to one party (creditor) of the contract. Contract Act, by permitting contractual parties to create rights for or impose obligations on a third party, to some extent loosens the requirement for privity. **18.28**

As mentioned above, an SSO and its members have a contractual relationship. An SSO's patent policy or a FRAND statement is part of the contract, in which an SEP owner promises to grant a FRAND license to third parties (standard implementers). Therefore, a court could hold that the SSO and SEP owner intend to create a right for the third party. For example, in *Microsoft Co. v Motorola, Inc.*, the US court held that Motorola, after having made a FRAND **18.29**

22 Wang Liming, above note 16, 209.

commitment, entered a legally binding contract with IEEE and ITU respectively, in which standard implementers are third-party beneficiaries.[23]

**18.30** As to the legal nature of the third party's right, two possible interpretations exist. The third party has either a right to require an SEP owner to grant a FRAND license, or a right to use the SEP directly. The Contract Act does not provide a clear answer; therefore a court has some discretion in its decision.

**18.31** If a court adopts the first interpretation, that is, that the contract confers on the third party a right to request the patentee to grant a patent license with FRAND terms, not a license to use the patent, the third party has to obtain patent licenses before implementing a technical standard. Otherwise, implementing a standard would infringe the SEPs, and the patent owner could seek injunctions against the third party (at least so under Contract Act). In *Microsoft Co. v Motorola, Inc.*, the court seemingly believed, Microsoft as a third-party beneficiary had the right to require a patentee to grant a license, not having a right to use the patent directly.[24] Such a right itself could not counter the claim of patent infringement. Nevertheless, the existence of this right will affect a court's decision as to whether to grant injunctive relief in the third party's favor, namely, excluding the application of injunctive relief.[25]

**18.32** In theory, if an SEP owner refuses to grant a patent license to a third party, the latter can request a court to enforce the contract against the SEP owner. Regrettably, the Contract Act does not specify such a remedy. Article 64 provides: 'Where the parties prescribed that the obligor render performance to a third person, if the obligor fails to render its performance to the third person, or rendered non-conforming performance, it shall be liable to the obligee for breach of contract.' This provision remains silent on the key question – whether the third party can claim its right under the contract against the obligor (the SEP owner). Scholars are split over its interpretation. Some believe the above provision only stipulates rights and obligations of contractual parties (the creditor and the debtor), and it does not affirm a third party's right to claim against the parties, so the third party has no such right.[26] Others take the opposite point of view, that the third person shall be entitled to claim its right against the contractual parties, otherwise it would be unnecessary for the

23 *Microsoft Corp. v Motorola, Inc.*, 696 F.3d 872, 878 (2012).

24 'The court has already determined that Motorola's declarations to the ITU created an enforceable contract requiring Motorola to license its H.264 Standard-essential patents on RAND terms, with Microsoft as a third-party beneficiary to that contract.' *Microsoft Corp. v Motorola, Inc.*, 871 F.Supp. 2d 1089, 1098 (2012).

25 *Microsoft Corp. v Motorola, Inc.*, 696 F.3d 872, 884 (2012).

26 Yin Tian, 'Lun sheta qiyue: jianlun woguo xin hetongfa do 64 tiao, di 65 tiao zhi guiding (On Contracts with a Third Party Beneficiary: Comments on the Articles 64 and 65 of the Contract Act)', **1/2001** *Faxue yanjiu* (Chinese Journal of Law) 48 et seq.

legislator to specify such a provision at all.[27] Currently, the latter seemingly represents the mainstream view among Chinese scholars. So, if necessary, a third party may directly notify an SEP owner, requiring the latter to fulfill its contract with the SSO, grant a patent license to the third party, and set reasonable licensing fees and so on.

If a court adopts the second interpretation that the contract confers on a third party a right to use the SEP directly, a third party's implementation of a technical standard would not constitute a patent infringement. An SEP owner cannot seek injunctive relief unless the third party (standard implementer) openly refuses to perform its ancillary duties, such as timely notifying the SEP of the third party's plan to implement the standard and to pay a reasonable royalty for such a use, and so on, under the contract between the SSO and its members. **18.33**

In China, when interpreting a FRAND statement under the theory of contract involving a third-party beneficiary, a court might trigger theoretical disputes. Some scholars are of the opinion that through such a contract, the parties can only grant rights or benefits to the third party, but may not impose duties.[28] According to the contract between an SSO and a patentee, if a third party (standard implementer) plans to use an SEP, it has to pay reasonable royalty to the patentee. What the third party obtains from the contract seemingly is not only a pure right to use the patent, but also a substantive obligation to pay a royalty. Does this violate the above-mentioned principle that contractual parties could not impose duties on a third party? **18.34**

When analyzing whether a third party only benefits from a contract, a court should not simply focus on whether the third party needs to fulfill any obligation under the contract. Instead, the court should consider from a third person's perspective whether the contract overall makes it better off than not having the contract in the first place. As we know, without the contract between an SSO and its members, a third party would not be allowed to use the patent. To implement a technical standard, the third party should bear liability for patent infringement. It is the contract that avails the third party of an additional option – paying a reasonable royalty and then being allowed to use the patent. Compared with having no right to work the patent, the contract actually makes the third party purely a beneficiary of the contract. **18.35**

---

27 Han Shiyuan, *Hetongfa zonglun* (On General Parts of Contract Act), *Falü chubanshe* (Law Press) 2004, 312 et seq.

28 Ibid., 307.

**18.36** In practice, it would be unthinkable that a contract involving a third-party beneficiary could solely grant rights to the third party without setting any ancillary obligation. In most transactions, a third person to a contract, when receiving a performance by one party of the contract, will inevitably perform some ancillary obligations, such as promptly notifying the debtor to perform its duty, taking delivery timely and so on. The existence of these ancillary obligations usually would not change what the third party obtains from the contract as a whole into an obligation.

### 3. The Supreme People's Court's possible attitude

**18.37** So far, the Supreme People's Court of China has never clarified the legal nature of a FRAND statement. Nevertheless, the court has come very close to doing so in a well-known judicial interpretation which is the court's official reply to a lower court's request for instruction on an SEP infringement case. In this reply, the Supreme Court said:

> In view of the actual situation that the standard-setting body in China has not established relevant rules on the public disclosure and use of patent information in a relevant standard, if a patentee has participated in setting a standard or has agreed to include his patent into a state, industry or local standard, it shall be deemed that the patentee has permitted others to exploit such a patent while implementing the standard, and therefore the relevant exploitation by others shall not constitute the patent infringement prescribed in Article 11 of the Patent Act. The patentee may require the person exploiting the patent to pay a royalty, which, however, shall be evidently less than a normal royalty.[29]

**18.38** In the above reply, the Supreme Court says a standard implementer is 'deemed' to have a patent license but it does not clarify the legal basis of the so-called license. This is a regrettable omission. Furthermore, unlike a typical SSO the SSO here had not set clear patent policies and the patent owners had not made a FRAND commitment. So this is not a typical dispute on a FRAND commitment. Nevertheless, the Supreme Court still holds that standard implementers have a license. It seems reasonable for us to believe that Chinese courts, in a typical FRAND commitment case, will be more likely to hold that standard implementers would obtain a patent license after an SEP owner has made a FRAND commitment to an SSO. Then, the remaining issue would be how to rationalize such a decision under the framework of China's Contract Act.

---

29 The Supreme Court of China, 'Letter on the Issue of Whether the Exploitation of a Patent in the Specification for the Design of Ram-compaction Piles with a Composite Bearing Base, an Industry Standard Issued by the Ministry of Construction, by Chaoyang Xingnuo Company Which Has Conducted Design and Construction according to the Standard Constitutes a Patent Infringement', (2008).

As discussed in Section C.1 and C.2, an SEP owner's FRAND commitment might be viewed as an offer to standard implementers or a contract between an SSO and its members aiming to benefit a third party, that is, standard implementers. Under either situation, standard implementers, after having informed the patent holder, will have the right to implement the standard. Even if the standard implementer and the SEP owner later failed to state the FRAND licensing terms, the SEP owner could not seek injunctive relief. Instead, he could only request the court to determine a reasonable royalty. **18.39**

It should be noted that the content of a FRAND commitment and the context of SSO patent policies in specific cases might vary considerably.[30] Thus, the above analysis is not necessarily applicable to all FRAND commitments in all cases. Especially when an SSO's patent policies are clear enough as to eliminate the legal ambiguity of a FRAND commitment, a court's discretion would be significantly restricted. For example, an SSO's patent policies might clarify that any standard implementer needs to obtain a patent license before implementing a standard. This statement basically excludes the possibility for a court to treat a FRAND commitment as an offer or contractual clause granting a license to a third party. **18.40**

In addition, the Supreme Court might change its attitude to a FRAND commitment in the future. As we already know, the court actually says nothing about FRAND commitment in the above reply. So, if wished, the court could easily distinguish a FRAND case from the above one. As discussed above, the Contract Act is ambiguous enough to provide such flexibility for a court. Around the world, some courts have already taken such an approach. For example, in *Philips v SK Kassetten*, the Dutch court held that after having made a FRAND commitment, an SEP owner can still seek injunctive relief.[31] Some US courts have similar opinions.[32] **18.41**

30 Hill Wellford and Bingham McCutchen, 'Reasons to Reject a "No Injunctions" Rule for SEPs and FRAND-Obligated Patents', *CPI Antitrust Chronicle*, April 2012 (2) at 2, available at http://www.bingham.com/Publications/Files/2012/04/No-Injunctions-Rule.

31 *Koninklijke Philips Electronics N.V. v SK Kassetten GmbH & Co. KG*, Infringement, FRAND, District Court The Hague, The Netherlands, 17 March 2010, Joint Cases No. 316533/HA ZA 08–2522 and 316535/HA ZA 08–2524.

32 See *Commonwealth Scientific and Industrial Research Organisation v Buffalo Technology Inc.*, 492 F.Supp.2d 600 (E.D.Tex. 2007). In this case, CSIRO promised to grant RAND licenses to all companies wanting to implement the IEEE's 802.11a standard. After IEEE ratified the standard, CSIRO brought suit against Buffalo Technology, Inc. The court granted a permanent injunction for CSIRO.

## D. INJUNCTIVE RELIEF UNDER THE CHINESE PATENT ACT

**18.42** When a FRAND commitment does not lead to a patent license between a patentee and a standard implementer, the latter's implementation of the standard would infringe the SEP's. Under conventional civil law theory, a patent right is viewed as a quasi 'real right', which by nature is a right to exclude others from interfering with a patented technology. Once it is infringed, the default remedies include compensatory damages plus injunctive relief. In other words, if an SEP infringement were established, an injunction would be almost automatically granted against a standard implementer.

**18.43** The default rule under the Chinese Patent Act is apparently in favor of the patentee, which differs greatly from the US law. In the United States, a patentee who seeks injunctive relief in a patent infringement case has to demonstrate:

(1) that it has suffered an irreparable injury;
(2) that remedies available at law are inadequate to compensate for that injury;
(3) that considering the balance of hardships between the plaintiff and defendant, a remedy in equity is warranted;
(4) that the public interest would not be disserved by a permanent injunction.[33]

That is, in terms of injunctive relief, the US law does not have a default rule favourable to a patentee.

**18.44** However, it should be noted that Chinese law does allow a court to divert from the above default rule, by staying an injunctive relief in a patent infringement case. To do so, a court usually requires an accused infringer (not the patentee) to prove that an ongoing royalty is enough to compensate the patentee. The Patent Act does not stipulate the elements to be considered by a court when determining whether to grant an injunction. Judicial practice suggests that a court might consider similar elements as mentioned by the US Supreme Court in the *eBay* case, such as the hardship to the infringer caused by an injunction, the effect on public interest, and the adequacy of monetary compensation for patent infringement, and so on.

**18.45** For example, in the *Wuhan Jingyuan* case, the court emphasized the element of 'public interest' and denied the patentee's request for injunctive relief:

---

33 *eBay Inc. v MercExchange, L.L.C.*,547 U.S. 388 (2006).

> Given that the Flue gas desulfurization system has been installed in the Huayang company's power plants and has actually been put into operation, if being ordered to stop, it will directly have a significant impact on the local public's interest. Thus, the trial court, having taken … full consideration of the interests of right holder and the public, rejected Jingyuan Company's request for ordering the defendant to stop infringing behaviour, but ordered Huayang Company to pay 240,000 RMB per unit and per year until the patent term expires. Nothing in this decision is wrong.[34]

In the *Shenzhen Airport* case, the court considered the hardship to the airport in dismantling a patented glass curtain wall and refused to grant an injunction: **18.46**

> Considering the particular situation of the Shenzhen Airport, the court finds it is unrealistic for the airport to stop using the patented glass curtain, therefore order the defendant to pay a reasonable royalty to the plaintiff.[35]

In the *Baiyun Airport* case, the court took a similar position.[36]

Next, let us return to FRAND commitment cases. If a patentee, after having made a FRAND commitment, seeks an injunction against a standard implementer, a court might place more weight on the factor of the FRAND commitment. As a matter of fact, once a patentee makes a FRAND commitment, to a large extent, it gives away the right to choose licensees and price patent licenses. This fact would likely convince a court that a denial of injunctive relief is unlikely to cause irreparable harm to the patentee. In a case where a technical standard was a *de jure* or *de facto* standard, an implementer's only choice would be to infringe the patent or leave the industry. Under this circumstance, the patentee has a strong negotiating position in a patent licensing negotiation. If an injunctive relief were available, the patentee would be encouraged to take a strategic act to delay a license negotiation for as long as possible to the detriment of standard implementers. To avoid such an unintended consequence, a court might stay an injunctive relief. **18.47**

Of course, if a standard implementer explicitly refuses to pay a reasonable license fee, is unable to afford a reasonable license fee, or has other integrity problems, a court's staying injunctive relief will cause irreparable harm to the patentee. Under such situations, the court should apply the default rule, granting injunctive relief to the patentee. **18.48**

---

34 *Wuhan Jingyuan Environmental Engineering Co., Ltd. v Japan Fujikaisui Engineering Co., Ltd.*, No.8 Decision of the IP Tribunal of the Supreme Court (2008).

35 *Zhuihai Jingyi Glass Engineering Co., Ltd. v Shenzhen Airport Co., Ltd.*, No. 587 of the IP Tribunal of the Shenzhen Intermediate Court (2004).

36 *Zhuihai Jingyi Glass Engineering Co., Ltd. v Guangzhou Baiyun International Airport Co., Ltd.*, No. 581 of the IP Tribunal of the Guangzhou Intermediate Court (2004).

## E. SEP HOLDERS' LIABILITIES UNDER THE CHINESE ANTI-MONOPOLY LAW

**18.49** As we know, once a technological standard has been widely implemented, an SEP owner's negotiating power in patent licensing will be drastically increased. How a patentee obtains and exercises such an increased market power has significant implications under the AML. If an SEP owner chooses to breach its FRAND statement made to the SSO by refusing to license its patents on FRAND terms and seeking injunctive relief after a failed patent license negotiation, it might incur legal liability under the AML. Here an SEP owner's act may constitute two types of anti-trust violations: seeking a dominant market position through fraudulency or abusing market dominance by discriminatory pricing against standard implementers.

**18.50** As a basic principle under competition law, to be a monopolist by itself is not illegal. But one should not be allowed to acquire a monopoly through illegal means. In a standard-setting process, a patentee might deliberately make a false FRAND statement and so induce an SSO to include its patents in a technological standard. Later on, the patentee would ignore the FRAND statement and insist on imposing unreasonable licensing terms on standard implementers. The patentee's fraudulency would harm the interest of the SSO, the patentee's competitors and standard implementers. For the SSO, if it had known from the start that the patentee would not honour the FRAND statement, it would have terminated the standard-setting process or have chosen another patentee's alternative technologies, rather than wasting time and money in setting a standard held up by the uncooperative patentee. For the patentee's competitors, its false statement misleads the SSO into making a technological choice unfavourable to them. For standard implementers, if the SSO were forced to re-set a standard after it has been widely adopted, they would suffer high switching costs. Thus, a patentee's false FRAND statement could substantially harm market competition in a standard-setting process and violate competition law.

**18.51** However, the current AML does not clearly ban one from seeking monopoly through fraudulency. The Law specifies that it might be illegal for one to acquire market dominance through monopolistic agreements or business centralization.[37] A fraudulent FRAND statement seemingly does not fall into the two categories. So it is uncertain whether such a behavior would be a violation against the AML.

37 Arts. 13, 14 and 17 AML (2007).

In the SAIC's fifth draft of a 'Guide to Anti-Monopoly Law Enforcement in the Field of Intellectual Property Rights', the above uncertainty has been removed. The draft provides that if an enterprise's exercising patent rights in standard setting or implementation process results or may result in excluding or restricting competition, the AML will be applied.[38] If this draft matured into a regulation in the future, a patentee's false FRAND statement would be viewed as a violation under the AML. Before the draft becomes law, a court might apply the general principle set forth in Article 2 of the Anti-Unfair Competition Act to hold a patentee liable for making a false FRAND statement.[39] In China, this article has been frequently applied to fight against unfair competition conduct that has not been specified by the Anti-Unfair Competition Act. Of course, it would not be easy for a standard implementer (potential licensee) to prove that the patentee has a malicious intent when making its FRAND statement in a standard-setting process, which is a prerequisite for establishing such a violation. That means the possibility of a patentee being held liable for a false FRAND statement would be relatively low. **18.52**

Even though the AML does not expressly regulate the act of seeking a monopoly by illegal means, it has a clear rule against a monopolist's excessive pricing or discriminatory behaviors. The first paragraph of Article 17 reads as follows: **18.53**

> A business operator with a dominant market position shall not abuse its dominant market position to conduct the following acts: (1) selling commodities at unfairly high prices … (3) refusing to trade with a trading party without any justifiable cause … (6) applying dissimilar prices or other transaction terms to counterparties with equal standing …

Theoretically, there is no legal hurdle for these anti-monopoly rules to be applied to the licensing of standard-essential patents. If a patentee breaches its FRAND commitment by seeking an excessive royalty from or refusing to grant a license to some standard implementers, this would be a discriminatory behavior or a refusal to deal under the AML. In normal patent licensing cases, a patentee enjoys freedom in choosing its licensees and determining a royalty rate. Once a patentee joins an SSO and makes a FRAND statement on SEPs for a standard, its freedom in licensing SEPs and seeking injunctive relief would be restricted significantly. In the famous *Orange Book Standard* case, the German Federal Supreme Court also illustrates this point of view: **18.54**

38 State Administration for Industry and Commerce Task Force, 'Guide on Antimonopoly Act Enforcement in the Field of Intellectual Property Rights', 5th Draft, R. 22(1), (2013).

39 Art. 2 Anti-Unfair Competition Act (1993).

> If a company with a dominant position on the market discriminates the company seeking a license in a commerce usually accessible to similar companies, or if it inequitably obstructs the proposed licensee by refusing to conclude a patent license agreement it has been offered, the enforcement of the patent-law claim for injunctive relief constitutes an abuse of its dominant position on the market, because the dominant company prevents the other company from gaining the very access to the market that it is obliged to grant by entering into the license agreement.[40]

**18.55** In the above-mentioned draft Guide, SAIC adopts the so-called essential facilities doctrine to deal with a patent owner's refusal to license:

> [F]or acts of refusal to license intellectual property rights which fall within one of the following conditions, the State Council Anti-Monopoly Law enforcement agencies can conclude that the undertaking has violated the provisions of the Anti-Monopoly Law on the abuse of dominant market position: (1) Undertakings with dominant market position unfairly, discriminatorily refuse to license their intellectual property rights; (2) The intellectual property right which the undertakings with dominant market position refuse to license is an essential element for the licensee to compete in the relevant market, and the refusal to license that intellectual property right will prohibit the licensee from competing effectively in the relevant market, which adversely impacts on competition and innovation in the relevant market, and as a result reasonable demands from customers cannot be satisfied.[41]

**18.56** In judicial practice, a Chinese court has also accepted the essential facilities doctrine in a high-profile case, *Huawei v IDC*.[42] The court of first instance held that since IDC's patents had become essential ones for the standard, IDC had obtained dominant power in the market. IDC treated its potential standard implementers differently and required Huawei to pay excessive royalty, 19 times the royalty paid by Apple and 7 to 8 times the royalty paid by Samsung.[43] Therefore, IDC, in violation of Article 17 of the AML, should bear legal liability. Upon request of the plaintiff, Huawei Company, the court prohibited the patentee from seeking an excessive licensing fee and ordered it to compensate the plaintiff with 20 Million RMB. In another parallel suit between Huawei and IDC, the court refused to grant injunctive relief and determined a reasonable royalty rate for IDC, in which the court considered the following elements, such as the average profit margin in the wireless telecommunication

---

40 German Federal Supreme Court Decision on the Orange-Book-Standard, case number KZR 39/06 (2009).

41 State Administration for Industry and Commerce Task Force, 'Guide on Antimonopoly Act Enforcement in the Field of Intellectual Property Rights', 5th Draft, R. 17 (2013).

42 *Huawei Technology Co. Ltd. v InterDigital Technology Corporation*, The No. 858 Decision of the IP Tribunal of the Shenzhen Intermediate Court, Guangdong Province (2013).

43 Ibid.

industry, the amount and quality of ESPs owned by the defendant, the defendant's position in this industry, and its R&D investment.[44]

## F. CONCLUSION

The enforcement of standard-essential patents is a new challenge for the whole world. China, like other major countries, needs more time to accumulate experiences in reconciling the protection of standard-essential patents and incentivizing standard-setting activities. As a large developing country, China is currently switching from a labour-extensive economy to an innovation-oriented one. China is beginning to participate more vigorously in the standard-setting activities of major international SSOs. But so far, China's influence in the major SSOs' standard-setting activities is still limited. Most international standards remain under the control of foreign companies, which own most of the standard-essential patents. **18.57**

Against this background, it is unrealistic to expect China's courts in the foreseeable future to adopt a very pro-patent attitude in interpreting an SSO's patent policy in general and the so-called FRAND statement in particular. On the contrary, it would not be surprising to see the courts taking a pro-standard-implementer's position, restricting a patentee's ability to seek injunctive relief in SEP disputes. However, China is already the second largest global market. The stake for setting a judicial position to an SSO's patent policy is extremely high. When doing this, China's courts should move very carefully within the lawful scope of their discretionary power, being mindful of the possible impact of their decisions on international trade. Otherwise, a court's decision might trigger a muddy international trade dispute. **18.58**

As the foregoing has discussed, most SSOs' patent policies are inherently ambiguous, with no hope of being clarified in the short term. This leaves enough leeway for China's courts to import policy considerations into the interpretation of the legal nature of a FRAND statement and the determination of the availability of injunctive relief in an SEP licensing dispute. Under the existing Chinese Contract Act, there is no legal barrier for a court to interpret a FRAND statement as a public offer to all standard implementers, or a contract term conferring on all standard implementers as third-party beneficiaries a right to use the SEPs. As a result, the court could refuse a patentee's request for injunctive relief under the Contract Act. Of course, a presumption is that the FRAND statement itself or the SSO patent policy does not eliminate **18.59**

44 Ye Ruosi, Zhu Jianjun and Chen Wenquan, above note 18.

the ambiguity. Otherwise, the court should respect the patentee's true intent expressed or implied in the FRAND statement or the SSO's patent policy.

**18.60** In addition to the Contract Act, the Patent Act and the AML also provide a legal basis for a court to stay or deny injunctive relief. Compared to a contract law approach, the Patent Act or AML approach provides less certainty because it is relatively difficult for standard implementers to predict the result of a court's discretion in a specific case. Nevertheless, the availability of a patent or anti-monopoly remedy remains an effective counter measure against an SEP owner's possible abuse of market power.

## G. APPENDIX – COMMENTS FROM A EUROPEAN PERSPECTIVE

### Heinz Goddar, Jan Bernd Nordemann and Christian Czychowski

The injunctive relief rule of Chinese Law (see above, paras. 18.42 et seq.) is followed by major European procedural jurisdictions such as Germany. Under the so-called 'Orange-Book-Standard' doctrine of the German Federal Supreme Court, in principle, the patentee keeps its injunction claims against anybody using the patent, although the patentee may be obliged by contract or by anti-trust law to license. Rather, the party seeking the license is in general forced to go to court and ask for a license to be granted.[45] An exception is allowed only when observing two (strict) requirements. First, the infringer (seeker for a license) must have made an unconditional offer to the patentee to enter into a license agreement, which may not be revoked and which may not be refused by the patentee without breaching anti-trust law or its contractual obligations. Second, in a case where the patent is already used, the infringer (seeker for a license) must comply with the obligations which are set out in the license agreement offered. In a case where the patentee asks for a royalty of an abusive amount or where the patentee refuses to specify the royalty, it is sufficient for the infringer to offer to the patentee a licensing agreement with the right for the patentee to set the royalty at an adequate amount; the infringer must then pay the royalties due into an account under the disposal of the patentee. However, there are tendencies to weaken these strict requirements for an exception from an injunction claim. This is in particular true for SEPs and for the requirement of an unconditional offer; some voices argue that the infringer must be allowed to make reservations as to a non-infringement and as to a possible cancellation of the patent. After a reference by the District Court Dusseldorf, this will now be decided by the Court of Justice of the European Union.[46] **18.61**

Another comparative look at European anti-trust law shows that patentees enjoying a monopoly due to an SEP may come under Article 102 of the Treaty of the Functioning of the European Union (TFEU). Article 102 TFEU prohibits the abuse by one or more firms of a dominant position within the Common European Market, or in a substantial part of it, where this may affect trade between Member States. Establishing or maintaining a dominant position is not prohibited. Article 102 TFEU only attacks the abuse of a dominant **18.62**

45 BGH **2009** *GRUR* 694 note 22 et seq. – 'Orange-Book-Standard'.

46 District Court (Landgericht) Dusseldorf **2013** *WRP*, 681 note 15 et seq.; see also European Commission, press release of 22 December 2012 – 'Samsung'; Court of Appeal Karlsruhe **2010** *GRUR-RR* 120, 121 et seq. – 'Patentverwertungsgesellschaft'.

position. Such abuse could include: predatory pricing; limiting production, markets or technical development; refusal to supply; or the imposition of discriminatory trading conditions to the competitive disadvantage of others. In relation to intellectual property, Article 102 TFEU has developed extensive case law to assess the competitive activity of dominant IP owners. Roughly said, EU competition law recognizes in principle the exclusivity of intellectual property rights. Exercising exclusive intellectual property rights can only under exceptional conditions constitute an abuse of market power.

**18.63** Most important case law concerning the abuse of exclusive intellectual property rights comes from the extended application of what is known as the 'essential facilities doctrine' and here in particular as to IP licenses as an essential facility. The European Court of Justice has decided several cases where an abusive refusal to license an IP right was claimed.[47] As to the standardization agreements, which create a dominant position, the European Commission requests the participants to ensure non-abusive access to the standard under FRAND conditions. Their IPR policy would need to require participants wishing to have their IPR included in the standard to provide an irrevocable commitment in writing to offer to license their essential IP rights to all third parties on fair, reasonable and non-discriminatory terms.[48] In particular, prices charged by a dominant IP owner can be abusive. The specific subject matter of IP rights merely guarantees the owner an *equitable* remuneration, not *any* remuneration.[49]

47 CJEU 29 April 2004 C-418/01 – 'IMS Health'; CJEU 5 October 1988 C-53/87 – 'CICRA i.a. /Renaul'; ECJ 5 October 1988 C-238/87 – 'Volvo/Veng'; CJEU 6 April 1995 C-241/91 and 242/91 – 'RTE and ITV/ Commission'; see also Court of First Instance 17 September 2007 T-J02/04 – 'Microsoft/Commission'.

48 See further European Commission, Guidelines on the applicability of Art. 101 TFEU to horizontal co-operation agreements, para. 257 et seq., OJ EU C 011, 14/01/2011 P. 0001–0072.

49 CJEU 4 October 2011, joint cases C-403/08 and C-429/08, C-403/08, C-429/08 paras.108–109 –'Football Association Premier League/Murphy'.

# Part F

# UTILITY MODEL AND DESIGN PROTECTION

# 19

# UTILITY MODELS

**Toby Mak**



## A. INTRODUCTION

The Chinese Patent Act protects the following three types of patents: **19.01**

- invention patent, which is equivalent to 'patents' according to European and US terminology;
- design patent, which is equivalent, for example, to the European Community Design or the US design patent; and
- utility models.

Utility models are in fact a common form of patent protection throughout the world and not unique to China. Utility models are available in many countries in Europe (for example, Austria, Belgium, Denmark, Finland, Germany, Italy, the Netherlands), Latin America (for example, Argentina, Brazil, Mexico), South East Asia (for example Malaysia, Indonesia, Vietnam), as well as in Japan, South Korea and Australia. The two most important developed countries which do not provide such protection are the UK and the US. **19.02**

The primary purpose of utility models is to enable quick patent protection for inventions with a short commercial life. The short commercial life also justifies a shorter protection term as compared to the protection term for invention patents. This is because invention patents in China are usually granted after **19.03** three to six years from the date of filing with SIPO, depending on when the request for examination is made. In contrast, utility models are normally granted after 10 to 16 months from filing. In exchange for quick grant, utility models only have a maximum protection term of 10 years instead of 20 years for invention patents.

**19.04** From 2008 to 2012, the total number of utility model patents granted by SIPO has increased from 176,675 to 571,175, that is, their number has been more than tripled. During the same period, the number of utility model patents granted to foreign entities also increased by three times, from 1,506 to 4,425. Even though the interest of foreigners in utility model protection has increased, the increases in absolute numbers (391,581 for domestic Chinese utility model patentees *v* 2,919 for foreign utility model patentees) are still out of proportion. Apparently, foreign entities are not using utility models as actively as Chinese entities. According to this author's insights which are based on discussions with foreign practitioners, the following appear to be the reasons for the lack of use of utility model protection by foreign entities:

- Lack of awareness of utility model protection – many foreign practitioners are simply not aware of the existence of utility model protection in China.
- Incompatibility of utility model protection with the PCT – as mentioned, international applications can enter China as utility models (*Mak*, Chapter 10). However, if the applicant uses the full period of 30 months, he would obtain utility model protection within 40 to 48 months from the earliest priority date. Such proceedings would run counter to the purpose of filing a utility model application, which is to obtain protection as soon as possible. It should be noted, however, that the PCT is a major route for foreign filings to enter China. As the PCT forms a major route for foreigners to obtain patent protection in China, its incompatibility with the purpose of utility model protection renders utility models comparably unattractive for foreign applicants.
- Lower quality and patentability requirements as compared to invention patents elicit the incorrect assumption that utility models are inferior to invention patents.

**19.05** However, it should be noted that utility models already have resulted in very high damage awards. In the case of *Chint v Schneider*, a recorded high compensation of RMB 330 million (about €50 million) had been awarded to the patentee for infringement of Chint's utility model. The decision has demonstrated that utility model protection can also be very useful and valuable.

This chapter will outline the pros and cons of utility model protection and peculiarities of utility model prosecution. In particular, the following issues will be treated: 19.06

- Why should utility model protection be considered?
- Subject matter of utility model protection.
- Patentability requirements – are patentability requirements on utility models lower than those of invention patents? Can less effort be used in preparing the patent specification of utility models?
- Peculiarities of utility model prosecution.
- Simultaneous filing of utility model and invention patent application.
- Commercial use of utility models.

## B. WHY SHOULD UTILITY MODEL PROTECTION BE CONSIDERED?

If any of the following questions can be answered with 'yes' … : 19.07

- Can the invention be easily copied?
- Is early infringement expected?
- Is the commercial life of the invention short?

… an application for a utility model protection should be considered, as the applicant should have an interest in quick grant of a patent and be content with a shorter protection term.

## C. SUBJECT MATTER OF UTILITY MODEL PROTECTION

Utility models are only granted for products with a new shape and/or new structural features, that is, not all inventions can be protected as utility models. Moreover, such new shape/structural features must form a technical solution. That is, mere ornamental solutions, for example, a vessel in the shape of a famous landmark like the Tower of London, cannot be protected. 19.08

Accordingly, the following inventions cannot be protected as utility models: 19.09

- inventions involving mainly methods, in particular those which use existing products, for example inventions pertaining to computers or systems which use already existing components to carry out a new procedure (that is, software programs) to perform a new function, or an existing product manufactured by a new method;

- products defined by processes, properties or functional limitations *per se*; and
- chemicals or chemical compositions.

**19.10** In contrast, the following inventions are considered to possess structural features, so that they can be protected under a utility model:

- electronic circuitry structure defined by the definite connections between various electronic components; and
- composite layer structures.

**19.11** Therefore, electronic products or products involving new composite materials are not absolutely excluded.

**19.12** In general, in order to be protected as a utility model, the invention must possess a new feature which pertains to the shape and/or structure of the product incorporating the utility model or, in this author's words, 'can be seen or touched'. The mere fact that the product has shape and/or structure *per se* is *not* sufficient for utility model protection, but the shape/structural feature must be new.

## D. PATENTABILITY REQUIREMENTS

**19.13** Utility models and invention patents have literally the same patentability requirements except inventiveness. More precisely, the requirements on novelty, utility, and disclosure (on sufficiency, support and clarity) are exactly the same for utility models and invention patents.

**19.14** For the sake of clarity, the current Chinese Patent Act requires all kinds of inventions, including utility models, to be absolutely novel. That is, an invention must be new over anything available within China or abroad to the public before the application date or priority date if priority date is claimed.

**19.15** On the other hand, the inventiveness requirements towards invention patents and utility models according to Article 22(3) of the Chinese Patent Act are only literally different. More specifically, the inventiveness requirement requires invention patents to possess '*prominent* and substantive distinguishing features and to represent a *remarkable* improvement' whereas utility models only have to 'possess substantive distinguishing features and represent an improvement'. However, in practice such differences are negligible (see different opinion of *Bu*, chapter 3).

The Chinese Patent Examination Guidelines[1] substantiate the lower inventiveness requirement as to utility models as follows: 19.16

(1) Only literature in the technical field to which the utility model belongs shall be considered, unless prior art documents from neighboring or relevant technical fields prompt the skilled artisan to also consider these neighboring or relevant fields. In practice, however, prior art from neighboring or relevant fields is quite frequently considered.
(2) Normally, only one or two prior art documents shall be cited when assessing the inventive step, unless the utility model forms a simple combination of more than two pieces of prior art. In practice, however, the Re-examination Board actually invalidated various utility models by combining three or even four prior art documents.[2]

Therefore, patentability requirements on invention patents and utility models are basically the same, and if an invention patent has been found to be invalid, the corresponding utility model (if such exists) would also be found to be invalid, and *vice versa*. Therefore, when preparing the specification of a utility model, the same level of care should be applied as in the case of invention patent applications. 19.17

## E. PECULIARITIES OF UTILITY MODEL PROSECUTION

Utility models undergo a mere preliminary examination before grant. During such preliminary examination, in practice, only objections based on absolute grounds will be raised, for example if the invention contravenes public morale, pertains to non-patentable subject matter or if the application lacks clarity. No prior art search will be carried out during such preliminary examination. 19.18

By contrast, invention patents will be examined substantively. As for European or US patents, during substantive examination, prior art searches will be done, and a Chinese examiner may raise objections against non-conformity with any patentability requirements under the Chinese Patent Act, including novelty, inventiveness, clarity, sufficiency, and so on. 19.19

As mentioned, the above preliminary examination mechanism allows quick grant of utility models within 10 to 16 months from filing, which satisfies the major purpose of utility model protection. 19.20

1 Part IV, Chapter 6, 4.
2 See invalidation decisions WX14469 and WX14412 issued in 2010.

**19.21** Accordingly, as long as care has been taken to prepare the utility model application in a manner which avoids absolute grounds for objections, in particular by ensuring that the subject matter of the application can be protected as a utility model, a utility model application will proceed smoothly until grant.

**19.22** However, as no prior art search is carried out, patents are also granted in utility models which apparently lack novelty or inventiveness. In fact, a lot of apparently invalid utility models have already been granted. In one notorious case, the specification of a later granted utility model had been an exact copy of the specification of another, already granted utility model.

**19.23** Another difference between prosecution of utility models and prosecution of invention patents is that utility models are *not* published before grant. Utility models are only published once, in the course of grant, whereas invention patents are published twice (similar to EP and US patents). Therefore, it is not possible to submit third party observations during the prosecution of a utility model, as third parties cannot be aware of subject matter filed for utility model protection.

## F. SIMULTANEOUS FILING OF UTILITY MODEL AND INVENTION PATENT APPLICATION FOR THE SAME INVENTION

**19.24** It should be first noted that 'the same invention' according to the Chinese Patent Examination Guidelines[3] refers to those having exactly the same claims. Second, at present in China, there is no mechanism to convert a utility model to an invention patent, or *vice versa*.

**19.25** The advantages of simultaneous applications for both utility model and invention patent protection are:

- quick grant of a utility model patent;
- maintaining the chance of obtaining long term protection through an invention patent;
- the extra filing costs involved due to a utility model application are relatively low, in particular for foreign applicants, as the same Chinese specification will be used; and
- extra prosecution costs are relatively low, as utility models will not be substantively examined.

3 Part II, Chapter 3, 6.

Therefore, it is advisable to apply for both utility model and invention patent protection for the same invention whenever possible. To do so, the Chinese Patent Act requires the two applications (one for the utility model, one for the invention patent) to be filed on exactly the same date and to indicate that both utility model and invention patent applications are applied for for the invention at issue. However, the following restrictions should be noted: 19.26

- Filing one utility model application in China and one PCT application on the same date is *not* considered as fulfilling the above requirement.
- A PCT application cannot enter China and then be filed as both a utility model and invention application.

Therefore, it is currently not permitted to apply for both utility model and invention patent protection for the same invention through the PCT. In other words, such filing can only be done within the domestic priority period of 12 months. This may be another reason why foreign entities do not actively procure utility model protection, as they cannot use the PCT to file both utility model and invention patent applications in China. 19.27

## G. COMMERCIAL USE OF UTILITY MODELS

Just like inventions, utility models can be used to stop other parties from practicing the invention without the patentee's consent. Furthermore, the same provisions in the Chinese Patent Act on claim interpretation and remedies apply to both utility models and inventions. Therefore, as an enforcement tool, utility models are as effective as invention patents. 19.28

Of course, also when it comes to utility models as the subject matter of technology transfer, for example licensing or assignment, utility models are not treated differently from invention patents. 19.29

Also litigation procedures in People's Courts are basically the same with regard to both utility models and invention patents, except that where a utility model is at issue, the patentee is required to furnish a patentability evaluation report. Such report is to be elaborated by SIPO at the request of the patentee. The format of the report is similar to the International Search Report plus the Written Opinion pertaining to PCT applications. That is, the report quotes the relevant prior art documents and comments on the patentability (mainly novelty and inventiveness). The introduction of this report in the course of the 2008 amendment to the Chinese Patent Act aimed at mitigating the problem of too many junk utility models. 19.30

**19.31** Patent litigation in China follows a double-track system which is similar to the German separation principle. That is, infringement proceedings are handled by the courts, whereas invalidation proceedings are handled separately and independently by the Re-examination Board. Invalidation proceedings are usually used to stay infringement proceedings at the courts. Naturally, a negative patentability evaluation report will deter the patentee from enforcing the utility model, as such negative reports will be used in the corresponding invalidation proceedings. In contrast, the court will usually not stay the infringement proceedings if the patentee can present a positive evaluation report.

**19.32** Even though the vast majority of foreign entities refrain from seeking utility model protection, they should be aware of the fact that one day they may face infringement allegation based on a utility model owned by a Chinese entity, as in *Chint v Schneider*. In such a case, the patentability evaluation report is useful to assess the enforceability of the utility model.

## H. CONCLUSION

**19.33** The major differences between utility models and invention patents lie in the subject matter of protection, term of protection and peculiarities of prosecution. In any other respect, utility models and invention patents are not much different from each other, in particular when it comes to enforcement. As utility model patents are granted much quicker than invention patents, and as it is possible to apply for both utility model and invention patents for the same invention, this author suggests that applicants, in particular foreign applicants, should be more enthusiastic about utility model protection, provided that the subject matter of the respective invention is protectable under a utility model and also because the extra costs of utility model prosecution are comparably low.

# 20

# DESIGNS

**Deng Ming**



## A. INTRODUCTION

The Chinese patent system provides for easily and quickly obtainable industrial design protection. Designs are protected under the same Patent Act which also comprises invention patent and utility model protection. A separate Design Act does not exist in China. A design patent will be granted after passing a formality examination. The State Intellectual Property Office (SIPO) which is in charge of such examination has accelerated formality examination in recent years, so that it currently takes six months on average until a design patent is granted. The examination period may even be shortened to three months if the application is filed online. **20.01**

China does not provide for protection of unregistered designs as, for instance the European Community does, so that filing a design application forms the only path to industrial design protection. The maximum protection term for a design patent in China is currently ten years, which is shorter than in many other countries, so that the legislature is considering an extension to 15 **20.02** years in the course of the coming amendment to the Chinese Patent Act.[1] Such amendment would be a prerequisite for China to become a member of the Hague system.

**20.03** Twenty eight years after the entry into force of the Patent Act, China leads the world in terms of design applications. The huge number of design applications received by the Patent Office (657,582 in 2012 alone) and the fact that more than 90 per cent of these applications have been filed by domestic applicants demonstrate a huge domestic interest in design protection.[2] This phenomenon is, without doubt, due to the maturing of economic development in China, as well as being catalysed by the innovation stimulation policy of the central government and local authorities. On the other hand, many granted design patents are of low value, which is also reflected by recent official statistics which show that a large number of design patents owned by domestic holders are only maintained for a short period of time. 35.2 per cent of them expire within two years, 39.7 per cent within three years after the date of filing.[3] The Chinese government and legislature acknowledge the necessity of improving the quality of design patents filed by Chinese entities and individuals, and have taken various measures which become evident from the newly amended Patent Act and the relevant regulations.

**20.04** In comparison with many western countries, the Chinese practice of industrial design protection turns out to be peculiar in a number of aspects. This chapter aims at providing an insight into these peculiarities, that is, into the special aspects of the legal framework, examination, procedures related to the maintenance of the design, as well as enforcement-related issues of the Chinese design protection system.

## B. LEGAL FRAMEWORK

### 1. Definition of a design

**20.05** Article 2(4) of the Patent Act provides the following definition for designs:

> 'Design' means any new design of the shape, the pattern or their combination, or the combination of the colour with shape or pattern, of a product, which creates an aesthetic feeling and is fit for industrial application.

1 Draft of the fourth amendment of the Patent Act, issued by SIPO in January 2013.

2 Annual Report of SIPO 2012.

3 *China Intellectual Property News*, 7 April 2012.

In the course of interpreting this definition of designs, Chinese examiners and judges have developed a common understanding of the three elements of a design, namely shape, pattern and colour. However, their perception of the terms 'product', 'aesthetic feeling' and 'industrial application' may diverge. **20.06**

In accordance with the Examination Guidelines issued by SIPO in 2010,[4] the carrier of a design must be a product (which excludes articles of handicraft that cannot be reproduced in identical form), farm products, livestock products, and articles of nature. Products of parts and components, large scale equipment and two-dimensional matters of print are all products in the meaning of the Chinese Patent Act, even though some commentators put this into doubt.[5] **20.07**

The term 'aesthetic feeling' apparently constitutes a general limitation to design protection. In practice, it is neither possible nor necessary to use a uniform standard to judge whether or not a design evokes aesthetic feelings. So far, neither the Patent Re-examination Board (PRB) nor the courts have ever declared a design patent invalid due to lack of aesthetic appeal. The word 'aesthetic' means that in practice, when assessing whether a design meets the criteria to be protected as a design patent, the visual sensation of the appearance of the product shall be taken into consideration, not the function or technical effect of the product. **20.08**

Finally, to be fit for 'industrial application', the product which incorporates the design shall be capable of being used in industry and manufactured in quantity. **20.09**

### 2. Non-patentable designs

Generally, according to Article 5(1) of the Patent Act, a design patent shall not be granted for designs which are contrary to Chinese laws, contrary to Chinese social morality, or detrimental to the public interest. For example, a design of a bedsheet containing the pattern of the Chinese currency Renminbi, a design containing drawings of violence, or a design containing a famous building, for example, the Tian'anmen Gate, shall not be granted a design patent. **20.10**

4 Examination Guidelines, Part I, Chapter 3, 7.

5 Zhong Hua, 'A Study on Design Patent-eligible Subject Matters in China', [2012] **2** *China Patents & Trademarks* 56.

**20.11** In addition, the Examination Guidelines provide a long list of non-patentable subject-matter.[6] Foreign applicants should pay attention to the following three items contained in this list, because they can be protected in certain western countries:

(1) A design which is applied to a plain printed matter, made of patterns, colours, or their combination, and used mainly to identify the origin of the related product or service, except wallpapers and textiles;
(2) A component part of a product, which cannot be partitioned, or sold and used independently such as the heel of socks, the peak of a hat, the handle of a cup;
(3) A computer game interface or a pattern shown by a display device which is neither related to the interaction between humans and computers nor associated with the functions of a product, for example a wallpaper shown on an electronic screen, a picture showing the status 'turned on' or 'turned off' or the layout design of a webpage.[7]

Item (3) has been softened only recently, on 1 May 2014, in response to demands from foreign and domestic companies to extend design protection to graphical user interfaces (GUI), due to increased investment in this area.

## 3. Substantive requirements for design protection

**20.12** In accordance with Article 23 of the Patent Act, a patent design shall meet the following requirements:

(1) It shall not correspond to a prior design, which means any design known to the public before the filing date of the application of the design patent. No other application must have been filed for the same design with SIPO before the filing date of the application.
(2) It shall significantly differ from prior designs or the combination of features of prior designs.
(3) It must not be in conflict with a legitimate right obtained before the filing date of the application.

As there is no substantive examination carried out before the grant of a design patent, these requirements can be examined when the granted design patent is challenged by an invalidation request.

---

6 Examination Guidelines, Part I, Chapter 3, 7.4.

7 Order of SIPO Nr. 68

*(a) Absolute novelty*

The above requirement (1) means that China applies the absolute novelty standard to design patents. As defined in the Examination Guidelines, a prior design means any design known to the public through publication, use or any other way before the date of filing or the priority date. The absolute character of the novelty prerequisite is reflected by the absence of any restriction with regard to the means of disclosure, time, worldwide location and circles to whom the prior art has been made available.[8] **20.13**

There are two exceptions to the absolute novelty standard, however. First, a Chinese application for the same design which has been filed before but published on or after the filing date of the design patent at issue is considered to be a conflicting design patent application. In fact, such a conflicting application is to be considered by the examiner to assess whether or not its design is identical or substantially identical to the design patent concerned, even though it has not been available to the public before the filing date of the application at issue. The second exception is the grace period granted to designs published within six months before the filing date of the application. Pursuant to Article 24 Chinese Patent Act, such non-prejudicial disclosures are disclosures made at an international exhibition sponsored or recognized by the Chinese government, at an official academic or technological meeting or by any person without the consent of the applicant. **20.14**

It should be noted that apart from the two exceptions, no general grace period prior to filing a design application during which the applicant may disclose his or her design without destroying the novelty of the later-filed design application is available. **20.15**

*(b) Significant difference*

Requirement (2) mentioned above was introduced in the course of the third amendment to the Chinese Patent Act of 2009 with the purpose of improving the quality of Chinese design patents. Correspondingly, a new section has been added to the Examination Guidelines to introduce the approaches which may be used in invalidity procedures to assess whether or not a design is significantly different from a prior design or the combination of features of prior designs. These relatively new approaches will be further discussed in Section D.3 of this chapter. **20.16**

8 Examination Guidelines, Part IV, Chapter 5, 2.

*(c) No conflict with existing rights*

**20.17** A design patent which is in conflict with any other person's legitimate right obtained before the filing date of the design application shall be declared invalid. 'Legitimate right' refers to rights or interests which are recognized by Chinese laws and which are still valid at the filing date of the design application. They include trademark rights, copyright, rights to portrait and rights in special packaging or decoration of well-known goods.[9]

**20.18** 'Conflict' means that the design patent interferes with the subject-matter of a prior legitimate right in such a manner that its exploitation infringes upon the prior legitimate right. In the relevant invalidation procedure, the petitioner shall bear the burden of proof. He or she must prove, *inter alia*, that he or she is the legitimate holder of such right and that the right is valid.[10]

## C. PRELIMINARY EXAMINATION[11]

**20.19** The preliminary examination of design applications appears to be extremely strict from the point of view of many applicants, particularly those from western countries. In practice, it happens often that a foreign applicant, after filing a Chinese design application based on the corresponding application filed abroad, receives a notification to make rectification. Since communications between SIPO and the applicant due to the rectification of defects take at least two months, the design application should be prepared carefully according to the requirements of SIPO in order to get a grant of the design patent without a delay and additional costs. All possible defects of a design application are exhaustively listed in the Examination Guidelines as follows:

### 1. Drawings or photographs[12]

**20.20** The following circumstances are considered as defects of the drawings or photograph:

(1) The relation of projection of the views is wrong, for example, it is not in conformity with the rules of exact projection.

---

9 Examination Guidelines, Part IV, Chapter 5, 7.

10 Zhang Peng and Qian Yijun, 'Mechanism for and Application of Law to Design Patent Right Conflict Resolution', [2010] **2** *China Patents & Trademarks* 46.

11 Examination Guidelines, Part I, Chapter 3.

12 Examination Guidelines, Part I, Chapter 3, 4.2.

(2) The content of the design cannot be correctly expressed, because the drawings or photographs contain defects such as blinking, shadow and reflection.
(3) Lines which are used to show the product do not meet formality requirements, such as unallowable shadow line, indicative line, dotted line, central line, dimension line, or dot-dash line.
(4) The scale of various views is inconsistent, or the views are not sufficient to show the essential features involving multiple sides.
(5) In the case of a long and thin product, the middle part of the product which is omitted in the drawing is not illustrated using the double-parallel dash lines or using the natural geosutures.
(6) At the section or section surface of a sectional view, a line or symbol showing the place of the section is absent or incomplete.
(7) Where an enlarged view is provided, the location of the corresponding part is not indicated.

## 2. Request[13] and the brief explanation[14] [15]

The request shall indicate a name for the product incorporating the design. Such name is crucial for interpreting the protection scope of the design, as it is used to identify the category of the product as shown in the drawings or photographs. For example, an application may contain the same drawings or photographs displaying an automobile, but depending on whether it is named 'automobile' or 'toy automobile', the design would be assigned to totally different classes of product. **20.21**

In general, the name is required to be in conformity with the names listed in the subclass of the International Classification for Industrial Designs pursuant to the Locarno Agreement. In general, the use of the following names shall be avoided: **20.22**

(1) name of a person, a place, a nation, an entity, a trademark, a code or a model;
(2) improper generic or abstract names, such as 'musical instrument';
(3) names which describe the technical effect of the product, for example, 'fuel-saving engine';

13 Examination Guidelines, Part I, Chapter 3, 4.1.
14 Examination Guidelines, Part I, Chapter 3, 4.3.
15 Zhong Hua, 'Tentative Analysis of Role of Brief Description of Design in Patent Right Affirmation and Infringement Determination', [2010] 3 *China Patents & Trademarks* 17.

(4) names which specify size, scale, or numerical unit of the product, for example, '21-inch TV'.

**20.23** Since the third amendment of the Chinese Patent Act, it is mandatorily required that a design application shall contain a brief explanation as an integral part of the disclosure of the design application. It shall consist of different parts, which will be examined by the examiner according to the following requirements:

(1) Name of the product, which shall be the same as the name indicated in the request.
(2) Usage of the product, which determines the class of the product. The class of the product is an important basis for determining the protection scope of the design, which covers all identical and similar designs of identical or similar classes. Indication of the usage of the product is extremely important, in particular when the information on the usage of the product cannot be found in or cannot be directly and unambiguously derived from other documents of the application.
(3) Essential design features, that is, the major differences of the design in comparison with prior designs. However, the protection scope of a design should not depend on how the essential design features are described in the explanation, but on the class of the product incorporating the design as well as on the drawings or photographs. The described essential features should serve the purpose of helping the public to understand the design.
(4) Designation of one drawing or photograph for publication in the Design Patent Gazette, which should present the essential features of a design in the best way.
(5) Indication of colours if protection is also claimed for colours. It is worth noting that defining the extent of protection by colour is not necessarily tantamount to narrowing the protection scope, which is to be determined comprehensively in the light of the total visual effect the design creates. Usually, in the case of three-dimensional products, the shape attracts the most attention of normal consumers, whereas pattern and colour have a weaker impact on the whole visual effect. In contrast, if a two-dimensional product is at issue or if the entire shape of a three-dimensional product is a common design, pattern and colour have a stronger impact.
(6) Indication of other peculiarities, if applicable, such as symmetric view, omitted views, the basic design in case of applications of multiple similar designs, the name of a set of products, transparent material and new materials with a special visual effect.

### 3. Multiple designs in one application[16]

Article 31 Patent Act provides that a design application shall be limited to one design. Two or more similar designs for the same product or two or more designs which are incorporated in products belonging to the same class and are sold or used in sets may be filed as one application. 20.24

According to Rule 35(1) Implementing Regulations to the Chinese Patent Act, the specific requirements for filing an application containing multiple similar designs for the same product are: 20.25

(1) one of the designs shall be designated as the basic design;
(2) the other designs shall be similar to the basic one in the sense that the former ones differ from the latter only due to slight changes in some fine details, in the usual design of the product category, in the repeated and continuous arrangement of the same design unit or in colour elements;
(3) an application should not contain more than ten similar designs.

According to Rule 35(2) Implementing Regulations to the Chinese Patent Act, the specific requirements for filing an application with a plurality of designs which are incorporated in products sold or used in sets are: 20.26

(1) The products belong to the same class as defined in the International Classification for Industrial Designs but are independent from each other.
(2) The products shall be customarily sold and used at the same time, and shall have a collective value through their combination, for example, a bedding set which consists of a bedspread, a sheet and a pillow case, or a coffee set comprised of cups, coffee pot, milk pot and sugar pot.
(3) The products are designed with the same concept of design. This means that the designs of the shape, the pattern or their combination, or the combination of the colour with shape or pattern for all the products are unified.

In order to avoid confusion with practice in some other countries, the applicant should note that a design application with multiple designs incorporated in the products in a set shall not contain two or more similar designs of a product. If the examiner detects such cumulation of designs, he or she will require the applicant to delete the relevant designs or to file a divisional application.[17] If the 20.27

16 Examination Guidelines, Part I, Chapter 3, 9.

17 Wu Su, 'Examination of Designs for Products in Set Including Similar Designs', [2011] **2** *China Patents & Trademarks* 26.

requirements are not met, the examiner will issue a notification to amend the application. Where the applicant fails to eliminate the defect, the application will be rejected.

### 4. Priority

**20.28** In accordance with the Paris Convention, design applicants enjoy a priority period of six months. A prerequisite for a later-filed Chinese design application to enjoy a priority right over an earlier application is that the former claims priority for the subject-matter disclosed in the latter. To examine whether this prerequisite is met, the documents of the two applications, including drawings, photographs, brief explanations, and claims (in case of an earlier utility model application or a US design application), are compared with each other. In practice, foreign applicants should pay attention to the following issues when claiming priority:[18]

(1) In some foreign countries, several designs may be included in one application, whereas the Chinese provisions permit only one design per application, except for the two scenarios discussed in Section 3 above. That is, if the applicant wants to protect all the designs which are disclosed in an earlier-filed foreign application, he has to file a separate application for each design contained in the foreign application and base the priority for each of these designs on the foreign application.
(2) If the earlier foreign design application relates to a partial design which is indicated by using broken lines in the drawings, the applicant must change the broken lines to solid lines in the corresponding drawings of the Chinese application to enable priority of the foreign application. It may also happen that the examiner instructs the applicant to change the product name accordingly.
(3) Priority of an earlier foreign application can also be claimed if the foreign application lacks clarity or if its drawings or photographs contain errors as long as the foreign application still displays the entire design of the product and discloses the subject-matter to be claimed by the later application.
(4) If the earlier application contains a colour element, the later application which claims priority may or may not contain such colour element, as both versions, the one with and the one without the colour element, are considered to be disclosed by the earlier application. In contrast, if the

18 Zhong Hua, 'Exploration of Design Priority Examination', [2006] 1 *China Patents & Trademarks* 32.

earlier application does not contain such colour element, the later application may not add a colour element if it claims priority over the earlier application.

(5) Priority may also be claimed for earlier applications which do not contain a brief explanation. The Chinese application, however, must contain such brief explanation. The content of such explanations shall not go beyond the disclosure of the earlier application.

## D. ESSENTIAL PATENTABILITY REQUIREMENTS

A design patent can only be challenged in an invalidation procedure in the course of which the essential requirements for design protection are substantively examined. Similar to the novelty and the inventive step requirements with regard to invention and utility model patents, novelty and 'significant difference' are the two most important requirements for the patentability of a design. The approaches used by the SIPO to assess if a design meets these requirements are specified in the Examination Guidelines.[19] They can be outlined as follows: **20.29**

### 1. The 'normal consumer'[20]

The assessment of novelty and significant difference as compared to prior designs should be based on the knowledge and abilities of a hypothetical person, the 'normal consumer'. **20.30**

Depending on the kind of design product, the notion of the normal consumer may change but, in general, a normal consumer is characterized as follows: **20.31**

(1) He or she has a common knowledge of the design patent incorporated in the same or similar product and of the relevant commonly used designing methods such as the knowledge of the transformation, mosaic or replacement of a design. For example, a normal consumer in the area of the automotive industry will be aware of car models on the market and will have general information about cars available from frequently shown advertisements in the media.

(2) He or she will have a certain capability to distinguish differences in shape, pattern and colour between products of the same class which incorporate different designs, without having to pay attention to minor differences in shape, pattern and colour.

19 Examination Guidelines, Part IV, Chapter 5.

20 Examination Guidelines, Part IV, Chapter 5, 4.

## 2. Assessment of novelty[21]

20.32 Assessment of the novelty of a design patent according to Article 23(1) Chinese Patent Act means to examine whether prior art comprises a design which is identical or substantially identical with the patented design. It will be made by combining overall observation of and comprehensive judgment to the patented design and the prior design as a whole rather than some parts or locations of the two designs, on grounds of the cognitive capability of the hypothetical normal consumer, as mentioned above.

20.33 Identity between the two designs means that they pertain to the same product category and that all their design elements, that is, shape, pattern and colour, are identical. Other product elements, such as different materials, functions, internal structures or product dimensions do not impact on the assessment of identity. Products of the same category refer to the products that have completely the same use. For example, a mechanical watch and an electronic watch are of the same category, since they have the same use, although they have different internal structures. In practice, in order to determine whether the two designs pertain to the same product category, the examiner may refer to the titles of the designs, the international classification for the designs and the shelf classifications of the relevant products.

20.34 The assessment as to whether the two designs are substantially identical will not be made unless they pertain to the same product category or to similar categories. If two products have similar uses, for example, a toy and a tiny ornament, they are considered to be products of similar categories. If two products have multiple uses, some of which are the same, the examiner will also consider them to be products pertaining to similar categories. For example, a watch equipped with an MP3 player and a watch with other functions are regarded as belonging to similar categories. The two designs will be considered to be substantially identical if a normal consumer, upon comparing the two designs, only sees the following minor differences:

(1) The difference is only in a slight change of some fine details which cannot be noticed by paying normal attention to the product, for example, the difference in the number of slats between two designs of venetian blind.
(2) The difference exists in the parts which cannot be seen easily or at all when the designs are in use, unless, exceptionally, there is evidence showing that the special design in those parts has a notable visual effect on a normal consumer.

21 Examination Guidelines, Part IV, Chapter 5, 5.

(3) The difference is due to the substitution of one design element by a design element which is commonly known for the relevant product category, for example, a difference resulting from changing the shape of a cookie jar from a cube to a cuboid.
(4) The design patent is simply a repeated and continuous arrangement of the other design following the conventional arrangement of the relevant category of product, for example, the repeated arrangement of the rows of the seats in a cinema.
(5) The two designs form a mirror image.

The comparison of the designs will be based on the immediate visual impression, not on the use of magnifiers, microscopes, chemical analysis or other instruments or methods. That is, parts or elements which are not immediately perceived by eye shall remain unconsidered. Only the appearance of the product shall be taken into account, that is, the visual effect produced by the elements of shape, pattern and colour of a product, or the combination thereof. **20.35**

The patented design is identified as outlined in the drawings or photographs, with the help of the brief explanation. Where the drawings or photographs of the comparative prior design do not display all the views of the product, the extent of the disclosure of the prior design will be determined based on the cognitive capability of a normal consumer. If differences between the patented design and the potentially identical or similar design pertain to parts of the latter which remained undisclosed in the drawings or photographs and which usually do not draw the attention of a normal consumer when using the design product, they will not be considered to be sufficient to influence the overall visual effect of the product. **20.36**

Generally, in the examination of the novelty, the design patent will be compared with only one prior design, rather than with two or more in combination. If the design patent, however, contains several designs for a set of products or several similar designs for a product, each of these designs is to be separately compared with potentially identical or similar designs pertaining to prior art. **20.37**

In specific cases where a design patent at issue has been granted for a product comprising at least two components, the novelty of the design patent will be assessed differently in dependence on the impression of the product given to a normal consumer. If the components of the product are used in a fixed form of assembly, a normal consumer will have an impression of the overall design of the assembled product, for example, an electronic kettle assembly comprising a kettle and a heater. In such a case, the design patent may be compared with a combination of as many prior designs as the number of the components, as long **20.38** as those prior designs have a clear interrelation of assembly constituting a single design. In contrast, where the components of the product can be assembled with different options so that a normal consumer obtains separate impressions of the designs for the components, for example, some toy comprising many plug-in units, or where the product can be used without the need to assemble its components together, such as poker cards and chess pieces, the normal consumer will have an impression of the design of each individual component. In such a case, the assessment will target the appearance of each component.

### 3. Assessment of significant difference[22]

**20.39** A further essential and substantive prerequisite for design protection is that the design patent should significantly differ from the prior design or from the combination of features of the prior designs. The Examination Guidelines categorize all the circumstances where this prerequisite is not fulfilled into the following three scenarios:

(1) The patented design is not significantly different from a comparative prior design incorporated in a product in the same or approximate category.
(2) The patented design is obtained through a transformation of a prior design, where the design features of the former are identical to or only slightly different from those of the latter and the transformation has been inspired.
(3) The patented design is obtained through a combination of prior designs or of features of the prior designs, where the design features of the combination are identical to or only slightly different from those of the corresponding part of the patented design and the combination has been inspired.

**20.40** In scenario (1), the examiner will assess whether the difference between the patented design and the comparative prior design has a notable impact on the overall visual effect of the product. The examiner will make such assessment from the point of view of a normal consumer on a comprehensive observation of the designs. Only when the examiner establishes a significant difference based on the assessment, can the design at issue be considered patentable. In order to make an objective judgement, the following factors will be taken into account:

22 Examination Guidelines, Part IV, Chapter 5, 6.

(a) A high degree of attention will be paid to those design parts which can be easily perceived while the design product is in use. Differences pertaining to these parts shall have a more notable influence on the overall visual effect than differences which cannot be easily seen or not be seen at all.
(b) If the design of certain parts turns out to pertain to a commonly known design with respect to the product category at issue, the differences pertaining to the other parts should be given special weight when assessing the impact on the overall visual effect.
(c) A specific shape which is exclusively determined by the function of the product shall, in general, not have a notable impact on the overall visual effect.
(d) Minor differences with regard to fine details do not suffice to notably impact on the overall visual effect.

It should also be mentioned that the significant difference between a patented design and a prior design may be emphasized by additional views of different working states of the design patent, if appropriate, such as an adjustable height baby pushchair and a fold-type mobile phone. In a recent invalidation case, PRB concluded that the different working states, for example, the extendable and retractable configurations of the design for a key ring, are of interest and use to the normal consumer and should therefore be considered as a whole when compared with prior designs. In this case, the design patent with different working states was upheld, since PRB considered that none of the prior designs cited by the invalidation requester was of such different working states.[23] Based on this decision of PRB, applicants should, where a design has one or more working states, file additional views of the design to demonstrate its different states, which makes the design less vulnerable in an invalidation procedure. **20.41**

In scenarios (2) and (3), the examiner may determine one comparative prior design pertaining to a product category which may be the same as, similar to or different from the category of the product which incorporates the patented design. The examiner will then compare the selected comparative prior design or its design features with the corresponding parts of the design at issue and, if he or she finds no or only minor differences upon comparison, decide whether the transformation or combination has been inspired by the compared prior design (or by other prior designs in scenario (3)). If the inspiration is available, the examiner shall judge that the patented design is not significantly different from the prior design or from the combination of features of the prior designs, unless the transformation or combination produces a unique visual effect. **20.42**

---

23 The PRB's Examination Decision No. 16897/2011.

**20.43** The above-mentioned transformation is considered to have been inspired by the prior design if the design at issue obtained through the transformation merely adopts basic geometric shapes, with slight changes, displays a natural object or scenery, simulates the entire shape, pattern and colour of a well-known building or work, or is a design for a product such as a toy, decoration or food, which is obtained through the transformation from a design of another category of product. An obvious inspiration of the above-mentioned combination is given if the design patent is obtained by merely aggregating multiple prior designs, possibly with slight changes, or by replacing, with slight changes, some features of one prior design by features of another prior design of a product belonging to the same or similar category.

**20.44** Recently, some senior examiners of PRB have further developed the approach for assessing the significant difference of designs obtained through a combination of prior designs.[24] [25] Similar to the approach to assessing the inventive step of a patent, this approach consists of following three stages:

- Selecting the closest design from the prior designs, that is, the design which is most relevant to the design patent at issue, pertaining to the same or approximate category of product, the most similar composition of product and the most relevant overall visual effect.
- Identifying the distinctive features of the patented design, that is, those which distinguish it from the closest prior design.
- Determining whether the identified distinctive features are obvious to the normal consumer, that is, whether there is an inspiration given by prior designs to add the distinctive features to the closest prior design so as to obtain the design patent. Hereby, the inspiration shall be considered to be given if the distinctive features:
  - are only insignificant differences in small details without substantial impact on the overall visual effect;
  - can be combined to the closest prior design based on the common knowledge of design;
  - are identical with or differ only slightly from the features of another prior design which pertains to the same product category or does not take a product as its carrier.

24 Zhong Hua, 'A Study on Improvement of Design Determination Methods', [2011] **3** *China Patents & Trademarks* 30.

25 Wu Bing, 'Determination of "Combination" in Assessment of Design Patentability', [2012] **4** *China Patents & Trademarks* 39.

In fact, the approach mentioned above has been used by the examiners of PRB in some invalidation procedures.[26 27 28] It may find its way into the Examination Guidelines in the course of a coming amendment. 20.45

## E. DEBATED ISSUES WITH REGARD TO DESIGN ENFORCEMENT

### 1. 'Normal consumer' as the reference person who determines infringement

Article 59(2) of the Chinese Patent Act provides that 'the drawings or photographs of a design patent incorporated in a product shall determine the extent of protection of the design …', that is, it clearly states that the subject-matter of protection shall be the design incorporated in a product. Based on Items 8 and 11 Judicial Interpretation of Several Issues Concerning Application of Law to Trial of Cases of Dispute Arising from Patent Infringement Issued by the Supreme People's Court (SPC) in December 2009 ('the Judicial Interpretation of the SPC'), the determination of design infringement depends on the assessment of whether the design of the allegedly infringing product is identical with or similar to the subject-matter of the design patent. However, a clear definition of the reference person in the eyes of whom another design infringes upon the patented design is not available. The 'normal consumer' according to the Examination Guidelines (see also Section D.1 above) only decides whether a patented design corresponds to prior designs. 20.46

In a set of non-binding interpretation guidelines issued in 2001 (*Ganea*, chapter 16), the Higher People's Court of the City of Beijing provides that 'The establishment of infringement of a design patent should be based on the aesthetic and observational capability of a normal consumer, not on that of a person skilled in the art of the design patent. The normal consumers, as a group of particular consumers, refer to those who buy or use the products which are identical with or similar to the product of the same class incorporating the design patent.'[29] However, this provision still does not provide a clear definition of the normal consumer, when the buyer and the user of the product are different persons. Such ambiguous definition of the normal consumer may entail different conclusions in similar cases as to whether a design is identical with or similar to the design patent, that is, whether it constitutes infringement. 20.47

26 The PRB's Examination Decision No. 17909.

27 The PRB's Examination Decision No. 17904.

28 The PRB's Examination Decision No. 17447.

29 Opinions on Several Issues Relating to Patent Infringement Adjudication issued by the Beijing Higher People's Court in 2001.

This problem can be demonstrated by a recent case decided by the Higher People's Court of Jiangsu Province[30] which will be outlined below.

**20.48** The plaintiff, holder of the design patent 'a flying-like high pressure sodium lamp', accused the defendant of infringing his patent by making street lamps and installing them on the street. The Higher People's Court, as well as the court of previous instance held that infringement should be determined from the perspective of pedestrians who were to be regarded as the normal consumers and users with regard to this product category, not from that of the purchasers of street lamps. As the pedestrians could observe the street lamp only from a certain distance, they should not be able to distinguish the allegedly infringing product from the product incorporating the design patent from the main and bottom views which both showed only minor differences between the two products. Therefore, the Higher People's Court's judgment confirmed the decision of the previous instance, stating that normal consumers were likely to visually confuse one product with the other, so that infringement must be established.

**20.49** If the courts had instead determined that the purchasers of street lamps should be regarded as normal consumers who would have been capable of looking at the lamps from a closer distance, more significant differences between the two designs may have been observed.

**20.50** In accordance with Item 10 Judicial Interpretation of the SPC, the People's Courts should assess identity or similarity on grounds of the knowledge and cognitive capacity of normal consumers of the products incorporating the design. This provision, however, also remains silent on the question of how to proceed if buyers and users belong to two different groups of people.

**20.51** Actually, there are two different views about the reference person who determines infringement. One view is that design infringement should be determined from the perspective of a normal consumer with regard to the question of whether the allegedly infringing product creates confusion with or misidentification of the product which incorporates the protected design. The other view is that determination of infringement should be made from the perspective of a person who is ordinarily skilled in the art and who comprehensively considers mode and state of use of the product at issue. The former view seems to point to direct users or those who appreciate the aesthetic appeal of designs, whereas the

30 The Jiangsu Higher People's Court's Civil Judgment No. Suminsanzhongzi 0061/2007.

latter seems to regard the normal user as a person with a certain degree of specialization in the respective design field.[31]

A clearer definition of the normal consumer seems to be necessary and should be considered by future Judicial Interpretations of the SPC. **20.52**

## 2. Design protection of invisible products

Also with regard to the question as to whether or not design elements which are invisible in the course of use of the design product shall be protected, there are currently two opposing views in China. **20.53**

On the one hand, many patents in such designs could be granted by SIPO. For example, around 30,000 design patents have been granted in section steel components which become invisible after construction is finished. The Examination Guidelines,[32] for instance, provide that 'as the contour of the cross section of section steel is usually rectangle, the change in other parts of the cross section has a more notable effect' whereby they affirm that such invisible designs are patentable. This view is also supported by the argument that such designs are based on people's technical invention-creations which should be encouraged.[33] **20.54**

The other view, however, is that the shape of the cross section of the section steel is entirely dictated by functional considerations, so that it should not be the subject-matter of design patent protection. The technical solution incorporated in such a shape may instead be protected by an invention patent or utility model. The legislative aim of design protection would not be to promote technical progress, but to spur the creation of aesthetically appealing product designs. Supporters of this view even suggest that a court which handles an infringement case does not even need to suspend the infringement procedure due to a parallel invalidation request if the design patent at issue remains invisible in the course of using the product. The court should instead directly decide that the accusation of infringement is not tenable, as a hidden design could not cause any visual confusion among consumers.[34] **20.55**

---

31 Zhou Xiaobing, 'Issues Relating to Standards for Determination of Design Patent Infringement', [2008] **4** *China Patents & Trademarks* 40.

32 Examination Guidelines, Part IV, Chapter 5, 6.1.

33 Wang Xiajun (ed.), 'Protection of Design of Section Steel Products carried in the Design Examination Department of SIPO', *Designs and IP Protection*, the Publishing House of Intellectual Property 2002, 40.

34 Zhang Xiaodu, 'How to construe "Aesthetic Appeal" in Definition of Design in the PL', [2013] **1** *China Patents & Trademarks* 42.

### 3. Deviating designs

**20.56** The creative leeway of a designer to develop a design can also be regarded as the extent of possible design variations subject to technical constraints such as type, material and function of the design product. Even though the Chinese Patent Act, the Implementing Regulations and the Examination Guidelines do not contain any provision on such leeway, it has become one of the factors considered in the judicial assessment of the patentability of designs.[35] It can be expected that the consideration of the leeway a designer has will soon be introduced to China's design protection system. Hereby, two recent landmark cases which had been reviewed by the SPC in the final instance are likely to play a guiding role.

**20.57** In 2010, the SPC reviewed an administrative case involving the invalidation of a design patent for the product category 'motorcycle wheel'. When determining the similarity of the disputed design and the prior design, the courts at three levels arrived at different conclusions. The Intermediate People's Court No.1 of the City of Beijing and the Higher People's Court of the City of Beijing both considered the leeway for designing a motorcycle wheel comprehensively as a whole and concluded that as the design leeway of a motorcycle wheel is considerably limited by the function of the product, the disputed design should be patentable.[36] [37] The SPC, however, analysed the rim, spoke and hub of the wheel separately and concluded that as a motorcycle wheel was limited by its function, the design of the rim and hub were also limited with regard to possible variations, but the spoke could have been made in a variety of shapes as long as it met the requirement of equilibrium of forces. All three decisions were based on the consideration of the leeway for possible designs, yet the SPC arrived at a decision which is completely different from the opinion of the two lower courts.[38]

**20.58** In another recent administrative case involving a dispute over the invalidation of a design for an SUV made by Honda, the SPC considered the high density of the prior designs in the automotive field, the convergence of the contours of automobiles, and, therefore, the limited space for design variations in this area. Accordingly, it ruled that a relatively small difference as compared to prior designs could also be regarded as a notable innovation in the eyes of 'average

35 Mao Jin and Qian Yijun, 'Reflection on Introduction of Design Space Element in Determination of Design Patent', [2012] **4** *China Patents & Trademarks* 31.

36 The Beijing Nr. 1 Intermediate People's Court's Administrative Judgment No. Yizhongzhixingchuzi 2556/2009.

37 The Beijing Higher People's Court's Administrative Judgment No. Gaoxingzhongzi 448/2010.

38 The Supreme People's Court's Administrative Judgment No. Xingtizi 6/2010.

consumers', and that even such comparably slight difference would be likely to produce a distinctive overall visual effect.[39] Obviously, this ruling has enhanced the eligibility of SUV designs for patent protection.

## 4. Evaluation report

According to Article 61(2) Chinese Patent Act, where an infringement dispute relates to a design, the People's Court or the administrative authorities for patent affairs may ask the patentee or any interested party to furnish an evaluation report produced by SIPO. At the request of the patentee or an interested party, SIPO shall conduct a formality examination and a search on the relevant design patent, analyse and evaluate whether the design patent is in conformity with all the requirements of the Patent Act, and issue an evaluation report within two months from receiving the request.[40] **20.59**

It should be mentioned that 'interested party' refers to a person who has the right to file a law suit or to request the administrative authority to handle the patent dispute, for example, the patentee, the exclusive licensee or the non-exclusive licensee who has been authorized by the patentee to act in his or her name. **20.60**

In order to evaluate the design, all requirements to be met by a design patent should be examined, and, if necessary, a search should be carried out in respect of all the drawings or photographs of the design, whereby the brief explanation should also be considered. If the design is found to be not patentable, the report should contain a corresponding evaluation and conclusion and, where applicable, the reference documents should be cited. **20.61**

Mistakes in the report may be corrected at the discretion of the responsible department of SIPO or at the request of the petitioner. In such case, the petitioner shall file a request for review of the report. However, the report may not be challenged by the petitioner, as it does not form an administrative decision of SIPO. **20.62**

Where two or more persons request an evaluation report in respect of the same design, SIPO will make only one evaluation report. Upon issuance, the report will be made available for inspection by any third party. **20.63**

39 The Supreme People's Court's Administrative Judgment No. Xingtizi 6/2010.

40 Examination Guidelines, Part V, Chapter 10, 3.

**20.64** In practice, in order to determine whether it is necessary to suspend the infringement procedure, the courts always consider both the evaluation report as an important piece of evidence and other evidence provided by the alleged infringer supporting the invalidation of the design patent.

**20.65** Even though the Patent Act has specified that the evaluation report can be used as evidence, its effect is definitely not equivalent to an invalidation decision. Even if the evaluation report concludes that the patent in suit is valid, such conclusion does not oblige the People's Courts to refrain from suspending infringement litigation. The courts can decide at their own discretion, taking into account the likelihood of an invalidation of the disputed patent. From a People's Court's point of view, the evaluation report is not the only factor to be considered when deciding about a suspension. Instead, the court should comprehensively assess the likelihood of an invalidation based on the evaluation report and the grounds of invalidation raised by the defendant, as well as any other relevant evidence he or she presents. If the report evaluates the patentability of the design positively also on grounds of the other evidence raised by the defendant, the infringement procedure should not be suspended. Otherwise, if the alleged infringer provides new evidence which has not been considered by the report, in particular evidence which, in the eyes of the judge, renders invalidation likely, infringement litigation should be suspended. This way to proceed corresponds exactly to the handling of utility model search reports by the Intermediate People's Court No.1 of the City of Beijing before the third amendment to the Chinese Patent Act, when a search report had to be furnished only in the case of utility model disputes. Due to the good experience of utility model search reports in the past, design evaluation reports should be handled in the same manner.[41]

### 5. 'Prior design defence'

**20.66** As a judicial doctrine, the prior art or prior design defence had been in existence before the third amendment of the Patent Act. Making such defence against a design patent seems to be more justifiable than a corresponding defence against an invention patent which has been examined as to substance. In the case of a prior design defence, the court does not examine the patentability of the disputed design but only determines whether or not the alleged infringer uses a design which has been in public use or been published before the application date of the disputed design. In practice, alleged infringers often refrain from initiating an invalidation procedure which is costly and time consuming, but

41 Zhang Guangliang, 'Reflection on Patent Evaluation Report System in China', [2010] **3** *China Patents & Trademarks* 84.

prefer to simply raise such a prior design defence. The prior design defence has the potential to effectively restrain the abuse of design patents and open a simple procedural route for the resolution of patent disputes.[42]

In the past, however, some controversies have evolved around the application of the prior art or prior design defence in judicial practice. In some cases, the defence has even given rise to abusive practices, for example, by courts which protected local infringers (so-called 'local protectionism') or to confuse judges.[43] **20.67**

Meanwhile, in the course of the third amendment to the Chinese Patent Act, the prior art defence (which includes the prior design defence) has been elevated to a legal provision. Article 62 of the Chinese Patent Act provides that 'in a patent infringement dispute, if the alleged infringer has evidence proving that the technology or design he exploited is a prior technology or design, the exploitation does not constitute an infringement of the patent right'. To enhance the enforceability of this provision, Item 14(1) Judicial Interpretation of the SPC provides that 'Where all the technical features allegedly falling within the extent of protection of the patent right are identical with or not substantially different from the corresponding technical features of one existing technical solution, the courts shall conclude that the technical art exploited by the alleged infringer belongs to prior art or prior design as provided by Article 62 Patent Act'. Obviously, the above provisions of the Patent Act and the Judicial Interpretation of the SPC are different in the steps for applying the prior art defence. The express provisions now contained in the Patent Act and the Judicial Interpretation of the SPC should reduce the danger of controversial interpretations and enhance the predictability of court decisions. **20.68**

Assessing the conformity of a prior art defence with Article 62 requires a comparison of the allegedly infringing design with the prior design, whereas the corresponding assessment based on Item 14(2) Judicial Interpretation of the SPC is to be made by two steps, that is, to determine which features of the allegedly infringing design fall within the protection scope of the design patent in suit, and to compare those features, which fall within the protection scope of the design patent, with the prior design. Obviously, the judgement under Article 62 Chinese Patent Act may be stricter for the alleged infringer than that under Item 14(2) Judicial Interpretation of the SPC, since the latter may be made only with respect to features falling within the scope of the design patent, **20.69**

42 The Intellectual Property Tribunal of the Beijing Higher People's Court, 'Several Issues in Hearing Design Patent Cases', [2009] **2** *China Patents & Trademarks* 17.

43 Cheng Yongshun, 'Legislative Progress in Protection of Design Patent and Exploration of Enforcement', [2009] **2** *China Patents & Trademarks* 40.

which may be less than all features of the design of the alleged infringing product and which, thus, may be more easily found to be disclosed by a prior design. Which of these judgement methods will be applied should depend on the choice of the accused infringer, since the prior art or design defence is a cause of a defence.[44]

**20.70** This means that, if the prior design defence were to be based on Article 62 Chinese Patent Act alone, the alleged infringer would find it more difficult to prove that his or her design pertains to prior art, since all features of the exploited design have to be compared with prior art. Only if the whole design corresponds to such prior art can the prior art defence be successful. Item 14(2) Judicial Interpretation of the SPC, however, facilitates the situation of the alleged infringer, as it clarifies that only those parts of his or her design which fall into the scope of the patented design should become subject-matter of the comparison with prior art. Only if the defendant holds that all features of the design he or she uses pertain to prior art, will the court consider solely on grounds of Article 62 Chinese Patent Act whether the defence is tenable. In cases where the alleged infringer can find a prior design which comprises only those features which fall within the scope of the design patent in suit but not all features of the alleged design, the court should decide about the tenability of the defence in accordance with Item 14(2) Judicial Interpretation of the SPC.[45]

**20.71** In a design infringement case, which was recently reviewed by the SPC, the defendant who was accused of infringing upon a patented design over a tyre, made his prior design defence according to Item 14(2) Judicial Interpretation of the SPC. The first and second instance courts held the prior design defence tenable on the grounds that the design of the alleged infringing product was similar to the prior design as a whole because the difference between the two designs, on which the owner of the design patent insists, had no significant impact on the overall visual effect.[46, 47] Interestingly, the decisions of the previous courts were overturned by the SPC, the ruling of which can be summarized as follows.

**20.72** The previous two courts did not correctly compare the design used by the defendant with the prior design, which ignored the distinguishing features of the former over the latter and thus led to the wrong judgment. In the present case, where the design used by the defendant, the prior design and the design

---

44 Zhang Guangliang, 'Rules Applicable to the Prior Art Defence: Difference in Law Provisions and Analysis Thereof', [2010] **2** *China Patents & Trademarks* 55.

45 Ibid.

46 Beijing No. 2 Intermediate People's Court (2007) Civil First Instance No. 391.

47 Beijing Higher People's Court (2007) Civil Final No. 1552.

patent are similar to each other, these three designs should all be compared with each other. After comparing the design patent with the prior design, the impact on the overall visual effect created by the distinguishing features of the former over the latter can be determined. Upon this determination, it can be judged comprehensively that the design used by the defendant is of the same distinguishing features as mentioned above and, thus, differs from the prior design. Therefore, the prior design defence is not tenable according to Item 14(2) Judicial Interpretation of the SPC.[48]

Without doubt, the totally new method adopted by the SPC to judge the tenability of the prior design defence in this case will have a large impact on the courts, particularly those that have handled cases of prior design defence using different methods in the past. **20.73**

### 6. Design of a product consisting of several components

In a case where a design application pertains to a product consisting of several components, called also a combination product, the individual components have to be shown in the different views indicated in the application, which seems to be somewhat similar to the requirements raised with regard to designs for products sold in sets or for similar designs under one application. Such similarity, however, is only superficial, as the single components of a combination product are not protected in the same manner as the designs for products sold in sets or similar designs filed in one application. **20.74**

One difference between the above-mentioned design categories becomes evident in the course of the invalidation procedure. Whereas a design patent related to products in sets or to several similar designs in one application can be partially invalidated if one of the respective designs is found to be non-patentable, non-patentability of one component of a combination product inevitably results in the invalidity of the whole combination design.[49] **20.75**

To date, courts have dealt with designs pertaining to combination products by referring to the practice of invalidation proceedings in SIPO, as the Chinese Patent Act and its accompanying regulations do not contain express provisions on this issue. Designs for products sold in sets or similar designs filed in one application are enforceable in respect of each of the products in a set or each of the similar designs in the application. That is, infringement can be determined **20.76**

48 The SPC's Decision (2012) Civil Arraignment No. 189.

49 Wang Meifang, 'Protection of and Application for Patent for Designs incorporated in Combination Products', [2012] **3** *China Patents & Trademarks* 60.

if only one of the products pertaining to the set or only one of the similar designs has been imitated. However, in the case of combination products, the components will be considered to be parts of the product, so that they cannot be separately enforced. That is, if only one component is imitated, the design patent for the combination product is not necessarily infringed upon, as infringement should be established on grounds of all components of the combination product. For example, in a case which involved a steam cleaner comprising a main part, to which a glass-cleaning head or an ironing brush were optionally assembled as further components, the court decided that 'the plaintiff's design is different from the defendant's product only in that one part, the glass cleaning head, is absent from the defendant's product, so that the defendant's product is similar to the plaintiff's product if it is used in one of two possible manners of use. Hence, the defendant's design is to be regarded as similar to the plaintiff's design.' Obviously, this judgment was based on the overall appearance of the patented design to which further components were added for specific uses, not on the designs of the separate components.[50]

**20.77** That is, if certain components of a combination product can be sold and used independently, the design applicant is well-advised to file additional applications for each component to seek protection for both the combination product as well as for its individual components. Hereby, it is important to note that a design application for a whole combination product cannot be based on foreign design applications for the individual components, that is, the later Chinese application will not meet the requirement of claiming priority if only such applications for each component were filed abroad. In order to avoid such problem, the applicant is recommended to file an additional foreign application for the design of the whole combination product which would then serve as the basis for a priority claim in the later Chinese application.

50 The Beijing No. 1 Intermediate People's Court Civil Judgment No. Yizhongminchuzhi 10522/2003.

# Part G

# INTRODUCTION TO THE PATENT SYSTEM IN CHINESE TAIPEI (TAIWAN)

# 21

# INTRODUCTION TO THE PATENT SYSTEM IN CHINESE TAIPEI (TAIWAN)

**Liu Kung-Chung and Lee Su-Hua**



## A. GENERAL OBSERVATIONS

The shelf life of a statutory IP law in Chinese Taipei (Taiwan) is rather short. So far, the Trademark Act has been revised 13 times in 84 years, with an average life cycle of 7.2 years. The Patent Act has been revised 11 times in 70 years, with an average life cycle of 6.3 years, whereas the Copyright Act has seen 16 revisions 21.01

in 86 years with an average life cycle of only 5.4 years. The frequent amendment of statutory IP laws cannot be explained by the rapid pace of technological change and societal needs alone. The inability of the judiciary to further the development of IP law by clarifying the existing provisions and pointing out the new direction of IP law,[1] and the activism on the part of the IP Office (TIPO) and its technocrats to alleviate pressure from the US by constantly revising IP laws also play an important role. The activism of technocrats pre-empts the judiciary and destabilizes the IP statutory law itself. As a consequence, the development of IP law in Taiwan is largely equivalent to 'new amendment' of statutory IP law. The proper balance between statutory IP law and adjudicated IP law has yet to be struck. The IP technocrats need to wait patiently and the judiciary needs to decide cases on their merit and substantively solve the legal disputes.

**21.02** A recent empirical study of decisions on patent adjudicated by the IP Court from 1 July 2008 to 31 October 2010 shows a disturbingly low success rate. Of 154 first instance cases, only 10 decisions favoured plaintiffs, 11 decisions partially favoured plaintiffs, and in as many as 133 cases the rulings were against plaintiffs. The statistics in second-instance cases are quite similar, namely, in most cases the plaintiffs lost.[2] Whether the trend will continue is worthy of further study.

## B. SUBSTANTIVE PATENT LAW: THE NEWLY AMENDED PATENT ACT

**21.03** Beginning from 2006, TIPO conducted 23 public hearings and came to the conclusion that there was a need to overhaul the Patent Act. After five years of preparation, the Patent Act was revised and promulgated by the President on 21 December 2011 and took effect on 1 January 2013.

### 1. Driving force

#### *(a) Viewing the Patent Act as an economic policy instrument*

**21.04** The main driving force behind this was the following consideration: 'In order to encourage *industrial innovation and R&D*, to enhance the *economic strength and*

---

1 Taiwan has a so-called 'precedent' system which allows the Supreme Courts (including the Supreme Administrative Court) to choose from the decisions they rendered the precedent status which legally binds all courts until the Supreme Courts think otherwise. To date, there has not been any precedent on the Patent Act, which to some extent means that the Supreme Courts have failed to solve legal disputes authoritatively and conclusively.

2 Ming-Yan Shieh and Su-Hua Lee in Kung-Chung Liu and Reto Hilty (eds.), *The Enforcement of Patents*, The Hague: Kluwer Law International 2012, 205–206.

*industrial competitiveness*, to promote domestic industries that are listed among the Six Newly Developed Industries such as biotechnology, green energy and high-end agriculture, to improve the *patent examination quality* and to *further harmonize* the highly international patent regime with international norms to cope with the impact from globalization.'[3] In a nutshell, the revision was driven by the perception that with the improvement of patent examination quality and further harmonization with international standards, patent law can work as a policy instrument for economic policy.

#### (b) *The obsession of technocrats with wording*

The revision was large in scale, deleting 15 articles, amending 108 articles, and adding 36 new articles. Only 15 articles remained unchanged. As a consequence, the articles have again been totally renumbered. The Patent Act in its renumbered form looks less familiar. One cannot help wondering the wisdom of such a massive revamping. Would it not make the Patent Act less constant and stable and less readily accessible to its users?[4] It might have been the mentality of the technocrats that perfection in wording makes the law more professional to them. **21.05**

### 2. The thrust of the revision

Among other things, such as reinstatement of rights[5] and adding a grace period for disclosing an invention in a publication by the applicant, the following points are worth mentioning: **21.06**

#### (a) *Remedy for infringement*

Provisions have been amended to clarify the subjective requirements (with intent or due to negligence) for the patentee to claim the damages of patent infringement (Article 96(2)). As in torts law, the burden of proving the infringer's intent or negligence is on the patentee. **21.07**

The methods of calculating damages and the regulation of the patent marking have also been revised. The presumption of the infringer's profit ('The entire income derived from the sale of the infringing articles shall be deemed the **21.08**

3 All the unspecified quotations in B.1–B.2 are from the General Explanation for the 2013 Patent Revision Act.

4 For a similar opinion see Ming-Yan Shieh, 'Comments on and Analysis of the Newly Revised Patent Act' (in Chinese), [2012] **205** *Taiwan Law Review*, 57. However, some perceive the frequent amendment of IP law quite positively: 'all of the amendments had the same goal – to comply with international protection standards, to avoid more IP suits and to modernize'. See Paul C.B. Liu, in Paul Goldstein and Joseph Straus et al. (ed.), *Intellectual Property in Asia*, Berlin: Springer Verlag 2009, 282.

5 Pursuant to reinstatement of rights mechanism (Art. 52), applicants who lost their patent rights because they unintentionally failed to claim priority rights at the time of application or failed to pay an issue fee or patent annuities on time may apply for reinstatement of rights.

infringer's profit, provided that the infringer is unable to produce proof to justify his/her costs or necessary expenses') was deleted and 'the equivalent amount of royalty that may be collected from exploiting the invention patent under licensing' was added as the third method of calculating damages.

**21.09** In order to adhere to the principle of torts in Taiwan, the provisions that the patentee may make an additional claim for reasonable damages due to loss of reputation and that triple damages may be awarded for intentional infringement were deleted on 1 January 2013. However, the provision of punitive damages was re-introduced into the Patent Act on June 13, 2013, to strengthen the protection of patentees.[6] The special regulations governing the granting of a provisional seizure were also deleted so that the Civil Procedure Law can govern.

#### *(b) Patent invalidation*

**21.10** The provision that allowed the TIPO to revoke a patent right *ex officio* was deleted. However, a new article was added that allows the TIPO to examine *ex officio* the reason(s) and evidence not submitted by the invalidation requester if the said reason(s) and evidence are within the scope of the invalidation statement when conducting an invalidation proceeding. The TIPO shall notify the patentee to submit a response within a time limit. The invalidation proceedings shall be conducted directly if the patentee fails to submit a response within the time limit (Article 75).

#### *(c) Overhaul of the design patent regime*

**21.11** 'In order to encourage traditional industry to design creatively based on existent resources and to meet the needs of domestic industrial development and design of products which are in their maturity', the so-called 'partial design', has been introduced in Article 121(1), following Article 3 of the EU Design Regulation: '"Design" means the creation made in respect of the shape, pattern, colour, or any combination thereof, of an article as *a whole or in part* by visual appeal'.

**21.12** In addition, 'given the fact that domestic industry's ability to develop and utilize consumer electronic products and computers and information and communication products with electronic images is maturing, and that computer images or *graphic user interfaces (GUI)* are inseparable from the use and operation of the said products', Article 121(2) allows filing for design patents on computer generated icons (Icons) and GUI applied to an article, although they lack what

6 TIPO's News 'Patent Act Amendment: Introducing Punitive Damages' available at http://www.tipo.gov.tw/ct.asp?xItem=472220&ctNode=6687&mp=2.

is required of a 'normal' design, namely the three dimensions of the object to which the design is applied.

The derivative design system is also introduced into Article 127 to satisfy the domestic demands for protection of a series of designs which stem from the same design concept or which are an improvement over previous designs. **21.13**

### (d) Clear adoption of international exhaustion

Before the revision, the Patent Act used to have a unique and much-criticized exhaustion regime in Article 57(1) and (2) which provides in the first place that a patent right shall exhaust, and the exhaustion is not limited to the domestic market. However, it then prescribed that the area in which exhaustion takes place is for courts to decide based on facts. It left the exhaustion subject to the court's decision, running against the public policy nature of exhaustion. Now Article 59(1) provides: 'The effects of an invention patent right shall not extend to the following circumstances: 6. where, after the sale of a patented product made by the patentee or made under consent of the patentee, using or reselling such product. *The making and selling as stated above are not limited to acts done domestically*,' deleting the provision that subjects exhaustion to a court's decision. The legislative reason is very concise, simply citing Article 6 of the TRIPS Agreement which allows Members to freely decide the scope of exhaustion. **21.14**

### (e) Limiting compulsory licensing and government use[7]

TIPO initiated the amendment of the Patent Act to limit its power to grant compulsory licences and government use. Article 87 largely closes down the possibility of granting compulsory licences upon application to three narrowly defined situations: (1) non-commercial exploitation for enhancement of public interest; (2) exploitation of dependent patents; (3) where a patentee has been found committing acts restricting competition or unfair competition acts determined by a court or by the Fair Trade Commission.[8] Article 88 prescribes **21.15**

7 For more see Kung-Chung Liu, 'Regressing Compulsory License and Government Use in Taiwan' in Reto M. Hilty and Kung-Chung Liu (eds.), *Compulsory Licensing – Practical Experiences and Ways Forward*, Max Planck Asian Intellectual Property Law Series, Berlin: Springer Verlag (forthcoming).

8 Art. 87(2)-(5) provides: '2.Under any of the following circumstances, for which a compulsory patent licensing is necessary, the Specific Patent Agency may, upon request, grant compulsory licensing of a patent: (1) where the patented invention is exploited non-commercially for the enhancement of public interest; (2) where a later invention or utility model patent cannot be exploited without infringing a prior invention or utility model patent, and where the later invention or utility model patent involves an important technical advancement of considerable economic significance in relation to the prior invention or utility model patent; (3) where a patentee has been found committing acts restricting competition or unfair competition acts by a court or by the Fair Trade Commission. 3. Application for compulsory license of a patent covering semiconductor technology shall be filed based on the grounds set forth in Subparagraphs 1 and 3 of the preceding Paragraph. 4. Application for compulsory license of a patent in accordance with Subparagraphs 1 through 2 of Paragraph 2 may only be permitted if the requestor for compulsory license has made efforts to obtain authorization from the

the procedure, scope, and duration and so on of compulsory licences. Article 89 deals with the termination of compulsory licences. Article 90 prescribes grounds of and procedures for compulsory licensing of pharmaceuticals, while Article 91 deals with export and remuneration of compulsory licensing of pharmaceuticals.

**21.16** The 2013 Patent Act related to government use was mainly driven by the need for government authorities to respond to national emergency or other circumstances of extreme urgency immediately without having to file an application for a compulsory licence. According to Article 87(1), in response to national emergency or other circumstances of extreme urgency, TIPO shall, in accordance with an Emergency Order or upon notice from the competent central government authorities, grant a compulsory licence, and notify the patentee as soon as reasonably practicable. In other words, TIPO no longer has to make a decision and will just issue a compulsory licence automatically.

**21.17** By and large, the new provisions on compulsory patent licensing and government have regressed rather than progressed in terms of furthering public interests, mainly because a more general and broader clause for compulsory licences is missing, such as Article 67 of the 1949–1994 Patent Act and provisions in Mainland China, Germany, Japan, Korea and the UK. In addition, it deprives the patentee of the procedural right to be heard prior to the granting of government use in case of national emergency, relieves TIPO of its gatekeeper role in case of national emergency, and erroneously limits public interest use to not-for-profit.[9]

### *(f) Remaining issue: animal and plant patents*

**21.18** The Steering Group of the Executive Yuan[10] for the Biotechnology Industry, understandably a strong advocate for patenting biotechnology inventions, decided in 2005 that full recognition of the patentability of animals and plants was one of the important coherent policies for the promotion of bio industry. TIPO followed that decision and issued a draft which deleted the provisions

---

right holder on reasonable commercial terms and conditions, and if such efforts have not been successful within a reasonable period of time. 5. Request for compulsory licensing of a patent in accordance with Subparagraph 2 of Paragraph 2, the owner of the prior patent may propose reasonable terms and conditions and seek grant of compulsory license of the later patent owned by the requestor.'

9 The provision on not-for-profit practice that would enhance public interest stands out for two reasons: (1) It does not elaborate on the meaning or scope of public interest, which provides courts with little guidance on its application. Without clear guidance courts tend to interpret public interest narrowly. (2) It limits such compulsory licence to not-for-profit use, a limitation that is in itself infeasible in a market economy and therefore cannot be found in the much looked-up German and UK patent law.

10 The Executive Yuan is the executive branch of Taiwanese government, and its legal status is similar to the Cabinet.

that prohibited the patentability of animals and plants. But the proposal met with heavy resistance. Despite many efforts by TIPO and political parties to draft exemption clauses that would dampen the impact on farmers and plant breeders, the concern over such expansion was so huge that the government was compelled to drop the proposal. It is foreseeable that lobby and interest groups for animal and plant patents will not give up their joint mission easily.

### 3. Some practices of TIPO

#### *(a) Extension of patent term for pharmaceutical and agrochemical inventions*

The Regulation Governing the Extension of Patent Terms (of Pharmaceutical and Agrochemical Related Invention Patents) was amended on 28 December 2012. The main points of the amendment are as follows: (1) the so-called time periods spent for conducting clinical trials or field trials in Taiwan or foreign countries are limited to those confirmed by the Department of Health (for medicines) and Council of Agriculture (for farm chemicals) to be needed for issuing drug licences or agrochemical licences; (2) if the review has confirmed that the time period within which a patent cannot be exploited due to the need to obtain related licences surpasses the extension term that the applicant has applied to extend, the extension shall be limited to what the applicant has applied for (Rule 9). **21.19**

#### *(b) Adjustment to regulations of patent fees*

In order to conform to the 'user-pays' principle, a clause was inserted to the Regulations of Examination Fees governing substantive examination of invention patent application on 1 January 2010. TIPO will charge fees according to the number of claims respectively. The objective of this adjustment is to establish a sound and reasonable mechanism of payment. Hence, a sustainable environment of patent application and examination would be reached. **21.20**

In harmonization with international norms and to establish a fair mechanism of patent fees, a clause is inserted in the Regulations of Examination Fees governing fees in cases of applications for re-examination, invention and utility model patent invalidation and technical report of a utility model patent. TIPO will charge the applicant according to the number of claims. **21.21**

#### *(c) 'Implementation Regulation Governing Foreign-Language Patent Applications'*

To regulate the types of languages used and other relevant matters of foreign-language patent applications, the TIPO promulgated on 3 July 2012 the **21.22**

Implementation Regulation Governing Foreign-Language Patent Applications, which took effect along with the new Patent Act. Key points of this Regulation include:

- With reference to the types of languages stipulated in the Patent Cooperation Treaty (PCT), upon receiving a filing date, the languages of the application shall be limited to Arabic, English, French, German, Japanese, Korean, Portuguese, Russian or Spanish.
- Invention and utility model applications filed in foreign languages shall include specifications (at least one), claim, graph, and title of the creation.
- Applicants shall not replace foreign-language applications with foreign-language patent gazettes or priority documents.

*(d) Online search for Re-examination history available*

**21.23** Starting on 1 December 2011, online search for invention patent re-examination history will be available. Patent applicants and the public may use this online service to search for re-examination history. This service will help make patent examination more transparent and comprehensive. Businesses may use search results to gain a better grip of the patent examination process, which in turn would be helpful towards their R&D.

*(e) Launch of Patent Prosecution Highway with USPTO and JPO*

**21.24** TIPO and USPTO on 21 December 2012 jointly announced the launch of a permanent TIPO-USPTO Patent Prosecution Highway (PPH), which began on 1 September 2011 and commenced fully on 1 September 2012, after a successful one-year trial period. The PPH between TIPO and the Japan Patent Office (JPO) was launched on 1 May 2012. Such PPH will allow applicants to obtain patents faster and more efficiently.

*(f) Establishment of the Patent Search Center*

**21.25** In 2012 the TIPO established a new entity named the Patent Search Center (PSC), which is similar to the Industrial Property Cooperation Center (IPCC) in Japan and the Korea Intellectual Property Rights Information Service (KIPRIS). The PSC is a non-profit organization and designed to enhance the quality of patent examination and to accelerate TIPO's examination process. It is expected that the PSC will provide useful patent information for industries and R&D activities in the foreseeable future.

## C. PATENT PROSECUTION

21.26 Requirements for patent application under the Patent Act in Taiwan are no different from those of other countries, including patentable subject matters (inventions) (Article 21) and subject matters excluded from patent protection (Article 24). Also, patentable subject matters should meet the requirements of industrial application, novelty (Article 22(1)) and inventive step (Article 22(2)). Furthermore, the description of inventions should sufficiently disclose contents of the invention so as to enable persons skilled in the art to practise such invention (Article 26(1)).

21.27 Following the European Patent Convention (EPC) and the PCT, the Patent Act introduced in 2001 the early publication of applications for invention patents. The 2004 Patent Act made only minor literal and editorial changes. What is still overlooked is that, in order to keep outsiders fully informed, to help define the scope of claims and to determine whether the 'file-wrapper' estoppels apply, the early publication of applications must also include amendments made to applications. This is already the case in the European Patent Office (EPO)[11] and UK Intellectual Property Office.[12] However, the revised Patent Act and its implementing regulations have not yet recognized the necessity of publishing amendments made to the applications for invention patents.[13]

21.28 TIPO's decisions to grant or reject patent applications are administrative action (Article 92 paragraph 2 Administrative Procedure Act), and those dissatisfied with such decisions could resort to administrative remedy proceedings. In other words, patent applicants can file for a re-examination of TIPO's decision (Article 48 Patent Act). If the applicants are still dissatisfied with the reviewed decision and believe that their rights or interests are not adequately protected, they can then appeal to the Board of Appeal of the Ministry of Economic Affairs (MOEA) (Article 1(1) Administrative Appeal Act). Moreover, if the appellants (that is, the patent applicants) are still dissatisfied with the appeal decision, under Article 4(1) of the Administrative Litigation Act, they may appeal to the IP Court which has jurisdiction over administrative matters (Article 3 paragraph 3 IP Court Organization Act). Those dissatisfied with decisions made by the IP Court may appeal to the Supreme Administrative Court (Article 238(1) Administrative Litigation Act).

---

11 Margarete Singer and Dieter Stauder, *European Patent Convention*, 3rd edn., London: Sweet & Maxwell 2003, Art. 93 note 17.

12 William Cornish, David Llewelyn and Tanya Aplin, *Intellectual Property: Patents, Copyright, Trade Marks and Allied Rights*, 7th edn., London: Sweet & Maxwell 2010, 4–21.

13 This problem has already been pointed out in 2005, see Kung-Chung Liu, 'Of the Latest and Future Taiwanese IP Pilgrimage After Acceding Into the WTO', [2005] **2** *Tsing Hua Journal of Law and Technology Policy* 3, 5, 13.

**21.29** After the patent grant, any third party who believes that an invention should not have been granted a patent, may request a revocation with TIPO (Article 71(1) Patent Act). Neither ordinary courts nor the IP Court can invalidate a patent by declaratory judgments in patent infringement cases.[14] The administrative proceedings regarding issues over patent validity are adversarial in nature and TIPO is always a party to the proceedings. If TIPO decides that there should be a revocation but the original patentee is dissatisfied with TIPO's decision, the patentee may seek remedies from the Board of Appeal of the MOEA, the IP Court and the Supreme Administrative Court. On the other hand, if TIPO believes a revocation is unnecessary and the patent right is valid, the party requesting the revocation may have recourse to the aforementioned administrative remedy proceedings. Unless the invalidation proceeding has been exhausted and a patent rendered invalid, no one, including a court that handles civil infringement cases, can deny a patent's validity.

## D. ENFORCEMENT[15]

**21.30** Taiwan's administrative and civil proceedings of patent enforcement are modelled on German laws, in particular the dual systems of administrative and civil adjudication. Disputes of patent prosecution and validity are administrative matters governed by administrative proceedings, while patent infringement matters are under the jurisdiction of ordinary courts and follow the related provisions of torts stipulated by the Civil Code and the Civil Procedure Act.

### 1. The IP Court

#### *(a) Establishment of the IP Court*[16]

**21.31** From 1992 onward the Judicial Yuan[17] ordered courts to establish special divisions to handle IP lawsuits. In July 1998 the Taipei District Court followed suit and dedicated a division to dealing with IP cases.[18] However, the Taipei District Court was handicapped by the ineffective procedural rules that were

---

14 By contrast, in Germany any third party, believing that a patent should not be granted, is entitled to file a request for a declaration of invalidity before the German Federal Patent Court (Bundespatentgericht). The invalidation proceedings before the Federal Patent Court differ from the opposition proceedings before the German Patent and Trade Mark Office (Deutsches Patent- und Markenamt).

15 Ming-Yan Shieh and Su-Hua Lee in Kung-Chung Liu and Reto Hilty (ed.), *The Enforcement of Patents*, Berlin: Springer Verlag 2012, 180–7.

16 Ibid., 191–2.

17 The Judicial Yuan is the highest supervision authority in charge of the judiciary, and exercises the power to interpret the constitution and the judicial administration power.

18 Zhong-Sen Yang, *Theory and Application of Patent Law*, 2nd edn. Taipei: Sanmin Publishing Company 2007 (Chinese), 535.

applicable to ordinary courts and could not live up to the expectations of IP professionals. Strong need was felt to establish effective adjudication proceedings and a specialized IP court, particularly in the field of patent law. In 2007 the Legislative Yuan[19] passed the Intellectual Property Court Organization Act and the Intellectual Property Case Adjudication Act (IP Adjudication Act), which contains *lex specialis* of criminal, civil and administrative litigation laws. The IP Court began operating on 1 July 2008.

#### *(b) Comparison with the IP Courts in other countries*

Unlike the IP High Court in Japan[20] but similar to the US Court of Appeals for the Federal Circuit, the German Federal Patent Court and the IP & International Trade Court (IP & IT Court) in Thailand, the IP Court in Taiwan is a separate court. Remarkably, the IP Court in Taiwan has a broad jurisdiction over patent, trademark, copyright, trade secret, integrated circuit, plant variety right cases and cases governed by the competition law. Different from the IP High Court in Japan and IP & IT Court in Thailand which serve exclusively as the second instance in charge of appeal cases,[21] the IP Court in Taiwan serves as the first and second instance in civil cases, appeal instance in criminal cases and the first instance in administrative cases. Due to this broad jurisdiction, the case load for the 15 IP Court judges is extremely heavy. **21.32**

### 2. Civil infringement proceedings

As from 2004, following the complete decriminalization of patent infringement, there is only civil liability for patent infringement.[22] **21.33**

#### *(a) Definition of infringement*

Patent infringement is a kind of tort stipulated in Article 184 of the Civil Code and is handled by ordinary courts, which follow the adversarial system. Similarly to many other countries' legal systems, Taiwan's civil and criminal cases go through three instances and three trials in the district court, high court and the Supreme Court respectively. Various district courts have jurisdiction over patent **21.34**

19 The Legislative Yuan is equivalent to the parliament.

20 It should be noted that in spite of its title the IP High Court in Japan is not a separate court but only a special branch within the Tokyo High Court.

21 In contrast, the Tokyo District Court (29th, 40th, 46th and 47th Divisions) and the Osaka District Court (21st and 26th Divisions) have IP-specialized divisions that have had exclusive jurisdiction over cases on patents matters in the first instance since 2004. Judgments made by the Tokyo District Court and the Osaka District Court can be appealed before the IP High Court. For more details of the specialized courts in Japan, see Masabumi Suzuki and Yoshiyuki Tamura, *Patent Enforcement in Japan*, in Kung-Chung Liu and Reto M. Hilty (eds.), *The Enforcement of Patents*, Berlin: Springer Verlag 138.

22 For more see Kung-Chung Liu, 'Of the Latest and Future Taiwanese IP Pilgrimage After Acceding Into the WTO', [2005] **2** *Tsing Hua Journal of Law and Technology Policy* 3, 5, 11.

infringements. In addition, the IP Court also has jurisdiction over patent infringement cases.

**21.35** Following Article 34 of TRIPS Agreement, Article 99 of the Patent Act also foresees the presumption of infringement of a method patent. It is noteworthy that Taiwan's Patent Act only has regulations on direct infringement and does not have regulations on indirect infringement in contrast to the United States and Germany. Aiding, abetting or inducing patent infringement is only covered by Article 185 paragraph 2 of the Civil Code. In practice, it is difficult to prove that a person has acted as a joint tortfeasor by helping or inducing patent infringement. For instance, patent holders often cannot prove that such behaviour was the direct cause of patent infringement; it is also difficult to prove that the abettor acted intentionally or negligently.

*(b) Determining patent infringement*

**21.36** The core of a civil patent enforcement lies in determining the connection between the scope (claims) protected by the patent and the allegedly infringing product or method; in other words, determining whether the allegedly infringing product or method is covered by the scope protected by patent rights (Article 58(4) Patent Act). When conducting claim construction, the interests of the patent holder and third parties should be taken into account. The following are important issues considered by courts when they determine the patent scope in patent infringement cases: (1) adequate protection for the patent holder; (2) allowing third parties to enjoy sufficient protection of legal certainty. After determining the scope of the patent claims, principles such as the all elements rule, literal interpretation, the doctrine of equivalents, and the reverse doctrine of equivalents[23] should be used to determine whether the allegedly infringing product or method falls under the protected scope asserted by the patent rights holder.

**21.37** From the above-mentioned process of determining patent infringement, it is clear that other than applying laws, a more in-depth understanding of technical knowledge is also necessary during the adjudication and litigation of patent infringement which requires the assistance of experts. Thus, Article 103(2) and (3) of the Patent Act provide that the Judicial Yuan may appoint specific professional institution(s) to perform expert verification work; when a court adjudicates patent litigation cases, it may ask these institutions for expert

23 The reverse doctrine of equivalents acts as a defense to a charge of literal infringement. The doctrine absolves an accused infringer from infringement liability where the accused device, although literally falling within the scope of the asserted patent claim, is so far changed in principle from the claimed invention that a finding of liability cannot be justified as a policy matter; Janice M. Mueller, *Patent Law*, 4th edn., Alphen aan den Rijn: Wolters Kluwer 2013, 476.

verification. After the verification by expert institutes or professionals, judges can then decide whether to recognize the results at their discretion.

### (c) *Remedies and procedures*

When there is patent infringement, the patentee and the exclusive licensee may bring suit against the infringer. In a case where a patent is co-owned by more than one party, the Patent Act does not provide provisions on whether any one of the co-owners is able to individually resort to civil remedies against a third party. However, an affirmative answer could be inferred from Article 821 Civil Code, which specifies that co-ownership will allow any one of the patent co-owners to file civil remedies against a third party for the common interests of all the co-owners. In addition to claiming damages an invention patentee or an exclusive licensee may request destruction of the infringing products or the raw materials or implements used in infringing the patent, or request other necessary forms of disposal (Article 96(3) Patent Act). When the inventor's right to indicate his/her name is infringed, he/she may request a ruling to indicate the inventor's name or otherwise to recover his/her reputation (Article 96(5) Patent Act). The right to claim provided in this Article shall become extinguished if not exercised within two years from the time the patentee became aware of the infringing act and the person responsible for the damages, or within ten years from the time of the infringement (Article 96(6) Patent Act). **21.38**

### (d) *Position of competitors and third parties*

Similar to other countries, Taiwan's Patent Act prescribes that patent rights cannot be extended to certain circumstances, such as acts done privately and for non-commercial purpose, research and development on patented subject matter (Article 59). When legal conditions given in such provisions are met, the practice of invention by a third party will not constitute an infringement to a patent right. **21.39**

Regarding patent validity issues, not only the patentee's competitors but also any third party can request administrative remedies to revoke the patent, or raise patent invalidity as a defence in a civil infringement suit. **21.40**

### (e) *International jurisdiction*

Article 25 Taiwan's Conflict of Law Act states: 'The laws at the place of tort shall apply to liabilities for tort, but other laws shall prevail which have the closest relation to the tort.' Therefore, as long as the patent is granted by TIPO, Taiwanese courts have jurisdiction over the infringement to the patent, regardless of whether the infringement occurs in Taiwan or in other countries. **21.41**

**21.42** In addition, according to the principle of territoriality, a patent granted by a foreign patent authority does not enjoy patent right in Taiwan. However, when the patentee and the infringer of a foreign patent are both in Taiwan, it will be a question of whether the patentee is allowed to file a suit in Taiwan. According to the amendments to Taiwan's Conflict of Law Act on 26 May 2010, Taiwanese courts seem to have jurisdiction and shall adjudicate the case by applying foreign patent laws.[24]

### *(f) Alternative dispute resolution and border measures*

**21.43** Patent right disputes may be resolved through alternative dispute resolution (ADR), such as mediation and arbitration. As for arbitration, the Arbitration Association of the Republic of China has an Intellectual Property Right Dispute Arbitration Research Committee. However, because some patent disputes are concerned with arbitrability, in practice there are few patent disputes resolved through arbitration.

**21.44** TIPO's decision to grant patent application is an administrative action. In this regard, the patent validity issue cannot be subject to a mediator or arbitrator. Therefore, patent disputes resolvable through ADR are limited to contractual disputes such as licensing or patent ownership. However, in practice such agreements in Taiwan rarely have mediation or arbitration clauses.

**21.45** Article 51 TRIPS Agreement provides that member countries may take necessary border measures against infringing products. Different from the comprehensive border control measures of the European Union and International Trade Commission in the USA, Taiwan had only started such measures in 2004 and these measures are limited to products infringing trademark, copyright, and plate rights.[25] It is worth noting that four provisions (Article 97–1 to 97–4) governing border measures against patent infringing products were introduced into the Patent Act on 22 January 2013 and took effect on 24 March of the same year.[26]

---

24 Art. 42 Conflict of Laws Act provides: 'For the right which has intellectual property as its subject matter, the laws at the locality where protection is claimed shall apply (para. 1). For the ownership of the intellectual property made by an employee in the performance of his/her duties, the laws applicable to the employment agreement apply (para. 2).'

25 A plate maker who arranges and prints a literary or artistic work that has no economic rights or for which the economic rights have extinguished, or who photocopies, prints, or uses a similar method of reproduction and first publishes such reproduction based on such original artistic work, and duly records it in accordance with the Copyright Act, shall have the exclusive right to photocopy, print, or use similar methods of reproduction based on the plate ten years from the time the plate is completed (Art. 79 of Copyright Act).

26 TIPO's News 'Legislative Yuan Passes Patent Act Amendment Concerning Border Protection Measures for Patents' available at http://www.tipo.gov.tw/ct.asp?xItem=504561&ctNode=6687&mp=2.

### (g) Wrongful enforcement[27]

The Patent Act had provisions for criminal penalties before 2003, which were often used by patentees in patent infringement cases as a threat to competitors or to urge an infringing party to reach a settlement or take a licence. Since the removal of criminal penalties from the Patent Act civil remedies have become the major resort in patent infringement cases. Another form of wrongful enforcement is via false patent marking (such as falsely claiming oneself as patentee, bearing patent marking after the patent has expired, or marking a 'utility model' patent as an 'invention' patent), in case of which Article 21 or 24 of the Taiwan Fair Trade Act (TFTA) may apply.[28] The TFTA also applies to warning letters issued by the patentee. Therefore, if the patentee issues warning letters in an improper way and does not comply with the TFTA, the victim can seek remedies according to the competition law. 21.46

One recent case is noteworthy: A patentee filed several infringement suits based on a patent granted by TIPO. In one infringement suit, the defendant raised the patent invalidity as a defence and the civil court agreed with the defendant but left the patent intact. Later the patentee filed a new complaint against other parties based on that patent. The court opined that there was an abuse of right against good faith condemned in Article 148 of the Civil Code and dismissed the new complaint out of hand.[29] 21.47

Regarding spurious litigation such as wrongful seizure or interim relief that is subsequently overturned, the provisions of torts stipulated by Article 184 of the Civil Code and Article 531 paragraph 1 of the Civil Procedure Act may apply. However, there has been no case where the victim claims damages against the actor, since the victim often cannot prove that such behaviour was the direct cause of damage and that the patentee has intended to cause the damage. However, it should be noted that in a recent case[30] the victim of a wrongful enforcement was granted damages for losses resulting from a baseless preliminary injunction where no infringement was found. 21.48

27 Ming-Yan Shieh and Su-Hua Lee,above note 15, 191.
28 Art. 21 prohibits misleading advertisement and Art. 24 is a general ban of all deceptive and overly unfair acts.
29 IP Court Civil Decision 2010 *Min-Zhuan-Shan-Tze* No. 58.
30 IP Court Civil Decision 2010 *Min-Kon-Shan-Tze* No. 3.

## E. LICENSING AGREEMENTS AND ANTI-TRUST LAW

### 1. Refusal to license and warning letters

**21.49** Before 2013, the Patent Act used to have a provision related to patent misuse.[31] But in 2013 Article 60 was deleted and the issue will now be dealt with exclusively by competition law. Disputes arising from the enforcement of patent rights or licensing could also be resolved through other provisions of the TFTA. The TFTA condemns the abuse of a monopolistic market position which can derive from an 'essential patent'. Accordingly, the monopolistic patentee's refusal to license may constitute an abuse of its monopolistic market position. If found so by a court or the Taiwanese Fair Trade Commission (TFTC), the interested party could even apply for a compulsory licence based on Article 87(2) of the Patent Act.

**21.50** The TFTC promulgated the Guidelines on Technology Licensing Agreements (TFTC Guidelines) on 20 January 2001, to explain how it would treat patents and/or know-how licensing agreements according to the TFTA. In 2009 the TFTC Guidelines completely abolished the *per se* illegal position it had taken from the beginning. The determination of the listed examples of prohibited clauses in Point 6 is either subject to the condition that it is 'in a manner sufficient to influence the functions of the relevant market' or it is 'likely to lessen competition or to impede fair competition in relevant markets'.

**21.51** The CD-R cases involving Philips, Sony and Taiyo Yuden (with a uniform royalty rate and a sole licensing channel) prompted the TFTC to interpret and apply Article 10 to the refusal to license the pooled patents.[32] In 2000, Philips et al. were accused of abusing their monopoly power in the CD-R market through the joint licensing agreement by demanding excessive royalties and obscuring information about the patents to be licensed. Philips et al. were further accused of engaging in cartels by bundling patents and licensing in packages, tying in

---

31 Art.60 of the old Patent Act stipulated that: 'An assignment or a licensing of an invention patent shall not take effect if the contract signed therefor contains any of the following circumstances that will give rise to unfair competition: (1). To prohibit or restrict the assignee from using any specific article or process not furnished by the assignor or licensor; or (2). To require that the assignee purchase products or raw materials of the assignor which is not under patent protection.' According to this provision, assignment or licensing agreements shall be treated as invalid under certain circumstances. However, there has been no case in which Art.60 was put to use.

32 TFTC Decision 2001 *Kon-Chu-Tze* No. 21, TFTC Decision 2002 *Kon-Chu-Tze* No. 69 and the following numerous administrative appeal and administrative litigation proceedings. For more details of the case and some critique, see Liu Kung-Chung and Chien Wei-Ke, 'CD-R, Analysis of and Comments on CD-R-related Cases: Focusing on Competition Law and Patent Compulsory Licensing Issues' (in Chinese), *Fair Trade Q.* Jan. 2009, 1; Wu Shiu-Ming, 'Patent Pool and the Regulation of Cartel According to the Fair Trade Act' (in Chinese), [2009] **174** *Taiwan Law Review* 120; [2009] **175** *Taiwan Law Review*, 85.

patents that had already expired. In January 2001 the TFTC found that Philips et al. had a joint monopoly power in the CD-R patent-licensing technology market because they own all the important patents for the manufacture of CD-R. From the drastic price drop and the 60-fold growth in volume worldwide, the TFTC concluded that the maintenance of the minimum royalty of 10 Japanese Yen and the refusal to negotiate on a royalty scheme to match the market situation would give rise to the situation where Philips et al. would earn royalties between 20 and 60 times more than the expected amount; hence Philips et al. were guilty of abusing their joint monopoly power and violated Article 10(2) of the TFTA. The Taipei Administrative High Court and the Supreme Administrative Court concurred with this finding.[33]

To deal with the practice that before the patentee files a lawsuit against the infringer, the patentee usually issues a warning letter to ask to 'cease and desist' from the infringement, the TFTC promulgated Guidelines on the Reviewing of Cases Involving Enterprises Issuing Warning Letters for Infringement on Copyright, Trademark, and Patent Rights on 7 May 1997. **21.52**

### 2. Patent pools

The TFTC Guidelines do not address the issue of patent pool at all. However, the TFTC has held in the CD-R cases that patent pools comprising potentially substitutable patents by competitors, namely Philips, Sony and Taiyo Yuden, are cartels in disguise. However, the Taipei Administrative High Courts overruled on the following grounds: local CD-R manufacturers must use all the patents owned by Philips et al. in order to make CD-R; using patents of any one of the three companies would not be sufficient to manufacture CD-R; therefore, patents owned by Philips et al. were complementary in nature and every pooled patent was indispensable, which made the patented technology no **21.53**

33 TFTC *Kon-Chu-tze* 098156. Upon appeal, the TFTC's determination of the relevant product market has not been upheld. But on remand the TFTC reached the same conclusion, which was appealed to and upheld by the Executive Yuan, the Taipei Administrative High Court and the Administrative Supreme Court. However, the Taipei Administrative High Court took into consideration the fact that the TFTC imposed different fines on Philips, Sony and Taiyo Yuden respectively in one administrative decision (not three administrative decisions) and found itself unable to render an 'affirmed-in-part, vacated-in-part' decision and instead compelled to rescind the TFTC's decision as a whole. Both the TFTC and Philips et al. appealed the case to the Supreme Administrative Court which rejected both the appeal in 2007 and the retrial appeal by the TFTC in 2009. So the case was remanded back to the TFTC for further treatment. On 29 October 2009 the TFTC again came to the same conclusion that Philips et al. had violated Art. 10(2) and (4) of the FTA in the following exploitative abuse of monopoly power: refusing to renegotiate royalty with licensees while there have been significant changes in the market, available at http://www.ftc.gov.tw/uploadDecision/faed94a8–34ce-4f8e-b59a-239a9eaece1d.pdf. For more details see Kung-Chung Liu, 'The Taiwanese "Philips" CD-R Cases: Abuses of a Monopolistic Position, Cartel and Compulsory Patent Licensing', in Christopher Heath and Anselm Kamperman Sanders (eds.), *Landmark Intellectual Property Cases and their Legacy* The Hague: Kluwer Law International 2010, 83–104.

longer substitutable, therefore no horizontal competitive relationship existed between Philips et al. and Article 14 of the TFTA which bans cartels could not be applied.[34] The Taipei Administrative High Court's finding of 'no substitutability for the patented technology and no competition relationship between Philips et al' was upheld by the Supreme Administrative Court as 'ascertaining the facts according to the law'.[35]

**21.54** On 30 March 2011 the TFTC cleared the first patent pool that sought its approval. The TFTC decided not to oppose the merger between Hitachi, Panasonic, Philips, Samsung, Sony and Cyberlink which took the form of a new company, One-Blue, with each company controlling a one-sixth share. One-Blue will act as a licensing agent for the patent pool to license essential blue-ray disc (BD) patents for the manufacturing of backward compatible BD products (such as CD, DVD and so on). One-Blue made assurances that (1) the patent pool will be composed exclusively of patents that will be periodically reviewed by independent patent experts (selected by the Administrative Commission from independent and professional patent experts of different countries. The patent experts will provide their patent evaluation service on an hourly charge basis, and the outcome of their evaluations on the patents essentiality have nothing to do with their compensations for the service) to be necessary, complementary and valid; (2) the patent pool will be open to all patent holders; (3) licensors of the patent pool are required to conduct individual licensing activities to any licensee on a FRAND (fair, reasonable, and non-discriminatory terms) basis; (4) licensors of the patent pool are prohibited from disclosing their confidential information, and shall not get access to licensee's information provided in the application of a per-batch licence before each shipment of the product; (5) grant back is limited to essential patents, the royalties will be paid under the same royalty rate as the patent pool, and licensors of such grant back licensing are free to individually license their patents.

**21.55** In order to ensure that the overall economic benefit of the merger outweighs the disadvantages resulting from competition restraints and to ensure that participating parties will not restrain competition through the patent pool, the TFTC imposes the following conditions on participating parties and One-Blue:[36] (1) not to engage in any concerted action by entering into any agreement that restricts the quantities or prices of the BD products or by exchanging important

34 Article 14 is equivalent to Article 101 of the TFEU.

35 For more details of the case and some critique, see Liu Kung-Chung and Chien Wei-Ke, above note 32; Wu Shiu-Ming, above note 32.

36 Resolution of the TFTC's 1012th Commissioners' Meeting. available at http://www.ftc.gov.tw/upload/657b824b-ad69–4ded-ae32-b9a962a7d72f.pdf.

transaction information; (2) not to restrict licensees' use of technology, trading counterparts and product prices; (3) not to restrict licensees from challenging the essentiality and validity of the licensed patents; (4) not to restrict licensees from researching and developing, manufacturing, using and selling competitive products and/or adopting competitive technologies within the licence term or after the expiration of the licence; (5) not to refuse to provide licensees with the content, scope and term of the licensed patents; (6) to provide executed copies of the pool agreements for the TFTC's review.

It is evident that the TFTC puts much emphasis on the fact that substitute patents are not included in the patent pool, and strives to avoid restraint of licensees' freedom to decide prices, use or challenge the pooled patents and to research and develop competitive products or technologies. In addition, it is noteworthy that the TFTC has abandoned its prior scepticism about the sole licensing channel through a particular pool member which it exhibited against the CD-R patent pool and concludes that 'Therefore, licensing the essential BD patents through a patent pool is expected to make it easier for Taiwanese manufactures to obtain the licence of essential patents, to lower the transaction cost and to avoid the risk of infringement and litigation, which will make it easier for Taiwanese manufactures to compete with each other for consumer's interest.'[37] **21.56**

## F. EXCURSUS: IP PROTECTION ACROSS THE TAIWAN STRAIT

The Cross-Strait Agreement on Intellectual Property Right Protection and Cooperation (IPR Agreement) was signed on 29 June 2010 between the Strait Exchange Foundation (representing Mainland China) and the Association for Relations across the Taiwan Strait (representing Taiwan) and came into effect on 12 September of the same year. Pursuant to the IPR Agreement both sides agree to strengthen exchange and cooperation based on the principle of equality and reciprocity to protect IPR such as patents, trademarks, copyright and plant breeders' right, negotiate resolution for relevant problems, and enhance the innovation, application, management and protection of IPR across the Strait. **21.57**

It is further agreed that both sides shall establish a coordination and assistance mechanism for law enforcement, and each side shall follow its own laws and **21.58**

37 For more details see Kung-Chung Liu, 'A More Economic and Cross-Jurisdiction Study on Patent Pools', [2012] **7** (1) *NTU Law Review* (March) 49.

regulations to appropriately handle the following IPR protection issues: crackdown on piracy and counterfeiting, especially of books, audio-video products, software through websites and of pirated and counterfeited goods circulating on the market, protection of well-known marks and Geographical Indications (GIs), prevention of trademark squatting, protection of the right to apply for cancelling the registration of squatted trademarks and strengthening up market oversight and control measures for false GI labelling of fruits and other agricultural products.

**21.59** The patent offices of both sides began accepting requests for priority claims of patents, trademarks and plant varieties on 22 November 2010 and adjusted their internal operations respectively. From then up until 31 December 2012, there were 10,320 priority claims filed from Taiwan: 10,235 for patents, 82 for trademarks and 3 for plant variety rights; priority claims from Mainland China totalled 7,186: 6,929 for patents and 257 for trademarks.

**21.60** Branch offices or constituent companies of foreign enterprises in Taiwan may also claim priority right with Mainland China as long as they are a juridical person of Taiwan (for example, Siemens Taiwan). Furthermore, if in a multiple-applicant case one of the applicants is a Taiwanese national and filed as first applicant, such application may request priority claim with Mainland China, regardless of the nationality of the remaining applicants. Branch companies may also request priority with Mainland China as long as they have been certified under related Taiwanese regulations and the related technological R&D was completed in Taiwan.

**21.61** With regard to mutually accepted plant variety right applications, Taiwan hopes to add ten more plant varieties to the published list of protected plant varieties; Mainland China has agreed to review five such plant varieties.

**21.62** As of the end of February 2013, the number of successful negotiations of disputes by TIPO via the consultation mechanism is 317, with 290 trademark cases (55 have been processed and completed), 19 copyright cases (14 have been processed and completed), and 8 patent cases (3 have been processed and completed).

# Part H

# PATENT PROTECTION IN HONG KONG SAR

# 22

# INTRODUCTION TO THE PATENT SYSTEM IN HONG KONG SAR

**Douglas Clark**



## A. INTRODUCTION

The Hong Kong Special Administrative Region of the People's Republic of China came into existence on 1 July 1997. Immediately prior to that Hong Kong had been a British colony for over 150 years. Hong Kong Island and the Kowloon Peninsula had been ceded to Great Britain in 1842 and 1860 respectively. In 1898, Britain leased the much larger New Territories for 99 years. **22.01**

In 1984 Britain agreed with China to retrocede Hong Kong Island and Kowloon Peninsula when its lease on the New Territories expired on 1 July 1997. Under the agreement, called the Joint Declaration, China agreed that Hong Kong would become a Special Administrative Region of China with a high degree of autonomy and that the previous British common law legal system would remain in place for at least 50 years. In 1990, China enacted the Basic Law for the HKSAR which implemented the Joint Declaration. The Basic Law acts as Hong Kong's mini-constitution and provides that Hong **22.02**

Kong courts shall exercise judicial powers independently from the mainland of China. A Court of Final Appeal was created in Hong Kong as a final appellate court to replace the Privy Council.

**22.03** Prior to 1997, Hong Kong did not have its own patent system. UK patents (or European patents designating the UK) were re-registered in Hong Kong under the Registration of Patents Ordinance. Infringement actions were brought under the 1977 UK Patents Act which was extended to Hong Kong.

**22.04** In order to localize laws as part of the handover of Hong Kong, on 27 June 1997 the Hong Kong Patents Ordinance was enacted. The Patents Ordinance is modelled closely on the 1977 UK Patents Act. In addition, Article 69 European Patent Convention and its protocol have been effectively reproduced in section 76 (Extent of Invention) Patents Ordinance to provide a guide to the interpretation of patents.

**22.05** Hong Kong patent law is, therefore, essentially based on UK patent law. For this reason, UK authorities and pre-1997 Hong Kong authorities are generally followed in Hong Kong and UK text books, such as *Terrell on Patents*, are regularly referred to and cited in Hong Kong.[1]

**22.06** However, where a UK statutory provision differs from the Hong Kong provisions, such as those regarding unjustified threats, UK case law cannot be applied.

## B. GRANT OF PATENT RIGHTS IN HONG KONG SAR

**22.07** There are two types of patents in Hong Kong: Standard Patents and Short-Term Patents. They are granted by the Patents Registry, part of the Intellectual Property Department.

**22.08** At present there is no local substantive examination of patents in Hong Kong. A recent report has recommended that some changes be made to this system.[2]

**22.09** Standard Patents are granted as re-registrations of Mainland PRC or UK patents (either directly registered in the UK or through the European Patent Office (EPO) designating the UK). For a European patent to be registered in

1 See *Tanashin Denki Co Ltd v King Long Industrial Ltd* [1997] **4** *HKC* 217 as an example of a case where English authorities were followed under the 1997 Patents Ordinance.

2 The report is available at http://www.ipd.gov.hk/eng/intellectual_property/patents/review_report.pdf.

Hong Kong the specification is required to be translated into English or Chinese. Mainland PRC patents are re-registered in Chinese. The original patent office is referred to in the Ordinance as the 'designated patent office'.

An application for re-registration called a 'request to record' must be filed within six months from the date of publication of the application by the designated patent office.[3] The request to record should include a copy of the published designated patent application, the title of the invention in both English and Chinese and an abstract in both English and Chinese. **22.10**

A further 'request for registration and grant' must be made within six months of grant in the home office.[4] The request should include a copy of the published specification of the designated patent and the title of invention in both English and Chinese.[5] **22.11**

Applications to re-register standard patents are only examined as to form. There is no substantive examination of the patent. **22.12**

All patents re-registered in Hong Kong are treated as stand alone local patents. If the underlying patent registered in the designated patent office is invalidated or amended in proceedings in its home jurisdiction this does not directly affect the validity of the patent in Hong Kong. **22.13**

Short-term patents are filed directly in Hong Kong. They are not substantively examined and are not prima facie considered to be valid.[6] Short-term patents have an initial term of four years and may be extended for another four years, giving a total life of eight years. A short-term patent is in almost all other respects treated in the same way as a standard patent. The same tests for validity apply. The patent may, however, have only one independent claim. **22.14**

There are no validity proceedings before the Patents Registry. Any challenge as to the validity of a patent must be brought in the Court of First Instance of the High Court. **22.15**

The remainder of this chapter, therefore, deals with patent court proceedings in Hong Kong. **22.16**

---

3 S. 15 Patents Ordinance.

4 S. 23 Patents Ordinance.

5 Full details of the application procedures may be found on the Hong Kong Intellectual Property Department's website at:http://www.ipd.gov.hk/eng/intellectual_property/patents/how_to_apply.htm.

6 S. 129(1) Patents Ordinance.

## C. PATENT LITIGATION IN HONG KONG SAR

### 1. Courts with jurisdiction

**22.17** The Court of First Instance in the High Court has sole first instance jurisdiction over patent cases in Hong Kong.[7] There is no patents or intellectual property court in Hong Kong. The Hong Kong High Court does have certain specialist lists to handle cases related to specialist areas, such as admiralty or administrative law. At present, there is no patent or intellectual property list, although some practitioners are lobbying for one. Accordingly, patent (and other intellectual property) cases are filed as general High Court actions and handled by generalist judges.

**22.18** There is an automatic right of appeal to the Court of Appeal against final decisions of the Court of First Instance. Interlocutory decisions may only be appealed with leave of either the Court of First Instance or the Court of Appeal. With leave, interlocutory and final decisions of the Court of Appeal may be appealed to the Court of Final Appeal. The Court of Final Appeal generally only deals with questions of law, but it may also deal with questions of fact if it considers it necessary. The Court of Final Appeal will very rarely hear appeals on procedural issues.

### 2. Language of proceedings

**22.19** Both English and Chinese are official languages in Hong Kong and patent cases may be filed in Chinese or English. Parties may make applications for the language of proceedings to be changed or for certain documents to be translated. The court will determine whether one language or both will be used depending of the circumstances of the case. Where documents are in English and Chinese a request for a bilingual judge can be made.

**22.20** Generally, given that the law is based on English law, most cases relating to patents are filed and conducted in English even if the patent is in Chinese.

**22.21** Witnesses have a complete right to elect whether to use English or Chinese in court. If witnesses give evidence in Cantonese or Mandarin dialects of Chinese, the court will provide an interpreter. They are generally highly skilled. For interpretation from other languages, the parties are required to arrange interpreters.

---

7 S. 2 Patents Ordinance (definition of 'Court').

### 3. Actions in the court

22.22 The principal patent actions that may be brought in court in Hong Kong are:

(1) Infringement proceedings.
(2) Invalidation proceedings.
(3) An action for unjustified threats.
(4) Declaration of non-infringement.

### 4. Infringement proceedings

22.23 Actions for infringement may be brought under sections 73 and 74 Patents Ordinance. Section 73 provides for direct infringement (for example, making, disposing of, using or importing a patented product or using a patented product). Section 74 provides for indirect infringement (for example, supplying a means relating to an essential element of the invention).

22.24 Both the registered proprietor (s. 80) and an exclusive licensee (s. 86) may bring an action. In the case of an exclusive licensee the patentee must be joined as a party (s. 86(3)). Where title is assigned or an exclusive licence is granted this should be registered at the Patent Registry under section 87. If this is not done within six months the court may refuse to award damages or an account of profits for the period the licence was not registered.

22.25 A claim for infringement (whether for a standard or short-term patent) can only be brought following grant. In the case of a standard patent damages may be claimed in respect of acts done following publication of the application provided the scope of the claims has not been varied substantially in examination.[8]

#### *(a) Rules of court*

22.26 The Rules of the High Court govern civil procedure in the High Court of Hong Kong. It is divided into 'Orders' that set out rules for different procedural steps. Order 103 which provides rules for patent actions was enacted under the pre-1997 Registration of Patents Ordinance. Even though the new Patents Ordinance was enacted more than 17 years ago, the Rules of Court have not been updated other than two amendments made as part of the enactment of Civil Justice Reforms in 2008. In *Wing Yick Bamboo Scaffolders Ltd v Wui Loong Scaffolding Works Co Ltd*[9] it was held that Order 103 had no direct application

8 S. 88(1) as qualified by s. 88(3).
9 [2002] **1** HKLRD 166.

under the new Patents Ordinance. In *Re Low Ban Chai*[10] the court held that where the Rules of Court did not make provision, the then English equivalent Rule of Court, then Order 104, could be applied. Order 104 has now been replaced by Pt 63 Civil Procedure Rules, which can also be applied as far as necessary and relevant. In some recent cases the courts have also applied provisions of Order 103 as far as they appear applicable.[11]

*(b) Test for infringement*

**22.27** Section 76(1)(b) Patents Ordinance provides the basic test for claim construction to determine infringement of a patent. This is:

> (1) For the purposes of this Ordinance–
>
> (b) an invention for which a patent has been granted shall, unless the context otherwise requires, be taken to be that specified in a claim of the specification of the patent, as interpreted by the description and any drawings contained in that specification.

**22.28** Section 76(3) provides further guidance. This subsection is based on the Protocol on the Interpretation of Article 69 European Patent Convention. Section 76(3) provides:

> (3) Subsection (1) should not be interpreted in either of the following senses, namely–
>
> (a) in the sense that the extent of the protection conferred by a patent is to be understood as that defined by the strict, literal meaning of the wording used in the claims, the description and drawings being employed only for the purpose of resolving an ambiguity found in the claims, on the one hand; or
>
> (b) in the sense that the claims serve only as a guideline and that the actual protection conferred by a patent may extend to what, from a consideration of the description and drawings by a person skilled in the art, the patentee has contemplated, on the other hand,
>
> but rather is to be interpreted as defining a position between these extremes which combines a fair protection for the proprietor of the patent or the application for a patent with a reasonable degree of certainty for third parties.

**22.29** Hong Kong courts adopt the approach to patent construction used by English courts, that is: 'purposive construction'. In *Improver Corp v Raymond Industrial*

10 [1999] HKLRD 166.

11 In both *Kooniinklijke Philips Electronics NV v Orient Power Holding Ltd* HCA) No. 945/2005) and *SNE Engineering Co Ltd v Hsin Chong Construction Co Ltd* [2013] **1** HKC 60 the court applied Order 103 in relation to pleading questions.

*Ltd*[12] the Hong Kong Court of Appeal adopted the tests used in *Catnic Components Ltd and Another v Hill & Smith Ltd*[13] where the House of Lords held:

> My Lords, a patent specification is a unilateral statement by the patentee, in words of his own choosing, addressed to those likely to have a practical interest in the subject matter of his invention (i.e. 'skilled in the art'), by which he informs them what he claims to be the essential features of the new product or process for which the letters patent grant him a monopoly. It is those novel features only that he claims to be essential that constitute the so-called 'pith and marrow' of the claim. A patent specification should be given a purposive construction rather than a purely literal one derived from applying to it the kind of meticulous verbal analysis in which lawyers are too often tempted by their training to indulge. The question in each case is: whether persons with practical knowledge and experience of the kind of work in which the invention was intended to be used, would understand that strict compliance with a particular descriptive word or phrase appearing in a claim was intended by the patentee to be an essential requirement of the invention so that any variant would fall outside the monopoly claimed, even though it could have no material effect upon the way the invention worked.

In 2004, the House of Lords comprehensively reviewed the principles for patent construction in *Kirin-Amgen v Hoechst Marion Rousell.*[14] Of most importance, the decision found that there is no place for the doctrine of equivalents in English patent law, rather the claim is to be interpreted according to the meaning the audience it was directed to would understand. No Hong Kong decision has yet applied the *Kirin-Amgen* case, but it will almost certainly be followed in Hong Kong. **22.30**

Once the scope of the claims has been construed it is a relatively simple matter to then determine if the alleged infringing product or process is covered by the claims; or on the other hand, whether the prior art discloses the invention. **22.31**

#### *(c) Relief for infringement*

Section 80(1) Patents Ordinance sets out the relief obtainable, namely: an injunction to restrain infringement; an order for delivery-up or destruction of an infringing product or of any article in which such product is inextricably comprised; damages, alternatively, an account of profits; and, a declaration that the patent has been infringed. **22.32**

12 [1991] **1** HKLR 251.
13 [1982] RPC 183.
14 [2005] RPC 9.

**22.33** Injunctions will generally be ordered, but, being an equitable remedy, the court retains a discretion not to grant an injunction.

**22.34** It is possible to apply for interlocutory injunctions where the patentee can show they will suffer irreparable harm and cannot be compensated in damages. The court will generally not grant an interim injunction where the validity of the patent can be shown to be disputed on meritorious grounds. Cases where the court has been willing to grant interlocutory injunctions have included cases of infringement of mechanical patents and pharmaceutical patents that are near the end of their term.[15]

*(d) Split trial on liability and damages*

**22.35** The general practice in all intellectual property cases in Hong Kong is to bring a case on liability alone in the first instance. If after trial, the defendant is found to have infringed, the plaintiff may proceed with an inquiry as to damages or an account of profits.[16] However, the plaintiff may also choose to proceed with a damages claim at trial if they believe they have all the evidence of infringement by the defendant and therefore do not need further discovery. This could be the case, for example, if following the execution of a search or seizure order (better known as *Anton Piller* Order) they have obtained all the records of the defendant.

**22.36** Following a decision on liability the defendant may be ordered to make limited disclosure in order to allow the plaintiff to make an informed choice between an assessment of damages or account of profits.[17] It is also possible to seek an interim payment following a decision on liability.

*(e) Summary judgment*

**22.37** The Hong Kong courts have also in certain cases been willing to grant summary judgment in patent cases, even where validity has been put in issue.[18] The test for obtaining summary judgment is that the defendant has no defence to the action. In the cases where summary judgment has been granted the defendants have relied on very narrow defences which allowed the court to decide the case

15 See for example: *Dyson Technology Ltd & Anor v German Pool Group Co Ltd* HCA838/2011 (mechanical patent, an injunction prevention copyright infringement was also granted at the same time); and, *Abbott GmBH & Co v Pharmareg Consulting Co Ltd* [2009] **3** HKLRD 524 (end of life pharmaceutical patent). The test for grant of an interlocutory injunction is also set out in these cases.

16 *Auto-Treasure Ltd v Noble Diamond Ltd* [1992] **1** HKC 17, *Nintendo Co Ltd v Supreme Factory Ltd* [2008] 2 HKC 129, per Rogers VP and *Canon Kabushiki Kaisha v Green Cartridge*, HCA 7844/1993, 15 July 1994, para. 2.

17 *Island Records Ltd v Tring International Plc* [1995] FSR 560 and *Canon Kabushiki Kaisha v Green Cartridge*, HCA7844/1993, 22 June 1995, para. 20.

18 See for example: *Koninklijke Philips Electronics N.V. v Wealth Full Technology Ltd* [2002] **3** HKC 87.

at a summary stage. In general, it is very unlikely that a court will grant summary judgment in most patent cases.

### *(f) Liability of directors*

In some cases plaintiffs wish to sue not only an infringing company but also the directors. The company may not have assets, so making the directors personally liable will help in recovery of damages. Further, the plaintiff may wish to stop the directors setting up another company to infringe. **22.38**

In *Canon v Green Cartridge*[19] the Hong Kong Court of Appeal found a director was not liable for infringement of patents by the company on the grounds that he was only one of the directors and could not be said to have personally directed the acts of infringement. In *KK Yakult Honsha v Yakudo Holdings Ltd*,[20] Lam J considered the law on directly liability in detail and held the director in that case liable. He held that it is necessary to show that such directors were personally involved in the infringing transactions in the sense that they personally directed or procured the company's infringing acts. **22.39**

### *(g) Liability of foreign parent companies or manufacturers as joint tortfeasors*

Many plaintiffs will want to join foreign parent companies or suppliers as joint tortfeasors in Hong Kong. The best way to do so is to seek to establish an act of infringement in Hong Kong. Without an act of infringement in the jurisdiction, the English and Hong Kong courts have been reluctant to allow foreign defendants, even parent companies who control the subsidiaries, to be joined to actions. Liability as a joint tortfeasor will only be imposed where there is evidence the party has conspired with the primary infringer or procured or induced his infringements or joined in a common design pursuant to which the infringements were committed.[21] **22.40**

In *Sabaf SpA v MFI Furniture Centres Ltd*,[22] the House of Lords held that a foreign seller did not import a patented product into the UK even if it made the arrangements for shipping the product to the UK. The House of Lords left open the question of whether the foreign seller could be a joint tortfeasor. **22.41**

There is, however, an argument that this case does not apply in Hong Kong. The definition of 'import' in the UK legislation was to 'bring into the United Kingdom'. In Hong Kong 'import' is defined more broadly as meaning 'to bring **22.42**

19 [1996] **1** HKLRD 69.
20 [2004] HKLRD 587. This was a trademark case, but the principles apply to patent cases.
21 See, for example, *Unilever v Gillette* [1989] RPC 583.
22 [2004] UKHL 45; [2005] RPC 10.

or cause to be brought into Hong Kong by air, land or water'.[23] In *Sabaf v MFI* the plaintiff sought to rely on a Dutch case, *Probel v Parke Davis*, to establish there was importation. Under Dutch Law, 'bringing the goods into the market' was an act of infringement. The House of Lords found *Probel v Parke Davis* did not apply because 'bringing the goods into the market' was 'a much wider expression than importing the goods'. The Hong Kong act of infringement: 'bringing or causing to be brought into Hong Kong' is even wider. *Sabaf v MFI* arguably is not applicable in Hong Kong.

*(h) Goods in transit*

**22.43** It should be noted that importation under Hong Kong law includes bringing goods into Hong Kong temporarily with the intention to re-export them. This was confirmed in the case of *Bang & Olufsen v To Huk Chung*,[24] where goods that were brought into Hong Kong by truck for immediate air freighting to Denmark were held to infringe. This means that goods that are brought in from Mainland China (or other places) with the intention of onward shipping are considered to infringe. The only generally accepted exception is if the goods enter and exit Hong Kong on the same vessel or vehicle.[25]

*(i) Grounds of defence*

**22.44** The two main grounds of defence to a claim for infringement are a denial of infringement and a denial of validity and/or counterclaim for revocation of the patent.

**22.45** Denying infringement essentially challenges the scope of the claims of the patent or alleges that one of the integers of the claim or claims alleged to be infringed is not present in the alleged infringing device or method being used.

**22.46** Because infringement and validity are tried together the defendant will often try to 'squeeze' the plaintiff between arguments that support validity of a patent and the prior art or other arguments that the patent is invalid.

**22.47** There are other limited defences provided in the Patents Ordinance. These include: non-infringement of importation of pharmaceuticals if done under an import compulsory licence (s. 72I Patents Ordinance); private use, experimentation, clinical trials, use on board vessels, aircraft or vehicles temporarily entering (s. 75 Patents Ordinance); prior use defence (s. 83 Patents Ordinance)

---

23 Sec. 3 Interpretation and General Clauses Ordinance.

24 *Bang & Olufsen AS v To Huk Chung* [2007] **1** HKLRD 85.

25 This exception is provided for statutorily in the Trade Marks Ordinance and Copyright Ordinance, but has not been enacted in the Patents Ordinance. The courts would most likely, however, hold that this is not infringement.

and limitation on damages or account of profits if exclusive licence is not registered (s. 87 Patents Ordinance).

### 5. Challenging validity of a patent

Under section 91 Patents Ordinance, all claims for revocation of a patent must be made to the Court of First Instance of the High Court. They cannot be made to the Patents Registry. Section 91 Patents Ordinance provides the grounds on which a patent may be revoked. Most claims for revocation of a patent arise in existing claims for infringement and accordingly are made by way of counter-claim. **22.48**

If no infringement proceedings are on foot, an application may be made for revocation of the patent directly to the court. The application must be brought by originating summons.[26] **22.49**

Following UK practice, particulars of the objections to the validity of the patent are generally served with the counterclaim or originating summons. These specify the grounds on which validity of the patent is challenged. **22.50**

The burden of proof of invalidity of a standard patent lies on the party alleging invalidity. The burden of proof of validity of a short-term patent is on the patentee (s. 129(1)(a) Patents Ordinance). However, under section 129(1)(b) Patents Ordinance, 'evidence by the proprietor which is sufficient to establish prima facie the validity of the patent shall in the absence of evidence to the contrary be sufficient proof of such validity'. **22.51**

#### *(a) Grounds of invalidity*

The grounds of invalidity are set out in section 91(1) Patents Ordinance. They are: **22.52**

(a) the invention is not a patentable invention;
(b) the patent was granted to a person who was not the only person entitled to be granted that;
(c) the specification of the patent does not disclose the invention clearly enough and completely enough for it to be performed by a person skilled in the art;

26 Order 103 Rule 29 and *Re Wing Yick Bamboo Scaffolders Ltd* [2002] **1** HKC 395. An originating summons is a simplified means for issuing proceedings. The summons is issued with a supporting affirmation and then proceeds to a hearing before a judge who will then either grant the relief sought or give directions for further conduct of the action.

(d) that the matter disclosed in the specification of the patent extends beyond that disclosed in the application for the patent as filed or, if the patent was granted on a new application filed under section 55(4) or as mentioned in section 22 or 116, in the earlier application for a patent as filed;
(e) that the protection conferred by the patent has been extended by an amendment of the application for the patent or the specification of the patent which is invalid;
(f) that the patent is one of two standard patents for the same invention, the applications for which were filed by the same person and have the same deemed date of filing;
(g) that the patent is one of two short-term patents for the same invention, the applications for which were filed by the same person and have the same date of filing;
(h) that (i) the patent is one of two patents for the same invention, one such patent being a standard patent and the other being a short-term patent, the applications for which were filed by the same person and have the same deemed date of filing or date of filing; and (ii) the two patents are not under the proprietorship of the same person;
(i) in the case of a standard patent, that the corresponding designated patent has been revoked following prescribed opposition or revocation proceedings in the designated patent office.

**22.53** 'Not a patentable invention', referred to in sub-paragraph (a), covers the grounds of lack of novelty, obviousness, and 'incapable of industrial application' (sometimes referred to as 'insufficiency').[27]

**22.54** In Hong Kong, two cases have considered obviousness in infringement proceedings. Both cases applied UK case law. These are *Canon v Green Cartridge*[28] and *Tanashin Denki Co Ltd v King Long Industrial Ltd.*[29] In *Tanashin*, which was decided in 1997 under the old and new law, Rogers J applied the test set out in *Windsurfing International Inc. v Tabur Marine (Great Britain) Limited* (**59** *RPC* at p. 73):

> There are, we think, four steps which require to be taken in answering the jury question. The first is to identify the inventive concept embodied in the patent in suit. Thereafter, the court has to assume the mantle of the normally skilled but unimaginative addressee in the art at the priority date and to impute to him what was, at that date, common general knowledge in the art in question. The third step is to identify what, if any, differences exist between the matter cited as being 'known or used' and the alleged

27 See ss. 93(1), 94, 95 and 97, Patents Ordinance.
28 [1996] 1 HKLRD 69.
29 [1997] 4 HKC 217.

invention. Finally, the court has to ask itself whether, viewed without any knowledge of the alleged invention, those differences constitute steps which would have been obvious to the skilled man or whether they require any degree of invention.

### (b) *Non-invalidating disclosure*

The Patent Ordinance provides certain exceptions that prevent certain types of disclosure from invalidating a patent. Section 95 (for standard patents) and section 109 (short-term patents) provide that disclosures at certain international exhibitions are not considered disclosure to the public. Both provisions also provide that a disclosure which has been made where there has been 'evident abuse' in relation to the applicant will not invalidate the patent provided that the disclosure has occurred within six months of the filing of the patent. Neither provision has been considered in Hong Kong to date. These provisions match Article 55 European Patent Convention (EPC). European practice, particularly in relation to what amounts to 'evident abuse' is likely to be followed in Hong Kong. For example in T 173/83[30] the Board of Appeals ruled that there would be evident abuse within the meaning of Article 55(1)(a) EPC 1973 if it emerged clearly and unquestionably that a third party had not been authorized to communicate to other persons the information received. **22.55**

## 6. Unjustified threats of infringement

Under section 89 Patents Ordinance there is a statutory right for a person aggrieved by unjustified threats of patent infringement proceedings to sue for a declaration that the threats were unjustified, an injunction and damages. Unjustified threats actions are one area where Hong Kong law and UK patent law differ. The equivalent section in the UK section has been very substantially amended by section 12 Patents Act 2004. **22.56**

It is a defence to the action if the patentee can show that the threats are justified because there was infringement of the patent. A threats action also cannot be brought in relation to threats made against a manufacturer of a product or the user of a process. **22.57**

The provision is principally intended to stop threats being made against wholesalers and retailers of products to force them to stop dealing with a product without the patentee backing up their threats with legal action. Under the threats provision, the manufacturer (or another party affected by the threats) could bring action to have the threats declared unjustifiable. **22.58**

30 **1987** *OJ EPO* 465.

**22.59** Under section 89(5) Patents Ordinance, the mere notification of the existence of a patent does not of itself constitute a threat of proceedings. However, if any wording is added that suggests that what is complained of is infringement of a patent, this will constitute a threat.

**22.60** In *Nano World (HK) Ltd v Nano Biotechnology Holdings Ltd*[31] the court granted an interim injunction preventing threats of infringement being sent after a joint venture had broken down between two parties. However, in *Shanghai Reeferco Container Co Ltd v Wagonbau Elze GMBH & Co Besitz KG*,[32] the court struck out a threats action for lack of jurisdiction because the letters threatening action on the Hong Kong patent had not been sent to recipients in Hong Kong. The court allowed a claim for a declaration of non-infringement to proceed.

## 7. Declaration of non-infringement

**22.61** Declarations for non-infringement may be sought under two statutory provisions or the inherent jurisdiction of the court.

**22.62** Under section 90 Patents Ordinance an application may be made for a declaration that certain acts do not infringe a patent, notwithstanding that no assertion of infringement has been made. Under this provision, the party seeking such a declaration must first apply in writing to the patentee for a written acknowledgement that the proposed acts do not infringe and the patentee must have refused or failed to give such an acknowledgement.

**22.63** Section 89 Patents Ordinance which provides for threats actions also provides a mechanism for seeking a declaration that threats of infringement proceedings are unjustified (which includes a ground that the patent is not infringed), as well as damages.

**22.64** Under the inherent jurisdiction of the court an application for a declaration for non-infringement may be brought where a patentee has threatened infringement proceedings or, even when there has been no specific threat of proceedings.[33]

---

31 HCA 2797/2004.

32 [2005] **2** HKLRD 711.

33 *Messier-Dowty Ltd v Sabena* SA [2000] 1 WLR 2040; [2001] **1** All ER 275.

## D. PROPOSED CHANGES

In early 2013 a Committee appointed to review Hong Kong's patent system issued a report recommending changes.[34] In summary the relevant recommendations were: 22.65

### 1. Standard Patents

(a) An 'original grant' patent system should be established in Hong Kong with substantive examination outsourced to other patent offices; and 22.66
(b) the current re-registration system should be retained.

### 2. Short-term Patents

(a) The short-term patent system should be retained. 22.67

(b) The following refinements to the short-term system should be made:
  - (i) Substantive examination should be made a pre-requisite to commencement of infringement proceedings.
  - (ii) A short-term patentee, when making a threat of infringement proceedings, should furnish the person to whom the threat was made with full particulars about the short-term patent in question in support of the threat.
  - (iii) A failure to comply with the requirement in (ii) above should have the legal effect of rendering the threat groundless which enables the party aggrieved by the threat to seek a legal remedy.
  - (iv) Both the patentees and third parties having a legitimate concern or doubt about the validity of a short-term patent should have the right to apply to the Hong Kong Patents Registry for substantive examination of a short-term patent.
  - (vi) The official fees for substantive examination of a short-term patent should be payable by the person making the request for such examination.

The Hong Kong Government has announced that these changes will be adopted and should come into force in around 2017. 22.68

34 Report of the Advisory Committee on Review of the Patent System in Hong Kong.

**22.69** No recommendations were made as to improvements to the system for litigating patents, although a number of practitioners are pushing for, at the least, an Intellectual Property List to be created in the High Court.

## E. CONCLUSION

**22.70** By virtue of its adoption of English statute and case law, Hong Kong has a sophisticated legal system for handling patent disputes. Unlike the UK there is, however, no Patents Court or Intellectual Property Enterprise Court meaning that there is no specialist tribunal to handle patent cases. This can lead to delays and inconsistent decisions. It is hoped that as part of the Review of the Patent System the government and the judiciary will take steps to change this.

# Part I

# PATENT PROTECTION IN MACAU SAR

# 23

# INTRODUCTION TO THE PATENT SYSTEM IN MACAU SAR

**Carlos D. Simões**



## A. GENERAL

With the enactment of the Industrial Property Code (IPC) in June 2000, Macau Special Administrative Region (Macau SAR) was provided with a legal framework to promote registration and protection of IP rights in an expedited way. **23.01**

Registration procedures in Macau are handled by the Intellectual Property Office (IPO) of the Department of Economic Services (DSE), including the registration of patents. **23.02**

There are two ways of getting a patent for Macau: **23.03**

(a) an application – for a patent or utility model – is filed in Macau and will be examined by the Chinese State Intellectual Property Office (SIPO), or
(b) a patent granted by SIPO – only with regard to patents and not utility models – is extended to Macau.

Regardless of the chosen approach, the legal concept behind the patent protection is the same, that is, the patent rights and their effects do not differ. However, as the only difference it should be noted that a patent – based on an extension of a patent granted by SIPO – may be invalid in Macau if the Chinese patent was revoked. **23.04**

**23.05** The application and examination procedure under the first option (option (a)) will be explained under Section C of this chapter.

**23.06** The second option for a patent protection – the extension of patents examined and granted by SIPO – makes clear that Macau has a patent system similar to the one of Hong Kong (see in this regard *Clark*, Chapter 22).

**23.07** The registration and substantive examination of the originating or supporting patent to be extended to Macau is made by SIPO under the laws of mainland China. The laws of Macau only deal with the procedures and conditions as regards the extension. Consequently, a substantive examination under Macau laws only takes place when a patent is filed directly in Macau, not when dealing with extensions from mainland China patents.

**23.08** Chinese patents can be extended to Macau within three months from the date of publication of the granting decision in China. Within this period it is necessary to submit to the IPO, together with the request for extension of the patent, a certified copy of extracts from SIPO and a certified copy of the Chinese patent issued by SIPO. It is necessary to pay a fee for the extension application, which is substantially smaller than the fee payable for a patent filed in Macau directly.

**23.09** Because there is no substantive examination and the procedures are entirely formal, it usually takes less than six months for the entire extension procedures to be completed.

**23.10** Once the extension is published in the Macau Official Gazette – as well as a summary of the patent to be submitted by the applicant – the patent extension will become final and effective in Macau.

## B. SUBSTANTIVE PATENT LAW

**23.11** The patentability requirements in Macau are three: novelty, inventiveness and industry applicability or use (Section 60 IPC).

**23.12** Similar to other jurisdictions, there are a number of matters excluded from patentability in any circumstances (as per Section 62, no. 1, IPC):

(a) scientific discoveries, as well as scientific theories and mathematical methods;
(b) materials or substances already existing naturally and nuclear matter;

(c) aesthetic creations;
(d) schemes, rules and methods for performing mental acts, playing games or doing business as well as computer programs, as such; and
(e) presentation of information.

23.13 To these exceptions one should also add the following, of public order (pursuant to Section 62, no. 2, IPC):

(a) inventions whose commercial exploitation would be illegal, contrary to public order, public health or morality;
(b) methods for the surgical or therapeutic treatment of the human or animal body and methods of diagnosis applied to the human or animal body, excluding products, substances or compositions used in any of those methods; and
(c) plant varieties or breeds of animal, as well as essentially biological processes for the production of plants or animals.

The law (under Section 62, no. 3, IPC) further details what is deemed to be illegal, contrary to the public order or health and morality:

(a) the human body, in the various stages of its formation and development, as well as the simple discovery of one of its elements, including the sequence or partial sequence of a gene;
(b) human cloning processes;
(c) human germinal genetic identity modification processes;
(d) the use of human embryos for industrial or commercial purposes;
(e) processes for the modification of the genetic identity of animals that can cause them suffering without any substantial medical benefit to mankind or animal kind, as well as the animals obtained by those processes.

23.15 For the purposes of assisting to determine how to fulfil the requirement of novelty, IPC contains a definition of prior art (Section 65 IPC):

1. An invention shall be considered novel when it is not known in the prior art.
2. Prior art comprises everything that, inside or outside Macau, has been made accessible to the public before the date of the patent application, by description, use or any other means.
3. Prior art shall also be considered to include the content of patent applications filed at a date prior to that on which the patent in question is applied for and which produce effects in Macau and is not yet published.

23.16 A number of disclosures are also deemed not to affect the issue of novelty (as per Section 68 IPC):

(a) disclosures to scientific societies, professional technical associations, or for the purpose of competitions, exhibitions and trade fairs in Macau or abroad which are official or officially recognized, if the application for the granting of the respective patent be filed in Macau within 12 months;
(b) disclosures resulting from obvious abuse of the inventor or his successor in any capacity, or if improperly published by the IPO.

**23.17** Finally, the law also includes definitions of inventiveness, under Section 66 IPC (an invention is considered to involve an inventive step if, for a person skilled in the art, the result is not obvious from the prior art) and industrial use or application, under Section 67 IPC (an invention is considered industrially applicable if its subject-matter can be manufactured or used in any type of industrial or commercial activity).

## C. PATENT REGISTRATION: APPLICATION AND EXAMINATION PROCEDURE

**23.18** We shall now focus on the patent examination procedure before IPO. It should be noted that Macau is not a party to the Patent Cooperation Treaty (PCT) and, therefore, it is not possible to file international applications with the IPO.

**23.19** Macau is, however, a contracting party to the Paris Convention, making it possible to claim the priority in Macau of an application filed in or for any state party to the Paris Convention or in or for any member of the WTO that is not party to the Paris Convention.

**23.20** As mentioned above, a patent in Macau may only be granted for an invention (a product or a process) which is:

(1) new,
(2) involves an inventive step, and
(3) which is industrially applicable.

**23.21** The relevant patent application must contain (Sections 77 to 79 IPC):

- the applicant's name;
- the applicant's address;
- the name and country of residence of the inventor if the applicant is not the inventor;
- a heading summing up the subject-matter of the invention;
- a summary of the invention in no more than 150 words or 400 characters;
- a description of the subject-matter of the invention;

- drawings necessary for the perfect understanding of the description;
- a claim of what is considered new and characteristic of the invention;
- priority claim, if any (documentation has to be filed within three months from the filing date of the application);
- possibly a declaration of the inventor stating that his identity is not to be revealed;
- possibly a declaration of the applicant summing up the facts that entitles him to apply for registration if the applicant is not the inventor or the sole inventor.

After submission of the application, the IPO will proceed with a formal examination of all the documents within a two-month period. The application for the registration of the patent is published in the Macau Official Gazette after the expiry of 18 months from date of filing, or, if a priority has been claimed, from the priority date. **23.22**

Within seven years counting from the filing date, a request for an examination report must be submitted to the IPO, otherwise the patent application will be rejected. **23.23**

From the publication date of the application in the Official Gazette until the decision to grant the patent, any third party may submit observations on the patentability of the invention (under Section 84, no. 1, IPC). There are no specific requirements to such observations but the same should necessarily detail why the application does not meet the legal requirements for registration as a patent and enclose examples of prior art, if any, to support the claim, if made, of lack of novelty (Section 65 IPC). The patent applicant may reply to such observations within four months (Section 84, no. 2, IPC). **23.24**

A patent application entitles the applicant to provisional protection and, from the date of its publication in the Official Gazette, gives the applicant the protection of a granted patent. However, this protection is limited to the right to claim compensation reasonable in the circumstances (Section 7 IPC). This same protection is also given, even before the publication date, if the applicant informs the potential infringer of the patent submission and serves the documents filed. The court handling the infringement case will, however, stay the proceedings until the patent is granted (Section 7, no. 3, IPC). This means that the filing of a patent application does not vest the applicant with the right to seek an injunction or any other immediate enforcement right, such as the right to exclusively exploit the invention in Macau. A decision will only be made after the grant of the patent. **23.25**

**23.26** Once the IPO has registered the patent, it will be valid for 20 years from the application date, provided, in particular, that the renewal fees are paid in a timely manner.

## D. ENFORCEMENT OF PATENT RIGHTS

### 1. Introduction

**23.27** Patent rights can be enforced in the Macau courts through civil proceedings and criminal proceedings. However, as all the evidence has to be obtained by the parties in the civil proceedings, criminal proceedings are most commonly used to enforce patent rights in Macau.

**23.28** As a special feature of the enforcement system of Macau SAR, Macau Customs (MC) is the most important body to assure protection of intellectual property rights in Macau SAR (including patents), with a correspondingly broad range of competences. These competences were originally allocated to several entities but since the enactment of the IPC they have been concentrated with MC.

**23.29** Within its powers, MC shall:

- take the necessary actions to assure compliance with the intellectual property rights protection system;
- supervise the manufacturing of IP-relevant products within Macau SAR; and
- apply penalties as stipulated by the IPC (see detailed explanations below).

**23.30** Within its supervision powers, at its own initiative or by request of a third party, MC may request other entities such as the police, to seize any products that might infringe industrial property rights, including goods being imported or exported.

### 2. Criminal proceedings

#### *(a) General*

**23.31** The criminal courts in Macau have jurisdiction to hear criminal actions in relation to patent infringements. However, criminal actions to stop infringement of patent rights have to be investigated and instructed by MC, in coordination with the Public Attorney. Thus, MC collects relevant evidence supporting any wilful infringement.

Natural persons who have carried out the infringement are criminally prosecutable, as well as directors, managers, employees or representatives of infringing companies, with whom the company shall be held individually and subsidiarily liable for the payment of the fine. The directors of the company who did not take action or voted against the offence committed, being able to do so, shall also be individually and subsidiarily liable for the payment of the fine (Section 312 IPC). 23.32

MC submits the results of its investigations in a report to the Public Attorney for further prosecution and possibly for the hearing in trial, if the defendant is indicted. 23.33

The patent owner will be given the opportunity to report to the Public Attorney during the investigation and to submit a request for compensation. The request for compensation will be examined and awarded by the responsible criminal courts. 23.34

Often, when the patent infringements involve technical matters, the Public Attorney and the courts request the patent holder to provide additional evidence which proves the infringement, such as copies of the infringed products or expert evidence. 23.35

The parties may recommend or propose to the court to appoint a technical expert in order to deal with technical issues. Due to the fact that there are no specialized patent courts in Macau SAR, courts often face real difficulties in handling the technical issues at stake in an infringement case and therefore often need to request the assistance of court appointed experts. 23.36

Injunctions are regulated in a rather unspecified manner and can be requested in order to preserve evidence which might otherwise be irretrievably lost, or in order to prevent damage which may otherwise not be recovered. 23.37

They can be requested during a pending trial but also before a patent right makes part of pending infringement proceedings. In case of urgency, injunctions have to be issued within two months or 15 days from the request at the soonest (in case the defendant was not summoned). 23.38

### *(b) Punishable acts*

The following acts are punishable under the IPC: 23.39

- manufacturing of copies of products protected by a patent or semiconductor product topography; or

- using or applying methods or processes protected by a patent or by a semiconductor product topography; or
- importing and distributing products obtained by any of the above referred means.

**23.40** The IPC foresees in its Section 289 a penalty of imprisonment up to two years or a fine accumulating for between 60 to 120 days to those who act on a commercial scale and with the purpose of obtaining illegal gains for themselves or for third parties. Typically, the imprisonment convictions awarded by the courts are redeemable through monetary fines payable as an alternative.

**23.41** Moreover, Section 294 IPC also provides for imprisonment of up to six months or fines accumulating for between 60 to 90 days for those who, in bad faith, have obtained for themselves or for a third party a patent that by law or contract belongs to another entity. Upon conviction, the court will revoke the patent or, where applicable, determine its transfer to the lawful proprietor upon his/her request. Such transfer of right may also be requested in separate civil proceedings.

**23.42** Section 303 IPC also foresees fines of MOP$20,000 to MOP$250,000 if the convicted is a natural person, or MOP$50,000 to MOP$500,000 if the convicted is a company, for the following acts:

- presenting oneself as the holder of any patent right, without being its legal holder or alleging rights which have already been revoked or forfeited;
- falsely using or applying the indication of having a registered patent right;
- being the legitimate holder of the patent right but using such rights with regard to products that are not protected by the patent right.

**23.43** In case of lighter offences or other particular circumstances, the administrative penalties as provided for by the IPC may be reduced or even waived. Such special circumstances should have occurred before or after the offence, or may still be present when the court issues the punishment.

**23.44** In case of repeated offences (meaning a similar offence by the same party within one year from the penalty decision) the minimum limit applicable to the offence can be increased by one-third. This increase may not exceed the highest penalty applied in the previous sentence and the maximum limit shall remain the same.

**23.45** Administrative fines must be paid within 15 days from the notification of the penalty decision. The awarded party may initiate enforcement proceedings if the compensation is not voluntarily paid.

### 3. Civil proceedings

Under civil proceedings, parties have greater control over the process and do not depend on the Public Attorney and Macau Customs' initiatives. Therefore, if the writs were duly submitted and instructed, both authorities will have to proceed. Notwithstanding, civil proceedings have the disadvantage of not benefiting from public authority and thus, as a general principle, all relevant evidence should be obtained by the parties and submitted with the writs. As mentioned earlier, there are no specialized patent courts in Macau SAR. **23.46**

Once the claim is filed with the civil court having jurisdiction, the defendant has the possibility to lodge a statement of defence, usually followed by a first decision (the 'discovery order') of the judge on what has to be proved by the parties. As in criminal proceedings, the parties may recommend or propose to the court to appoint an expert in order to deal with technical questions at stake. This first decision will guide the parties through the production of evidence and the hearing sessions. Afterwards there will be a hearing and a final decision, which is subject to appeal. **23.47**

# BIBLIOGRAPHY

## A. BOOKS AND ARTICLES


Bu Yuanshi, *Einführung in das Recht Chinas*, JuS Schriftenreihe, Band 191, Munich: C.H. Beck Verlag 2009.

Bu Yuanshi, *Patentrecht und Technologietransfer in China*, Munich: C.H. Beck/ Helbing Lichtenhahn 2010.

Cao Jingjing, *Die Durchsetzung von Patenten in China*, Cologne: Carl Heymanns 2010.

Chen Albert, 'How Should Chinese Businesses Pay Remuneration for Inventions Created by Their Employees?', *Bridge IP Law Commentary*, 7 January 2013.

Chen Ping-Hsun (Quincy), 'China as a Technology Exporter: A Question Mark after the Third Amendment of the China Patent Law in 2009', [2012] **34** *EIPR* 853

China IPR SME Helpdesk, Technology Transfer to China, Guidance for Businesses, 2012, www.china-iprhelpdesk.eu.

Clark, Douglas, *Patent Litigation in China*, Oxford: Oxford University Press 2011.

Cui Zhou, 'Recent Developments in Litigation Involving Intellectual Property in China', [2012] **43** *IIC* 21.

Deng Jianzhi, 'Study on the Efficiency of Patent Administrative Enforcement in China', [2012] **2** *China Soft Science* 80.

Department of SIPO for Regulations and Laws (ed.), *Guide to the Newly Amended Patent Law*, Beijing: Intellectual Property Publishing House 2001.

Department of SIPO for Regulations and Laws (ed.), *Introductory Remarks on the Third Revision of the Patent Act*, Beijing: Intellectual Property Publishing House 2009.

EU-China IPR2, Third Revision of China's Patent Law. Legal texts and documents on the drafting process 2006–2008, 2010, www.ipr2.org.

Fan Xiaobo and Meng Fanxing, *Research on Patent Infringement Through Experimental Use*, Beijing: Fengxiaoqingip, 2012.

Ganea, Peter, 'China's amended legal regime on patents for inventions and utility models', [2010] **5** *JIPLP* 650.

He Huaiwen, 'Patent Invalidation Procedure: Limits of Judicial Power and Judicial Certainty', [2009] **3** *China Patents & Trademarks* 10.

Heide, Nils, 'Harmonisierungsaufgaben im internationalen Technologietransfer – Zum Schutz von Herstellungstechnologien in der Volksrepublik China', **2008** *GRUR Int.* 12.

Jaeschke, Wayne C., Lu Zhun, and Paul Crawford, 'Comparison of Chinese and U.S. Patent Reform Legislation: Which, if either, got it right?', [2012] **11** *J. Marshall Rev. Intell. Prop.* 567.

Li Zhang and Xu Liming, 'The Administrative Mediation of Patent Infringement Issues, Right or Wrong?', [2010] *Administration and Law*, July 2010, 84.

Luginbuehl, Stefan and Thomas Pattloch, 'The Awakening of the Chinese Patent Dragon – the Revised Chinese Patent Act 2009', [2011] **42** *IIC* 130.

Luginbuehl, Stefan and Thomas Pattloch, 'China's New Patent Policy', [2011] **33** *EIPR* 274.

Meng Hongzhi, *Study on New Development of Administrative Protection of Intellectual Property Rights*, Beijing, 2011.

Milner, Gordon and Claire Elizabeth Robley, 'Employees' rights to inventions and rewards under the revised Patent Law', *Association of Corporate Counsel*, 30 April 2010.

Moga, Thomas T., *China's utility model patent system: innovation driver or deterrent*, Asia, U.S. Chamber of Commerce, November 2012.

Prud'homme, Dan, *Dulling the Cutting Edge: How Patent-Related Policies and Practices Hamper Innovation*, European Chamber of Commerce in China 2011.

Schüler, Margot, *Technologietransfer nach China – ein unkalkulierbares Risiko für die Länder der Triade Europa, USA und Japan?*, Bonn/Berlin: Friedrich Ebert Stiftung 2008.

Tang Zongshun, *A Course in Patent Law*, 3rd ed., Law Press 2003.

Trade Lawyers Advisory Group, *China's Laws, Regulations and Practices in the Areas of Technology Transfer, Trade-related Investment Measures, Subsidies and Intellectual Property Protection which Raise WTO Compliance Concerns*, 2007.

Yin Xintian, *Protection of the Patent Right*, 2nd ed., Beijing: Intellectual Property Publishing House 2005.

Yin Xintian, *Detailed Commentary on China's Patent Law*, Beijing: Intellectual Property Publishing House 2011.

Yu Xia and Matthew Murphy, 'Employee Inventor Rights Under the New Chinese Patent Regulations', *MMLC Group*, 29 July 2010.

## B. USEFUL WEBPAGES AND PERIODICALS

### 1. China

#### *(a) Additional background information*

The following webpages provide further background information to patenting in China, including Chinese laws and English translations thereof.

*(i) State Intellectual Property Office*

- English: http://english.sipo.gov.cn/
- Chinese: http://www.sipo.gov.cn/

*(ii) Intellectual Property Protection in China*

- www.chinaipr.gov.cn

*(iii) China IPR SME Helpdesk*

- www.china-iprhelpdesk.eu

*(iv) EU-China IP Cooperative programme, IP Key*

- www.ipkey.org

*(v) EU-China project on the protection of Intellectual Property Rights (IPR2)*

- www.ipr2.org

#### *(b) Case law*

For patent case law of major Chinese courts, also including interactive statistics on the performance of courts (English):

- www.ciela.cn

For case law of the Patent Re-examination Board, also including national and regional patent legislation, as well as patent infringement litigation (Chinese):

- http://reexam.souips.com/

#### *(c) Newsletters*

The following newsletters provide interesting news relating to patents and other IPRs.

*(i)* China intellectual Property newsletter of the UK Government:

- www.gov.uk/government/publications/china-ip-newsletter

*(ii)* IP Key newsletter

- www.ipkey.org

#### *(d) Periodicals*

##### *(i) Official resources*

- *Gazette of the Standing Committee of the National People's Congress of the People's Republic of China* (Chinese), with the official versions of Chinese IP laws.
- *Gazette of the State Council of the People's Republic of China* (Chinese), with the official versions of administrative legislation, acts, opinions, etc., by the State Council and by the ministries and administrations it supervises.
- *Gazette of the Supreme People's Court of the People's Republic of China* (Chinese), with a selection of important cases decided by the Supreme People's Court and lower People's Courts, also in the area of IP.

##### *(ii) Journals*

- *China Patents & Trademarks* (Chinese/English), with a selection of articles which have been made accessible online: http://www.cpt.cn/en/pdf_list. aspx?m=20100223163922653225
- *China Intellectual Property Magazine:*
    - English: www.chinaipmagazine.com/en/
    - Chinese: www.chinaipmagazine.com/
- *China Law & Practice* (English), with translations of and comments/articles on current legislation also in the area of IP

*Intellectual property (Chinese)*:

- www.chips.org

### 2. Chinese Taipei (Taiwan)

*(a) Intellectual Property Office*

- English: www.tipo.gov.tw/mp.asp?mp=2
- Chinese: http://www.tipo.gov.tw/mp.asp?mp=1

### 3. Hong Kong (SAR)

*(a) Intellectual Property Department*

- English: http://www.ipd.gov.hk/eng/home.htm
- Chinese: http://www.ipd.gov.hk/chi/home.htm

## 4. Macau (SAR)

### *(a) Department of Economic Services*

English:

- http://www.economia.gov.mo/web/DSE/public?_nfpb=true&_pageLabel=Pg_IP_Index&locale=en_US

Chinese:

- http://www.economia.gov.mo/web/DSE/public?_nfpb=true&_pageLabel=Pg_IP_Index&locale=zh_CN

# INDEX